# Physiology and Behaviour of Marine Organisms

# Physiology and Behaviour of Marine Organisms

*Proceedings of the 12th European Symposium on Marine Biology*
*Stirling, Scotland, September 1977*

*Edited by*

## D.S. McLUSKY and A.J. BERRY

*Department of Biology, University of Stirling, Stirling, Scotland*

## PERGAMON PRESS

OXFORD · NEW YORK · TORONTO · SYDNEY · PARIS · FRANKFURT

| U.K. | Pergamon Press Ltd., Headington Hill Hall, Oxford OX3 0BW, England |
|------|-----------------------------------------------------------------------|
| U.S.A. | Pergamon Press Inc., Maxwell House, Fairview Park, Elmsford, New York 10523, U.S.A. |
| CANADA | Pergamon of Canada Ltd., 75 The East Mall, Toronto, Ontario, Canada |
| AUSTRALIA | Pergamon Press (Aust.) Pty. Ltd., 19a Boundary Street, Rushcutters Bay, N.S.W. 2011, Australia |
| FRANCE | Pergamon Press SARL, 24 rue des Ecoles, 75240 Paris, Cedex 05, France |
| FEDERAL REPUBLIC OF GERMANY | Pergamon Press GmbH, 6242 Kronberg-Taunus, Pferdstrasse 1, Federal Republic of Germany |

First edition 1978
Reprinted 1978

**British Library Cataloguing in Publication Data**

European Symposium on Marine Biology, 12th,
Stirling, 1977
Physiology and behaviour of marine organisms
1. Marine biology - Congresses 2. Marine
fauna - Behavior - Congresses
I. Title II. McLusky, Donald Stewart
III. Berry, A J
574.1'09162  QL120  77-30559
ISBN 0-08-021548-3

*In order to make this volume available as economically and as rapidly as possible the authors' typescripts have been reproduced in their original forms. This method unfortunately has its typographical limitations but it is hoped that they in no way distract the reader.*

*Printed in Great Britain by William Clowes & Sons Limited
London, Beccles and Colchester*

# CONTENTS

METABOLISM

## HEAVY METALS AND POLLUTION

## BEHAVIOUR

# FOREWORD

The 12th European Marine Biology Symposium was held at the
University of Stirling (Scotland) from September 5th until
September 12th, 1977.

150 participants from 15 countries were welcomed to the
University by Dr. W.A. Cramond, the University Principal, who
reminded them that, although the University of Stirling was only
10 years old, there was a long-standing connection between the
local area and Marine Biology, as Sir John Murray, the scientific
director of the pioneering "Challenger" expedition had resided
for many years close to the site of the University.   Today,
the University has strong interests in teaching and research
in Marine Biology, which are particularly fostered through its
links with the Scottish Marine Biological Association's laboratory at Oban.   Professor B. Battaglia, President of the
"International Committee for the European Symposia on Marine
Biology" also welcomed the participants, and expressed thanks
to the University for organising the 12th Symposium, especially
in view of earlier uncertainty about the location of same.

46 papers were presented on the topic of "Physiology and
Behaviour of Marine Organisms".   In addition 9 displays were
given during a poster session, and several films and slides
were given in an evening session.

The "camera-ready copy" system has been employed in publishing
the proceedings and most of the contributions remain, substantially, as they reached us.   We thank the authors for their
assistance in this process, designed to reduce costs and increase
the speed of publication.   We gratefully acknowledge the pat-
ience of the many typists who have prepared the manuscripts.

We express our thanks to the Department of Biology and our
colleagues for their assistance, in particular the support of
Professors Hans Meidner and Bill Muntz, and the forebearance of
our typists, Margaret Keilt and Jessica Liddell.   We gratefully
acknowledge the assistance of the Scottish Tourist Board, the
Bank of Scotland, the Central Regional Council Tourism Dept.,
and the staff of A.K. Davidson Hall of Residence.

Donald S. McLusky
Anthony J. Berry
Editors

Stirling, October 1977.

# LIST OF PARTICIPANTS

## Austria

Klepal, W.

## Belgium

Pequeux, A.
Persoone, G.

## Denmark

Hagerman, L.
Hagerman, C. Mrs.
Larsen, M.M.Z.
Rasmussen, K.J.
Salling, P.
Ursin, E.
Ursin, E. Mrs.

## Eire

Aldrich, J.C.
Keegan, B.F.
O'Ceidigh, P.

## France

Beaumartin, Mrs.
Boucher, J.
Cabioch, L.
Cabioch, J. Mrs.
Ceccaldi, H.
Gaudy, R.
Gaudy, Mrs.
Guerin, J-P.
Guerin, Mrs.
Masse, H.
Moal, J.
Pavillon, J-F.
Pavillon, Mrs.
Samain, J-F.
Thirior-Quieureux, C.

## Germany

Flügel, H.
Heimbach, F.
Kinne, O.

Kuhl, H.
Kunz-Kuhl, Mrs.
Schlichter, D.
Schriever, G.
Schulz-Baldes, M.
Svoboda, A.
Zander, C.D.

## Greece

Moraitou-Apostolopoulou, Maria
Moraitou-Apostolopoulou, Mr.

## Israel

Ben-Eliahu, N.

## Italy

Battaglia, B.
Bilio, M.
Canzonier, W.J.
Colombo, G.
Della Croce, N.
Relini, G.
Relini, Mrs.
Rossi, R.
Rossi, S.R.A. Mrs.
Sara, M.

## Malaysia

MacIntosh, D.J.

## Netherlands

De Blok, J.W.
Creutzberg, F.
Dankers, N.
Drinkwaard, A.C.
Drinkwaard, E. Mrs.
Essink, K.
Everaarts, J.M.
Kuipers, B.R.
Mulder, M.
Stam, A.
Van Arkel, M. A.
Vink, G.J.

De Wilde, P.A.W.J.
De Wolfe, P.
Wolff, W.J.
De Zwaan, A.

### Norway

Baake, T.
Christiansen, M.E.
Gulliksen, B.
Gulliksen, E. Mrs.
Hognestad, P.
Hopkins, C.C.E.
Schram, T.
Skjoldal, H.R.

### Switzerland

Pabst, B.

### United Kingdom

Allen, J.A.
Ansell, A.D.
Armitage, M.E.
Barnes, H.
Barnes, M. Mrs.
Blackstock, J.
Blaxter, J.H.S.
Bottoms, A.
Berry, A.J.
Boyd, R.J.
Briggs, R.P.
Bruce, R.W.
Coombs, T.L.
Cumberlidge, N.
Dunn, G.M.
Eleftheriou, A.
Elliott, M.
Emson, R.H.
Garwood, P.R.
George, S.G.
Gordon, J.D.M.
Grigg, H.
Gudmundsson, H.
Hartnoll, R.G.
Herbert, R.A.

Holmes, R.H.A.
Jamieson, A.
Jobling, M.
Jones, J.M.
Langford, T.E.
Meadows, P.S.
McCaul, S.
McLusky, D.S.
Muntz, W.R.A.
Naylor, E.
Naylor, Mrs.
Newton, J.
Olive, P.J.W.
Pearson, T.
Pirie, B.J.S.
Ross, L.
Sargent, J.R.
Smaldon, G.
Smaldon, P.R. Mrs.
Stewart, M.
Taylor, A.C.
Thornton, S.D.
Tytler, P.
Uglow, R.F.
Utting, N.J.
Warnes, J.
Webb, J.E.
Webb, J.E. Mrs.

### U.S.A

Bookhout, C.G.
Calabrese, A.
Edwards, C.
Forward, R.B. Jr.
Lawrence, G.C.
Sastry, A.N.
Selby, T.
Vargo, S.L. Mrs.
Vargo, G.A.

### YUGOSLAVIA

Hrs-Brenko, Mirjana
Lucu, C.
Valentincic, T.

# PREVIOUS EUROPEAN SYMPOSIA ON
# MARINE BIOLOGY

1st EUROPEAN SYMPOSIUM ON MARINE BIOLOGY

Helgoland Fed. Rep. Germany, Sept. 26-Oct. 1, 1966.
Biologische Anstait Helgoland.

TOPICS  - *Experimental ecology, its significance as a marine biological tool.*

- *Subtidal ecology particularly as studied by diving techniques.*

- *The food web in the sea.*

Kinne, O., and H. Aurich (Editors).
Helgoländer wissenschaftliche meeresuntersuchungen 15 (1967). 721 p.


2nd EUROPEAN SYMPOSIUM ON MARINE BIOLOGY

Bergen, Norway, Aug. 24-28, 1967.
Biological Station, Espegrend.

TOPICS  - *The importance of water movements for biology and distribution of marine organisms.*

Brattström, H. (Editor).
Sarsia, 34 (1968). 398 p.


3eme SYMPOSIUM EUROPEEN DE BIOLOGIE MARINE

Arcachon, France, 2-7 Sept., 1968.
Station Biologique d'Arcachon.

THEMES  - *Biologie des sediments meubles (Vol. 1).*

- *Biologie des eaux a salinite variable (Vol. 11).*

Soyer, J. (Editeur).
Vie et Milieu (1971), Suppl. 22:  1-464.
Vie et Milieu (1971), Suppl. 22:  464-857.


4th EUROPEAN MARINE BIOLOGY SYMPOSIUM

Bangor, North Wales, Great Britain, Sept. 14-20, 1969.
Marine Science Laboratories of the University College
of North Wales, Menai Bridge.

TOPICS  - *Larval biology.*

*Light in the marine environment.*

Crisp, D.J. (Editor).
Cambridge University Press (1971). 599 p.

5th EUROPEAN MARINE BIOLOGY SYMPOSIUM

    Venice, Italy, Oct. 5-11, 1970.
    Institute of Marine Biology, Venice.

    TOPICS   - *Evolutionary aspects of marine biology.*

             - *Factors affecting biological equilibria in the
               Adriatic brackish water lagoons.*

    Battaglia, B. (Editor).
    Piccin Editore, Padova (1972).   348 p.


6th EUROPEAN SYMPOSIUM ON MARINE BIOLOGY

    Rovinj, Yugoslavia, Sept. 27-Oct. 2, 1971.
    Marine Biological Station (Center for Marine Research of
    the Rudjer Boskovic Institute), Rovinj.

    TOPICS   - *Productivity in coastal areas of the sea.*

             - *Dynamics in benthic communities.*

    Zavodnik, D. (Editor).
    Thalassia Jugoslavica 7(1) (1971). 445 p.


7th EUROPEAN SYMPOSIUM ON MARINE BIOLOGY

    Texel, The Netherlands, Sept. 11-16, 1972.
    The Netherlands Institute for Sea Research, Texel.

    TOPICS   - *Mechanisms of migration in the marine environment.*

             - *Respiratory gases and the marine organism.*

    de Blok, J.W. (Editor).
    Netherlands Journal of sea Research 7 (1973).   505 p.


8th EUROPEAN SYMPOSIUM ON MARINE BIOLOGY

    Sorrento, Italy, Oct. 1-7, 1973.
    Zoological Station of Naples.

    TOPIC    - *Reproduction and sexuality in the marine environment.*

    Bonaduce, G., and G.C. Carrada (Editors).
    Pubblicazioni della Stazione Zoologica di Napoli 39,
    Suppl. 1(1975). 727 p.

9th EUROPEAN MARINE BIOLOGY SYMPOSIUM

Oban, Scotland, Great Britain, Oct. 2-8, 1974.
The Dunstaffnage Marine Research Laboratory, Oban.

TOPIC   - *The biochemistry, physiology, and behaviour of marine organisms in relation to their ecology.*

Barnes, H. (Editor).
Aberdeen University Press (1975). 760 p.


10th EUROPEAN SYMPOSIUM ON MARINE BIOLOGY

Ostend, Belgium, Sept. 17-23, 1975.
Institute for Marine Research, Bredene, Belgium.

TOPICS  - *Research in mariculture at laboratory - and pilot scale (Vol. 1).*

- *Population dynamics of marine organisms in relation with nutrient cycling in shallow waters (Vol. 11).*

Personne, G. and E. Jaspers (Editors).
Universa Press, Wettern, Belgium (1976), 620 p. (Vol. 1),
710 p. (Vol. 2).


11th EUROPEAN SYMPOSIUM ON MARINE BIOLOGY

Galway, Ireland, Oct. 5-11, 1976.
University College, Galway.

TOPIC - *Biology of benthic organisms.*

B.F. Keegan, P. O'Ceidigh & P.J.S. Boaden (Editors)
Pergamon Press, Oxford (1977), 630 p.

# METABOLISM

# EFFECTS OF NUTRITIVE STRESS UPON DIEL RHYTHMS, TOTAL TISSUE METABOLISM, AND TISSUE METABOLIC RATES IN *CARCINUS MAENAS* (L.) (CRUSTACEA: DECAPODA)

**John Carlson Aldrich**

*Department of Zoology, University of Dublin, Trinity College, Dublin 2, Ireland*

## ABSTRACT

Crabs were collected in 1974 and their excited rates, diel rhythms, tissue weights, and tissue metabolic rates were measured after 3-5 weeks under controlled conditions. More crabs were collected in 1977 and measured immediately. Summated tissue rates were similar in both fed and starved crabs, as were the average rhythmic rates. However, the rhythmic pattern varied or was nonexistent, depending on feeding or prior condition. Gill and hepatopancreas tissue rates were higher in rhythmic crabs than in arhythmic ones, and there was a correlation between hepatopancreas tissue rates and the total crab dry wt/wet wt ratio.

## INTRODUCTION

The fact that starvation suppresses metabolism in crustaceans is now well known (Ref. 13). There is a reduction of activity in the early stages of starvation (Ref. 7), there is a decrease in tissue weight, or loss of reserves during periods of low feeding levels (Refs. 2, 8 & 11). The reduction in activity following starvation is manifested both by a decrease in the average level of oxygen consumption, e.g. Aldrich (3), and by decreased time spent in the nocturnal active phase of the diel rhythm as found by Ansell (7). There are also reductions in the magnitude of the oscillations of semi-lunar rhythms, including changes in metabolic rate without overt changes in activity. The phasing and overall pattern of these changes is characteristic of the individual crab (Ref. 3). Starvation-induced reductions of metabolic rates in whole invertebrates may be manifested in the rates of oxygen consumption per gram in isolated tissues, as has been found in Littorina homogenates by Newell and Pye (14). Marsden et al. (12) studied this in Carcinus maenas, but comparisons were made with the routine rate of intact crabs. Neither they, nor Wallace (16) included the influence of starvation on metabolic rhythms and the possible influence of such individual behavioural characteristics upon the tissue metabolic rates.

In the present study, three possible causes for the reduction of oxygen consumption due to starvation were therefore examined simultaneously:
(1) reduction in tissue weight
(2) reduction in metabolic activity associated with rhythms
(3) reduction of the rate of oxygen consumption per gram in the gill, hepatopancreas, and muscle tissues.
These causes were examined against the background of the natural variation in organ sizes, and the differing dry wt/wet wt ratios of individual crabs,

3

indicative of their previous nutritional history and stage within the
intermoult cycle, respectively.

## MATERIALS AND METHODS

### Crabs

Carcinus maenas were collected on two occasions; June, 1974, and August, 1977.
In the 1974 collection, individuals were immediately segregated and numbered.
Crabs to be fed were given fresh cod ad libitum every second day, and were
kept separately from starved specimens. Crabs were kept at $18^{o}$C under a 16
hr dark/8 hr light regime for an average of four weeks. In 1977, crabs were
collected and measured under ambient light conditions, at $12^{o}$C without long
storage. None of these were fed. The 1974 collection was made at Burnham-
on-Crouch, Essex; and the 1977 collection at Seapoint, Co. Dublin.

### Respiration of Intact Crabs

Excited rate measurements. These were measured in 1974 on the day of
collection, excitement being automatically produced when placing the crabs in
the respirometer. Oxygen consumption was measured in a closed system with a
Gilson 'Oxygraph' and a Clark electrode (Ref. 5).

Diel rhythm recording. Two different sets of apparatus were used for this
purpose, both employing oxygen electrodes and intermittently closed
respirometers. Timers controlled the action of recorders, pumps and valves,
to either record the ambient level of oxygen in a temperature-controlled tank,
or the decline in oxygen in the temporarily closed respirometer. Crabs were
measured every 30 minutes in 1974, every 15 minutes in 1977, for 24 hrs total.

Rates of oxygen consumption per gram of tissue. These were measured with a
Gilson Differential Respirometer (Model GR20). Following the recording of
rhythms on the previous day, crabs were killed by spiking (Ref. 9), and the
total live weight and the wet weight of the chelae recorded. All the gills
were removed, blotted and weighed, the entire hepatopancreas was removed and
weighed without draining, and the chelae were dissected to obtain muscle
tissue. The total weight of muscle in each crab was later estimated from the
chela weight and the total dry wt/wet wt ratio (Ref. 5). The tissues were
measured in the respirometer by standard methods (Ref. 12).

## RESULTS AND DISCUSSION

### Activity and Diel Rhythms

Patterns of oxygen consumption, collection of 1974. Individual diel rhythms
were measured in 5 starved and 5 fed crabs, after 3-5 weeks storage. An
examination of the rhythmic patterns of individual crabs revealed patterns
that could be associated with nutritive condition. Most of the fed crabs had
no obvious rhythm, the exception being a crab that had not been fed for three
days prior to measurement (No. XIII, Fig. 1A). In contrast, three of the
starved crabs exhibited marked fluctuations in oxygen consumption over the
24 hr period (Fig. 1B). The average live weights of the two groups were
virtually identical, 60.1 g starved, 60.3 g fed. Surprisingly, the average

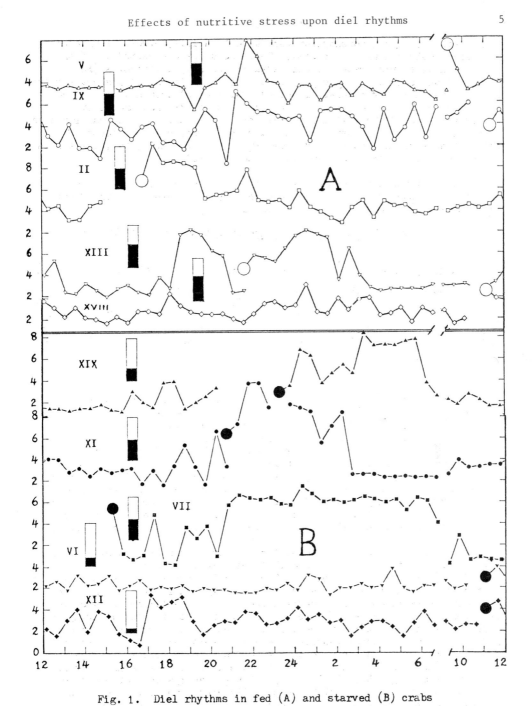

Fig. 1.  Diel rhythms in fed (A) and starved (B) crabs

Hepatopancreas wet wt relative to 'parametric' wt shown by shaded portions of rectangles.  Y axis = ml $O_2$/crab/hr, X axis = hr of day.

24 hr rates of oxygen consumption were also identical, 0.0624 ml $O_2$/g/hr
starved; 0.0630 fed (wet wt basis). This was quite unexpected since the
depression of starved rates is well established in poikilotherms (Ref. 13),
and was found earlier in Cancer pagurus (Ref. 3). The similar average rates
for both fed and starved crabs resulted from the fed ones having a steady
rate at a level intermediate between the quiescent diurnal and active
nocturnal rates of the rhythmic starved crabs. If only the diurnal rates had
been measured, as has often been the case when studying the effects of
starvation, e.g. Wallace (16), Marsden et al. (12), Aldrich (4), the starved
rates would have been considered lower than the fed ones.

These similarities between the average rates in fed and starved crabs
reappeared in comparisons of these average rhythmic rates with the excited
rates measured on the day of collection (Table 1).

TABLE 1   Comparison of Average Rhythmic Rates with Excited Rates

| | Starved crabs | | | | Fed crabs | | |
|---|---|---|---|---|---|---|---|
| No. | Rhythmic rate* | Ex. Rate | Rr/Er | No. | Rhythmic rate | Ex. rate | Rr/Er |
| XIX | 3.47 | 6.14 | 57% | V | 3.58 | 8.08 | 44% |
| XI | 4.82 | 2.51 | --- | IX | 4.01 | 8.56 | 47% |
| VII | 5.85 | 9.50 | 62% | II | 4.94 | 7.38 | 67% |
| VI | 2.26 | 6.00 | 38% | XIII | 3.61 | 6.97 | 52% |
| XII | 2.82 | 6.68 | 42% | XVIII | 2.71 | 5.52 | 49% |

*Ml $O_2$/crab/hr

Starved rates averaged 49.5% of the excited values (No. 2 not included,
excited rate not obtained), whilst fed rates averaged 51.8% of the excited
rates. The similarity of these comparisons may be related to the generally
similar relative hepatopancreas sizes. These were compared with the
'parametric' weights established previously (Ref. 5). By parametric, is
meant the average organ weight in a large sample of freshly collected crabs.
Generally speaking, both fed and starved crabs had deteriorated in condition
in the laboratory (Fig. 1A & 1B). The hepatopancreas weights were about half
those found in freshly-collected specimens, except for the very low values in
the two starved crabs, Nos. VI and XII (Fig. 1B) which did not have a rhythm.
These two crabs also had the lowest values for the ratios Rr/Er (Table 1).

Since both the fed and starved conditons resulted in similar decreases in
organ weights, it can be concluded that the rate of feeding was too low for
significant differences to appear. The general decrease in condition implies
that both fed and starved crabs were undergoing a nutritive stress. Such
general changes in condition, despite feeding, may be common in laboratory
situations and may be responsible for changes in activity noted during the
first few weeks of captivity (Ref. 16). In contrast, the four crabs of the
1977 collection had hepatopancreas sizes averageing 92% of the 'parametric'
sizes. These crabs had no opportunity to decrease in condition. The
nocturnal elevation of rates is probably due to food-seeking activity in
starved crabs (e.g., No. XI, Fig. 1B). Cancer pagurus were observed to
increase their activity at night, especially when given a food stimulus but
not fed. On the other hand, the absence of a nocturnal elevation, and the
great overall depression of rates in the two starved arhythmic crabs (Nos.
VI & XII, Fig. 1B) may have resulted from an inability to maintain normal
activity due to extreme starvation.

The average elevation of diurnal rates in fed crabs was expected, a routine rate (Ref. 10). The absence of a nocturnal elevation in these fed crabs might be correlated with the lack of a need to seek food (e.g., No. V, Fig.1A).

**Effects of feeding on respiratory patterns.** As found previously in <u>Cancer pagurus</u> and <u>Maia squinado</u>, a single meal elevated the quiescent rate for several hours (Ref. 4). This response could be differentiated from that of excitement by the greater duration of the elevated rate, and similar results were obtained with the <u>Carcinus maenas</u> tested here (Refs. 5 & 6).

Knowing that starved crabs were generally rhythmic, and that fed ones were not, experiments were run to ascertain the effects of single meals upon these patterns of respiration. A previously fed crab was recorded for 24 hrs and its arhythmic pattern established. A perforated bottle of cod was then introduced into the respirometer and the pattern was recorded for a further 24 hrs, but no rhythm appeared. The crab was then fed, producing a slight rise in metabolic rate, but not a good rhythm. No rhythm appeared during the next 24 hrs and the slight rise declined. Another previously fed crab was tested similarly but with even less result, feeding would not induce rhythms in these arhythmic crabs. This experiment was repeated with a starved crab that initially exhibited a slight rhythm. Nocturnal repiratory rates increased slightly when the crab was exposed to the closed container of cod, and increased greatly after feedin ad libitum. This nocturnal elevation decreased during the subsequent 24 hr period without food, and remained at the same level during the following days (four in all) despite two more feedings. Only one arhythmic starved crab was available for testing but it died before a result could be obtained. (Note; the three crabs used for these feeding experiments were not part of the ten crabs used in the preceding experiment.)

In general then, single meals did not induce rhythms in arhythmic crabs, but a single meal did induce or enhance the pattern in a weakly rhythmic crab.

**Rhythms in freshly-collected crabs, collection of 1977.** Here the object was to measure rhythms as close to the time of collection as possible. Crabs 1 and 2 were measured after two weeks, but 4 and 5 were measured within 1-4 days. Crab No. 1 exhibited a very clear tidal rhythm, No. 2 had no obvious rhythm, whilst 4 and 5 exhibited diel rhythms. The hepatopancreas of these crabs averaged 91% of the 'parametric' values, so their condition was good. From these results it is obvious that even when crabs are collected from a region of marked tidal fluctuation (Seapoint, Co. Dublin), their patterns of oxygen consumption are individually variable. Indeed there was only one proper tidal rhythm amongst the four.

## Tissue Respiration Rates

**Summated tissue metabolism, collection of 1974.** Having characterized the rhythms, the ten crabs were dissected and the oxygen consumption rates of the gill, hepatopancreas, and muscle were measured. The rates per gram were multiplied by the total dry weights of each tissue to give the proportional contribution of each to the total tissue metabolism (the blood and exoskeleton were neglected here although their contributions may be material). There appeared to be regular changes in these proportional contributions as the total crab dry wt/wet wt ratios increased, but the summated tissue metabolism (the total of the three tissue rates) was virtually identical for

fed and starved crabs.  The tissues measured in vitro accounted for 36.0% of
the 24 hr average rates in starved crabs, and 37.6% in fed ones (0.0224 and
0.0222 ml $O_2$/g/hr, respectively).  Two major points appear in these data;
first, the in vitro measurements are much lower than the in vivo ones, as had
been found previously (Ref. 12), second, there is no overall difference
between the starved and fed conditions, repeating the findings of the
rhythm measurements.

Tissue respiration rates per gram.  When these rates were looked at by
themselves they at first corroborated the picture given by the summated
tissue metabolism.  The rates per gram of the three tissues did not differ
significantly between the starved and fed crabs of the 1974 collection
(Table 2), a result previously found for this crab by Marsden et al. (Ref.
12).  Such independence of nutritive condition in vitro may be interpreted as
respiration at a standard rate when tissues have been isolated from the
sensory control of the intact crab (but see below, rhythmic-arhythmic crabs).

TABLE 2   Tissue Oxygen Consumption    (ul $O_2$/mg/hr, dry wt basis, 18°C)

| Tissue | Fed $\bar{X}$ | S.D. | Starved $\bar{X}$ | S.D. | Value of t (8 d.f.) | Sig. level |
|---|---|---|---|---|---|---|
| Gill | 1.745 | 0.299 | 1.474 | 0.264 | 1.96 | N.S. |
| Hepatopancreas | 1.010 | 0.271 | 1.620 | 0.589 | 1.45 | N.S. |
| Muscle | 0.179 | 0.041 | 0.239 | 0.109 | 1.16 | N.S. |

Summated tissue metabolism, comparison on rhythmic-arhythmic basis, all crabs.
The tissue rates from the 1977 collection were treated similarly to the above.
There was no fed or starved distinction here so their rates were added to the
previous ten after being raised to the equivalent of 18°C (assuming a $Q_{10}$ of
2).  Comparisons were then made of the basis of rhythmic versus
arhythmic crabs, but again, there were no significant differences in the
average rates.

Despite the similarity of the average rates in fed and starved, and rhythmic
and arhythmic crabs, there were marked differences in the proportional
contributions of the three tissues to the summated tissue rate, when rhythmic
crabs were compared with arhythmic ones.  The results were the same for the
1974 collection by itself, and when combined with the 1977 collection, so the
combined data are given (Table 3).  The contribution of gill tissue to the
whole was higher in rhythmic crabs than in arhythmic ones (significance level
0.06).  The percentage contribution of the hepatopancreas was was higher in
rhythmic crabs (sig. level 0.02) too.  The contribution of muscle tissue was
correspondingly lower in rhythmic crabs (sig. level 0.03).  These results
suggest that there are real metabolic differences between rhythmic and
arhythmic crabs, and that starvation or feeding under laboratory conditions
do not eliminate these differences.

An attempt was made to explain these differences on the basis of differing
total crab dry wt/wet wt ratios.  The oxygen consumption per gram (dry wt
basis) of each tissue was plotted against the dry wt/wet wt ratio of each
crab.  A marked correspondence of of low crab dry wt/wet wt ratios and high
metabolic rates was found in the hepatopancreas.  A corner test for
association (Ref. 15 indicated significance at the 0.02 level.  This
suggests greater hepatopancreas activity in crabs that are still developing
after a moult.  Significant results were not found for the other tissues,
although the apparent regression line was similar in muscle and

hepatopancreas tissues. The regression was opposite in sign in the gill tissue, and there was no obvious correlation between its metabolic rate and the crab dry wt/wet wt ratios.

TABLE 3   Proportional Contributions to the Summated Tissue Rates

| No. | Rhythmic crabs Gill* | Hepato. | Muscle | No. | Arhythmic crabs Gill | Hepato | Muscle |
|---|---|---|---|---|---|---|---|
| XIX | 12.9 | 30.4 | 56.5 | VI | 9.5 | 23.5 | 67.0 |
| XI | 13.8 | 38.6 | 47.6 | XII | 11.2 | 21.0 | 67.8 |
| VII | 28.6 | 41.0 | 30.4 | V | 17.8 | 29.8 | 52.4 |
| II | 26.2 | 42.4 | 31.4 | IX | 17.4 | 26.9 | 55.7 |
| XIII | 25.1 | 29.1 | 45.8 | XVIII | 26.9 | 41.1 | 32.0 |
| 1 | 24.1 | 44.7 | 24.0 | 2 | 16.8 | 24.9 | 58.4 |
| 4 | 34.5 | 38.3 | 27.3 | $\bar{X}$ | 16.6 | 27.9 | 55.5 |
| 5 | 39.3 | 60.7 | 0.0 | | | | |
| $\bar{X}$ | 25.6 | 40.7 | 32.9 | | | | |

*Tissue rates as percentages of the summated rate for each crab.

### CONCLUSIONS

Starvation appears to affect respiration through two of the aspects examined. It affects the level of activity, generally lowering the daily quiescent rate (Ref. 4), and in contrast to the findings of Ansell (7) using Cancer pagurus, the nocturnal respiratory rate tended to be suppressed in both fed and starved crabs. This could be enhanced by feeding for only a limited time, and then not in arhythmic crabs. Starvation acting through previous nutritional history (hepatopancreas size) may also be linked with the depression of oxygen consumption (Ref. 6).

However, the major determinant of the behavioural aspects appears to be the behaviour before collection. The presence or absence of a rhythm appears to be a characteristic of the individual crab. The finding that gills and hepatopancreas in rhythmic crabs had higher rates of oxygen consumption, whilst muscles had lower rates, bears out previous findings that these rhythms of oxygen consumption need not have a locomotory origin (Ref.3). This fact, plus the finding that the rate of oxygen consumption in the hepatopancreas increases with decreasing total dry wt/wet wt ratios, suggests that further work to elucidate the origin of these rhythms, and their control, must centre around the idiosyncrasies of individual crabs.

### Acknowledgements

I would like to thank Professor R. C. Newell, University of Odense, Odense, Denmark, who helped me with these investigations when I was at Queen Mary College, University of London. Thanks are also due to Mr. D. Collins, formerly of Coopers Company and Coborn School, Upminster, Essex, for his assistance in the laboratory.

### REFERENCES

(1)  Aldrich, J.C., 1972.  On the biology and energetics of Libinia emarginata, an omnivorous decapod.  145pp.  MA thesis, Boston Univ.

(2)  -  (1974).  Allometric studies on energy relationships in the spider crab Libinia emarginata (Leach).  Biological Bulletin of the Marine

Biological Laboratory, Woods Hole, 147, 257-273.

(3) - 1975. Individual variability in oxygen consumption rates of fed and starved Cancer pagurus and Maia squinado. Comparative Biochemistry and Physiology, 51A, 175-183.

(4) - 1975. On the oxygen consumption of the crabs Cancer pagurus and Maia squinado (Herbst). Comparative Biochemistry and Physiology, 50A, 223-228.

(5) - 1975. Endogenous factors affecting the metabolism of marine decapods. 239pp. PhD thesis, University of London.

(6) - 1975. On the relationship between oxygen consumption and feeding level in decapods. In Proceedings of the 9th European Marine Biology Symposium, 407-418. (Ed. H. Barnes).

(7) Ansell, A.D., 1973. Changes in oxygen consumption, heart rate and ventilation accompanying starvation in the decapod crustacean Cancer pagurus. Netherlands Journal of Sea Research, 7, 455-475.

(8) Armitage, K.B., A.L. Buikema Jr. & N.J. Willems, 1972. Organic constituents in the annual cycle of the crayfish Orconectes nais (Faxon). Comparative Biochemistry and Physiology, 41A, 825-842.

(9) Baker, J.R., 1955. Experiments on the humane killing of crabs. Journal of the Marine Biological Association of the United Kingdom, 34, 15-24.

(10) Bayne, B.L., 1973. Physiological changes in Mytilus edulis L. induced by temperature and nutritive stress. Journal of the Marine Biological Association of the United Kingdom, 53, 39-58.

(11) Heath, J.R. & H. Barnes, 1970. Some changes in the biochemical composition with season and moulting cycle of the common shore crab Carcinus maenas (L.). Journal of Experimental Marine Biology and Ecology, 5, 199-233.

(12) Marsden, I.D., R.C. Newell & M. Ahsanullah, 1973. The effect of starvation on the metabolism of the shore crab, Carcinus maenas. Comparative Biochemistry and Physiology, 45A, 195-213.

(13) Newell, R.C., 1973. Factors affecting the respiration of intertidal invertebrates. American Zoologist, 13, 513-528.

(14) - and V.I. Pye, 1971. Temperature-induced variations in the respiration of mitochondria from the winkle, Littorina littorea (L.). Comparative Biochemistry and Physiology, 40B, 249-261.

(15) Olmstead, P.S. & J.W. Tukey, 1947. A corner test for association. Annals of Mathematical Statistics, 18, 496-513.

(16) Wallace, J.C., 1973. Feeding, starvation and metabolic rate in the shore crab Carcinus maenas. Marine Biology, 20, 277-281.

# ACTIVITIES OF SOME ENZYMES ASSOCIATED WITH ENERGY YIELDING METABOLISM IN *GLYCERA ALBA (MÜLLER)* FROM THREE AREAS OF LOCH EIL

**John Blackstock**

*Dunstaffnage Marine Research Laboratory, P.O. Box No. 3, Oban, Argyll, Scotland*

## INTRODUCTION

Loch Eil forms the inner part of the Firth of Lorne, an extensive fjordic system on the west coast of Scotland. It is an enclosed sea loch with access to Loch Linnhe and the Firth of Lorne only through the Annat Narrows which are some 5-9m. deep and approximately 100m. wide. The physical environment and distribution of macrobenthic fauna in the system have been described in detail by Pearson (1970). The loch system receives effluent from the wood pulp and paper mill situated at Annat Point (see Fig. 1). Effects of the effluent input on the macrobenthic fauna have been assessed by Pearson (1972, 1975) who has observed that fluctuating amounts of effluent discharge were related to subsequent successional changes in the distributions of several species.

Loch Eil is currently being utilised as an experimental area in which detailed effects of organic discharges on the sediments and sediment populations are being studied. The polychaete worm <u>Glycera alba</u> (Müller) has a wide distribution in the sediments of Loch Eil, and a comparative biochemical investigation of this species from three areas of the loch has been initiated, with the object of assessing sub-lethal effects of the effluent discharge on the animals from the most affected sediments. The initial approach has been to estimate enzyme activities in crude extracts of whole animals and some results from these initial studies are reported in this paper.

## MATERIALS AND METHODS

### The sampling stations

<u>Glycera alba</u> were obtained, by means of a Naturalist's dredge, at the three stations indicated in Fig. 1. Some of the physical conditions prevailing during the sampling period (April 1976 to June 1977) are shown in Table 1.

Station 2 in the deep basin of Loch Eil is situated some 2.5 km from the effluent outfall where the sediment is most affected by the deposition of organic material from the pulp mill. Conditions are frequently anoxic at the sediment surface, and the sediment is normally dark in appearance and smells of hydrogen sulphide.

Station 1 is some 5 km from the effluent outfall and at the sediment surface conditions are only intermittently anoxic. At station 24, some 9 km from the outfall at the upper end of the loch the sediment condition is thought to be the least influenced by the effluent input. During the sampling period considerable variation in redox potential (Eh) has been observed at this station, possibly as a consequence of natural inputs of organic material from

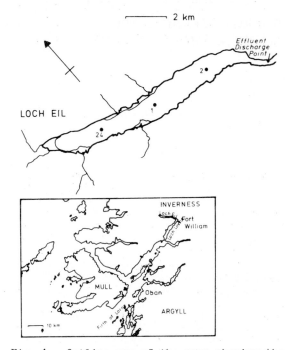

Fig. 1.  Outline map of the area showing the
sampling stations.

| Station | Sediment | Depth(m) | T(°c) | pH 1cm above sediment | Eh(mv) at sediment surface | 4cm in sediment |
|---------|----------|----------|-------|----------------------|---------------------------|-----------------|
| 2  | silt + clay | 60–70 | 10 (8–13) | 7·80(7·5–8·0) | +139(−106,+370) | −94(−173+69) |
| 1  | silt + clay | 30–40 | 9 (8–13)  | 7·90(7·6–8·1) | +222(−33,+390)  | −5(−68+43)   |
| 24 | silt + clay | 30–40 | 8 (7–12)  | 8·00(7·8–8·6) | +305(−167,+418) | −44(−108+149) |

Table 1.  Physical conditions at the sampling stations:
mean values from monthly monitoring from January, 1976
to March 1977.  The observed ranges are shown in parentheses.

drainage of the surrounding landward area at certain times of the year.

The three sampling stations are therefore considered to represent a series of
environments, each affected to a different extent by the inputs of organic
material to Loch Eil from industrial and natural sources.

Specimen collection

Immediately after dredging, the _Glycera_ were carefully separated from the

sediment by gently sieving and their lengths were measured. They were then
transferred to petri dishes in dry ice within an insulated container. Only
immature individuals some 2-3cm in length were used for analyses. For the
seasonal study pooled samples containing at least 10 individuals were used.
For experimental work live specimens were returned to the laboratory in sea
water contained in vacuum flasks and assays of enzymes were done on
preparations of individual animals.

Estimations of enzyme activities

The frozen pooled specimens were chopped into fragments of 1-2mm$^3$, without
thawing, and the well mixed sample was homogenised for 3 min at 0$^o$C, with 5ml
buffer/g of tissue. The selection of the buffer depended on the assays to be
carried out and 0.1 M phosphate buffer, pH 7.5 and 0.01 M tris - HC1 buffer
pH 7.5 containing EDTA (2m M) and dithiothreitol (2m M) were used on separate
portions of the sample. The honogenates were centrifuged at 30,000 g for 20
min at 0$^o$C and the supernatant fluid used for the analyses which were
commenced immediately. For assays of enzyme activity in individual Glycera
3ml buffer were added to the frozen specimens and extracts were then prepared
in the same way as for the pooled specimens.

The assays of enzyme activity were carried out using essentially standard
coenzyme-linked spectrophotometric procedures with substrate concentrations
and other reaction conditions modified as required to obtain maximum reaction
rates. Details of these procedures are currently being prepared for
publication as are details of effects of specimen and extract storage and
other factors on the measured enzyme activities. All reactions were carried
out at 25$^o$C in the thermostatted cell housing of a Pye Unicam SP800
spectrophotometer. The enzyme activities are expressed in Units (U) per g
dry weight of tissue or milli-Units (mU) per mg soluble protein in the extracts
where 1 unit represents the conversion of 1 $\mu$ Mole of substrate per min under
the test conditions.

Experimental Studies

For preliminary assessment of the effects of low dissolved oxygen concentrations
and sulphide on G. alba specimens from station 2 were divided into 4 groups.
Each group were placed initially in an open 1l beaker containing 500ml sea
water at 7$^o$C.
Group A:  Control group retained for 72h at 9 mg O$_2$/l by continuous
          circulation of air through the water in the beaker.
Group B:  Retained for 72h at 3 mg O$_2$/l by continuous circulation of oxygen
          free nitrogen through the water in the open beaker.
Group C:  Retained for 48h at 3 mg O$_2$/l as for Group B, then rapidly
          transferred to Dreschel Bottle and the oxygen content of the water
          reduced to <0.05 mg O$_2$/l by continuous circulation of oxygen-free
          nitrogen through the  inlet of the closed vessel. Retained for 24h
          at <0.05 mg O$_2$/l.
Group D:  Treated as for Group C. After 24h at <0.05 mg O$_2$/l, 10ppm sulphide
          in the form of Na$_2$S. 9 H$_2$O were added to the water.
At the end of the experiment the G. alba were rapidly removed from the
experimental vessels, quick frozen with dry ice and phosphate buffer extracts
prepared as described earlier for individual Glycera. The assays of enzyme
activity were restricted to phosphofructokinase, pyruvate kinase, $\alpha$-glycero-
phosphate dehydrogenase, malate dehydrogenase, and aspartate aminotransferase
all of which had shown significant differences in the seasonal study. Alanine

aminotransferase and lactate dehydrogenase assays were also included due to
their frequently being associated with anaerobic metabolic pathways in various
animal tissues.

## RESULTS

### Enzyme activities in the seasonal samples

In Fig. 2 the activities of phosphofructokinase (PFK), pyruvate kinase (PK),
lactate dehydrogenase (LDH), NAD-dependant malate dehydrogenase (MDH), citrate
synthase (CS) and aspartate aminotransferase (AST) in the seasonal samples
are shown.  Of the 15 enzymes studied the above group exhibited most variation
on a seasonal basis.  With malate and lactate dehydrogenases similar seasonal
trends in activities were observed in the three different groups of G. alba;
phosphofructokinase and aspartate aminotransferase exhibited similar trends
in the specimens collected from stations 1 and 24.  In general, the patterns
of seasonal changes observed at these stations tended to show some
similarities for most of the enzymes studied, while the pattern observed for

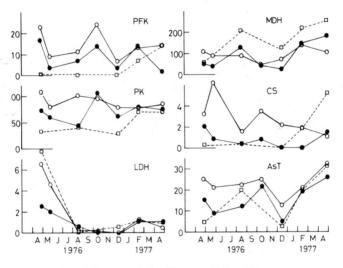

Station E1 o——o, Station E2 □---□, Station E24 ●——●

Fig. 2.  Glycera alba: seasonal changes in enzyme
activities (U/g. dry tissue).

G. alba from station 2 tended to differ considerably.  The most striking
example of this difference between the groups is shown by the phosphofructokinase activities which were extremely low (<0.1 - 0.4 units per g dry tissue)
in G. alba from station 2 between April 1976 and December 1976.  During this
period it was difficult to obtain sufficient numbers of G. alba from station
2 and insufficient material was available for the analyses in May and August.
In 1977, the phosphofructokinase activities recovered to values within the
range observed in the specimens from stations 1 and 24.  Similar, but less
pronounced trends were also observed for pyruvate kinase and fructose-1,6-
diphosphatase activities in the extracts of G. alba from station 2.  The
period of recovery in the station 2 specimens coincided with an observed
improvement in sediment conditions at station 2 and specimens were more

readily obtained. This may indicate an increase in the population of G. alba at station 2 in 1977, but the collecting technique used was not sufficiently quantitative to provide a valid indication of population changes.

Table 2 shows the mean values and standard deviations of the enzyme activities in the extracts of the seasonal preparations from G. alba collected at each sampling station. The mean activities of phosphofructokinase, pyruvate kinase, ∠-glycerophosphate dehydrogenase and fructose-1,6-diphosphatase in the specimens from station 2 are significantly lower (P <0.05) than the corresponding mean values for station 1, and the mean malate dehydrogenase activities are significantly higher in the station 2 samples.

| Enzyme | EC No | 1 | 2 | 24 |
|---|---|---|---|---|
| Hexokinase | 2.7.1.1. | 4·4 | 2·2 | 4·4 |
| Phosphofructokinase | 2.7.1.11. | 14·3 | ●4·6 | 8·5 |
| Pyruvate kinase | 2.71.40 | 89·1 | ●50·1 | 71·4 |
| Lactate dehydrogenase | 1.1.1.27 | 1·9 | 1·9 | 1·0 |
| ∝-glycerophosphate dehydrogenase | 1.1.1.8. | 6·1 | ●1·0 | 4·6 |
| Aspartate amino-transferase | 2.6.1.1. | 23·0 | 16·6 | ●15·4 |
| Alanine amino-transferase | 2.6.1.2. | 2·8 | 3·4 | 2·5 |
| Glutamate dehydrogenase | 1.4.1.3. | 31·6 | 28·2 | 27·6 |
| Citrate synthase | 4.1.3.7. | 2·8 | 1·6 | ●0·8 |
| Isocitrate dehydrogenase (NADP) | 1.1.1.42. | 3·8 | 3·4 | 3·7 |
| Malate dehydrogenase (NAD) | 1.1.1.37. | 94·2 | ●182·3 | 89·4 |
| Malate dehydrogenase (NADP, decarboxylating) | 1.1.1.40. | 0·5 | 0·9 | 0·6 |
| Phosphoenol-pyruvate-carboxykinase | 4.1.1.32. | 0·2 | <0·1 | <0·1 |
| Fructose-1,6-diphosphatase | 3.1.3.11. | 0·5 | ●0·1 | 0·4 |
| Glucose-6-phosphate dehydrogenase | 1.1.1.49. | 0·8 | 0·6 | 1·1 |

● indicates significant difference from mean values for samples from Station 1 (P < 0·05 calculated using "Student's" t test)

Table 2. Mean values of enzyme activities ($U/g$. dry wt. of tissue) estimated in extracts of the seasonal samples of G. alba collected between April 1976 and April 1977.

The mean activities in G. alba from station 24 tend to be intermediate between those in the animals from stations 1 and 2, and although phosphofructokinase and pyruvate kinase activities are lowest in the station 2 extracts only the mean ∠-glycerophosphate dehydrogenase (low at station 2) and malate dehydrogenase (high at station 2) activities show differences at the 5% level of significance from the mean values in the material from station 24.

## Effects of experimentally lowered oxygen concentrations and addition of sulphide.

The results (mean ± S.D.) of enzyme activity assays on 6 individual G. alba from each of the experimental groups are shown in Table 3. It was observed

that the supernatant fluids from the homogenates of individual worms contained
256 + 48 mg soluble protein/g. dry wt of tissue in the homogenate.  This
represents a much wider range of variation than was found in the seasonal
specimens (242 $\pm$ 12 S.D.).  A probable explanation for this variation is that

| GROUP | A | B | C | D |
|---|---|---|---|---|
|  | control | low oxgyen | anoxic | anoxic  sulphide |
| PFK | 10·1±4·6 | 13·3±13·0 | • 3·6±2·9 | 17·1±9·8 |
| MDH | 1057·0±103·5 | 1276·4±274·2 | 1064·8±61·7 | 1195·2±301·5 |
| LDH | 2·2±1·3 | 1·3±1·9 | 1·7±1·3 | 2·7±2·6 |
| AsT | 109·2±11·8 | 113·5±32·4 | • 76·9±8·0 | 114·9± 25·8 |
| AlT | 8·1±4·3 | 10·0±4·0 | 3·5±4·1 | 3·5±3·4 |
| ∝–GPDH | 49·3±7·3 | • 61·5±8·6 | 43·2±10·6 | 52·5±7·8 |

• indicates significant difference from mean value for the control group A.
( P < 0·05 calculated using "Student's" t test.)

Table 3.  Mean enzyme activities (m $^U$/mg soluble protein)
in extracts of G. alba maintained under experimental
conditions in the laboratory.

in contrast to the larger seasonal samples an accurate value for % tissue
water could not be obtained on a portion of the same sample as that used for
the analyses.  As a consequence enzyme activities expressed in terms of dry
weight of tissue would be subject to undesirably high errors.  The enzyme
activities estimated in experimental work are therefore expressed in mU per
mg soluble protein in the extracts.  Reliable estimates of pyruvate kinase
activity were not obtained due to a non-linear relationship between the
reaction rate and the quantity of extract contained in the reaction solution.
Livingstone (1975) has observed a similar effect with Mytilus edulis pyruvate
kinase in reaction mixtures containing small amounts of soluble protein, and
the effect observed in this work is therefore probably associated with the
low protein concentration ($\approx$ 0.1 mg) in the reaction mixtures.

Mean malate dehydrogenase, lactate dehydrogenase and alanine aminotransferase
activities were not significantly different in groups B, C or D compared with
the control group A.  The mean phosphofructokinase activity in group C was
significantly lower than in the control, as was the mean aspartate
aminotransferase activity.  Surprisingly, in group B which was subjected to
oxygen concentrations of 3 mg/l for 48h the mean ∡-glycerophosphate
dehydrogenase activity was higher than in the control group.

The group D results show a remarkable recovery of phosphofructokinase and
aspartate aminotransferase activities, to values similar to those observed
for groups A and C.  This group were retained under conditions identical to
the "anoxic" group C i.e. 48h at 3 mg $O_2$/l followed by 24h of anoxia.  During
this period the group C and D animals remained motionless.  Immediately after
addition of the sodium sulphide to group D, and before the crystals had
descended more than a few cm. the G. alba responded violently with continuing
repeated proboscis reactions and violent writhings of their entire bodies.
After about 1 minute, 2 of the animals had apparently died and the remainder

continued to react violently.  At this stage the remaining live specimens were rapidly removed and quick frozen.

Although the mean enzyme activities observed for Group A and D do not differ at the 5% level of significance the mean phosphofructokinase activity in Group D is the highest recorded among the experimental animals and is significantly higher ($P<0.05$) than the mean value for group C.  Aspartate aminotransferase activity was also significantly higher than in group C.

### DISCUSSION

The results suggest that in G. alba from station 2, which is the area most affected by the effluent discharge, the observed activities of certain enzymes (see Table 2) may primarily reflect effects of the effluent discharge on environmental conditions at this station.  Effects of the effluent on the Loch Eil system are well documented and the major elements which affect the benthic ecology of the system are considered to be long and short term biological oxygen demands (BOD) due to the quantity of suspended solids in the effluent and the amount of dissolved organic material respectively (Pearson, 1975).  In Fig. 3 the decrease in sulphide from 40ppm to 5ppm early in 1977, confirms the tendency towards an improvement in sediment conditions at station 2 concurrent with the commencement of the apparent recovery of the activities of the glycolytic enzymes phosphofructokinase and pyruvate kinase. The intermediate values observed at station 24 may be indicative of a less pronounced but essentially similar response to that observed at station 2 (see p.    ).

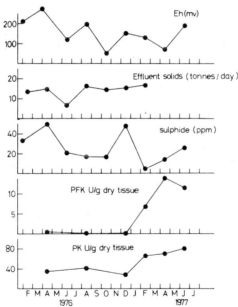

Fig. 3.  Station 2:  bimonthly averages of redox potential at the sediment surface (Eh), effluent solids discharged into L. Eil, water soluble sulphide in the first 4 cm of sediment, and the activities of phosphofructokinase (PFK) and pyruvate kinase (PK) in extracts of G. alba.

Glycera alba is a predatory polychaete which has a low energy requirement and
individuals may remain relatively inactive in their burrows for several days
when it wait for suitable prey (Ockelmann & Vahl, 1970).  There is little
information on the physiology of G. alba, but the intertidal bloodworm
G. dibranchiata has been observed to cease circulation of coelomic fluid at
low oxygen concentrations and all muscular activity ceased on immersion in
anoxic sea water (Mangum, 1970).  This species can tolerate virtual anoxia
for up to 3 days, and it has been suggested that a small reservoir of oxygen
is slowly depleted at low external $pO_2$ values (Mangum & Carhart, 1972).  The
present observations of the sublittoral G. alba at low external oxygen
concentrations are consistent with those made on G. dibranchiata.  A decrease
in glycolysis during anoxia would be consistent with the observed immobility
of G. alba under these conditions and also with the observed "apparent"
decline in phosphofructokinase activities, and it is possible that in G. alba
the capacity for survival during limited periods of anoxia is part due to a
low energy requirement when immobile.

Phosphofructokinase, pyruvate kinase and fructose -1,6-diphosphatase, are, in
most organisms, key enzymes involved in the regulation of carbohydrate
metabolism.  They catalyse unidirectional reactions and their activities are
finely tuned in vivo by the effects of allosteric modulators which include
various mucleotides and intermediate metabolites.  These considerations and
the complex kinetics of the enzyme reactions have the consequence that
activities measured in vitro using crude extracts may not reflect in vivo
activities.  Further work is therefore required to permit confident relation
of the observed "apparent" phosphofructokinase and pyruvate kinase activities
to possible changes of in vivo rates of glycolysis and fructose - 1, 6 -
diphosphatase activities to rates of gluconeogenesis.  The initial approach
utilising assays of enzyme activities in crude extracts has, however, largely
achieved the objective of indicating aspects of metabolism in G. alba which
merit more detailed investigation in relation to the effects of the inputs
of organic material to the Loch Eil system.  Detailed investigations,
involving enzyme kinetic studies and assays of metabolite concentrations
under appropriate conditions, have been initiated at this laboratory.

High malate dehydrogenase and low ⍺-glycerophosphate dehydrogenase activities
were a further characteristic of the seasonal specimens collected at station
2 (Table 2).  The observed activities of these enzymes did not respond to
experimentally induced anoxia (Table 3) and there was no parallel to the
recovery, in the seasonal samples, of the glycolytic enzyme activities early
in 1977.  It is thus possible that a longer term response is involved and it
is interesting to note that in Capitella capitata short term selection for a
single malate dehydrogenase genotype was observed after an oil spill (Grassle
& Grassle, 1974) and in Neanthes arenaceodentata experimenally lowered oxygen
concentrations for a period of 10 days elicited an increase in malate
dehydrogenase activity (Cripps & Reish, 1973).

The enzyme activity profiles observed in the seasonal specimens from station
2 and the more limited profile observed after experimentally induced anoxia
show similar responses in "apparent" phosphofructokinase activities and it is
conceivable that the profile observed in extracts of G. alba from station 2
may reflect more frequent periods of anoxia at station 2 compared with
stations 1 and 24.  However the relatively high sulphide concentrations in
the sediment at station 2 suggest that under anoxic conditions sulphide would
be present in the water column.  The reaction of the experimental G. alba
(group D) to minute quantities of sulphide suggests a low tolerance to

dissolved sulphide.  It is therefore probable that the results for G. alba from station 2 do not represent a response to periods of absolutely anaerobic conditions, but possibly to periods of low oxygen availability.

It must be emphasised that the biological oxygen demand created by the organic content of the effluent is only one of several possible effects e.g. the physical effects of fibrous and particulate matter and possibly toxic elements may exert an important influence on the metabolism of benthic fauna.  In addition effects on various aspects of metabolism are probable in view of the normal coordination of metabolic processes in any organism.  The low mean citrate synthase activity in G. alba from station 24 (Table 2) may be indicative of a more general metabolic response which may be induced by environmental influences at this station, possibly involving flux of carbon units (from lipid and/or carbohydrate) in aerobic metabolic processes.  The low aspartate aminotransferase activities observed in the extracts of G. alba from station 24 and also in the G. alba subjected to experimental anoxia possibly indicates effects on entry of amino-acid carbon to the citrate cycle. It is therefore possible that carbohydrate, lipid and protein metabolism are all affected, but further information on the consistency of the observed responses, in vivo reaction rates, metabolite concentrations and the enzymes associated with particulate cell fractions are required before the current limited data can be interpreted with reasonable confidence.

The results for the experimental G. alba, Group D, suggest that the sudden physical activity on addition of sulphide was accompanied by an apparent recovery of phosphofructokinase and aspartate aminotransferase activities in the crude extracts.  The wide range of enzyme activities observed in the seasonal study (Fig. 2) may also conceivably reflect short term responses to environmental fluctuations.  At present we have insufficient information on relevant short term fluctuations in the environment in Loch Eil. Interpretation of the enzymatic data in relation to short term oxygen depletion at station 2 must therefore remain speculative at present.

## Acknowledgements

I wish to thank Dr T.H. Pearson, Dr S.O. Stanley, Mr J. Leftley and the other members of the Organic Degradation Group of the Scottish Marine Biological Association, who supplied the environmental data included in Table 1 and Fig. 3.  The skilled technical assistance of Mrs N. Robertson is also gratefully acknowledged.

## REFERENCES

Cripps, R.A. & Reish, D.J., 1973.  The effect of environmental stress on the activity of malate dehydrogenase and lactate dehydrogenase in Neanthes arenaceodentata.  Comparative Biochemistry and Physiology, 46B, 122-133.

Grassle, J.F. & Grassle, J.P., 1974.  Opportunistic life histories and genetic systems in marine benthic polychaetes.  Journal of Marine Research, 32, 253-284.

Livingstone, D.R., 1975.  A comparison of the kinetic properties of pyruvate kinase in three populations of Mytilus edulis L. from  different environments.  In, Proceedings of the Ninth European Marine Biology Symposium (Ed. H. Barnes), 151-164, Aberdeen University Press.

Mangum, C., 1970.  Respiratory physiology in annelids.  American Scientist,
    58, 641-647.

Mangum, C. & Carhart, J.A., 1972.  Oxygen equilibrium of coelomic cell
    hemoglobin from the bloodworm Glycera dibranchiata.  Comparative
    Biochemistry and Physiology, 43A, 949-957.

Ockelmann, K.W. & Vahl, O., 1970.  On the biology of the polychaete Glycera
    alba, especially its burrowing and feeding.  Ophelia, 8, 275-294.

Pearson, T.H., 1970.  The benthic ecology of Loch Linnhe and Loch Eil, a
    sea loch system on the west coast of Scotland.  I.  The physical
    environment and distribution of the macrobenthic fauna.  Journal of
    Experimental Marine Biology and Ecology, 5, 1-34.

Pearson, T.H., 1972.  The effect of industrial effluent from pulp and paper
    mills on the marine benthic environment.  Proceedings of the Royal
    Society (B), 180, 469-485.

Pearson, T.H., 1975.  The benthic biology of Loch Linnhe and Loch Eil, a
    sea-loch system on the west coast of Scotland.  IV.  Changes in the
    benthic fauna attributable to organic enrichment.  Journal of
    Experimental Marine Biology and Ecology, 20, 1-41.

# STARVATION AND THE LACK OF HAEMOCYANIN IN *CANCER PAGURUS* L. (CRUSTACEA: DECAPODA) FROM SCOTTISH WEST COAST WATERS

**Adrian Bottoms**

*Dunstaffnage Marine Research Lab. PO Box 3, Oban, Scotland*

Published in abstract only

The population of Cancer pagurus occurring in the vicinity of Dunstaffnage Bay are shown to be more or less completely lacking in haemocyanin and haemolymph copper. It is suggested that this is a result of the lack of suitable feeding grounds resulting in starvation occurring in the wild population.

The daily rhythm of oxygen consumption under laboratory conditions is examined and shown to depend on day length, active periods being phased to dusk and dawn. A short period rhythm of heart and scaphognathite occurring during the resting phase is described. The period of this rhythm is about twenty minutes. The effects of laboratory starvation on this rhythm is described.

Measurements of respiratory performance during this short period rhythm show a surprisingly high value of oxygen utilisation from the ventilatory stream. The changes in circulatory performance in response to starvation and the lack of haemocyanin were examined and show that C. pagurus achieves the high utilisation mainly by an increase in effectiveness of oxygen removal from the ventilatory water (EW %) when compared to values from the literature. The methods of achieving this increase in a crab without haemocyanin are discussed.

# HEART AND SCAPHOGNATHITE ACTIVITY DURING THE DIGGING BEHAVIOUR OF THE SHORE CRAB, *CARCINUS MAENAS* (L.)

## N. Cumberlidge and R.F. Uglow

*Department of Zoology, University of Hull, Hull, U.K.*

ABSTRACT

Heart and scaphognathite activities, at various phases of the digging process, are described for Carcinus maenas. The activities described are discussed in terms of their possible advantages to a buried animal and compared with some similar data on Cancer pagurus.

INTRODUCTION

Sand-burrowing brachyurans use morphological and ventilatory adaptations to secure a stream of filtered seawater for irrigating the gills whilst the animal is buried. The tactic of reversing the postero-anterior flow, typical of non-buried animals, is used commonly by burrowing crabs. However, considerable interspecific variation exists of morphological specializations involved with the production of the ventilatory flow.

Bathynectes longipes and Portumnus nasatus are species with a body form similar to that of Carcinus maenas, and both establish a predominantly retrograde flow whilst buried (Garstang, 1897 a,b). Whilst buried, their chelipeds are held close to the carapace to form an 'exostegal channel' which, in conjunction with the setae around the Milne-Edwards openings, forms a filter for the inhalent stream - whether this be forwards or retrograde. It is not known whether a functional exostegal channel forms when Carcinus is buried, but it is known that this species adopts a similar posture in the sand as B.longipes and P. nasatus.

Corystes cassivelaunus and Albunea sp. have body forms specialized for the sand-dwelling mode of life, and both use retrograde ventilation and filtration whilst buried - although, here, filtration is effected by the antennal tube (Garstang, 1896, 1897c). Atelecyclus heterodon appears to use the antennal tube to filter a retrograde flow when buried just beneath the surface and, when more deeply buried, to use the folded legs to filter and retain a reservoir of water which is then pumped forwards.

Little attention appears to have been paid to the respiratory behaviour of Carcinus whilst buried and burying. Lim (1918) concluded that the direction of the ventilatory current was forwards, whether the animal was upon or buried in sand, and that scaphognathite reversals were more frequent in buried (cf. unburied) animals. Arudpragasam & Naylor (1964) have demonstrated that Carcinus, when partially-buried, irrigates by alternately drawing water in, and evacuating water out, through the normally exhalent openings. The authors are unaware of other reports of scaphognathite activities whilst this species is burying, or is buried, in sand.

Previous methods used to detect the directions of water flow through the gill chambers of buried crabs have consisted of using tracker dyes in the water and observing local movements of the sand above the margins of the carapace. These methods, plus the monitoring of branchial chamber pressures, have been used in the present studies. Additionally, the activities of the heart and both scaphognathites have been monitored in specimens throughout the burying/emerging processes. By these means it has been possible to identify better the ventilatory activities of Carcinus during the burying process and to provide records of long-term respiratory patterns of excited and quiescent buried crabs.

For comparative purposes, specimens of Cancer pagurus, which is known to ventilate its gills with a smaller proportion of its inflow through the Milne-Edwards openings than Carcinus (Arudpragasam & Naylor, 1966), were observed in a similar fashion. The aim of these investigations was to provide a fuller understanding of the ways Carcinus may survive long periods buried in a particulate substratum, and yet maintain branchial irrigation without clogging-up its gills.

## MATERIALS AND METHODS

Healthy, complete specimens of Carcinus were used in these studies. Specimens were maintained in aquaria supplied with a shallow (ca. 1 cm) layer of sand, circulating seawater (11°C) and aeration. All animals were held for at least 2 weeks under these conditions, with pertaining photoperiod, before being used in experiments.

The heart and both scaphognathites of individual specimens were monitored continuously by means of a modified impedance technique (Dyer & Uglow, 1977). Electrodes were of fine gauge (44s.w.g.) shellac-insulated copper wire. Branchial chamber pressure changes were monitored by means of fitted cannulae to Statham P23BB pressure transducers. The amplified impedance and pressure outputs were displayed as pen traces on a 'Physiograph' (Narco Biosystems Inc).

The routes of water currents were observed after pipetting a few drops of milk into the water in the vicinity of the animal. The position and postures adopted by the animals during the digging and burying sequence were recorded by visual observations.

Experiments were conducted in 10 l plastic tanks supplied with circulating seawater (11°C) and a deep (ca. 20 cm) layer of sand or gravel substratum.

Heart and scaphognathite recordings were made before, during and after burying, and records were made from these organs in animals adjudged to be at active or resting levels (see Cumberlidge & Uglow, 1977). Records were made also of animals with their inhalent apertures blocked artificially with sand, and also of animals which had been buried for some considerable time. In some instances, the digging behaviour and capabilities of animals without chelae were investigated.

## RESULTS

It was found that the digging activity of a crab could be induced usually by handling - which stimulated the crab to bury completely within 5 seconds. When digging normally, the burying process is less rapid and occurs usually in a series of stages, at any one of which the animal may pause for several minutes.

Table 1 shows that the increased proportion of time (from ca 5% to ca 50%) spent irrigating the gills with a reversed direction flow is brought about predominantly by an extension of reversal duration. Figure 1 illustrates similar data obtained from a single specimen and reveals approximately equal contributions from the 2 scaphognathites occurring at all phases in such 'active level' animals.

TABLE 1   Scaphognathite Activity Characteristics During Burying

| Activity | Reversals/10 min/ Scaphognathite | Mean Reversal Duration (sec) | Time spent Reversing (%) |
|---|---|---|---|
| On surface (5) | 7 | 4.8 | 5.6 |
| Partially-buried (5) | 8.5 | 37.2 | 53.1 |
| During burying (3) | 23.3 | 6.7 | 26.1 |
| Emerging (3) | 8.0 | 21.5 | 28.6 |
| Completely buried (5) | 8.0 | 34.9 | 45.0 |

Numbers in parentheses refer to number of traces sampled.

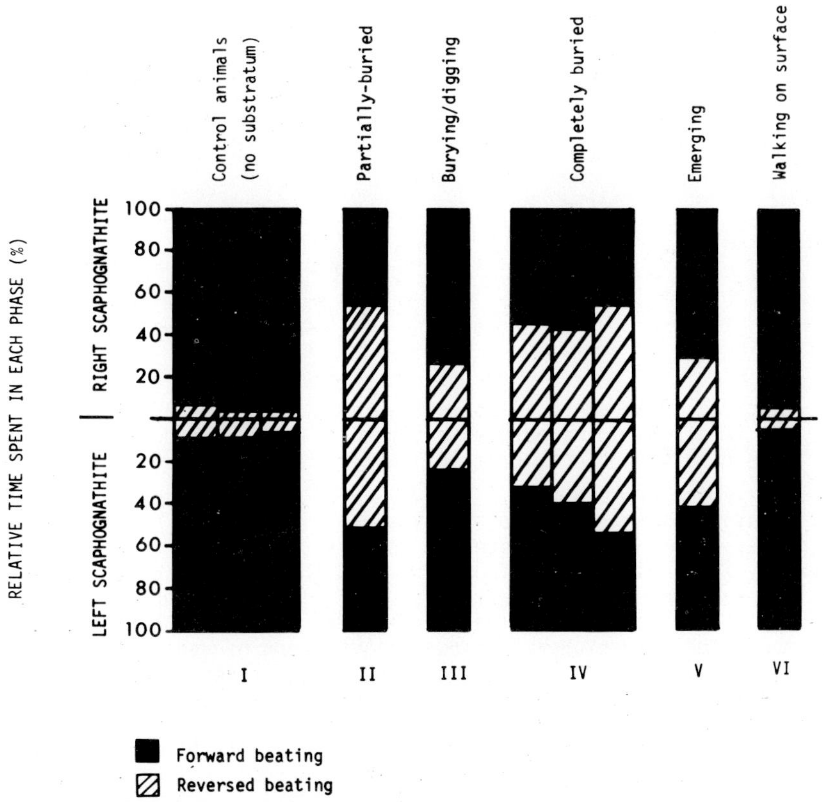

Fig. 1.   The proportion of time spent in forwards or reversed beating by the scaphognathites of Carcinus (active level) at various phases of the burying/emerging process.   Each column represents 10 minutes of recording.

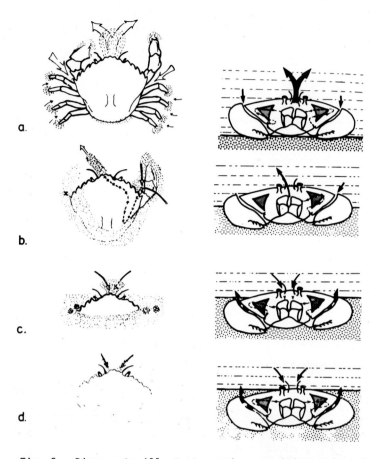

Fig. 2. Diagram to illustrate various positions adopted
by Carcinus during burying activities. Arrows indicate
the direction of the principal water currents.

Figure 2 illustrates the directions of the ventilatory flow of Carcinus at
various phases of the digging process. Animals on the surface maintain a
predominantly forwards-directed flow but, with the onset of digging, reversed
beating increases and a regular alternation of flow is set up with changes of
direction occurring about every minute (Fig. 3a). When in the fully-buried
position the animal may either continue this pattern of ventilation or, more
frequently, increase the duration of each period of reversed or forwards flow
to one of several minutes. These extended periods of reversed beating are
here termed retrograde beating. They are punctuated frequently by bursts of
high frequency forwards beating (analagous to reversals) so the term 'reversal'
is extended here to include brief changes in direction of the retrograde flow.

A partially- or fully-buried animal faces an increased risk of gill clogging
when using a retrograde flow. Small accumulations are dealt with by the
actions of the epipodite flagella of the maxillipeds whereas heavier blockages
evoke reversals of flow direction - accomplished by brief bursts of high-

frequency beating. Such events, including reversal bursts and scaphognathite slowing, can be induced by the deliberate obstruction with sand of the inhalent openings (Fig. 3b). If sand is piled above the inspiratory openings, in quantities too large for the animal to dislodge them immediately, the heart and scaphognathites have been observed to pause briefly and then to increase circulation and retrograde ventilation rates and to punctuate this activity with frequent, simultaneous bradycardia/reversal events. If the blockage persists the animal may emerge and revert to normal active level heart and forwards scaphognathite beating.

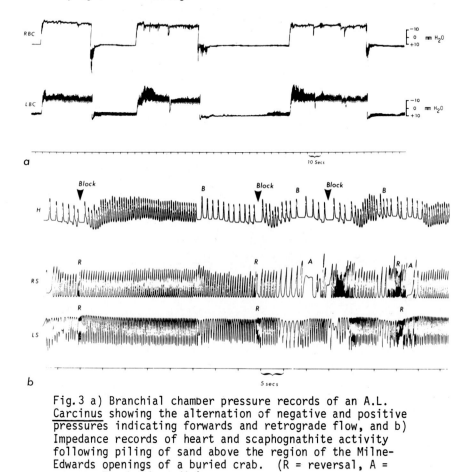

Fig. 3 a) Branchial chamber pressure records of an A.L. Carcinus showing the alternation of negative and positive pressures indicating forwards and retrograde flow, and b) Impedance records of heart and scaphognathite activity following piling of sand above the region of the Milne-Edwards openings of a buried crab. (R = reversal, A = apnoea, B = bradycardia).

When on the surface of a shallow substratum a resting level Carcinus displays slow beat rates of the heart with associated cardiac arrests and periods of bradycardia. At the same time the slow, forwards beating of the scaphognathites is marked by periods of apnoea and a low incidence of reversals. Resting level, buried animals, however, show characteristics associated with organ beating which differ from those described for an unburied animal. In such specimens the heart maintains an intermittent circulation of the blood whilst the ventilatory flow shows alternate changes of direction with accompanying periods of apnoea and thus display a 3-way interchange between retrograde, forwards and arrested flow.  Figure 4 illustrates the proportion of time each scaphognathite spent in each of these phases during 8 successive 10 minute periods by a resting level, buried Carcinus, and shows clearly the independent and intermittent ventilation of the 2 branchial chambers.

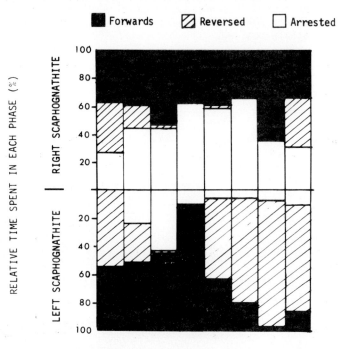

Fig. 4.  The proportion of time spent in forwards, reversed or arrested beating by the scaphognathites of a buried Carcinus (resting level).  Each column represents 10 minutes of recording.

It has been observed to be common at resting levels for such buried animals to cease beating with one scaphognathite for long periods, whilst the other continues 'normal' activities.  Commonly also, the 2 scaphognathites alternate in being the active partner.

The comparable study made on Cancer pagurus revealed that this species, normally, does not utilize extended retrograde ventilation to irrigate the branchial chambers whilst buried in sand.  Instead, the normally predominant forwards flow is maintained and the presence of the animal is indicated by disturbances of the sand above the mouth region only - often in 2 discrete areas corresponding to the outflow of each branchial chamber.  Paths of water flow, as evidence by milk tracer, indicated that the main intake of water in such specimens is through the openings above the pereiopods, and that the exhalent water is directed diagonally across the mouth region.  Although prolonged retrograde flow was not observed to occur in Cancer, it was noted that reversal frequencies were increased during digging movements, when partially-buried, or when the inhalent regions were blocked artificially.

Specimens of Carcinus deprived of both chelae were observed to dig readily into a deep, sandy substrate (using thoracic legs) and were seen to be capable of remaining completely covered for extended periods of time.

## DISCUSSION

These findings that Carcinus, when partially or completely buried, replace their normally predominant ventilatory flow with a pattern of alternating forwards and reversed flow, support the findings of Lim (1918) and Arudpragasam & Naylor (1964). Completely buried animals at active levels may increase the proportion of their retrograde beating to values between 40%-90% of their total irrigation time. When resting levels are re-established in such buried animals, the branchial irrigation is maintained by the integration of extended pausing with periods (of similar duration) of forwards and reversed flow. At resting levels also it is common for the animals to ventilate using one scaphognathite only.

The habit of establishing a reversed-direction ventilatory flow (cf unburied animals), complete with reversals and apnoeac periods, has been reported for other species of sand-burrowing brachyurans. The advantages to buried animals of these observed activities are related probably to the need to maintain a detritus-free ventilatory flow in situations where there is a likelihood of gill blockage due to the entry of particulate material into the gill chambers. The observation that there is no apparent preference for the direction of ventilatory flow in buried animals, suggests that the alternation of flow may be a tactic to equalize the filtration demands at each of the two major water intake areas. It is reasonable to assume that the reductions in gross movements, imposed on buried animals, are matched by reductions in tissue oxygen demands which, in turn, allow a reduction to be made in the amount of oxygenated water needed to supply the gills. In the present studies, the periods of extended apnoea observed in resting level, buried animals were seen to coincide with periods of bradycardia. Presumably these delays in the passage of blood through the gills, and water flow over the surfaces of the gills, serve to enhance the oxygen uptake (see also Larimer, 1964) and serve to provide intermittent increases in oxygen supply to the tissues. Besides maximizing the use of available oxygen, the reduced ventilation volumes will tend also to draw less detritus into the gill chambers, since the standing pressures developed at low scaphognathite beat rates are less than those at high beat rates (Hughes, Knights & Scammell, 1969).

The enhanced use of retrograde irrigation when buried may not be a general brachyuran feature, as the present observations on Cancer reveal. The different strategies employed by Carcinus and Cancer may be caused by morphological differences which, in Cancer, result in a greater retention of the functional use of the more posterior openings to the gill chambers (Arudpragasam & Naylor, 1966).

It is concluded that scaphognathite reversals in buried animals may serve the dual purpose of gill chamber sanitation and, in active level animals, enhancement of oxygen uptake. When the buried animal settles to resting levels there is a lessened need for a tactic to enhance oxygen extraction and the observation that buried, resting level animals have high reversal rates (whilst unburied, resting level animals do not) suggests that, in this situation, reversals serve principally in a cleansing capacity.

The possession of a repertoire of tactics, involving the manipulation of blood and ventilatory flows, so that the animal can satisfy tissue oxygen demands in a wide variety of environmental situations, may enable Carcinus to maximise its ecological distribution.

### ACKNOWLEDGEMENTS

This work was carried out whilst one of us (N.C.) held a SRC studentship.

### REFERENCES

Arudpragasam, K.D. & Naylor, E., 1964.  Gill ventilation and the role of reversed respiratory currents in Carcinus maenas (L).  Journal of Experimental Biology, 41, 299-307.

Arudpragasam, K.D. & Naylor, E., 1966.  Patterns of gill ventilation in some decapod crustacea.  Journal of Zoology, London, 150, 401-411.

Cumberlidge, N. & Uglow, R.F., 1977.  Heart and scaphognathite activity of the shore crab, Carcinus maenas (L).  Journal of Experimental Marine Biology and Ecology, 28, 87-107.

Dyer, M.F. & Uglow, R.F., 1977.  On a technique for monitoring heart and scaphognathite activity in Natantia.  Journal of Experimental Marine Biology and Ecology.

Garstang, W. 1896.  The habits and respiratory mechanisms of Corystes cassivelaunus.  Journal of the Marine Biological Association of the United Kingdom, 4, 223-232.

Garstang, W., 1897a.  The function of antero-lateral denticulations of the carapace of sand-burrowing crabs.  Journal of the Marine Biological Association of the United Kingdom, 4, 396-401.

Garstang, W., 1897b.  The systematic features, habits and respiratory phenomena of Portunus nasatus (Latreille).  Journal of the Marine Biological Association of the United Kingdom, 4, 402-407.

Garstang, W., 1897c.  On some modifications of structure subservient to respiration in decapod crustacea, which burrow in sand;  with some remarks on the utility of specific characters in the genus Callapa and the description of a new species of Albunea.  Quarterly Journal of Microscopical Science, 40, 211-232.

Hughes, G.M., Knights, B. & Scammell, C.A., 1969.  The distribution of $PO_2$ and hydrostatic pressure changes within the branchial chambers in relation to gill ventilation of the shore crab, Carcinus maenas (L).  Journal of Experimental Biology, 51, 203-220.

Larimer, J.L., 1964.  Patterns of diffusion of oxygen across crustacean gill membranes.  Journal of Cellular and Comparative Physiology, 64, 139-148.

Lim, R.K.S., 1918.  Experiments on the respiratory mechanism of the shore crab, (Carcinus maenas).  Proceedings of the Royal Society of Edinburgh, 48-56.

# ETUDE EXPERIMENTALE DE LA RESPIRATION, DE LA CROISSANCE ET DE LA FECONDITE DE *TISBE HOLOTHURIAE* (COPEPODE: HARPACTICOIDE) ELEVE A DES TEMPERATURES DIFFERENTES

**Raymond Gaudy et Jean-Pierre Guérin**

*Laboratoire d'hydrobiologie Marine et Station Marine d'Endoume, Centre Universitaire de Luminy, 13288 Marseille Cedex 2, France*

## ABSTRACT

The respiratory metabolic variations with **temperature** were studied in Tisbe holothuriae after or without preliminary acclimatization to high or low temperatures. Breeding of this species for the entire cycle was made under three different temperatures. The intrinsic growth rate and the respiratory rate increase with temperature, whereas the proportion of daughter females, the weight of individuals and the mean generation time decrease. Taking into account these results, the growth efficiency rates K1 and K2 were determined in females under different breeding temperatures.

## INTRODUCTION

Dans la recherche des conditions optimales d'élevage du copépode harpacticoïde *Tisbe holothuriae* Humes, nous avions envisagé initialement l'influence de la qualité de la nourriture offerte sur les paramètres de la dynamique des populations (Gaudy et Guérin, 1977) et sur la constitution chimique élémentaire des adultes obtenus (Guérin et Gaudy, sous presse). L'incidence de la température sur la plupart des processus biologiques intervenant chez les poïkilotermes est bien connue ; aussi nous proposons-nous, dans ce travail, d'étudier plus particulièrement son action au niveau de l'individu, aux différents stades de son cycle vital, et par rapport aux paramètres de croissance de la population.

## MATERIEL ET METHODES

### Respiration

Les expériences de respiration ne concernent que les femelles adultes obtenues en élevage au laboratoire à 19°C. Certains lots ont été acclimatés pendant une durée de 48 à 72 h. avant la mise en expérience, à une température "haute" (22 à 24°C), d'autres à une température "basse" (12 - 14 °C).

L'intensité respiratoire est établie d'après la teneur en $O_2$ de flacons d'eau de mer, certains contenant un nombre connu d'individus, d'autres servant de témoins, après un temps d'incubation de 24 h environ aux températures de 10, 14, 18, 22 ou 24°C. Les dosages d'oxygène dissous sont effectués grâce à une technique polarographique (électrode de Clark).

### Poids

Les estimations de poids sec chez les adultes nécessitent un tri par sexe des

animaux préalablement anesthésiés. Après rinçage rapide à l'eau douce, des
lots de 70 à 100 individus sont déposés sur une coupelle d'aluminium tarée,
déshydratés pendant 24 h à 60°C, puis conservés au dessicateur jusqu'à la pesée
à la balance de Cahn (précision de 0,01 mg). Le poids des oeufs a été obtenu
indirectement à partir de leur volume unitaire, lui-même établi par mensuration
au microscope, en tenant compte d'une densité de 1 et d'un rapport de conversion
poids sec/poids humide de 20 %. Les variations de diamètre des oeufs avec la
température étant négligeables, un poids de 0,04 mg par oeuf a été adopté uni-
formément. Cette valeur a été confirmée en déterminant la différence pondérale
entre des lots de femelles ovigères et non ovigères, élevées dans les mêmes conditions, et en se basant sur le nombre moyen d'oeufs par sac établi d'après les
élevages. Le poids ainsi déterminé est de 0,044 mg.

Les mesures pondérales ont été ramenées à leur équivalent carbone d'après les
résultats obtenus précédemment avec le même aliment (Guérin et Gaudy, sous presse), le taux de conversion poids sec/carbone étant de 0,42.

## Dynamique de la population

Les élevages ont été réalisés aux températures de 14, 19 et 24°C, à une salinité
de 38‰, en éclairement atténué, mais respectant le cycle naturel, dans des récipients de 40 ml environ. La nourriture est distribuée quotidiennement, en
quantité légèrement excédentaire par rapport aux besoins. Nous avons utilisé un
aliment synthétique destiné à la nourriture de crevettes (aliment "D", Guérin
et Gaudy, sous presse).

La destinée et la descendance de lots de femelles soeurs isolées après féconda-
tion, à raison d'une par récipient, sont suivies par des observations quoti-
diennes. Après éclosion de chaque sac ovigère, la femelle est transférée dans
un nouveau récipient, tandis que ses descendants, demeurés en place, sont observés et dénombrés lorsqu'il arrivent à l'état adulte. On peut ainsi établir sur
des séries de 12 lots par température : la longévité des femelles mères, le nombre de sacs ovigères successifs et le rythme de leur production, l'abondance et
le sex-ratio de la descendance, la durée du développement larvaire. Le nombre
d'oeufs produits lors de chaque ponte est calculé indirectement d'après l'abondance de la descendance adulte compte tenu d'une mortalité larvaire de 20 % en
moyenne (Gaudy et Guérin, 1977).

Les paramètres de croissance de la population pris en considération sont : le
taux de reproduction $R_o$, facteur par lequel la population de femelles se multi-
plie d'une génération à l'autre ; le temps moyen de génération T, calculé d'après
la formule $T = \Sigma x \cdot fx / \Sigma fx$, où x est l'âge des mères au moment de la production
des nauplii et fx le nombre de femelles issues de ces nauplii; et $r_m = Ln.R_o / T$.

### RESULTATS

## Respiration

L'augmentation du métabolisme respiratoire avec la température n'est pas régulière, la courbe tendant à former un plateau entre 14 et 18°C, quelle que soit
la température d'acclimatation. Les Q10 les plus élevés, dénotant une grande
sensibilité à la température, s'observent en-dessous de 14°C chez les individus
acclimatés au froid et à 19°C, alors que le Q10 maximum chez les individus acclimatés à 22-24°C est noté entre 18 et 22°C (tableau 1). Chez ces derniers, on
note les valeurs d'intensité respiratoire les plus basses pour une température
donnée, les plus élevées s'observant chez les individus acclimatés à 12-14°C.

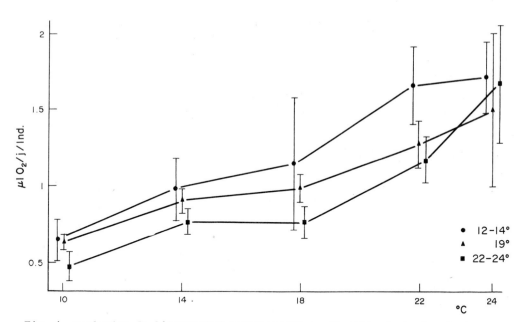

Fig. 1. Evolution de l'intensité respiratoire en fonction de la température.

Ce mécanisme a un effet homéostatique sur la respiration des individus élevés à des températures différentes.  Ainsi, le Q 10 basé sur la respiration à leur température d'élevage (14,19 et 24°C) des *Tisbe* considérés dans ce travail est-il plus réduit que celui correspondant à des individus acclimatés à une seule de ces températures (tableau 1).

TABLEAU 1 Q 10 pour différentes conditions d'acclimatation

| Intervalle de température | Individus acclimatés au froid | Individus acclimatés à 19°C | Individus acclimatés au chaud | Individus acclimatés à chaque température |
|---|---|---|---|---|
| 10 - 14°C | 2,92 | 2,52 | 1,95 | |
| 14 - 18°C | 1,42 | 1,36 | 1 | |
| 18 - 22°C | 2,61 | 1,87 | 2,98 | |
| 22 - 24°C | 1,07 | 1,51 | 2,45 | |
| 14 - 19°C* | 1,63 | 1,40 | 1,25 | 1,09 |
| 14 - 24°C | 1,74 | 1,71 | 2,12 | 1,69 |

## Dynamique des populations

Le tableau 2 et les figures 2 et 3 rassemblent les principaux résultats concernant la dynamique des populations.  On constate que la température a un effet accélérateur sur les différentes étapes du cycle biologique : développement larvaire, durée de la période précédent la première ponte chez les femelles, durée de la période de reproduction, fréquence des pontes.  Les poids des femelles adultes varient en raison inverse de leur temps de développement.

* d'après une intensité respiratoire à 19°C, calculée par interpolation

TABLEAU 2. Paramètres de la dynamique de la population aux trois
températures d'élevage (moyenne par lots de 12 femelles).

| Température (°C) | 14 | 19 | 24 |
|---|---|---|---|
| Poids sec des femelles (μg) | 6,97 | 6,67 | 5,97 |
| Durée du développement (ω/♀ adultes) | 19 | 8,75 | 5 |
| Age des ♀ à la première ponte (J) | 24 | 12 | 7 |
| Fréquence des ponte (J) | 4 | 2,6 | 1,6 |
| Nombre moyen de sacs ovigères | 4,75 | 3,41 | 4,92 |
| Nombre moyen d'oeufs/sac | 21,52 | 39,31 | 46,31 |
| Sex-ratio moyen (♀/Nb adultes) | 0,42 | 0,38 | 0,29 |
| $R_o$ | 36,08 | 43,33 | 56,66 |
| T (jours) | 34,51 | 17,09 | 10,74 |
| $r_m$ | 0,104 | 0,220 | 0,376 |

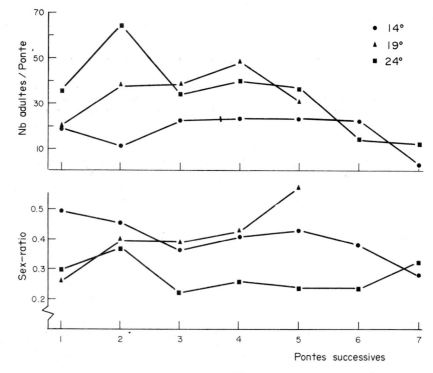

Fig. 2. Nombre moyen et sex-ratio des adultes obtenus au cours des pontes
successives.

Le nombre de sacs ovigères successifs présente une grande variabilité individuelle (de 1 à 7 sacs). Les derniers sont généralement plus réduits et peu prolifique (Fig. 2). La tendance à produire plus de descendants en début de cycle de ponte est surtout marquée à 24°C. Le sex-ratio est presque toujours en faveur des mâles.

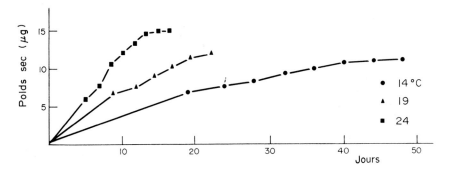

Fig. 3. Production cumulée de matière organique (croissance et production d'oeufs des sacs successifs), au cours du cycle vital de *T. holothuriae*.

C'est à 24°C que les taux les plus faibles s'observent. Malgré cette réduction du pourcentage de femelles, le paramètre $R_0$ croît avec la température, car la fertilité globale augmente rapidement avec la température, compensant ainsi largement l'effet défavorable du sex-ratio. T est largement dépendant de la température, diminuant de plus d'un facteur 3 entre 14 et 24°C. Ce paramètre joue le rôle principal sur la valeur de $r_m$, qui augmente sensiblement avec la température.

Compte tenu des éléments obtenus précédemment, il est possible de dresser un premier bilan des transformations matière-énergie intervenant au cours du cycle biologique chez les femelles, aux différentes températures (tableau 3).

Pour la période immature, la production de matière organique correspond à l'accroissement pondéral de l'oeuf à l'adulte. Les dépenses de la respiration sont établies en admettant une augmentation de la respiration R avec l'âge J (en jours) selon une relation de type parabolique $R = a.J^2$. La respiration cumulée au cours de la période de croissance correspond donc à l'intégrale :

$$R' = \frac{a.J^3}{3}$$

Connaissant R et J chez l'adulte d'après les expériences de respiration, on tire a, et il est possible de calculer R' pour un âge de J jours. Les valeurs de R' sont alors converties en équivalent carbone, en adoptant un QR de 0,8, ce qui donne un taux de conversion de 0,43 (Lasker et al., 1970).

Les pertes de matière dues aux mues sont estimées comme étant équivalentes à 6% du poids sec (Harris et Paffenhöfer, 1976), les poids des stades successifs étant dérivés de leurs mensuration en se référant à une relation taille-poids préétablie de type log. W = 1,915 log L - 2,253.

Pour la période fertile, nous avons tenu compte de la production cumulée d'oeufs en nous basant sur le poids unitaire d'un oeuf. La dépense respiratoire journalière est étendue à toute la période fertile. Le rendement net de croissance $K_2$ est le rapport de la quantité de matière organique produite sur la quantité de matière assimilée. Cette dernière équilibre la somme de la production organique, les mues et les dépenses respiratoires.

R. Gaudy and J-P. Guerin

TALEAU 3 Rendement brut ($K_1$) et rendement net ($K_2$) de croissance chez les femelles de *Tisbe holothuriae* aux 3 températures d'élevage

| T°C | Durée (J) | Production C ( µg) | Respiration | | Mues C ( µg) | $K_1$ | $K_2$ |
|-----|-----------|--------------------|-------------|---|--------------|-------|-------|
| | | | $O_2$ ( µl) | C ( µg) | | | |
| | | Période de croissance | | | | | |
| 14 | 19 | 2,91 | 6,33 | 2,72 | 0,21 | 0,37 | 0,50 |
| 19 | 8,75 | 2,78 | 3,04 | 1,30 | 0,21 | 0,47 | 0,65 |
| 24 | 5 | 2,49 | 2,80 | 1,20 | 0,21 | 0,47 | 0,64 |
| | | Période de reproduction | | | | | |
| 14 | 29 | 1,72 | 28,83 | 12,39 | – | 0,09 | 0,12 |
| 19 | 13,65 | 2,25 | 14,20 | 6,10 | – | 0,20 | 0,27 |
| 24 | 11,60 | 3,83 | 19,49 | 8,38 | – | 0,23 | 0,31 |
| | | Vie totale productive | | | | | |
| 14 | 48 | 4,63 | 35,16 | 15,11 | 0,21 | 0,17 | 0,23 |
| 19 | 22,40 | 5,03 | 17,24 | 7,40 | 0,21 | 0,29 | 0,40 |
| 24 | 16,60 | 6,32 | 22,29 | 9,58 | 0,21 | 0,29 | 0,39 |

Les valeurs de $K_2$ peuvent être converties en $K_1$ (rendement brut de croissance) selon la formule $K_1 = A.K_2$ où A est le taux d'assimilation. D'après la littérature A est souvent voisin de 0,8. Chez *Tigriopus* Harris (1973) calcule un taux moyen de 0,754. Chez *Tisbe holothuriae* nos propres estimations selon la méthode de Conover, mais avec un aliment inerte différent de celui utilisé dans ce travail, sont de 0,73. C'est d'après ce chiffre que les valeurs de $K_1$ du tableau ont été calculées.

## DISCUSSION

Ramenées à l'unité pondérale, les intensités respiratoires sont du même ordre que celles caractérisant les harpacticoïdes non interstitiels selon Coull et Vernberg (1970), soit 5,2 µl/mg/h en moyenne. L'acclimatation aux conditions thermiques d'élevage a un effet modérateur sur l'augmentation du métabolisme correspondant à une compensation partielle de type 2 (Precht, 1958). L'énergie ainsi économisée peut être consacrée à une plus grande production organique.

L'influence de la température sur le cycle biologique de *Tisbe* est plus particulièrement marquée au niveau des processus dynamiques, principalement la vitesse de croissance et la fréquence de ponte. Entre 14 et 24°C, la vitesse de croissance augmente dans une proportion de 3,8 tandis que la respiration présente un Q 10 de 1,69 seulement. La résultante de cette accélération est un raccourcissement marqué de la durée de génération T ( dans une proportion de 3,21 ) avec un effet notable sur les taux $r_m$   Parise et Lazzaretto (1966) chez *Tisbe furcata* et Heip et Smol (1976) chez deux harpacticoïdes d'eau saumâtre ont démontré également le rôle direct de la température sur les valeurs de $r_m$.

Les rendements de croissance obtenus pendant la période de croissance sont

généralement supérieurs à ceux des copépodes pélagiques. Ainsi Corner et al.
(1967) citent un $K_1$ de 0,34 chez *Calanus finmarchicus*. Chez l'espèce voisine
*C. helgolandicus* Paffenhöfer (1976) calcule des $K_1$ variant de 0,17 à 0,33 selon
la nature des algues proposées et le mode de calcul, alors que selon Corner et
al. (1976), ce taux peut monter à 0,53 en régime carnivore. Mullin et Brooks
(1967) trouvent un $K_1$ moyen de 0,35 au cours de la croissance de *Rhincalanus
nasutus*. Chez les petits calanoïdes, Harris et Paffenhöfer (1976) notent des
$K_1$ compris entre 0,13 et 0,17 chez *Pseudocalanus elongatus*, entre 0,17 et 0,27
chez *Temora longicornis*. Peu de données concernent les taux $K_1$ pour la période
de production d'oeufs. Ils sont inférieurs à 0,06 et 0,41 chez *Pseudocalanus*
et *Temora* (Harris et Paffenhöfer, 1976) et à 0,17 chez *Eurytemora affinis* (Heinle et al. 1977). Pour les Harpacticoïdes, nous ne disposons que des valeurs
calculées par Harris (1973) chez *Tigriopus brevicornis*, avec, pour la période de
croissance des valeurs $K_1$ et $K_2$ de 0,13 et 0,17 et pour la période de ponte,
des valeurs correspondantes de 0,22 et 0,29. Le rendement de production d'oeufs
comparativement très important, est, selon l'auteur, un mécanisme d'adaptation
à un biotope très fluctuant et sujet à dessication périodique. *Tisbe holothuriae*, espèce de taille et de biologie assez voisines, présente un taux similai-
re au niveau de la production d'oeufs, mais un taux très supérieur pour la
croissance, en raison du temps de développement plus court.

Les hauts niveaux des taux de conversion d'énergie chez *Tisbe* élevé sur nourriture inerte et l'importance du taux de croissance instantanée de la population
sont des éléments très favorables à une production organique maximale, qui
pourrait être utilisée comme nourriture vivante de complément en aquaculture.
Le rôle du facteur température apparaît prépondérant. Il serait utile dans des
études ultérieures de définir les limites supérieures dans lesquelles ce facteur reste favorable.

## REFERENCES

Corner, E.D.S., Cowey, C.B. & Marshall, S.M., 1967. On the nutrition and metabolism of zooplankton. V. Feeding efficiency of *Calanus finmarchicus*. *Journal of the Marine Biological Association of the United Kingdom*, 45, 429-442.

Corner, E.D.S., Head, R.N., Kilvington, C.C. & Pennycuick, L., 1976. On the
nutrition and metabolism of zooplankton. X. Quantitative aspects of *Calanus
helgolandicus* feeding as a carnivore. *Journal of the Marine Biological Association of the United Kingdom*, 56, 345-358.

Coull, B.C. & Vernberg, W.B., 1970. Harpacticoïd copepod respiration; *Enhydro-
soma propinquum* and *Longipedia helgolandica*. *Marine Biology*, 5, 341-344.

Gaudy, R. & Guérin, J.-P., 1977. Dynamique des populations de *Tisbe holothuriae* (Crustacea : Copepoda) en élevage sur trois régimes artificiels différents. *Marine Biology*, 29, 137-145.

Guérin, J.-P. & Gaudy, R., 1977. Etude des variations de poids sec et de constitution chimique élémentaire de *Tisbe holothuriae* (Copepoda, harpacticoïda)
élevé sur différents régimes artificiels. *Marine Biology*.(sous presse).

Harris, R.P., 1973. Feeding, growth, reproduction and nitrogen utilization by
the harpaticoïd copepod, *Tigriopus brevicornis*. *Journal of the Marine Biological Association of the United Kingdom*, 53, 785-800.

Harris, R.P. & Paffenhöfer, G.A., 1976.  The effect of food concentration on cumulative ingestion and growth efficiency of two small marine planktonic copepods. *Journal of the Marine Biological Association of the United Kingdom* 56, 875-888.

Heinle, D.R., Harris, R.P., Ustach, J.F. & Flemer, D.M., 1977.  Detritus as food for estuarine copepods. *Marine Biology*, 40, 341-353.

Heip, C. & Smol, N., 1976.  Influence of temperature on the reproductive potential of two brackish-water harpacticoïds (Crustacea : Copepoda) *Marine Biology*, 35, 327-334.

Lasker, R., Wells, J.B.J. & McIntyre, A.D., 1970.  Growth, reproduction, respiration and carbon utilization of the sand-dwelling harpacticoïd copepod, *Asellopsis intermedia*. *Journal of the Marine Biological Association of the United Kingdom*, 50, 147-160.

Mullin, M.M. & Brooks, E.R., 1967.  Laboratory culture, growth rate, and feeding behaviour of a planktonic marine copepod. *Limnology and Oceanography*, 12, 657-666.

Paffenhöfer, G.A., 1976.  Feeding, growth and food conversion of the marine planktonic copepod *Calanus helgolandicus*. *Limnology and Oceanography*, 21, 39-50.

Parise, A. & Lazzaretto, I., 1966.  Misure di popolazione sul copepode *Tisbe furcata* (Baird) (Harpacticoïda). *Atti i Memorie della Accademia patavina*, 79, 1-11.

Precht, H., 1958.  Concepts of temperature adaptation of unchanging reaction systems of cold-blooded animals in *Physiological adaptation*, edited by C.C. Prosser, pp 50-78, Washington D.C. : American Physiological Society.

# RESPIRATION OF *PATELLA VULGATA* ON THE SHORE

## D.F. Houlihan and J.R.L. Newton

*Department of Zoology, University of Aberdeen, Scotland*

### ABSTRACT

Limpets can respire in air and water, but laboratory determined rates of oxygen consumption are influenced by the disturbing effects of removing the animals from their normal habitat. A respirometer is described that can be used to measure the oxygen consumption of undisturbed limpets on the shore. Field results are compared with those from the laboratory and an analysis made of the changes occurring in *Patella* during tidal cycles.

### INTRODUCTION

The exchange of gases in intertidal animals is unusual in that it can occur in both air and water. Such animals are believed to show a range of air-breathing abilities related to their position on the shore [1]. *Patella vulgata* is found on the upper shore, where the animals may be exposed to air for several hours, twice a day. Experiments by Bannister [2] indicated that high level *P. lusitanica* had greater oxygen consumption in air, whereas with *P. vulgata*, oxygen consumption and heart beat had been reported as being maximal when the limpet was covered by the tide [3,4]. Laboratory experiments on a range of *Littorina* species have produced a similar set of contradictory data on the relative importance of air and water respiration [5].

Although it is the aim of many physiologists to describe the physiology of animals in their natural environment, there has been little effort to measure directly, the metabolism of intertidal invertebrates. This paper describes the results obtained from using relatively simple respiratory techniques on *P. vulgata in situ* on the shore and comparing these results with laboratory determinations.

### METHODS

Aerial respiration rates in the laboratory were measured with a Gilson respirometer, fitted with special wide-neck flasks. For larger limpets, the respiration caps shown in Fig. 1 were used. These limpets were positioned on small rocks in a constant temperature bath. A perspex cap was placed over the animal, held with plasticene and sealed with an overlying rubber solution. Filling the cap with nitrogen and subsequent analysis of the contained gas, indicated that there was no leakage for up to five hours. After fitting the caps, time was allowed for the temperature of the contained air to reach $10^{\circ}C$ before commencing the experiment. At its completion, gas samples were taken with a syringe filled with citrate buffer and analysed using a Scholander-Roughton [6] gas analyser, or an oxygen electrode. Finally the container

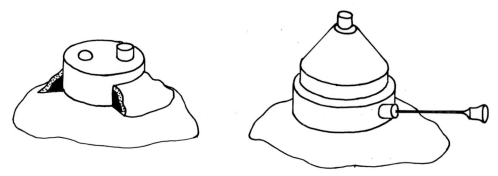

Air filled.                    Water filled.  Two part cap with piston-like
                               action allowing for volume changes.

Fig. 1   Perspex 'cap' respirometers for use on the shore.

volumes were determined by filling with water.

In the field, aerial respiration rates were determined using a respiration cap,
essentially as described for use in the laboratory.  Sample-syringes containing
nitrogen were first transported to the shore and back, without contamination.
To minimise disturbance, the limpet shell and surrounding rock were scrubbed a
few days before experimentation.  On the actual day the rock was blotted and
allowed to dry before positioning the perspex caps.  The ambient air temperature was always near to $10^{\circ}C$, but in order to prevent warming, the containers
were enclosed in a weighted polystyrene box, covered in aluminium foil.

Aquatic respiration rates produced in the laboratory were measured using 'closed
bottle respirometers';  the oxygen content of the water being determined by the
Winkler method, as described by Strickland and Parsons (7).  In all cases auto-
claved water was used and one control flask was run without an animal.  All
experiments were run at $10^{\circ}C$.  In the field, the closed volume, two part cap
shown in Fig. 1 was used.  This was filled with sea water and contained
approximately 50 cc.  Water samples were taken in duplicate using a 5 ml syringe
inserted through the rubber bung in the base ring and analysed by a modified
form of the Winkler method (7);  the dissolved oxygen being fixed chemically in
the field and the sample titrated in the laboratory.  A few days preceeding
experimentation, the chosen limpet and surrounding rock was scrubbed, washed
with sea water and allowed to dry, before the base ring was cemented into place
with 'Weatherproof Plastic Compound' (manufactured by BICC).  The open bung
hole allowed for water drainage after the base ring had been covered by the
tide.  Experiments, conducted a few days later, were commenced immediately after
the tide had receded from the chosen limpet.  The base ring was dried and the
lubricated upper cap turned into position, before filling with sea water to the
exclusion of the air bubbles.  At the same time, samples of this water were
fixed for oxygen analysis.  The piston-like action of the two halves of the cap
allowed for a reduction in volume when water samples were taken and also for
regular stirring by filling a sample-syringe and rapidly reinjecting this into
the container.  To avoid heating, polystyrene boxes covered with aluminium foil
were placed over the caps, but on each day, one cap which contained no animal
acted as a control.  Experiments were run for one to one and a half hours and
the ambient air temperature was always found to be near $10^{\circ}C$.  The data was
analysed according to Snedecor (8).

RESULTS

## Aerial respiration

Limpets that had just been collected at low tide were placed in the Gilson respirometer flasks and allowed one hour before measurements of oxygen consumption were begun.  These were conducted over a three hour period and found to be constant.  Only those animals that did not move have been included in the results.  The oxygen consumption of freshly collected limpets was also determined in the laboratory by use of the perspex caps.  Continuous gas sampling from one animal indicated that the rate became constant within an hour of positioning the cap, when the experiment would normally be commenced.  The data from these methods was subjected to regression analyses.  Covariance analysis reveals that the regressions are not significantly different in slope (P > 0.05) and thus the two methods produce a similar relationship between oxygen consumption and weight, over the weight range used.  The data from both methods thus pooled, gave a regression equation of:  $\log Y = 1.823 + 0.757 \log X$, where X is the wet flesh weight and Y is the oxygen consumption in $\mu$l of oxygen $h^{-1}$ (Fig. 2).  The analysis had a significant correlation coefficient (P < 0.05).

The use of the perspex cap on the shore did not seem to disturb the animals and they all had slightly raised shells at the end of the experiment, rather than being in the tightly clamped down state.  Only one animal moved inside the cap and this has not been included in the results.  Field results are shown in Fig. 2, with the relationship between oxygen consumption and flesh weight being expressed by the regression equation:  $\log Y = 1.482 + 0.644 \log X$.  This analysis has a significant correlation coefficient (P < 0.05).  Covariance analysis between the laboratory and shore determined rates reveals that the slopes of the regression analyses are not significantly different (P > 0.05), but that the elevation of the laboratory determined rates is significantly higher than those from the shore (P < 0.001).

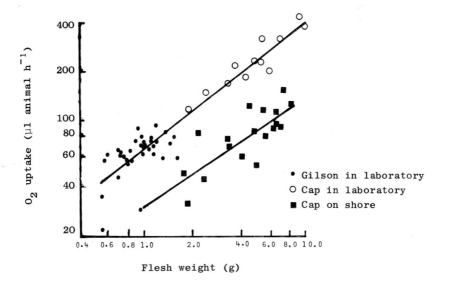

Fig. 2    Aerial respiration of *Patella vulgata*.

In view of the rapidity of the measurements made on freshly collected animals, their higher respiration rates in the laboratory compared with those on the shore, could be due to the disturbing influence of dislodging them.  However, the elevated rate remained constant for at least two days in limpets left undisturbed in the Gilson flasks.  Likewise, elevated rates were produced by limpets kept in flowing sea water for two days before being placed in the Gilson flasks.  In order to obtain values similar to those from the shore, it was eventually found necessary to place fresh animals in the flasks, keep them in flowing sea water for at least a day and then measure the aerial respiration rate, several hours after the sea water had been poured off the otherwise, undisturbed limpets.  The rates from animals treated in this way can be pooled with the shore values to yield a regression equation of log Y = 1.468 + 0.655 log X.  This is compared in Fig. 3 with that from the rates of freshly collected limpets in the laboratory. It has a significant correlation coefficient (P < 0.001) and is not significantly different in slope or elevation from the shore data (P > 0.05).  It is however, lower than the laboratory rate of freshly collected limpets (P < 0.001), but not significantly different in slope (P > 0.05).

The oxygen consumption in air, of a freshly collected limpet weighing 10g (flesh weight) and measured in the laboratory was 381 $\mu$l h$^{-1}$ ($\pm$ 1.09).  Whereas, a value of 250 $\mu$l h$^{-1}$ has been reported previously for a limpet of this size and temperature (9).  However, the same limpet treated in the laboratory in the manner described above, or measured on the shore produced a rate of 132 $\mu$l hr. ($\pm$ 1.10).

## Aquatic respiration

Freshly collected limpets were cleaned, placed on plastic dishes in aerated sea

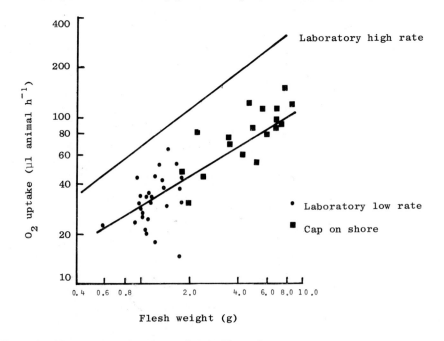

Fig. 3    Aerial respiration of *Patella vulgata*.

water and allowed one hour to acclimatize before the dish was transferred to a closed bottle respirometer.  Experiments were run for three hours which produced approximately, a 20% drop in oxygen concentration.  The limpets did not move during the experiments.  The respiration rates obtained were subjected to regression analysis and could be related to flesh weight by the equation log Y = 1.524 + 0.489 log X (Fig. 4. High rate).  This has a significant correlation coefficient (P < 0.001).

Alternatively, limpets were left undisturbed in flowing sea water for 24 hours before conducting the experiments outlined above.  In this case, the regression equation is log Y = 1.332 + 0.612 log X (Fig. 4. Low rate) and has a significant correlation coefficient (P < 0.001).

Covariance analysis shows that the respiration rates of those limpets measured after one day in the laboratory are significantly lower than from those freshly collected (P < 0.005), but that there is no significant difference in their slope (P > 0.005).

The perspex containers used in the field did not appear to disturb the limpets, since they were in a 'relaxed state' i.e. with raised shells, when the upper cap was removed at the end of the experiment.  On subjecting the results to regression analysis, respiration rates were found to relate to flesh weight by the equation log Y = 1.340 + 0.412 log X (P < 0.001).   (Fig. 5).   Covariance analysis of the regression analyses produced by the field and laboratory results shows that the field respiration rates are significantly lower than those of freshly collected animals, in the laboratory (P < 0.001).  They are not however, significantly different to those from limpets allowed to stand in sea water for a day (P > 0.05).  In neither case is there any significant difference in slope (P > 0.05).

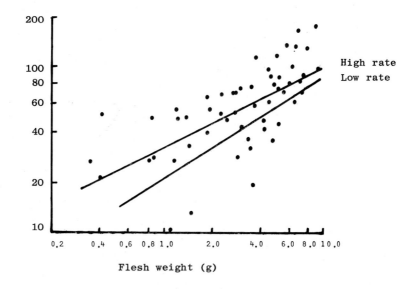

Fig. 4    Aquatic respiration of *Patella vulgata* in the laboratory.

Covariance analysis of the aquatic and aerial respiration rates of freshly
collected animals reveals that the regression analyses are significantly
different in slope (P < 0.05) and that the aerial rates are higher (P < 0.001).
When the analysis is made between the shore results, the aerial rates are also
found to be significantly higher than the aquatic, (P < 0.001) but there is no
significant difference in slope (P > 0.05).

In none of the experiments described were any animals observed to move, yet
there are seen to be large differences in oxygen consumption.  As a high proportion of an animal's tissue is taken up by the shell muscle and it is a common
experience that limpets can be in a relaxed or 'clamped down' state, it was
decided to investigate the metabolic activity of the shell muscle.

## Respiration and adhesion

All experiments were conducted in air.  Nylon fishing line was glued to the
shells of freshly collected limpets with 'Araldite' and after this had dried,
they were placed on plastic plates in flowing sea water of $10^{\circ}C$, for two days.
The respirometer was placed in a water bath of $10^{\circ}C$ and after 24 hours, carbon
dioxide absorber was added and the whole apparatus sealed with the bungs and
vaseline.  The respiration rates of the limpets were then measured over a three
hour period and found to be similar to those from the shore animals (Fig. 2).
A weight was attached to the end of the line using a system of wheels and left
in place for 30 minutes, while the oxygen consumption of the limpets was recorded as frequently as possible.  It was then removed and recording continued for
a further three hours.

With weights of up to 400g, the animals showed an immediate increase in oxygen
consumption which returned to the previous value as soon as the weight was
removed.  This has been expressed as a mean percentage increase above the mean

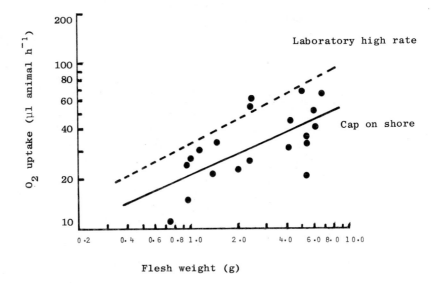

Flesh weight (g)

Fig. 5    Aquatic respiration of *Patella vulgata* on the shore.

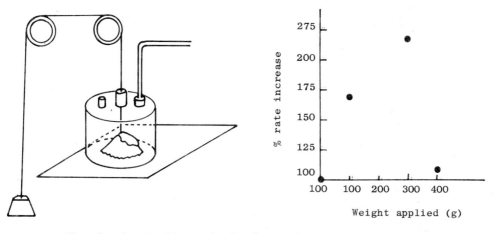

Fig. 6   Respiration and adhesion:   the apparatus and results.

before and after rate.   Each mean is from three to six different animals (Fig. 6).

### DISCUSSION

The experiments reported in this paper reveal the importance of making measurements on undisturbed animals *in situ*;   so providing a reference point for laboratory work.   The maintained, elevated aerial respiration rates of limpets simply placed in laboratory respirometers are in contrast to the reduced rates of animals on the shore and those of limpets in the laboratory which have been undisturbed and emmersed for a period in sea water.   When laboratory animals are so treated in their respirometer bottles, the subsequent decline in respiration rate can be correlated with an increase in weight.   This is rapid during the first four hours and thereafter, the weight remains fairly constant (unpublished results).   The elevated respiration rates of freshly collected animals in the laboratory seem to be related to the loss of a certain volume of necessary, 'extra corporeal' water.   This is probably held in the nuchal cavity (10) and its recovery would explain the subsequent decline in respiration rate that occurs within a day of collection, rather than does starvation (11).

All the shore and laboratory experiments were carried out at $10^{o}C$ and from what is known of the responses to temperature of standard and active metabolism (12), one would expect the elevated, laboratory rates of respiration to have higher $Q_{10}$ values than the shore, or lower laboratory rates.

At $10^{o}C$, *P. vulgata* appears to have higher respiration rates in air than in water.   If the limpet has to clamp down to the rock, as in an attempt to lessen desiccation or, when exposed to wave action its oxygen consumption would greatly increase.   However, if respiring from water, such an increased energy demand might well be associated with an oxygen debt because of reduced gas exchange between the animal and environment.   Such changes in oxygen consumption assume inactivity in the limpets, but they are known to move in both air and water (13) and accordingly, oxygen consumption approximately doubles above the levels recorded on the shore.

ACKNOWLEDGEMENT

We would like to thank Mr. Stephen Nicol for allowing us to use some of his data on aquatic respiration.

REFERENCES

(1) Newell, R.C., 1970. Biology of Intertidal Animals. 555 pp. London: Elek Books.

(2) Bannister, J.U., 1974. The respiration in air and in water of the limpets *Patella caerulea* (L.) and *Patella histicanica* (Gmelin). Comparative Biochemistry and Physiology 49, 407-411.

(3) Gompel, M., 1938. Recherches sur la consommation d'oxygene de quelques animaux aquatiques littoraux. Annls Physiol. Physiochim. biol. 14, 914-931.

(4) Jones, H.D., 1968. Some aspects of heart function in *Patella vulgata* L. Nature, London 217, 1170-1172.

(5) McMahon, R. and Russell-Hunter, W.D., 1977. Temperature relations of aerial and aquatic respiration in six littoral snails in relation to their vertical zonation. Biological Bulletin, Woods Hole, 152, 182-198.

(6) Scholander, P.F., Flemister, S.C., and Irving, L., 1947. Micro geometric estimation of the blood gases. V. Combined carbon dioxide and oxygen. Journal of Biological Chemistry, 169, 173-181.

(7) Strickland, J.D.H. and Parsons, T.R., 1972. A practical handbook of sea water analysis. Fisheries research board of Canada, Ottawa.

(8) Snedecor, G., 1959. Statistical Methods. 593 pp. Iowa, State College Press.

(9) Davies, P.S., 1966. Physiological ecology of *Patella*. 1. The effect of body size and temperature on metabolic rate. Journal of the Marine Biological Association of the United Kingdom, 46, 647-658.

(10) Wolcott, T.G., 1973. Physiological ecology and intertidal zonations in limpets (*Acmaea*): a critical look at "Limiting factors". Biological Bulletin, Woods Hole, 145, 389-422.

(11) Von Brand, T., McMahon, P. and Nolan, M.O., 1957. Physiological observations of *Australorbis glabratus* and some other aquatic snails. Biological Bulletin, Woods Hole, 113, 89-102.

(12) Newell, R.C. and Northcroft, H.R., 1967. A re-interpretation of the effect of temperature on the metabolism of certain marine inverte-brates. Journal of Zoology, London 151, 277-298.

(13) Fretter, V. and Graham, A., 1962. British Prosobranch Molluscs, pp. 755. London Royal Society.

# CONSUMPTION AND UTILIZATION OF FOOD BY JUVENILE PLAICE IN THE WADDEN SEA

**B. Kuipers and M. Fonds**

*N.I.O.Z., Texel, The Netherlands*

Published in abstract only

Recent studies on the density and food-intake of juvenile plaice in the western Wadden Sea have revealed the importance of young plaice as consumers of the high benthic invertebrate production on the intertidal mud-flats. Dense populations of O-, I- and II-group plaice are estimated to consume as much as half the amount of invertebrate food available to birds and fishes between March and July. From June onwards, after this period of heavy predation, juvenile plaice leave the intertidal zone in order of size - larger fish first - although the invertebrate macro-benthos has not even reached its maximum biomass.

One of the possible explanations for this rapid leave deals with the effects of increasing water-temperature on the energy balance of the rapidly growing young plaice, which in experiments showed optimal growth at lower temperatures. On basis of average and rough field data on gastric digestion and stomach-contents of the plaice, together with experimental data on the relationship between temperature, fish-size and rate of digestion, the consumption by O-, I- and II-group plaice in the intertidal zone from March to September was estimated.

On the other hand, laboratory data on oxygen consumption, and some generally accepted relationships between fish-size, temperature and respiration lead to curves of maximum and minimum respiration values for juvenile plaice during their stay in the intertidal zone and hence, to estimates on the average biomass respired.

A comparison of the results shows how increasing summer-temperatures in the intertidal zone are unfavourable for especially the larger plaice, since their energy available for growth decreases due to increasing respiration. The gradual shift of these larger plaice towards the deeper and colder water of the North Sea coastal zone might, therefore, be explained in terms of the "maximum power hypothesis", as it obviously leads to maximum possible growth in the juvenile plaice populations.

# SOME RESPONSES OF TROPICAL MANGROVE FIDDLER CRABS *(UCA spp.)* TO HIGH ENVIRONMENTAL TEMPERATURES

**D.J. Macintosh**

*Department of Zoology, University of Malaya, Malaysia*

ABSTRACT

Mud surface temperatures in open mangrove habitats in Malaysia reach 44°C which is above the thermal tolerance of resident fiddler crabs. Four species of *Uca* each inhabiting a distinct zone within the mangrove were studied to determine whether they differed in their behavioural and physiological responses to temperature.

The species were similar in their pattern of daily activity. Despite zonal variations in ambient temperature, fiddler crab burrows in all parts of the mangrove attained a thermal equilibrium of between 28° and 30°C at about 10 cm depth. Body temperatures were regulated in part by a burrow-retreat response in which the frequency of burrow visits by active crabs increased with environmental temperature. Measured upper thermal tolerances of the four *Uca* species differed only slightly; $LD_{50}$ varied from 13 to 15 minutes at 43°C.

Interspecific differences were evident in the metabolic response of *Uca* to temperature. In relation to their zonation on the shore the species showed a decrease in respiratory rate with increasing tidal position. In addition, the rate of each species was relatively independent of temperature over the thermal range most commonly experienced in its particular habitat.

From these findings, the probable influence of temperature on the intertidal distribution of mangrove fiddler crabs is discussed.

## INTRODUCTION

Comparisons between tropical and temperate fiddler crabs have indicated adaptive differences in their thermal tolerances (1,2) and respiratory response to temperature (3,4). In general, tropical fiddler crabs are less sensitive to high temperatures than temperate forms, while the reverse is true at low temperatures. Only a few studies have investigated similar adaptive physiological variation among fiddler crabs from different levels of the same shore (5,6,7) and some findings are not in agreement. Teal (5) recorded uniform upper lethal temperatures in three species of *Uca* from different thermal environments of the Georgia salt marshes whereas significantly higher upper lethal limits were reported for the more terrestrial species on a Mocambique shore (7).

A distinct intertidal zonation is shown by four species of *Uca* in the west coast mangroves of Peninsular Malaysia (8). The present paper describes the upper thermal tolerance, respiration rate-temperature response and behaviour of the Malaysian fiddler crabs in relation to their distribution and thermal environment on the shore.

D. J. Macintosh

STUDY SITE AND METHODS

Field observations were made in mangrove on the south shore of the Selangor
River estuary (3°21'N.,101°15'E.) at a point where the estuary widened in its
seaward approach to the Straits of Malacca. A mixed forest of *Avicennia* and
*Bruguiera* extended from E.H.W.M. to an open mud-flat below H.W.M.N. (Fig. 1).
The forest was modified considerably by timber extraction and the cutting of
access paths to the estuary. Fiddler crabs were common in all parts of the
mangrove. *Uca rosea* occurred throughout the forest but was most abundant in
unshaded areas cleared of vegetation; *U. triangularis* and *U. forcipata* occupied
the upper and lower forest respectively; both species favoured shaded habitats
although *U. triangularis* was also present on open soils. The fourth species,
*U. dussumieri*, was confined to unshaded regions of the foreshore.

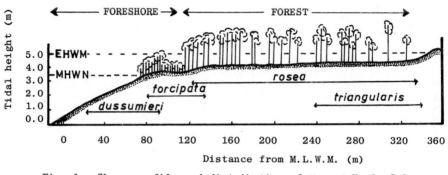

Fig. 1.    Shore profile and distribution of *Uca* at Kuala Selangor.

Laboratory determinations of respiration rate and upper thermal tolerance were
made on each species. Crabs were used in experiments one to three days after
collection from the study site to prevent acclimation to laboratory conditions.
The holding period allowed the crabs to expell faecal matter and recover from
handling. Experimental animals were not fed.

Temperature tolerance was measured at 39°, 41° and 43°C using 45 to 50 crabs in
each experiment; *U. rosea* was also tested at 42°C. Crabs were placed individually
in 150 ml conical flasks set in a constant temperature bath. Each flask
contained sufficient mangrove water (salinity 25 PPT) to two-thirds cover the
crab. The flasks were equilibrated to the test temperature prior to each
experiment. Observations were made at one minute intervals at 43°C and every
10 minutes at the other temperatures. The number of crabs dying during each
time interval was noted.

Oxygen consumption during respiration was measured in constant pressure
respirometers (9). Respiratory rates of each species were determined at five
temperatures within the maximum thermal range in the mangrove: 25°, 29°, 33°, 36°
and 39°C. Measurements were made at different times of day, and in various
periods of the lunar cycle, to randomise rhythms of oxygen consumption (10).

## RESULTS

### Thermal environment

Temperatures on the west coast of Peninsular Malaysia are high and uniform
throughout the year except for a slight monsoonal influence. The mean monthly
air temperature at Kuala Selangor varies by less than 2°C. The average diurnal
fluctuation is 9°C with recorded extremes of 20.6° and 34.4°C.

Thermal conditions at the study site are summarised in Table 1. Temperatures on
the mud-flat were moderated by a slight onshore breeze and almost daily flooding
of the habitat by tidal water (28° to 29°C). Maximum temperatures were higher
towards the upper shore. Unshaded soils at H.W.M. warmed as much as 8°C above
the surrounding air temperature and were up to 11°C hotter than shaded forest
soils. Burrow temperatures were taken 10 to 15 cm below the surface.

TABLE 1   Daily Maximum Temperatures in each Species-Habitat Zone

|  | Species | U.dussumieri | U.forcipata | U.rosea | U.triangularis |
|---|---|---|---|---|---|
|  | Habitat | unshaded mud-flat | shaded forest | unshaded forest | partial shade in forest |
|  | Air | 30-32 | 29-32 | 33-36 | 31-34 |
| t/°C | Surface | 32-37 | 32-33 | 39-44 | 36-42 |
|  | Burrow | 29-30 | 29-31 | 30-31 | 30-31 |

Despite variations in surface heating, temperatures inside *Uca* burrows on
different parts of the shore were remarkably similar. A consistant equilibrium
temperature of 28° to 30°C occurred at about 10 cm depth (Fig. 2). In unshaded
areas the average diurnal fluctuation in burrow temperature was only 3°C as
compared to 14°C at the soil surface (Fig. 3).

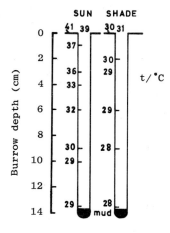

Fig. 2.   Temperature profiles
in *Uca* burrows.

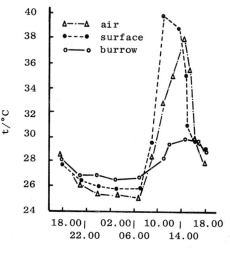

Fig. 3.   Average diurnal temperature
fluctuation in open mangrove.

### Behaviour in relation to temperature

The four species of *Uca* showed a similar pattern of activity. Each crab
constructed and maintained a burrow which it occupied at dusk or prior to
flooding by the tide. The crabs emerged onto the soil surface shortly after
dawn, or once the habitat was uncovered by the tide; most animals were active
throughout the hours of daylight (Fig. 4).

Active crabs made regular burrow visits of 15 to 50 seconds duration; these
were more frequent at higher ambient temperatures. In one observation period,
for example, the interval between burrow visits decreased from more than
30 minutes at 28°C to less than six minutes at 35°C (Fig. 5). The frequency of
the 'burrow-retreat' response varied considerably between neighbouring crabs
but was regularly timed in each animal. Wilkens and Fingerman (11) reported a
comparable burrow-retreat rhythm of 18 to 24 minutes in *U. pugilator* at 27.5°C
(average air temperature).

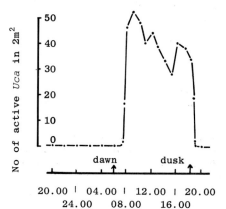

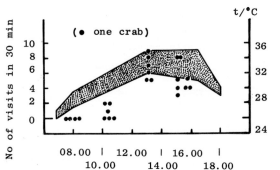

Fig. 4.  Daily activity period of
         *Uca* during neap tides.

Fig. 5.  Frequency of burrow visits in
         relation to ambient temperature.
         Shaded area is air-surface range
         of temperature.

Contrary to many other studies, *Uca* burrows at Kuala Selangor did not always
reach the water table. During some extreme neap tide periods seap water was
obtainable only at depths greater than 60 cm; adult fiddler crabs burrowed
only 20 to 40 cm. However the burrow walls remained damp even when the soil
surface at H.W.M. became dry and cracked during the drier months of the year.
In these conditions, high level fiddler crabs remained within their burrows
except for brief visits to the surface in the early morning. Normal feeding
activity was resumed after the first spring tide wetting of the habitat.

### Temperature tolerance

Results of the thermal tolerance experiments were plotted as probits of
percentage survival against time (Fig. 6a). $LD_{50}$ values obtained from these
plots show that slight increases in temperature above 39°C greatly reduced
survival time (Table 2). All the test animals survived more than 3 hours at
39°C. The variation in survival at 43°C was not significant (Chi$^2$ test:P > 0.95)
and at 41°C the range in $LD_{50}$ was within one time interval of survival (10
minutes at this temperature).

TABLE 2   Time to Thermal Death (minutes to $LD_{50}$) of *Uca*

| Species | Test temperature (°C) | | |
|---------|------|------|------|
|         | 41   | 42   | 43   |
| *Uca dussumieri*   | 97  |    | 14 |
| *U. forcipata*     | 98  |    | 15 |
| *U. rosea*         | 92  | 45 | 13 |
| *U. triangularis*  | 101 |    | 15 |

Other workers have expressed the upper thermal limit of *Uca* as the temperature causing $LD_{50}$ in one hour (5,11) or $LD_{100}$ in 15 minutes (7). The corresponding temperatures obtained for *U. rosea* were 41.6° and 43.3°C respectively (Fig. 6b). The upper thermal limits of the Malaysian species seem similar to those of *U. rapax* in Jamaica (1) and *U. inversa* in Mocambique (7). A number of other species have slightly lower limits in comparison (1,2,5,7).

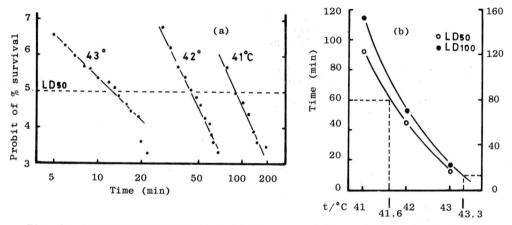

Fig. 6.   Upper thermal tolerance of *Uca rosea*. (a) survival against time, (b) time to lethal death ($LD_{50}$ and $LD_{100}$) against temperature.

## Respiration

The results and analysis of a typical respiration experiment are shown in Fig. 7. The rates of oxygen consumption of *Uca* were weight and activity dependent. Active crabs respired at higher rates than inactive (stationary) crabs of similar weight. The average respiration rate was obtained from a regression line fitted to all the points. A second line, fitted to only the lowest points, was used as an estimate of the minimum rate. Covariance analysis showed that temperature did not significantly alter the slope of either the average or minimum rate-weight regression for each species. The regression lines of the two rates were very nearly parallel in each experiment indicating that the rate-weight relationship was also independent of activity level. The regression equations were recalculated using a common slope for each species and each activity level. $Q_{10}$ values obtained from these adjusted equations are independent of body weight so that interspecific comparisons of the respiration rate-temperature response of *Uca* are facilitated.

The species differed both in their rates of oxygen consumption and respiratory response to temperature change. In relation to intertidal position, the species showed a decrease in respiration rate with increasing shore level. The highest

D. J. Macintosh

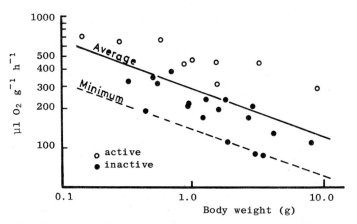

Fig. 7.   Rate of oxygen consumption of *Uca forcipata* at 36°C.
          Average rate regression (solid line) fitted to all points.
          Minimum rate regression (dashed line) fitted to lower points.

rate at 25°C was recorded in *U. dussumieri* and this species was also the most
sensitive to increase in temperature (Table 3).

TABLE 3   Respiration Rates ($\mu l\ O_2\ g^{-1}\ h^{-1}$) of 0.2 and 1.0 g *Uca*

| t/°C | Species and body weight (g) | | | | | | | |
|------|------|------|------|------|------|------|------|------|
| | *U.dussumieri* | | *U.forcipata* | | *U.rosea* | | *U.triangularis* | |
| | 0.2 | 1.0 | 0.2 | 1.0 | 0.2 | 1.0 | 0.2 | 1.0 |
| 25° | 280 | 140 | 182 | 100 | 193 | 122 | 132 | 68 |
| 29° | 260 | 130 | 287 | 158 | 384 | 244 | 212 | 109 |
| 33° | 607 | 303 | 371 | 204 | 493 | 313 | 402 | 207 |
| 36° | 1005 | 503 | 511 | 281 | 685 | 435 | 389 | 200 |
| 39° | 1599 | 800 | 851 | 467 | 767 | 487 | 700 | 360 |

Temperature coefficients of the minimum respiration rate are compared in
Table 4. In considering the minimum rate-temperature response of *Uca*, much of
the activity related variation in metabolism is eliminated. Low $Q_{10}$ values
were obtained for *U. forcipata*, *U. rosea* and *U. triangularis* over the range
29° to 36°C. A similar low $Q_{10}$ (1.7-1.9) also occurred for *U. rosea* over the
33° to 39°C range and for *U. dussumieri* between 25° and 33°C. Figure 8 (where
horizontal lines span the temperature intervals for which $Q_{10}$ was less than 2.0)
illustrates that partial respiratory compensation to temperature was shown
over more intervals within the measured thermal range by *U. rosea* and
*U. triangularis* than by the two lower level species.

TABLE 4   $Q_{10}$ of Respiration Rate of the Four Species of *Uca*

| Temperature range (°C) | *U.dussumieri* | *U.forcipata* | *U.rosea* | *U.triangularis* |
|------|------|------|------|------|
| 25-33 | 1.71 | 2.33 | 4.23 | 2.95 |
| 29-36 | 3.50 | 1.70 | 1.90 | 1.76 |
| 33-39 | 9.26 | 3.76 | 1.76 | 2.83 |

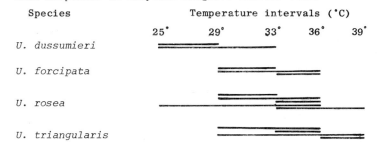

Fig. 8.   Temperature intervals with $Q_{10}$ less than 2.0.

DISCUSSION

High surface temperatures did not restrict the distribution of *Uca* at Kuala
Selangor. Similarly, Teal (5) reported no temperature limitations on the
habitats available to salt marsh fiddler crabs. As in the present study, Teal
also found no relationship between the thermal environments of the different
species and their tolerance of high temperature in the laboratory.

Fiddler crabs in unshaded mangrove were clearly dependent on their burrows for
survival. Their surface activity was further contingent on the presence of
standing water, either in the burrow or on the soil surface; high level *Uca*
were not active during extreme neap tides when these sources dried up. Active
crabs expended water in feeding (12) in addition to that lost from the body by
evaporation. Water losses from burrow-dwelling crabs were probably negligible
in comparison since the burrows served as humid microclimates almost independent
of surface fluctuations in temperature. Dembowski (13) has demonstrated that
*U. pugilator* can survive for several weeks in saturated air with no available
free water.

Wilkens and Fingerman (11) attributed a thermoregulatory function to the
burrow-retreat response of *Uca*. However its effectiveness in thermoregulation
was doubted by Smith and Miller (14) who suggested that a crab's body
temperature would change within seconds of the animal returning to the surface.
The primary function of the burrow-retreat response observed in mangrove
fiddler crabs was to replace water losses. In *Uca*, body water is lost by
evaporation more rapidly at higher temperatures (11) and this would explain the
relationship between the frequency of burrow visits and ambient temperature
(Fig. 5). While evaporation from wetted body surfaces is effective in lowering
the body temperature of *Uca* (6,14), the stimulus to replenish body water was
probably the requirement of water for feeding. The thermoregulatory advantage
which may also have resulted from this behaviour (i.e. wetting the body
surfaces) is considered to be coincidental. In support of this view, some
non-feeding crabs were observed to remain in direct sunlight for up to 20
minutes when temperatures at the soil surface were near maximum.

A significant relationship is evident between the thermal environments selected
by the four species of *Uca* in the mangrove (Table 1) and their metabolic
response to temperature. Respiration rates of the high level species, *U. rosea*
and *U. triangularis*, were relatively independent of temperature over the range
29° to 39°C. This respiratory adaptation would result in their metabolic rate
being insensitive to thermal fluctuations in the mangrove and particularly to
the rapid increase in temperature which was experienced in emerging from the
burrow microclimate onto the heated soil surface. In contrast, *U. forcipata*

and *U. dussumieri* showed no respiratory compenstion  over the range of high
temperatures encountered only in the upper mangrove and this may explain why
neither species extended above the seaward edge of the forest. It is noteable
that *U. rosea* is the most abundant and widely distributed fiddler crab on
mangrove shores in Malaysia (8) and, of the four species, its respiratory
compensation to temperature covered the widest thermal range.


REFERENCES

(1)    Vernberg, F.J. & Tashian, R.E., 1959.  Studies on the physiological
          variation between tropical and temperate zone fiddler crabs of the
          genus *Uca*. I. Thermal death limits. *Ecology*, 40, 589-593.
(2)    Vernberg, F.J. & Vernberg, W.B., 1967.  Studies on the physiological
          variation between tropical and temperate zone fiddler crabs of the
          genus *Uca*. IX. Thermal lethal limits of southern hemisphere *Uca* crabs.
          *Oikos*, 18, 118-123.
(3)    Tashian, R.E., 1956.  Geographic variation in the respiratory metabolism
          and temperature coefficient in tropical and temperate forms of the
          fiddler crab, *Uca pugnax*. *Zoologica*, 41, 39-47.
(4)    Vernberg, F.J., 1959.  Studies on the physiological variation between
          tropical and temperate zone fiddler crabs of the genus *Uca*. II. Oxygen
          consumption of whole organisms. *Biological Bulletin. Marine Biological
          Laboratory, Woods Hole, Mass.*, 117, 163-184.
(5)    Teal, J.M., 1958.  Distribution of fiddler crabs in Georgia salt marshes.
          *Ecology*, 39, 185-193.
(6)    Teal, J.M., 1959.  Respiration of crabs in Georgia salt marshes and its
          relation to their ecology. *Physiological Zoology*, 32, 1-14.
(7)    Edney, E.B., 1961.  The water and heat relations of fiddler crabs (*Uca*
          spp.). *Transactions of the Royal Society of South Africa*, 36, 71-91.
(8)    Macintosh, D.J.  The intertidal distribution of mangrove fiddler crabs
          (*Uca* spp.) on the west coast of the Malay Peninsula. In preparation.
(9)    Davies, P.S., 1966.  A constant pressure respirometer for medium-sized
          animals. *Oikos*, 17, 108-112.
(10)   Brown, F.A.,JR., Bennett, M.F. & Webb, H.M., 1954.  Persistent daily and
          tidal rhythms of $O_2$-consumption in fiddler crabs. *Journal of Cellular
          and Comparative Physiology*, 44, 477-505.
(11)   Wilkens, J.I. & Fingerman, F., 1965.  Heat tolerance and temperature
          relationships of the fiddler crab, *Uca pugilator*, with reference to
          body coloration. *Biological Bulletin. Marine Biological Laboratory,
          Woods Hole, Mass.*, 128, 133-141.
(12)   Miller, D.C., 1961.  The feeding mechanism of fiddler crabs with
          ecological considerations of feeding adaptations. *Zoologica*, 46, 89-100.
(13)   Dembowski, J.B., 1926.  Notes on the behaviour of the fiddler crab.
          *Biological Bulletin . Marine Biological Laboratory, Woods Hole,
          Mass.*, 50, 179-201.
(14)   Smith, W.K. & Miller, P.C., 1973.  The thermal ecology of two south
          Florida fiddler crabs: *Uca rapax* Smith and *U. pugilator* Bosc.
          *Physiological Zoology*, 46, 186-207.

# PHYSIOLOGICAL ADAPTATION
# OF *CANCER IRRORATUS* LARVAE
# TO CYCLIC TEMPERATURES

## A.N. Sastry

*Graduate School of Oceanography, University of Rhode Island, Kingston,
Rhode Island 02881*

## ABSTRACT

Larvae of the sublittoral crab, Cancer irroratus, cultured under the daily
cyclic temperatures developed at a faster rate with enhanced survival than
those larvae at a comparable constant temperature. The metabolic-temperature
responses of the larvae cultured in the cyclic regime were altered relative to
those at the constant temperature. These alterations included an extension of
metabolic rate compensation towards higher temperatures with a $Q_{10}$ close to
unity and a shift of tolerance range to higher temperatures. The differential
responses in metabolic adaptation of the larval stages at daily cyclic and
constant temperatures were accompanied by changes in activity of the enzyme
systems examined. Reorganization of metabolism by cyclic temperature-induced
biochemical changes appear to adapt larvae for development with enhanced survival under fluctuating temperatures.

## INTRODUCTION

The physiological and biochemical adaptations of adult poikilotherms to temperature variation have been well documented (Vernberg and Vernberg, 1972;
Hochachka and Somero, 1973; Hazel and Prosser, 1974), but relatively little is
known of the early life stages. Larvae of a number of benthic marine organisms are exposed to continuously varying environmental factors during their
planktonic development. Crustacean larvae are particularly useful for studies
on the adaptational phenomenon of early life stages because of the readily a-
vailable culture techniques and distinct stages of larval development. The
environmental requirements (Costlow and Bookhout, 1964; Sastry and Vargo, 1977)
and to a more limited extent, the physiological responses (Kalber & Costlow, 1966;
Vernberg and Costlow, 1966; Vargo and Sastry, 1977) and behavioral responses
(Forward and Costlow, 1973) have been determined. However, detailed knowledge
of the physiological adaptations of larvae to temperature variation is still
lacking. Studies on the adaptation of pelagic larvae to the environment are
significant to our understanding of their probable distribution and ecology,
and the ontogeny of mechanisms of adaptation and variation among geographically
separated populations. Larvae of two sublittoral crabs, Cancer irroratus and
Cancer borealis, cultured at the constant temperature and salinity which was
optimal for maximum survival of the respective species, showed interstage
variation in the patterns of metabolic responses to temperature (Sastry and
McCarthy, 1973). This interstage variation may adapt successive larval stages
for development and survival in a varying environment.

Larvae of the few crustaceans cultured at fluctuating temperatures survived
better than those at constant temperatures (Costlow and Bookhout, 1971; Sastry,

1976).  The physiological and biochemical effects of fluctuating temperatures
on the developing larvae are not known.  In this paper the results of some
recent studies on the effects of fluctuating temperatures on the development,
survival, and metabolism of C. irroratus are discussed.


## MATERIALS AND METHODS

Larvae of C. irroratus occur in the plankton from April to late June in
Narragansett Bay, Rhode Island (Hillman, 1964).  During planktonic development,
the larvae are exposed to a diurnal variation of +2.0 C between April and June,
a seasonal variation from 5-6 C in early April to 16-19 C in May (Hillman,
1964), and a vertical gradient of 5-6 in May (Hicks, 1958).  Eggs removed from
ovigerous C. irroratus collected between December and June and incubated at
15 C in 30 o/oo salinity under a photoperiod regime of 14:10 LD cycle develop
to hatching and release larvae.  The resulting larvae were fed daily with
newly hatched Artemia salina nauplii.  The procedures for larval culture have
been previously described in detail (Sastry, 1970).  The larvae pass through a
sequence of five zoeal stages and a megalops stage before metamorphosis to the
crab stage (Sastry, 1977).  Multifactorial experiments in the laboratory indicate that complete development with maximum survival occurs between 13 to
23 C and 28 to 38 o/oo salinity.  Below 9 C and above 28 C, and at salinities
below 20 o/oo and above 38 o/oo there is essentially no survival (Sastry, unpublished data).

To determine the effects of cyclic temperatures on development and survival,
the larvae were then cultured at 10-20, 15-25, 12.5-17.5 and 17.5-22.5 C
daily cycles and 10, 15, 20 and 25 C constant temperatures (Sastry, 1976).
The effects of cyclic temperatures on metabolism were determined by comparing
metabolic-temperature responses of larvae cultured at 10-20 cyclic and 15 C
constant temperatures.  The oxygen consumption rates of larvae were measured
over a graded series of test temperatures between 5 and 25 or 30 C using all
glass differential microrespirometers (Sastry and McCarthy, 1973).  The weight-
specific oxygen uptake rates of each larval stage were plotted against test
temperature to determine the patterns of metabolic response to temperature.
$Q_{10}$ values of oxygen consumption were calculated for 5 C test temperature intervals to reveal the alterations in metabolic rate to temperature.

Specific activities of lactate dehydrogenase, malate dehydrogenase and glucose-
6 phosphate dehydrogenase were assayed for pooled groups of larval stages
cultured at 10-20 C daily cyclic and 15 C constant temperatures.  Larvae were
homogenized in 1:5 w/v of 50 mM Tris-HCl buffer (pH 7.5) and the resulting
homogenate was centrifuged at 2,500 g in a refrigerated centrifuge for 20
minutes.  The resulting supernatant was used as the source of enzymes.  The
assays were performed using the following reaction mixtures: LDH, 0.01 mM NADH,
5 mM sodium pyruvate and 50 mM Tris-HCl (pH 7.5) in a total volume of 3.0 ml;
MDH, 0.01 mM NADH, 0.2 mM oxaloacetate and 50 mM Tris-HCl (pH 7.5) in a total
volume of 3.0 ml; G6PDH, 0.15 mM NADP, 1.66 mM glucose 6 phosphate, 5 mM $MgCl_2$
and 50 mM Tris-HCl (pH 7.5) in a total volume of 3.0 ml.  Enzyme assay mixtures were equilibrated to 15 C prior to assay in a Zeiss PMQ II Spectrophotometer.  Enzyme activities were expressed as μ moles per mg Biuret protein.


## RESULTS AND DISCUSSION

Development and Survival

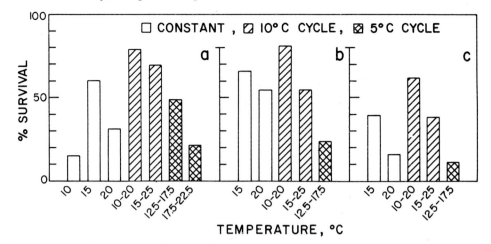

Fig. 1. The effects of daily cyclic and constant temperatures on the survival of C. irroratus larvae. a. hatch to megalops, b. megalops, c. hatch to crab. (After Sastry, 1976)

The daily cyclic and constant temperature regimes affected the development and survival of $\underline{C}$. $\underline{irroratus}$ larvae differently. Complete development to the crab stage was observed at 10-20, 15-25 and 12.5-17.5 C cyclic and 15 and 20 C constant temperatures. Larvae developed to the megalops stage under the 17.5-22.5 C cyclic and 10 C constant regimes, but only to the fourth zoeal stage at 25 C constant.

Survival of all the larval stages was higher at 15 C than at any other constant temperature (Fig. 1). Survival of larvae decreased on either side of 15 C optimum. Survival of all the larval stages was enhanced at 10-20 C cycle when compared with other constant and cyclic temperatures (Fig. 1). The decrease in mortality of the 10-20 C cycling larvae during fifth zoeal stage and megalops stage, relative to the 15 C larvae, contributed to the higher survival rate of the crab stage at the cyclic regime. At both 12.5-17.5 C cycle and 15 C, there was no significant difference in survival of larvae during the zoeal stages, but the mortalities were higher in the megalops stage at the cyclic regime. While survival of larvae during the zoeal stages was about the same at both 10-20 C and 15-25 C cycles, at the warmer temperature cycle the higher mortalities during the megalops stage decreased survival to the crab stage. However, survival of all larval stages was higher at the 15-25 C cycle than at constant 20 C. Survival of the third and fourth zoeal stages and megalops stage at 17.5-22.5 cycle was lower than at 20 C. In general, survival of zoeal stages, megalops stage, and hatch to crab stage was higher at the 10 C cycles ($\pm$5.0 C) than the comparable 5 C cycles ($\pm$2.5 C) or the constant temperatures. The megalops stage of $\underline{C}$. $\underline{irroratus}$ was relatively more sensitive to temperature variation than the preceeding zoeal stages.

The differential responses of larvae to constant and cyclic temperatures were also evident in the duration for complete development to the crab stage. The developmental time for all the stages decreased with increasing constant temperatures (Fig. 2). The first zoeal stage developed at a slower rate than the later zoeal stages. The rate of development of all the zoeal stages was predicted to decrease below 10 C, and remained nearly constant above 25 C. The

A. N. Sastry

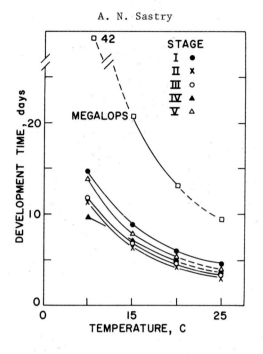

Fig. 2. The effects of constant temperatures on development time for larval stages of C. irroratus. (After Sastry, 1976)

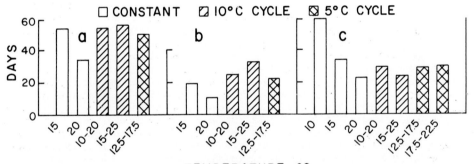

Fig. 3. The effects of daily cyclic and constant temperatures on the duration of C. irroratus larval development. a. hatch to crab, b. megalops, c, hatch to megalops. (After Sastry, 1976)

megalops stage developed at a much slower rate than the preceeding zoeal stages at any temperature. The rate of megalops development was directly dependent upon temperature between 10-20 C range. The developmental rate of megalops stage was predicted to decrease below 15 C, and remained nearly constant above 20 C in comparison to the zoeal stages.

The daily cyclic temperature regimes modified the duration of development differently than the comparable constant temperatures (Fig. 3). The duration of
the zoeal stages decreased and the megalops stage increased at 10-20 C and 12.5-
17.5 C cycles in comparison with that at 15 C. The fifth stage zoeae took
less time and megalops more time at both cyclic regimes than at the constant
temperature. However, the duration for total development was about the same
at both cyclic and constant temperatures. While the duration of zoeal stages
was about the same at 15-25 C cyclic and 20 C constant temperatures, the megalops stage was considerably delayed by the cyclic regime. The zoeal stages

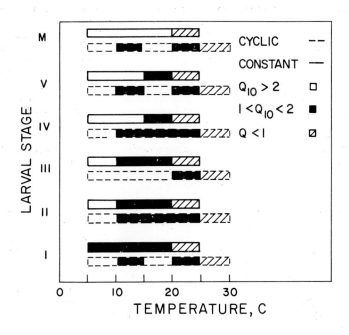

Fig. 4. The effects of daily cyclic and constant temperatures on metabolism of
C. irroratus larval stages. Metabolic responses are represented as $Q_{10}$ values.
(After Sastry and Vargo, 1977)

took longer time at 17.5-22.5 C cycle than at constant 20 C. The two warmer
temperature cycles have generally increased the duration of both zoeal and megalops stages compared to those larvae at constant temperature. The duration
of zoeal stages decreased and megalops stage increased at 15-25 C cycle compared to that at 10-20 C cycle. However, the duration for total development
was about the same at both 10 C cycles (+5.0 C) in spite of the differences in
the culture temperatures. The duration of zoeal stages at the 12.5-17.5 C
cycle was slightly less than at the 17.5-22.5 C cycle. The zoeal and megalops
stages were differentially sensitive to the amplitude and the mean temperature
of the cyclic regimes. This differential sensitivity of the larval stages
contributed to the variable duration for their total development and survival
at different cyclic regimes.

The effects of daily cyclic temperatures on the development and survival also seem to vary, interspecifically. Larvae of the estuarine crab, Rhithropanopeus harrisii, survived better at a 30-35 C daily cycle compared to those at constant 30 or 35 C (Costlow and Bookhout, 1971). However, the duration of development and survival of this species were not significantly affected within the temperature range of 10-30 C. Larvae of another estuarine species, Palaemonetes pugio, also showed no significant differences in the developmental and survival rates at daily cyclic and comparable constant temperatures (Sastry, unpublished data). It is possible that different species may adapt differently to a variable environment during the course of their development.

## Metabolic-Temperature Responses

The differences in the developmental and survival rates of C. irroratus larvae at daily cyclic and comparable constant temperatures indicate that adaptive capacities of the larval stages are altered by the fluctuating temperatures. The patterns of metabolic-temperature responses of the larval stages cultured under the 10-20 C cycle were different from those cultured at constant 15 C (Fig. 4). The larval stages at constant 15 C were characterized by major changes in the metabolic-temperature patterns between first and second stage zoeae, third and fourth stage zoeae, and between fifth stage zoeae and megalops stage (Fig. 4). The first zoeae compensated their metabolic rate between 5-20 C range. The zone of thermal sensitivity between 5-10 C in the second and third zoeae expanded to 5-15 C in the fourth and fifth zoeae. The temperature range for metabolic rate compensation narrowed from 10-20 C in the early zoeal stages, to 15-20 C in the later fourth and fifth zoeal stages. The megalops stage showed no compensation from 5-20 C range. The metabolic rate of all the larval stages cultured at 15 C was depressed between 20-25 C. The larval stages cultured at the 10-20 C cycle increased their compensatory range towards higher temperatures (20-25 C) and shifted their temperature range for depression of metabolic rate to higher temperatures (25-30 C) (Fig. 4). Physiological processes with $Q_{10}$'s close to unity and which are reversibly thermolabile, by definition exhibit immediate compensation (Hazel and Prosser, 1974). The larvae at 10-20 C cycle seem to exhibit immediate compensation of metabolic rate to a diurnally fluctuating thermal environment. Immediate compensation in some adult poikilotherms experiencing rapid or diurnal temperature changes in their environment has been reported to result from biochemical mechanisms such as changes in enzyme-substrate affinities, conformational changes, and varying effectiveness of branched metabolic pathways to compete for a common substrate (Somero, 1969; Hazel and Prosser, 1974). It would appear that enzymatic reactions inactive in the 15 C larvae may have been activated by the cyclic temperatures to allow metabolic activity in the upper range (Somero, 1969). It is possible that such biochemical mechanisms induced in the larvae at cyclic temperatures may be adaptive to the fluctuating thermal environment. Since larvae completed their total development at the respective constant and cyclic temperatures, it is also possible that quantitative and/or qualitative changes in enzymes may have occurred for optimal activity and metabolic regulation as observed in adult poikilotherms acclimated to different temperatures (Hazel and Prosser, 1974).

## Enzyme Activities

To examine the possibility that enzyme activities are affected by culturing larvae at constant and daily cyclic temperatures, the specific activities of lactate dehydrogenase, malate dehydrogenase and glucose 6 phosphate dehydrogenase were assayed in the larval stages at the 10-20 C cycle and constant 15 C.

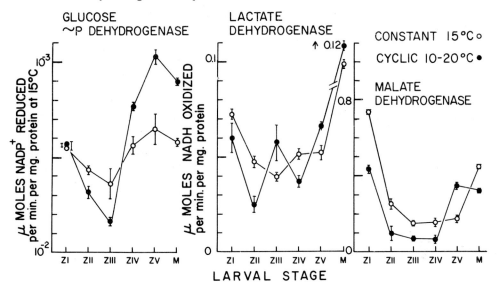

Fig. 5. The effects of daily cyclic and constant temperatures on the activities of lactate dehydrogenase (Sastry and Ellington, in press), malate dehydrogenase and glucose 6 phosphate dehydrogenase in C. irroratus larval stages. I-V, zoeae; M, megalops.

The activity patterns of the three enzyme systems were essentially U-shaped, with highest activity in the first zoeae and latter larval stages at both culture regimes (Fig. 5). Interstage variation of the three enzyme systems were differentially affected by the cyclic temperatures. Lactate dehydrogenase activity was enhanced in the third and fifth zoeal stages and megalops stage at 10-20 C cycle and compared to that in larvae at 15 C. The activity of lactate dehydrogenase was significantly increased in the megalops stage compared to that of the earlier zoeal stages regardless of temperature regime. The malate dehydrogenase activity decreased in all except the fifth zoeal stage at 10-20 C cycle compared to that in larvae at constant 15 C. The glucose 6 dehydrogenase activity decreased in the second and third stage zoeae, but increased in the fourth and fifth zoeal and megalops stages at the cyclic regime. These differences in the activity of enzymes in larvae at constant and cyclic temperatures may have resulted from changes in quantity, isozymes, kinetics, and allosteric effects (Hazel and Prosser, 1974). A great deal of further study is required to determine the biochemical mechanisms by which the metabolic responses to temperature in developing life stages are altered by the cyclic thermal regimes.

CONCLUSION

Daily cyclic and constant temperatures affected differently both larval development and survival of the sublittoral crab, C. irroratus. The amplitude and mean temperatures of the daily cycles produced variable responses in development and survival. The limited information available on the effects of cyclic temperatures on larval development of crustaceans shows that species react

differently with regards to development and survival. The basis of interspecific variation is not well understood. The survival rate of C. irroratus larvae was enhanced at favorable daily cyclic temperatures compared to that at
constant temperatures. The metabolic responses of larvae to temperature were
also altered relative to those of larvae at constant temperature. These alterations included an extension of metabolic compensation towards higher temperatures and an upward shift of the temperature range of metabolic activity. The
activities of lactate dehydrogenase, malate dehydrogenase and glucose 6 phosphate dehydrogenase were also altered in larvae cultured at the 10-20 C cycle
and constant 15 C. The differences in the activity of the three enzymes in
larvae at constant and cyclic temperatures did not follow the same trends.
This would indicate that enzyme systems in different metabolic sequences are
affected differently in each stage by the cyclic temperatures. The altered
metabolic responses of C. irroratus larval stages, presumably resulting from
cyclic temperature induced biochemical changes, appear to have adapted them for
development with an enhanced survival at fluctuating temperatures. Detailed
investigations on the physiological and underlying biochemical responses in
developing early life stages to varying thermal environments are needed to fully understand this facet of adaptational phenomena.

## ACKNOWLEDGEMENTS

This study was supported by a grant (R800981) from the U.S. Environmental Protection Agency. The author would like to thank Dr. Ross Ellington for the enzyme assays. A travel award (OCE 7721176) from NSF enabled the author to present this paper at the 12 European Marine Biology Symposium, Stirling, Scotland.

## REFERENCES

Costlow, J. D. & Bookhout, C. G., 1964. An approach to the ecology of marine
    invertebrate larvae. In Symposium on Experimental Ecology, Graduate School
    of Oceanography, University of Rhode Island, Occassional Publication No. 2,
    69-75.
Costlow, J. D. & Bookhout, C. G., 1971. The effects of cyclic temperatures on
    larval development in the mud crab, Rhithropanopeus harrisii. In Fourth
    European Symposium on Marine Biology, (Ed. D. J. Crisp), pp. 211-220,
    Cambridge: Cambridge University Press.
Forward, R. B. & Costlow, J. D., 1974. The ontogeny of phototaxis by larvae of
    the crab Rhithropanopeus harrisii. Marine Biology, 26, 27-33.
Hazel, J. R. & Prosser, C. L., 1974. Molecular mechanisms of temperature comp-
    ensation in Poikilotherms. Physiological Reviews, 54, 620-677.
Hicks, S. D., 1958. The physical oceanography of Narragansett Bay. Limnology
    and Oceanography, 4, 316-327.
Hillman, N. S., 1964. Studies on the distribution and abundance of decapod lar-
    vae in Narragansett Bay, Rhode Island with a consideration of morphology
    and mortality. M.S. Thesis, University of Rhode Island.
Hochachka, P. W. & Somero, G. N., 1973. Strategies of Biochemical Adaptation.
    358 pp. Philadelphia: W. B. Saunders Company.
Kalber, F. & Costlow, J. D., 1966. The ontogeny of osmoregulation and its
    neurosecretory control in decapod crustacean, Rhithropanopeus harrisii
    (Gould). American Zoologist, 6, 221-230.
Sastry, A. N., 1970. Culture of brachyuran crab larvae using a recirculating
    sea water system in the laboratory. Helgolander wissenschaftliche
    Meeresuntersuchungen, 20, 406-416.

Sastry, A. N., 1976. Effects of constant and cyclic temperature regimes on the pelagic larval development of a brachyuran crab. In Thermal Ecology II (Ed. G. W. Esch and R. W. McFarlane), pp. 81-87. ERDA Symposium Series, 40 (Conf. 750425).

Sastry, A. N., 1977. The larval development of the rock crab, Cancer irroratus Say, 1818, under laboratory conditions (Decapoda Brachyura). Crustaceana, (In the Press).

Sastry, A. N. & W. R. Ellington. Lactate dehydrogenase during the larval development of Cancer irroratus: Effect of constant and cyclic thermal regimes. Experientia (In the Press).

Sastry, A. N. & McCarthy, J. F., 1973. Diversity of metabolic adaptation of pelagic larval stages of two sympatric brachyuran crabs. Netherlands Journal of Sea Research, 7, 434-446.

Sastry, A. N. & Vargo, S. L., 1977. Variation in physiological responses of crustacean larvae to temperature. In Physiological Responses of Marine Biota to Pollutants. (Ed. F. J. Vernberg, A. Calabrese, F. P. Thurberg and W. B. Vernberg), pp. 401-423, New York: Academic Press.

Somero, G. N., 1969. Enzymatic mechanisms of temperature compensation: immediate and evolutionary effects of temperature on enzymes of aquatic poikilotherms. American Naturalist, 103, 517-530.

Vargo, S. L. & Sastry, A. N., 1977. Acute temperature and low dissolved oxygen tolerances of brachyuran crab (Cancer irroratus) larvae. Marine Biology, 40, 165-171.

Vernberg, F. J. & Costlow, J. D., 1966. Studies on physiological variation between tropical and temperate zone fiddler crabs of the genus Uca. IV. Oxygen consumption of larvae and young crabs reared in the laboratory. Physiological Zoology, 39, 36-52.

Vernberg, W. B. & Vernberg, F. J., 1972. Environmental Physiology of Marine Animals. 346 pp. New York: Springer Verlag.

# ANAEROBIC METABOLISM OF THE SCAVENGING ISOPOD *CIROLANA BOREALIS* LILLJEBORG. ADENINE NUCLEOTIDES

**Hein Rune Skjoldal and Torgeir Baakke**

*Institute of Marine Biology, University of Bergen, N-5065 Blomsterdalen, Norway*

## ABSTRACT

The oxygen consumption of *Cirolana borealis* decreased almost proportionally to the ambient oxygen tension, indicating no ability to regulate the rate of oxygen uptake. The concentration of ATP and the adenylate energy charge (EC) showed no change throughout 48 h as the metabolism shifted to anaerobiosis. When transferring *C. borealis* from oxygen-saturated seawater to deoxygenated water, the ATP concentration remained stable for 24 h, but decreased markedly after 48 h. This was reflected in a drop in EC from about 0.6 to 0.3. After transferring specimens back into oxygen-saturated seawater following 3 days of anaerobiosis, about 10 % of these individuals recovered and regained high ATP content and EC. These results demonstrate the ability of *C. borealis* to maintain balanced anaerobic metabolism for 1-2 days, after which continued lack of oxygen rapidly leads to death.

## INTRODUCTION

Many marine organisms live in oxygen poor environments and can survive long periods without oxygen even in the presence of hydrogen sulfide (Theede *et al.*, 1969). In many cases this is accomplished through facultative anaerobic metabolism, which has been studied in parasitic helminths (Saz, 1970), intertidal bivalves (Zwaan & Wijsman, 1976), and polychaetes (Zebe, 1975; Ruby & Fox, 1976).

The facultative anaerobic metabolism is ordinarily more complex than the classical fermentation leading to formation of lactate, and common end products are succinate, propionate and alanine (Hochachka, 1975).

The anaerobic metabolism of crustaceans has been little studied. Intertidal barnacles can survive for days under an atmosphere of nitrogen, during which time they accumulate lactic acid (Barnes *et al.*, 1963). We have found that the scavenging marine isopod *Cirolana borealis* (Lilljeborg) survives anoxia for about two days under experimental conditions. In this paper we present data on the adenine nucleotides under aerobic and anaerobic conditions as an approach to the study of the anaerobic energy metabolism of *C. borealis*.

## MATERIAL AND METHODS

Specimens of *C. borealis* were caught in large numbers in fish-baited traps at 90 m depth in Skogsvågen (60°16'N, 05°06'E) and were kept in running seawater (temperature 5-8 °C, salinity 33.0-33.5 ‰, oxygen 6.8-7.2 ml/l). One batch was trapped in September 1976 and kept for 8 months before being used for experiments in May 1977 ("laboratory" group). During this time they were fed pieces of frozen fish, though prior to the experiments they were starved for one week. Another batch of individuals was trapped in April 1977 and starved for one week before being used for experiments ("field" group).

In one experiment oxygen consumption and adenine nucleotides of individuals kept in closed 140 ml glass jars were measured as the oxygen tension decreased. The jars contained 9 individuals each and were kept immersed in running seawater at 6 °C. One jar without animals was included as a blank. At intervals during 48 h water samples of 0.5 ml were withdrawn with a syringe and analyzed with a Radiometer oxymeter equipped with an E 5046 oxygen electrode mounted in a D 616 thermostatted cell. To compensate for the removed water samples, equal amounts of saturated water were injected into the jars. At intervals jars were removed and the adenine nucleotides were extracted as described below. This experiment was carried out with individuals from both the "laboratory" and "field" groups.

In a second experiment 20 groups of 9 specimens each (of the "field" group) were placed in 370 ml jars with water deoxygenated to less than 0.5 ml $O_2$/l by bubbling with nitrogen gas. The jars were closed and immersed in seawater at 7.5 °C. The deoxygenated water was replaced every 24 h. Eight of the jars were used to test the effects of varying length of anaerobiosis (10 min to 4 days). The remaining 12 jars were used to test the recovery of the animals after transferring them back into oxygen-saturated seawater following 1 and 3 days of anoxia, respectively. At intervals jars were removed and the adenine nucleotides extracted.

Adenine nucleotides were extracted in triplicate by dropping groups of 3 individuals into 40 ml of hot Tris-buffer (96 °C, 0.02 M, pH 7.7) and macerating them with a forceps. After centrifugation subsamples of the extracts were frozen for subsequent analysis. The telson length of each of the extracted animals was measured to the nearest 0.05 mm, and the measurements were converted to ash-free dry weight by use of a regression based on measurements of 100 specimens.

The extracts were analyzed for ATP by the luciferase reaction, and for ADP and AMP by the same method after enzymatic conversion to ATP (Chapman *et al.*, 1971). The measurements were standardized by analyzing portions of the extracts to which known amount of ATP, ADP and AMP were added.

## RESULTS

### Oxygen Uptake

During the respiration experiment the oxygen content of the

water decreased rapidly from 6.85 ml/l at the onset to a mean of 0.70 ml/l after 14 h (Fig. 1 A). The rate of decrease then declined, and after 46 h the mean oxygen content was 0.30 ml/l.

The initial rate of oxygen uptake of *Cirolana borealis*, adjusted for change in the blank jar, were 77 and 78 $\mu l$ $O_2$/g ash-free dry weight·h for "field" and "laboratory" animals, respectively (Fig. 1 B). During the first 12 h the rate decreased almost linearily to 22 and 15 $\mu l$ $O_2$/g·h, respectively, and in 21 h the mean consumption rate had become 0.5 $\mu l$ $O_2$/g·h for both groups of animals. This rate was probably reached in about 13 h as judged from Fig. 1 A. The animals still showed normal behaviour with rapid pleopod movements and occational periods of swimming. The calculated consumption rate at any time was highest in the "field" group, even significant at one instance. However, when

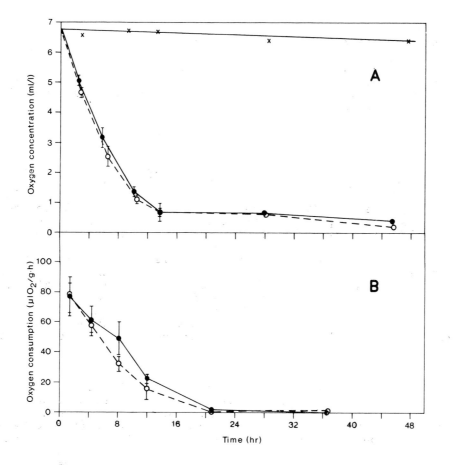

Fig. 1. *Cirolana borealis*. Decrease in oxygen concentration of the water (A) and rate of oxygen consumption (B) in closed jars during a 48 h period. ●——●: "field" group; o——o: "laboratory" group; x——x: blank. Vertical bars denote 95 % confidence intervals

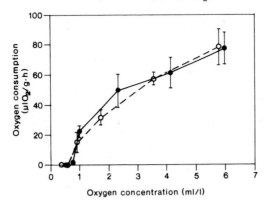

Fig. 2. *Cirolana borealis.*
The relationship between
rate of oxygen consumption
and oxygen concentration
of the water. Symbols and
vertical bars as in Fig. 1

the consumption rate was plotted against the corresponding
ambient oxygen content (Fig. 2), there was no significant
difference between the two groups. Both showed a decrease in
consumption which was almost proportional to the oxygen content
until the latter became less than 2 ml/l. When the content fell
below 1 ml $O_2$/l respiration ceased.

## Adenine Nucleotides

Concentrations of ATP and total adenine nucleotides and values of
EC (EC = ATP + $\frac{1}{2}$ADP / ATP + ADP + AMP) during the respiration
experiment are shown in Fig. 3. The "laboratory" group contained
about twice as much ATP as the "field" group. Also the average EC
of the former group was significantly higher (p < 0.01) than that
of the latter. There were no clear changes in ATP or EC during
the experiment.

C. *borealis* maintained a fairly stable concentration of ATP
during 24 h in deoxygenated water in the second experiment (Fig.
4 A). Subsequent anaerobiosis led to a decrease in the ATP pool.
At the same time the animals became inactive and would eventually
die; thus following 48 h of anoxia only 2 individuals remained
active and after 72 h all were inactive. The EC showed some
variation during the initial 24 h, ranging from 0.50 to 0.77, but
the decrease in ATP between 24 and 48 h was associated with a
decrease in EC to values below 0.4.

When returning individuals to oxygen-saturated seawater
following 23 h in deoxygenated water, ATP and EC were low in some
of the individuals during the initial 1$\frac{1}{2}$ h, but after 6 and 24 h
the values were generally high (Fig. 4 B). On returning individuals to saturated seawater following 72 h in deoxygenated water,
only 1 or 2 out of 9 individuals in each jar became active and
these individuals were analysed separately from the inactive
ones. The ATP content of the active individuals in some cases
was higher than observed in the previous experiments, while the
EC was in the normal range around 0.6. The inactive individuals
had low contents of ATP and total adenine nucleotides, as well
as low EC (Fig. 4 C).

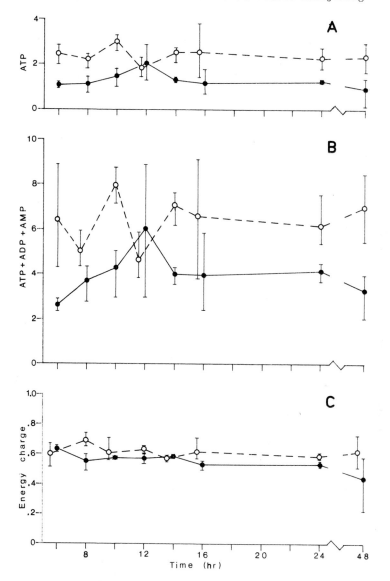

Fig. 3. *Cirolana borealis*. Concentrations of ATP (A) and total adenine nucleotides (B) (nmole/mg ash-free dry weight) and energy charge (C) during transition from aerobiosis to anaerobiosis. Symbols as in Fig. 1. Vertical bars denote the range of triplicate determinations

DISCUSSION

The pattern of change in respiration rate with decreasing oxygen tension (Fig. 2) reveals that *Cirolana borealis* to a large extent

H. R. Skjoldal and T. Baake

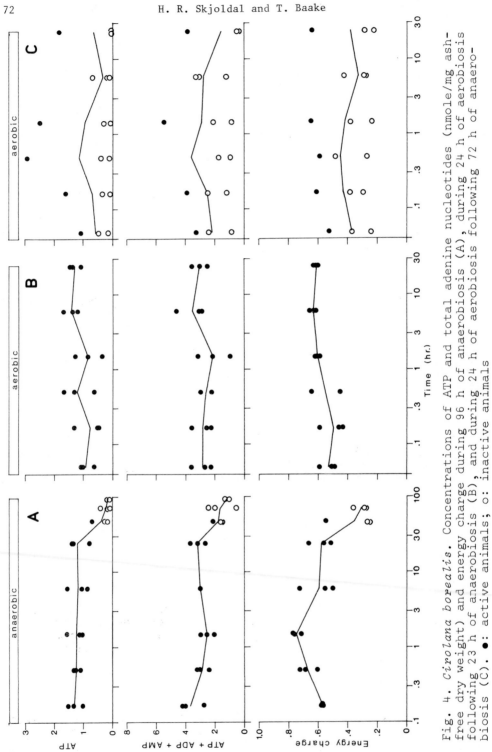

Fig. 4. *Cirolana borealis*. Concentrations of ATP and total adenine nucleotides (nmole/mg ash-free dry weight) and energy charge during 96 h of anaerobiosis (A), during 24 h of aerobiosis following 23 h of anaerobiosis (B), and during 24 h of aerobiosis following 72 h of anaerobiosis (C). ●: active animals; o: inactive animals

is unable to regulate its oxygen consumption. Many invertebrate
species that encounter low oxygen tensions in their environments
increase their respiratory efficiency at these low tensions
(Vernberg, 1972). *C. borealis* ceases to respire at an oxygen
tension of about 0.7 ml/l, thus showing more similarity to
organisms that are adapted to life in water that is permanently
rich in oxygen.

The transition towards zero oxygen consumption of *C. borealis*
did not coincide with any obvious change in behaviour or activity.
This apparent ease in changing from aerobiosis to anaerobiosis is
probably a result of its scavenging feeding habits. *C. borealis*
regularly encounters low oxygen tensions as it burrows into the
meat of dead fish to feed. Obviously it needs to be active during
this time and an increase in the circulation of water over its
respiratory surfaces must be difficult to accomplish inside the
fish. An efficient anaerobic metabolism would therefore be
advantageous to this species.

The observations on the adenine nucleotides can give some
indications as to the efficiency of the anaerobic metabolism of
*C. borealis*. As the ATP concentration and EC remained stable
during the gradual transition from aerobiosis to anaerobiosis
(Fig. 3) and during 24 h of anaerobiosis (Fig. 4 A), we conclude
that *C. borealis* has a balanced anaerobic metabolism, i.e. the
production of ATP equals the rate of its utilization. The anaerobic metabolism is thus efficient enough to provide the ATP for
the maintenance requirements and for a "normal" activity level.

A comparison of the ATP levels during anaerobiosis and
aerobiosis has been used as an argument for the high degree of
efficiency of anaerobic metabolism (Zs.-Nagy & Ermini, 1972;
Hochachka, 1975). One cannot conclude, however, from the similar
levels of ATP during aerobiosis and anaerobiosis (Fig. 3) that
the anaerobic energy metabolism is as efficient as the aerobic.
From the theoretical role of EC in metabolic regulation (Atkinson,
1969), it can be inferred that the ATP level will be strictly
poised as long as the minimum rate of ATP production is equal to
or higher than the minimum rate of ATP utilization. This has been
convincingly demonstrated for the blue-green alga *Anabaena
cylindrica* (Bottomley & Stewart, 1976).

At present the nature of the anaerobic metabolism of *Cirolana
borealis* is unknown as no analysis of anaerobic end products has
been performed. Although many invertebrate taxa have been shown
to possess a more complex and efficient anaerobic metabolism than
the classical glycolysis (Hochachka, 1975), the latter cannot be
ruled out as the mechanism used by *C. borealis*. Barnes *et al.*
(1963) found that the intertidal barnacles *Balanus balanoides*
and *Chthamalus stellatus* produced about 0.3 mg lactic acid/g wet
weight.h during anaerobiosis. The crab *Uca pugnax* can survive 24
h of anoxia and also accumulates lactic acid (Teal & Carey, 1967).


## ACKNOWLEDGEMENTS

We thank the Institute of Physiology, University of Bergen, for
providing facilities for doing the biochemical analyses, and Ms
Liz McLean for correcting the English text.

## REFERENCES

Atkinson, D. E., 1969. Regulation of enzyme function. *Annual Review of Microbiology*, 23, 47-68.

Barnes, H., Finlayson, D. M. & Piatigorsky, J., 1963. The effect of desiccation and anaerobic conditions on the behaviour, survival and general metabolism of three common cirripedes. *Journal of Animal Ecology*, 32, 233-252.

Bottomley, P. J. & Stewart, W. D. P., 1976. ATP pools and transients in the blue-green alga, *Anabaena cylindrica*. *Archives of Microbiology*, 108, 249-258.

Chapman, A. G., Fall, L. & Atkinson, D. E., 1971. Adenylate energy charge in *Escherichia coli* during growth and starvation. *Journal of Bacteriology*, 108, 1072-1086.

Hochachka, P. W., 1975. An exploration of metabolic and enzyme mechanisms underlying animal life without oxygen. In *Biochemical and Biophysical Perspectives in Marine Biology*, Vol. 2 (ed. D. C. Malins & J. R. Sargent), pp. 107-137. Academic Press.

Ruby, E. G. & Fox, D. L., 1976. Anaerobic respiration in the polychaete *Euzonus (Thoracophelia) mucronata*. *Marine Biology*, 35, 149-153.

Saz, H. J., 1970. Comparative energy metabolism of some parasitic helminths. *Journal of Parasitology*, 56, 634-642.

Teal, J. M. & Carey, F. G., 1967. The metabolism of marsh crabs under conditions of reduced oxygen pressure. *Physiological Zoology*, 40, 83-91.

Theede, H., Ponat, A., Hiroki, K. & Schlieper, C., 1969. Studies on the resistance of marine bottom invertebrates to oxygen-deficiency and hydrogen sulphide. *Marine Biology*, 2, 325-337.

Vernberg, F. J., 1972. Dissolved gases. Animals. In *Marine Ecology*. Vol. I: *Environmental Factors* (ed. O. Kinne), pp. 1491-1526. Wiley-Interscience.

Zebe, E., 1975. *In vivo*-Untersuchungen über den Glucose-Abbau bei *Arenicola marina* (Annelida, Polychaeta). *Journal of Comparative Physiology*, 101, 133-147.

Zs.-Nagy, I. & Ermini, M., 1972. ATP production in the tissues of the bivalve *Mytilus galloprovincialis* (Pelecypoda) under normal and anoxic conditions. *Comparative Biochemistry and Physiology*, 43 B, 593-600.

Zwaan, A. de & Wijsman, T. C. M., 1976. Anaerobic metabolism in Bivalvia (Mollusca). Characteristics of anaerobic metabolism. *Comparative Biochemistry and Physiology*, 54 B, 313-324.

# IN SITU MONITORING OF OXYGEN PRODUCTION AND RESPIRATION IN CNIDARIA WITH AND WITHOUT ZOOXANTHELLAE

**Armin Svoboda**

*Lehrstuhl für Spezielle Zoologie, Ruhr-Universität, Bochum, Postfach 102148, D-463 Bochum 1, F.R.G.*

ABSTRACT

24h in situ monitoring was carried out on Red Sea corals and other coelenterates with symbiotic zooxanthellae and some species lacking them. The individuals were enclosed in bell jars, and the water stirred continuously. In another experimental series the bell jars were flushed automatically at regular intervals. During a 24h cycle the species having zooxanthellae showed a conspicuous surplus in $O_2$ production at all depths down to 40m. In all species examined there was a maximum production and respiration below 5m depth, with an unexpected decrease of 25-50% in 1m depth. A slight decrease in production appeared following saturation light intensities in the morning if the closed bell jar system was used. In the flushed bell jars production remained constant until the evening saturation level. Xeniids showed a stepwise increase of $O_2$ output caused by diurnal colony contraction. Species lacking symbionts showed remarkable reduced metabolism compared with symbiotic species. It must be concluded that metabolism of symbiotic species is accelerated by the supply of photosynthetic products.

INTRODUCTION

Symbiosis between Gymnodinium microadriaticum (FREUDENTHAL) and various marine coelenterates has been known for about 100 years. Transfer of photosynthetic products from alga to host was demonstrated first by MUSCATINE & HAND (1958). Laboratory experiments on respiration and productivity were described by KANWISHER & WAINWRIGHT (1967), ROFFMANN (1968) and FRANZISKET (1969). Field monitoring, avoiding the problems of simulation of the natural light conditions, has been scarce until now, mainly because of equipment problems. Some field data are now available from WETHEY & PORTER (1977) and MERGNER & SVOBODA (1977). From productivity studies in the field the effectivness of the mutualistic nutrient exchange cannot be deduced directly (MUSCATINE & PORTER, 1977). In contrast the contribution of coelenterate species to the productivity of coral reefs is best measured in situ. The present experiments, carried out in the northern Red Sea at Aqaba, Jordan, and at Al Ghardaqa, Egypt, were carried out on as many species as possible and at various depths, to get a general survey.

MATERIAL and METHODS

24h in situ monitoring of $O_2$ was carried out on 12 coelenterate species with and 5 species without zooxanthellae. The experiments took place in February and March, 1976, at Aqaba at 1m, 5m, 10m, 20m and 40m depth; and in March 1977 at Al Ghardaqa at 5m and 10m depth. All recordings were run from noon to noon. The pressure-proof self-contained monitors for $O_2$, light and the perspex bell jars were inserted by SCUBA diving after calibration of the electrodes, and mounted close to the habitat of the individual selected for the experiment.

Fig. 1    Arrangement of monitoring units and bell jars in the field; junction
          from bell jars to $O_2$ probe-pump units by small tubes, to flushing
          pump by wide tubes; lightprobe(white opaque cover) attached to large
          bell jar

The average dry weight of the specimens enclosed in the 1,41 bell jars was about 0,5g, while those in the 3,21 bell jars were up to 1,0g in weight. After all air bubbles were removed from the circulation system the individuals were detached from their substrates and put on the bottom of the bell jar. The closed bell jars and the light probe were mounted on the site of detachment of the specimen. The bell jar was connected by rubber tubes to the circulation pump/$O_2$ electrode unit, and in the case of the Al Ghardaqa experiments to the automatically flushing pump unit as well. The whole procedure took 10-15 minutes, enough time to adjust the temperature compensating thermistors of the oxygen probe. After 24h monitoring the bell jar was detached from the pump units and brought to surface. A new experiment could be started immediately after the end of the preceding one by connecting the pump to a second bell jar which already contained a new test colony. All test animals were preserved in a 10% solution of formaldehyde in seawater for 24h and the skeleton dissolved in 10% HCl after determination of the wet weight. The tissues were rinsed with tap water for several hours and oven-dried at 105°C. The ash-free dry weight was calculated after combustion of the tissues at 1000°C in a muffle furnace. The $O_2$ recorder unit had junction boxes for 2 pressure and temperature compensated $O_2$ probes (YSI 5739) and 2 stirring pumps which could be connected to 2 bell jars. The light recorder unit could be connected to 4 light probes. Both units, each 16kg in weight, were driven by 12V - 12 Ah sealed lead batteries supplying more than 100h operation time. On each of the wax paper recorders 4 channels could be printed. 2 channels recorded $O_2$ content in the ranges 10mg or 20mg $O_2$ on full scale, 2 channels for the probe temperature in the range 5°-30°C of one channel instead of temperature for $O_2$ content differences between both bell jars, in the control experiments.

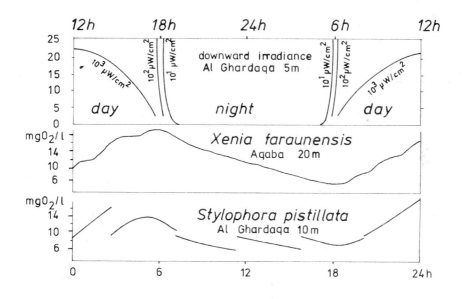

Fig. 2    24h light record and oxygen records. Xenia in the closed bell jar system, Stylophora in the flushed bell jar system.

The light recorder unit printed the current response of up to 4 cosine-corrected calibrated silicone lightprobes with linear response in the range of 400-950nm (PIN 10 DF-CAL, United Detector Company) on a linear scale. The instrument ranged over seven orders of magnitude. Each of them could be plotted over the full scale, fig. 2, or 5 orders could be covered by the full scale (fig. 6,

MERGNER & SVOBODA, 1977). The spectral composition of downward irradiance was measured by a calibrated underwater spectrophotometer. 13 interference filters in the spectral range of 400-700nm could be placed in front of the silicone cell. The instrument scale range of 2 orders of magnitude could be extended to 5 orders of magnitude by inserting neutral grey density filters.

The filter photometer was developed by K. Dietzel, Krefeld; the light- and $O_2$-monitoring units by R. Machan, Vienna, and the author.

TABLE 1　　List of Species with ($^+$) and without ($^-$) Zooxanthellae

Hydrozoa:　　Millepora dichotoma$^+$
Scyphozoa:　　Aurelia aurita$^-$, Cassiopea andromeda$^+$
Octocorallia:　Dendronephthya dollfusi$^-$, Dendronephthya rubeola$^-$,
　　　　　　　Lithophyton arboreum$^+$, Heteroxenia ghardaqensis$^+$,
　　　　　　　Heteroxenia fuscescens$^+$, Xenia faraunensis$^+$
Hexacorallia:　Palythoa mammilata$^+$, Tubastrea micrantha$^-$, Balanophyllia
　　　　　　　gemmifera$^-$, Fungia scutaria$^+$, Acropora variabilis$^+$,
　　　　　　　Stylophora pistillata$^+$, Favia pallida$^+$, Goniastrea pectinata$^+$

## RESULTS and CONCLUSIONS

Daily measurements in the lagoon and in the forereef of Aqaba indicated pronounced differences between the two areas in both oxygen and temperature conditions (MERGNER & SVOBODA, 1977). Below 5m depth temperature remained nearly constant at 21,5°C and the $O_2$ content similarly varied little from 8,5mg/l. During the experimental period wave action was minimal and the sky was cloudless. The meteorological conditions at Al Ghardaqa were similar.

The ratio between wet weight and dry weight was determined in order to compare the metabolic rates with data from literature. The highest values, of up to 7%, were obtained from the scyphomedusa Cassiopea. This ratio was as variable in Cassiopea as in alcyonarians because of a different degree of water loss by contraction in spite of prior formaldehyde fixation. The ratios in Alcyonaria varied from 2,5-4%. Within the Scleractinia the species lacking symbionts gave a ratio of 2-3%; the hermatypic species, Fungia, of 1-2%; and the branched species Acropora and Stylophora a lower ratio still, 0,5%. The massive genera Favia and Goniastrea were not easy to compare in this respect because only the living parts of the colony were dissolved to get the dry weight values. With increasing depth alcyonarians increased in percentage of dry weight, while in contrast the percentage dry weight decreased in the hermatypic coral species studied. Excepting the two medusa species considerable respiration differences were recorded between species which, although comparable in polyp and colony size, differed in the presence or absence of zooxanthellae. The two medusae, Cassiopea and Aurelia, consumed about 3mg$O_2$/g/h. Dendronephthya, without symbionts, consumed only about 1mg, compared with the Lithophyton, Heteroxenia and Xenia which consumed 3mg$O_2$/g/h. Tubastrea and Balanophyllia lacking symbionts, consumed 0,5mg compared with greater uptake rates in corals possessing symbionts. Thus, Fungia and Favia took up 1mg Goniastrea 2mg, Stylophora 3mg and Acropora up to 5mg$O_2$/g/h. Within a species individuals at 1m depth consumed 25-50% $O_2$ less than those at 5m depth or below. Another slight decrease of $O_2$ uptake could be observed in individuals below 20m depth.

TABLE 2   Results of O₂ Monitoring of Coelenterate Species from Aqaba and Al Ghardaqa (+)

| species | depth m | % dry wt./wet wt. | h productivity/24h | mgO$_2$/g/h consumption (24h average) | mgO$_2$/g/h production (24h average) | P max/R max | P/R (24h average) | species | depth m | % dry wt./wet wt. | h productivity/24h | mgO$_2$/g/h consumption (24h average) | mgO$_2$/g/h production (24h average) | P max/R max | P/R (24h average) |
|---|---|---|---|---|---|---|---|---|---|---|---|---|---|---|---|
| **Hydrozoa** | | | | | | | | **Hexacorallia: Scleractinia** | | | | | | | |
| Millepora d. | 1 | 1.1 | 11.5 | 2.4 | 2.9 | 1.9 | 1.2 | Tubastrea m. | 1 | 2.2 | | 0.6 | | | |
| " | 5 | 0.4 | 9.5 | 3.5 | 4.7 | 3.3 | 1.4 | Balanophyllia g. | 1 | 3.0 | | 0.5 | | | |
| **Scyphozoa** | | | | | | | | Fungia s. | 1 | 0.8 | 11 | 1.2 | 1.9 | 3.3 | 1.7 |
| | | | | | | | | " | 5 | 1.6 | 9.5 | 0.5 | 0.6 | 1.9 | 1.1 |
| Aurelia a. | 5 | 0.4 | | 3.2 | | | | " | 10 | 1.6 | 9.5 | 1.0 | 1.5 | 3.1 | 1.4 |
| Cassiopea a. | 5 | 4.5 | 10 | 2.8 | 4.1 | 3.1 | 1.5 | " * | 10 | 2.2 | 10.5 | 0.5 | 0.8 | 3.5 | 1.7 |
| " | 20 | 7.4 | 9 | 3.3 | 4.8 | 3.5 | 1.3 | " | 20 | 0.8 | 9.5 | 1.0 | 1.5 | 2.8 | 1.3 |
| " | 40 | 7.1 | 8.5 | 1.9 | 2.7 | 4.1 | 1.4 | " | 40 | 1.0 | 8 | 0.9 | 0.9 | 1.7 | 1.0 |
| **Octocorallia** | | | | | | | | Acropora v. | 1 | 1.5 | 11 | 1.5 | 2.2 | 2.4 | 1.4 |
| | | | | | | | | " | 5 | 0.5 | 10 | 5.4 | 6.7 | 3.1 | 1.2 |
| Dendronephthya d. | 40 | 3.8 | | 1.3 | | | | " * | 5 | 0.8 | 10 | 2.3 | 2.6 | 1.2 | 1.1 |
| Dendronephthya r. | 40 | 1.1 | | 1.5 | | | | " | 10 | 0.7 | 9.5 | 3.7 | 4.5 | 1.9 | 1.2 |
| Lithophyton a. | 1 | 4.9 | 10.5 | 2.3 | 2.5 | 1.5 | 1.1 | " * | 10 | 0.8 | 9.8 | 2.9 | 2.6 | 1.4 | 0.9 |
| " | 5 | 4.6 | 10 | 3.8 | 4.2 | 1.8 | 1.1 | " | 20 | 0.6 | 9.5 | 3.2 | 3.7 | 2.5 | 1.2 |
| " | 10 | 3.0 | 10 | 2.6 | 2.5 | 1.9 | 1.0 | " | 40 | 0.5 | 8.5 | 3.1 | 3.5 | 2.9 | 1.2 |
| Heteroxenia g. | 5 | 2.5 | 9.5 | 2.9 | 3.1 | 2.6 | 1.1 | Stylophora p. | 1 | 1.0 | 11 | 2.0 | 2.9 | 2.6 | 1.5 |
| " | 10 | 2.3 | 9 | 2.1 | 3.0 | 4.2 | 1.4 | " | 5 | 0.5 | 10 | 4.0 | 5.3 | 3.1 | 1.3 |
| " * | 10 | 2.8 | 9.8 | 2.6 | 2.8 | 2.6 | 1.1 | " | 10 | 0.6 | 9.5 | 3.0 | 3.9 | 3.1 | 1.3 |
| " | 20 | 3.4 | 9.5 | 2.8 | 3.3 | 3.2 | 1.2 | " * | 10 | 1.1 | 10.5 | 1.3 | 6.1 | 5.5 | 1.1 |
| Heteroxenia f. | 5 | 2.4 | 9.5 | 3.2 | 3.2 | 3.7 | 1.0 | " | 20 | 0.6 | 10 | 2.7 | 3.4 | 3.3 | 1.2 |
| " | 10 | 3.8 | 9 | 2.7 | 3.2 | 3.5 | 1.2 | " | 40 | 0.5 | 9 | 3.2 | 3.8 | 3.3 | 1.2 |
| " * | 10 | 2.5 | 9.8 | 2.4 | 3.2 | 2.3 | 1.3 | Favia p. | 1 | 1.2 | 10 | 1.3 | 1.4 | 2.1 | 1.1 |
| Xenia f. | 1 | 2.3 | 10.5 | 2.2 | 2.6 | 2.7 | 1.2 | " | 5 | 0.7 | 10 | 1.1 | 1.5 | 2.6 | 1.3 |
| " | 20 | 4.1 | 10 | 2.8 | 3.4 | 3.6 | 1.3 | " | 10 | 0.8 | 10 | 0.6 | 0.9 | 3.2 | 1.5 |
| | | | | | | | | " | 20 | 0.6 | 10 | 0.8 | 1.3 | 3.6 | 1.5 |
| **Hexacorallia: Zoantharia** | | | | | | | | " | 40 | 0.6 | 8 | 1.3 | 1.1 | 3.0 | 0.9 |
| | | | | | | | | Goniastrea p. | 1 | 0.7 | 8 | 1.8 | 1.5 | 1.2 | 0.9 |
| Palythoa m. | 1 | 4.7 | 10.5 | 0.5 | 0.7 | 1.9 | 1.2 | " | 5 | 0.4 | 10 | 2.0 | 2.3 | 1.8 | 1.2 |
| " | 20 | 3.4 | 10 | 0.7 | 0.9 | 2.4 | 1.3 | " | 10 | 0.3 | 9.5 | 1.8 | 2.1 | 2.1 | 1.2 |
| " | 40 | 4.5 | 9 | 0.5 | 0.6 | 2.7 | 1.1 | " | 20 | 0.4 | 9.5 | 2.0 | 2.2 | 2.3 | 1.1 |

In all symbiotic species respiration was 20-30% greater in the first four hours
of darkness than in the early morning. After 1-3h the $O_2$ consumption rates decreased and became constant, unless the $O_2$ content exceeded half saturation val-
vues. In some experiments corals survived several hours in $O_2$ depleted water
without apparent influence on the productivity the following morning. There
was no $O_2$ uptake difference between individuals of the same species used in
both closed and flushed bell jar methods. Parallel control probes did not record any measurable effects by bacterial or planktonic respiration or productivity.

In Aqaba the visibility below 5m depth was excellent during the experiments,
in contrast with the turbid lagoon areas there and at Al Ghardaqa. In the turbid layer the maximum downward irradiance occurred at about 570nm; and below
5m depth, in the clear layer, at 520nm, which is close to the wavelength of
the absorbtion and production maximum of the zooxanthellae (SVOBODA, 1973,
HALLDAL, 1968). At the end of February at noon the downward irradiance between
400-700nm was 64mW/cm$^2$ at the surface, decreasing to 46mW/cm$^2$ at 1m, to 24 at
5m, 18 at 10m, 12 at 20m and to 5,6mW/cm$^2$ at 40m depth. Under these light conditions all symbiotic species examined produced an $O_2$ excess in the 24h cycle.
The average surplus was about 10 - 40% of the total metabolism. The surplus
was larger in the shallow water of the lagoon and decreased with increasing
depths. In Acropora and Stylophora, which occurred to 50m depth in the gulf,
there was still 20% $O_2$ excess at 40m depth. In the other species there was an
obvious decrease in productivity close to their lower limits of depth distribution, but a P/R ratio less than 1.0 was never attained. Because of the decrease of downward irradiance with increasing depth the compensation points
were shifted towards noon. At 40m depth the daily duration of photosynthesis
was 1,5h; less, therefore, than in the lagoon area in at depth. The $O_2$ records
in all cases showed a strong increase in the morning, after passing the compensation point at 0,3-1,0mW/cm$^2$ up to 10mW/cm$^2$. In the closed bell jars the
production rate decreased slightly before noon despite still increasing downward irradiance, although remaining linear in the flushed bell jars after
passing the saturation valvue and only decreasing after passing the evening
saturation point. The $O_2$ production slightly decreased concurrently with a
contraction of the polyps; and actually stopped completely in the xeniids following their diurnal colony contractions (fig.2). Relative to biomass Stylophora and Acropora were among the most productive hermatypic species. They
produced up to 5mgO$_2$/g/h calculated from the 24h average. Less productive were
Cassiopea, Millepora, the xeniids, Lithophyton, Goniastrea, Fungia and Favia.
The lowest values were obtained in Palythoa. The sequence of species is hardly
changed by comparing by P max/R max values obtained from the maximum respiration and rates. At P max/R max values exceeding 1,7 and a daily sunshine of
11-12h the symbiotic species produce an excess in $O_2$ in a 24h cycle.


DISCUSSION

Because of remarkable intra-generic differences in metabolism between two Mediterranean Aglaophenia species (Hydrozoa), one having and the other lacking
zooxanthellae (SVOBODA, unpublished), several reef coelenterates were examined
in this respect. There were no differences between the two scyphomedusae, however. Aurelia (lacking symbionts) is a fast swimming species and Cassiopea,
having zooxanthellae is usually sedentary. In the Alcyonaria and Scleractinia
comparable species with zooxanthellae consumed 2 - 6 times more oxygen than
those lacking them. Since free living Gymnodinium species have a low respiration level (HUMPHREY, 1975) it seems probable that the increase in metabolism

results mainly from the host. The accelerated metabolism recorded may be caused by high concentrations of carbohydrates produced by the symbionts. The concentrations may be sufficient to cause prolonged high respiration rates in the first hours of darkness. The same effect occurs after strong illumination of hermatypic corals (ROFFMANN, 1968, fig. 5) and the anemone, Anemonia (SVOBODA, unpublished) with subsequent shading. The initially high consumption becomes linear after 1 hour at a 25-40% reduced level. Because of this effect the values for the daily respiration (Table 2) were summed from the average night rate and an assumed day rate which was calculated from the high values of the evening. Species without symbionts consumed $O_2$ apparently independently of the light conditions although the polyps were opened only at night. The lower respiration rate in most symbiotic species from the lagoon at 1m depth is correlated with reduced metabolism. Both may be caused by daily fluctuation in temperature, salinity and sedimentation rate. Another slight decrease in respiration observed in individuals below 20m depth may be due to reduced photosynthesis at low light intensities. This decrease probably results from the short fall in photosynthesis not being sufficiently compensated by the decreasing compensation point energy level, increase in numbers of zooxanthellae (DREW, 1972; SVOBODA, 1973), increase in chlorophyll content and changing pigment composition. Depth limits of most symbiotic species seemed to be dependet on maintaining autotrophic conditions by adaptation processes. Productivity in several species seemed to be effected by metabolic products enriched in the closed bell jars. The Aqaba values, therefore, need a slight correction of plus 5-10%. Such inhibitions in photosynthesis may have resulted in errors in calcification experiments as well (GOREAU, 1959), as CLAUSEN & ROTH (1975) showed experimentally.

In most of the 24h records the average P/R ratio exceeded 1,0. All these species, therefore, must be autotrophic, at least from the point of view of energy supply, as MUSCATINE & PORTER (1977) calculated from the amount of carbon transfer. It is not yet clear, however, whether the excess of fixed carbon is stored, or released as soluble or particulate organic matter (FRANZISKET, 1969). In several experiments Lithophyton and Favia consumed more than they produced and the xeniids showed a stepwise $O_2$ production. Most individuals of Lithophyton remained contracted after being chiselled off. The xeniids showed diurnal contractions connected with a stop in $O_2$ output. The low production rates recorded from both the alcyonarians when contracted may be caused by shading of the zooxanthellae with dyes, spicules or covering zooxanthellae; and by reduced water exchange through the locked gastral cavity. In Favia the contracted polyps were covered by a glossy membrane which may also have the effects of shading and inhibition of the water exchange. Future experiments in the northern Red Sea should concentrate on regulation processes and adaptation to the annual light condition changes. Sunshine duration there increases from 10h in December to 14h in June correlated with changes in the sun's altitude. Parallel experiments might be conducted on the speed of light level adaptation by artificially altering the downward irradiance and duration of exposure.

ACKNOWLEDGEMENTS


Grateful acknowledgements are due to Dr. Badran and Dr. N.C.Hulings, University of Jordan, for their hospitality in the Marine Science Station, Aqaba, to Dr.Bayoumi, Egyptian Academy of Sciences, for his invitation to the Marine Science Station at Al Ghardaqa; to Dr. J.Versefeldt, Zwolle, Netherlands, for determination of the alcyonaria; to the 'Deutsche Forschungsgemeinschaft' (program Dr. H.Mergner) and to the 'Österreichischen Fonds zur Förderung der wissenschaftlichen Forschung' grant 2202, for financial help with both field work and equipment.

LITERATURE

Clausen, C.H. & Roth, A.A., 1975. Estimation of coral growth-rates from laboratory $^{45}$Ca incorporation rates. Marine Biology, 33, 85-91.

Drew, E.A., 1972. The biology and physiology of alga-invertebrate symbiosis. II. Density of symbiotic algal cells in a number of hermatypic hard corals and alcyonarians from various depths. Journal of experimental marine Biology and Ecology, 9, 71-75.

Franzisket, L., 1969. Das Verhältnis von Photosynthese zu Respiration bei riffbildenden Korallen während des 24h-Tages. Forma et Functio,1, 153-158.

Goreau, T.F. & Goreau, N.I., 1959. The physiology of skeleton formation in corals. II. Calcium deposition by hermatypic corals under various conditions in the reef. Biological Bulletin of the marine biological Laboratory, Woods Hole, 117, 239-259.

Halldal, P., 1968. Photosynthetic capacities and photosynthetic action spectra of endozoic algae of the massive coral Favia. Biological Bulletin of the marine biological Laboratory, Woods Hole, 134, 411-424.

Humphrey, G.F., 1975. The photosynthesis: Respiration ratio of some unicellular marine algae. Journal of experimental marine Biology and Ecology, 18, 111-119.

Kanwisher, J.W. & Wainwright, S.A., 1967. Oxygen balance in some reef corals. Biological Bulletin of the marine biological Laboratory, Woods Hole, 133, 378-390.

Mergner, H. & Svoboda, A., 1977. Productivity and seasonal changes in selected reef areas in the Gulf of Aqaba (Red Sea). Helgoländer wissenschaftliche Meeresuntersuchungen, (in the Press).

Muscatine, L. & Porter, W., 1977. Reef corals: Mutualistic symbiosis adapted to nutrient-poor environments. Bio Science, 27, 7, 454-460.

Roffmann, B., 1968. Patterns of oxygen exchange in some Pacific corals. Comparative Biochemistry and Physiology, 27, 405-418.

Svoboda, A. Beitrag zur Ökologie, Biometrie und Systematik der mediterranen Aglaophenia Arten (Hydroidea). Ph. D. Thesis, Vienna 1972. Zoologische Verhandelingen, (in the Press).

Wethey, D.S. & Porter, J.W., 1977. Habitat-related patterns of productivity of the foliaceous reef coral, Pavona praetorta Dana. Coelenterate Ecology and Behavior. (Ed. G.O. Mackie). Plenum Press. New York.

# THE INFLUENCE OF SWIMMING PERFORMANCE ON THE METABOLIC RATE OF GADOID FISH

**Peter Tytler**

*Biology Department, University of Stirling, Scotland*

## INTRODUCTION

The value of the measurement of the relationship between oxygen consumption and induced, sustained swimming speed is that standardised minimal and maximal metabolic rates can be obtained by extrapolation.   These standard and active metabolic rates have been used to assess the responses of fish to abiotic factors such as temperature, ambient oxygen tension, and salinity (see Brett (9) and Fry (11) for reviews).   Also this approach has been used to gauge the influence of body size and to emphasise inter-specific differences (Brett (5) (9) and Morgan (18)).   In addition data from such measurements have been combined with field observations to estimate daily metabolic requirements (Brett (7), Holliday et al (15)) and the energy expenditure during migration (Brett (6)).   A recent application of this technique has been the estimations of the muscular and propulsive efficiency in fish locomotion (Webb (27)).

Most of the published work in this field has been confined to freshwater species.   The aim of this paper is to correct this trend in a small way by describing the relationship between oxygen consumption and swimming speed in the Gadidae, which contain many of our commercially important marine species.   The emphasis will be on the haddock, Melanogrammus aeglefinus, but comparisons with data from the Saithe, Pollachius virens and the cod Gadus morhua will be made.   Also an assessment of the importance of locomotor activity in the respiratory component of the energy equation will be made by applying these relationships to observations of the daily levels of swimming in the natural environment and to calculations of the average swimming speeds during spawning migrations.

## MATERIALS AND METHODS

The apparatus used in this study was a modification of the Blazka closed vessel tunnel respirometer (Blazka et al(4).  As can be seen from the section through the middle of the apparatus (Fig. 1) it consists of two concentric perspex tubes. The fish is introduced through a hatch into the inner tube down which a uniformly turbulent flow of water is forced by the rotation of a propellor.   During the measurement of oxygen consumption the continuous flow of air saturated water is stopped and the fish allowed to reduce the oxygen tension which is recorded by a polarograph electrode inserted in a by-pass

flow.    The fish was deprived of food for 24h before loading
into the respirometer and allowed a further 15 hours during
which to settle down in the new surroundings.    The velocity
of the water flow was increased in 10 cm/sec steps from the
familiarisation speed of 3.5 cm/sec.    Each step was held for
at least 45 minutes and the maximum sustained swimming speed
was taken as the highest velocity which could be maintained for
45 minutes.

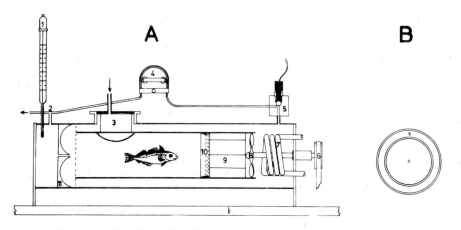

Fig. 1. A. The Blazka respirometer: 1. Contact
            thermometer, 2 outlet, 3 hatch with
            outflow, 4 peristaltic pump, 5 $PO_2$
            electrode, 6 belt drive, 7 cooling
            coil, 8 propellor, 9 radial plates,
            10 baffle screens, 11 flow former.
         B. Section through the middle of
            respirometer.

In general the fish had sufficiently strong optomotor responses
which eliminated the need for electric screens which is the
normal practise for freshwater fish.


## RESULTS AND DISCUSSION

### Saithe at $10^{o}$C

Fig. 2 shows the relationship between the logarithm of oxygen
uptake and swimming speed in 10 saithe (mean weight 151.8g and
mean length 25.5 cm) at $10^{o}$C.    The data represented by the
triangles were from 6 unexercised saithe.    The squares
represent data from four saithe pre-exercised at 0.5 Bl/sec for
7 days prior to measurement.    The regression line is for
unexercised fish data (Table 1).

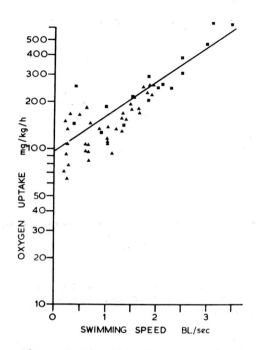

Fig. 2.   The relationship between the logarithm
          of oxygen consumption and swimming speed;
          exercised ( ■ ) and unexercised ( ▲ ).

The mean maximum swimming speed for the unexercised and
exercised fish were 1.8 and 3.1 Bl/sec respectively.    Both
values fall short of the critical swimming speed of 4.0 Bl/sec
Saithe found by Johnston and Goldspink (16).    The extrapolated
standard metabolic rate is 98 mg/kg/h and the active metabolic
rate is 648 mg/kg/h.       Thus swimming at the maximum sustained
swimming speed will increase the respiratory component of the
energy budget by a factor of six.

There are two points of interest arising from these data.
Firstly the measurements made at the higher swimming speeds
within the exercised group lie close to the extrapolated
regression for unexercised fish.       Secondly at the lower
velocities, below 1 Bl/sec there is considerable variability in
the data.       At these speeds the saithe swam less uniformly than
at the higher speeds.

Haddock and Cod at 10°C

Fig. 3 shows the data from five 2+ year group haddock with mean
weight 155.9g and mean length 24.8cm.       The remaining data
points are from 6 cod mean weight 440.9g and mean length 36.1 cm.
The continuous line is the regression for haddock data at 10°C.

The broken line is the regression for all the saithe data at 10°C.

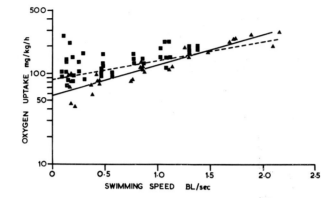

Fig. 3.  The relationships between the logarithm
         of oxygen uptake and swimming speed in
         haddock (▲) and cod (■) at 10°C.

The haddock were found to perform most satisfactorily in the respirometer and this is reflected in the quality of the data. The regression was significant at the 0.5% level and the maximum swimming speed was 2.2 Bl/sec without pre-exercise. The standard metabolic rate was 59 mg/kg/h and the active metabolic rate was 280 mg/kg/h, 4.5 times higher than the standard rate.    By contrast the cod fatigued earlier at velocities below 1.5 Bl/sec and consequently because of high variability at these speeds a significant regression could not be obtained.    Although the cod data fits that of the saithe more closely than that of haddock, the minimum values of oxygen uptake at the various speeds lie close to the regression line for haddock.

Influence of Temperature and Swimming Performance on the
Oxygen Consumption of Haddock

Fig. 4 shows the influence of temperature on the relationship between oxygen uptake and swimming speed in 2+ year group haddock (20-29 cm in length and 55 to 253g in weight).    The lines are the regression lines for all the data from groups of 10 fish at 5°C (▲), 10°C (■) and 15°C (□) (See Table 1). There is no significant difference between the standard rates at 5 and 10°C but between 5 and 15°C the $Q_{10}$ was 2.14.    On the face of it, it would seem that within this narrow range of 5 to 10°C, which represents the thermal zone of greatest abundance, the metabolic rate of haddock is virtually independent of temperature.    However, closer examination of the data at 5°C

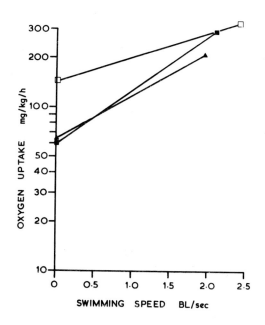

Fig. 4.    The relationships between the logarithm
of oxygen consumption and swimming speed
in haddock at 5°C (▲), 10°C (■) and
15°C (□).

shows a higher level of variability at the low velocities which
would tend to reduce the slope of the line and raise the
standard metabolic rate.    In order to avoid this source of
error the regressions were recalculated using only data obtained
at swimming speeds greater than 1 Bl/sec.    Even with this
adjustment the $Q_{10}$ for the increase in standard rates of oxygen
consumption between 5 and 10°C is only 1.05 and there is no
significant difference between standard rates at these
temperatures.    There is growing support in the literature for
narrow zones of thermal homeostasis in poikilotherms,
particularly in intertidal invertebrates (Newell & Northcroft
(20), Newell (21), Newell & Bayne (22)).    Examination of
most of the work with freshwater fish employing a technique
similar to that used in this study show similar zones of thermal
homeostasis in brown trout, perch and bass (Morgan (18),
Beamish (1).                            It is likely that this phenomenon
arises from adjustments in the utilisation of energy substrates,
metabolic pathways and rates of enzymic reactions previously
observed by Hochachka and Hayes (13), Hochachka and Somero (14)
during thermal acclimation in isolated tissue preparations.
Above 10°C in haddock this cellular process of thermal adjustment

appears to be inadequate.

With increase in temperature there is a progressive increase
in the maximum sustainable swimming speed from 1.9 Bl/sec at
5°C to 2.4 Bl/sec at 15°C.    Also the difference between
standard and active metabolic rates (the scope for activity)
increases to a maximum at 15°C.     Previous work with sockeye
salmon, bass and goldfish all showed that the scope for
activity reached a maximum at a temperature close to the
optimum for each species, after which it fell (see Brett (9)).
This decline in scope for activity has been attributed to the
limitations imposed on metabolism by the reduction in the
concentration of dissolved oxygen and the capacity of the
oxygen extraction mechanisms with increase in ambient
temperature.    It is possible,that by extending the
experimental temperature range this respiratory failure in
haddock might have been detected.


## Metabolic Cost of Locomotion in the Natural Environment

Finally I would like to consider the importance of the energy
cost of swimming of gadoid fish in the natural environment.  No
information on the day to day swimming activity of haddock in
the natural environment is available but recently Hawkins (12)
has described such information in cod, a closely related
demersal species of the gadidae.

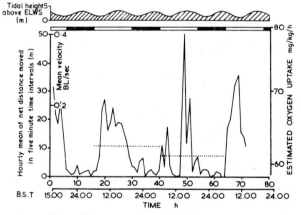

Fig. 5.    The fluctuations in locomotor activity
           and derived oxygen uptake of a 42 cm
           cod tracked ultrasonically in a Scottish
           Sea Loch.

In Fig. 5 is plotted the changes in the hourly mean of net
distance moved in five minute intervals and rhythmic changes
in tidal height and illumination.    The dark and light bars
indicate night and day respectively.    On the ordinate has been
superimposed the mean relative swimming speed in Bl/sec and its
conversion to metabolic rate from the relationship between
oxygen consumption and swimming speed in haddock at 10°C.   The
dotted lines are the mean swimming speed over the 24 h period
indicated by the extent of the line over the time scale.

As can be seen the maximum oxygen consumption due to locomotion
is only 130% of the standard.    This is somewhat lower than
the 5 times of standard estimated by Brett (7) for lake dwelling
juvenile sockeye salmon but is a similar situation to that
found by Holliday et al (15) for lake brown trout which was also
based on ultrasonic tracking.    It should, of course, be
recognised that these estimates of swimming speeds for free
swimming fish are derived from net movements over five minute
intervals and may be an underestimate of the actual distance
covered.    In fact Hawkins (personal communication) has found
the mean swimming speed during a 26 minute period of tracking
based on positional fixes every 30 secs can be as high as
0.7 Bl/sec for 50 cm cod.    However, even at this maximum
swimming speed, metabolic rate would not exceed 3 times the
standard metabolic rate.    Over a 24h period, even if the
values for swimming speed are doubled to account for under
estimation, the overall metabolic rate due to locomotor
activity will not exceed 120% of standard.

The spawning migration in haddock and cod although confined to
2 to 4 months in the year covers extensive distances and may
therefore contribute significantly to the energy equation.    In
the case of North Sea haddock whose seasonal movements have
been investigated by Jones (17) using conventional tagging
techniques the 2+ year group and older fish appear to begin a
northerly migration in early November.    The mean daily rate
of progress was estimated to be 0.7 miles, which when
transformed into relative swimming speed for 25 cm haddock
becomes 0.04 Bl/sec which cannot have much impact on the
respiratory component of the energy budget.

It would seem on the face of these observations that for the
demersal gadoid fishes the contribution from swimming activity
to the energy budget is so small as to be of no significance.
More detailed information from more species on the duration and
intensity of swimming activity in normal routine behaviour and
during migratory movements in the natural environment is
needed to develop this hypothesis further.    It may be possible
with the development of sophisticated biotelemetry techniques
to use physiological parameters such as heart rate (Wardle and
Kanwisher (26), Priede and Tytler (24)) or gill ventilation
rate (Oswald (23))to estimate indirectly the metabolic rate of
fish in the wild state and obtain a more accurate estimate of
the importance of the contribution of locomotion to the total
energy budget.

TABLE 1.   The linear regressions relating swimming speed
           (x Bl/sec) and oxygen consumption (Y mg/kg/h)
           for Haddock and Saithe.

| Species | Linear Regression | Temp °C | Standard Oxygen Uptake mg/kg/h | Active Oxygen Uptake mg/kg/h | Standard Error Y from x |
|---|---|---|---|---|---|
| Melanogrammus | Log Y = 0.26x + 1.81 | 5 | 65 | 200 | 3.0 |
| aeglefinus | Log Y = 0.33x + 1.77 | 10 | 59 | 280 | 3.2 |
| | Log Y = 0.13x + 2.16 | 15 | 144 | 400 | 4.2 |

REFERENCES

(1)   Beamish, F.W.H., 1970.   Oxygen consumption of largemouth
      bass, Micropterus salmoides, in relation to swimming
      speed and temperature. Can. J. Zool. 48, 122-1228.

(2)   Black, E.C., Connor, A.R., Lam, K.K.C. & Chiu, W.G. 1962.
      Changes in glycogen, pyruvate and lactate in rainbow
      trout (Salmo gairdneri) during and following
      musculature activity.  J. Fish. Res. Bd. Can. 19, 409-
      436.

(3)   Black, E.C., Bosomworth, N.J. & Docherty, G.E., 1966.
      Combined effects of starvation and severe exercise on
      glycogen metabolism of rainbow trout, Salmo gairdneri.
      J. Fish. Res. Bd. Can. 23, 1461-1463.

(4)   Blazka, P., Volt, M. & Cepela, M. 1960.   A new type of
      respirometer for the determination of the metabolism
      of fish in an active state.  Physiol. Bohemoslov.
      9, 553-558.

(5)   Brett, J.R. 1965.   The relation of size to rate of
      oxygen consumption and sustained swimming speed of
      sockeye salmon (Oncorhynchus nerka).   J. Fish. Res.
      Bd. Can. 22, 1491-1501.

(6)   Brett, J.R.,1970.  Fish - the energy cost of living.   In
      Marine Aquaculture, edited by W.J. McNeil, Oregon
      State University Press.

(7)   Brett, J.R., 1971.   Energetic responses of salmon to
      temperature.:  A study of some thermal relations in
      the physiology and freshwater ecology of sockeye
      salmon (Oncorhynchus nerka).   Amer. Zool. 11, 99-113.

(8)   Brett, J.R., 1964.   The respiratory metabolism and
      swimming performance of sockeye salmon.  J. Fish. Res.
      Bd. Can. 21, 1183-1226.

(9)    Brett, J.R. 1972.   The metabolic demand for oxygen in
        fish, particularly salmonids and a comparison with
        other vertebrates.   Respiration Physiology 14, 151-
        170.

(10)   Farmer, G.J. & Beamish, F.W.H., 1969.   Oxygen consumption
        of Tilapia nilotica in relation to swimming speed and
        salinity.   J. Fish. Res. Bd. Can. 26, 2807-2821.

(11)   Fry , F.E., 1970.   The effect of environmental factors
        on the physiology of fish.   In Fish Physiology vol.
        VI, edited by W.S. Hoar and D.J. Randall p. 1-98.

(12)   Hawkins, A.D., 1978.   Periodicities in feeding of
        juvenile cod, and in the behaviour of their prey.
        Journal of Fish Biology (in press).

(13)   Hochachka, P.W. & Hayes, F.R., 1964.   The effect of
        temperature acclimation on the pathways of glucose
        metabolism in the trout.   Can. J. Zool. 40, 261-270.

(14)   Hochachka, P.W. & Somero, G.N., 1970.   Biochemical
        adaptation to the Environment.   In Fish Physiology
        edited by W.S. Hoar and D.J. Randall p. 99-156.

(15)   Holliday, F.G.T., Tytler, P. & Young, A.H., 1974.
        Activity levels of trout in Airthrey Loch, Stirling
        and Loch Leven, Kinross.   Proc. R. Soc. Edin. 74B,
        315-331.

(16)   Johnston, I.A. and Goldspink, G.A., 1973.   A study of
        Glycogen and Lactate in the myotomal muscles and
        liver of the coalfish (Gadus virens L.) during
        sustained swimming.   J. mar. biol. Ass. UK 53, 17-26.

(17)   Jones, R., 1969.   A method of analysis of some tagged
        Haddock returns.   J. Cons. int. Explor. Mer., 25, 58-
        72.

(18)   Morgan, R.I.G., 1974.   The energy requirements of trout
        and perch populations in Loch Leven, Kinross.   Proc.
        R. Soc. Edin. 74B, 334-345.

(19)   Morgan, R.I.G., 1973.   Some aspects of the respiratory
        metabolism in trout and perch.   Ph.D. thesis,
        University of Stirling.

(20)   Newell, R.C. & Northcroft, H.R., 1967.   A re-interpret-
        ation of the effect of temperature on the metabolism
        of certain invertebrates.   J. Zool. London 151, 277-
        298.

(21)   Newell, R.C., 1969.   The effect of temperature
        fluctuation on the metabolism of intertidal

invertebrates *An. Zool.*, 9, 293-307.

(22)   Newell, R.C. & Bayne, B.L., 1973.   A review on
       temperature and metabolic acclimation in
       intertidal marine invertebrates.   *Netherlands
       Journal of Sea Research*, 7, 421-433.

(23)   Oswald, R.L., 1978.   Feeding and light synchronisation
       in wild brown trout.   *Journal of Fish Biology*
       (in press).

(24)   Priede, I.G. and Tytler, P., 1977.   Heart rate as a
       measure of metabolic rate in teleost fishes; *Salmo
       gairdneri, Salmo trutta* and *Gadus morhua*.   *Journal
       of Fish Biology* 10, 231-242.

(25)   Rao, G.M.M., 1969.   Oxygen consumption of the rainbow
       trout (*Salmo gairdneri*) in relation to activity and
       salinity *Can. J. Zool*. 47, 131-134.

(26)   Wardle, G.S. and Kanwisher, J.W., 1974.   The significan-
       ce of heart rate in free swimming *Gadus morhua*:   Some
       observations with ultrasonic tags.   *Mar. Behav.
       Physiol*.  2, 311-324.

(27)   Webb, P.W., 1971.   The swimming energetics of trout.
       I Thrust and Power output at cruising speeds.
       II Oxygen consumption and swimming efficiency.
       *J. exp. Biol*. 55, 489-540.

## ACKNOWLEDGEMENTS

I am grateful to the Natural Environment Research Council for
financial support, during this study, in the form of a
Postdoctorate Research Fellowship.   I am also indebted to
Mr. R.I. Currie the director of the Scottish Marine Biological
Association for providing facilities for part of this work.
Acknowledgements are also due to Dr. A.D. Hawkins and Mr. G.G.
Urquart for generously supplying the information on cod
movements.     Finally I am particularly grateful to Professor
F.G.T. Holliday for his encouragement during this study and his
criticism of the initial manuscript.

# OSMOTIC AND PERMEABILITY STUDIES

# SODIUM BALANCE AND SALINITY TOLERANCE OF THE MYSID *LEPTOMYSIS MEDITERRANEA*

## Cedomil Lucu

*Institute "Rudjer Boskovic", Centre for Marine Research, YU 52210 Rovinj, Yugoslavia*

ABSTRACT

Sodium fluxes and salinity tolerance in the mysid Leptomysis mediterranea
Sars. have been studied.  Sodium and chloride concentrations in the blood of
L. mediterranea are equal to the concentration of these particular ions in
diluted sea water (322.7 mEq Na/l), and slightly lower when the animals are
maintained in sea water (470.3 mEq Na/l) or concentrated sea water (554.4 mEq
Na/l).

Sodium influxes are extremely high in all investigated sea water concentrations
($0.232 - 0.632$ uEq Na mg$^{-1}$ h$^{-1}$).  The activation energy of sodium in the sea
water amounts to 8.9 kcal mole$^{-1}$.  Measured electrochemical potentials and
potentials calculated by the Goldman equation agree closely with each other.
The permeability coefficient ratio Na: Cl = 1 : 0.76.  The results are discussed in the light of an explanation already proposed.

## INTRODUCTION

Mysids are widely distributed species mostly living in sea water, but several
representatives also inhabit brackish water and freshwater.  The effects of
limiting physico-chemical factors, such as temperature, salinity and oxygen
on Amphipoda, Decapoda and Isopoda have been extensively studied from an
ecophysiological viewpoint (Refs. 1,2,3.4,5).  There is however little information concerning the effects of environmental factors on crustaceans such as
mysids, copepods and euphausids, despite their enormous biomass, and ecological importance in the food chain.  The tolerance of the euryhaline mysid
Neomysis intermedia to salinity and temperature variations depends on multiple
inter-relationships of weight, sex, season, growth and reproductive phases
(6).  The euryhaline mysid Praunus flexuosus (7) and calanoid copepods (8)
regulate hyper-hypoosmotically over a wide range of salinities.  Euphausia
pacifica (9) collected from different localities showed physiological variations in salinity-temperature responses reflecting different adaptational
characteristics to the environment.  Since mysids are some of the more important prey of inshore fish and invertebrates in the Adriatic Sea (10), there are
good reasons to investigate the ionic regulatory abilities and tolerances of
environmental factors in this group, which are regarded as a primitive division
of the Crustacea (11).

## MATERIALS AND METHODS

Leptomysis mediterranea Sars. were collected from sandy bottoms in the vicinity
of Rovinj (Nothern Adriatic) during March and August 1977.  Several hundred

animals were caught by net from one aggregation and transported to the laboratory which was supplied with running sea water.    Mysids were fed "ad libidum"
with Tetramin synthetic food and algae.    The animals were gradually acclimated
to various sea water concentrations for at least one week before the experi-
ments.    Acclimation was carried out at a constant temperature of $20 \overset{+}{\phantom{}} 2^{\circ}C$, in
aerated sea water, and in darkness, since under these conditions moulting is
not so frequent and survival of animals higher.    Diluted sea water (DSW) was
prepared by appropriate dilution with distilled water.    Concentrated sea
water (CSW) was prepared by addition of oceanic salts (Pag island) into the
sea water (SW).

Blood samples were collected by piercing the carapace at the dorsal position
of the median cephalic artery.    The drop of haemolymph was sucked off by
microcaps (Drummond) and a pooled sample of the haemolymph from 3 or 5 animals
(1 $\mu$l) was diluted with 1 ml of redistilled water for the Na, K and Cl measurements.    Determinations of the whole body Na, K and Cl were carried out after
whole body digestion in 100 - 200 $\mu$l of conc. $HNO_3$, and made up to 10 ml with
redistilled water.    Na and K were measured by Varian Atomic Absorption (Model
AA-6) and Cl by a chloride analyser (Model IL-279).

The rate of $^{22}$Na uptake in 6 to 8 mysids was monitored for 8 min in polyethylene tubes (20 ml) in an appropriate sea water concentration and specific
radioactivity ($^{22}$Na impulses / $\mu$Eq Na).    At the mean time (4 min) a sample of
the loading medium for radioactive and stable measurements was taken.    After
8 min mysids were transferred to a similar composition of non-radioactive sea
water for an additional 2 min to wash off superficial radioactivity.    The
zero point of influx was obtained by extrapolation over the initial linear
range.

The rate of $^{22}$Na was calculated in the following way:

$$^{22}Na \text{ uptake} = \frac{^{22}Na \text{ radioactivity in mysid x 7.5}}{\text{mean specific radioactivity in medium}}$$

After the $^{22}$Na steady state in the animals had been reached, mysids were
transferred to polyethylene tubes (3 ml) with running sea water (17 ml/min)
where the radioactivity was washed out in efflux experiments.    Polyethylene
tubing was inserted in a well-type scintillation crystal Hershaw (1 x 1")
combined with a single channel analyser for radioactive measurements.    Radioactivity was counted every 2 min.    The rate of sodium efflux was calculated
as described elsewhere (5).    The potential difference between haemolymph and
sea water was measured by Hg-HgCl electrodes in a 3M KCl agar bridge connected
with an electrometer (Keithley, Model 601).    One electrode was connected via
an agar bridge with a 0.1 mm microcapilary tube which was inserted in the
blood sinus by a micromanipulating device adjusted on a binocular microscope,
at a place where the carapace had been previously pierced by a pin.    The
second electrode was immersed in the **sea water**.    After a few seconds the steady
state potentials were recorded.

### RESULTS

#### Temperature and Salinity Tolerance

Stepwise acclimation to the salinity reduction down to $21^{\circ}$/oo did not influence
mortality, while salinity stress in the range of 21 to $31^{\circ}$/oo caused lethal

effects at 10°C (Table 1)

Table 1.    Percentage survival of the mysid Leptomysis mediterranea at various
            salinities (t = 10°C).   Stepwise acclimations were provided by
            gradually increased (CSW) or decreased (DSW) salinities.   In the
            stepwise acclimated animals survival values were taken 24 h after
            exposure.

| TEST SALINITY °/ooNaCl. | | 19 | 22 | 31 | 44 |
|---|---|---|---|---|---|
| SURVIVAL  -  STRESS | % | 40 | 70 | 95 | 100 |
| SURVIVAL  -  STEPWISE ACCLIM. | % | 60 | 100 | 100 | 100 |

Previously unpublished results have revealed that in the winter population of
mysids the combined stress of temperature and salinity cause a decreased
tolerance at 25°C, in the salinity range of 25 to 37°/oo.   The genetic capacity for the adaptation of mysids to temperature might be greater than to
salinity since temperature fluctuations in the area investigated are much more
marked than salinity changes.   The curve representing mortality rate consists
of one fast component and a second slower component suggesting different
causes of death.

## Ionic Composition, Sodium Fluxes and Electrochemical Potentials

Haemolymph Na and Cl concentrations are isoionic with the medium in the DSW
(322.7 mEq Na/l), and slightly hypoionic in the SW (470.3 mEq Na/l) and CSW
(554.4 mEq Na/l) (Table 2).   A similar type of regulation was observed in the
isopod Ligia occidentalis (12).   Furthermore, paralellism is evident in the
whole body and haemolymph sodium and chloride concentrations at all sea-water
concentrations investigated.

Table 2.    Sodium, potassium and chloride concentration in mysids Leptomysis
            mediterranea acclimated to different sea water concentrations.
            Mean ± S.D., number of observations (in brackets).

|  | HEMOLYMPH (mEq/l) | WHOLE BODY (mEq/kg body $H_2O$) | SEA WATER (mEq/l) |
|---|---|---|---|
| $Na^+$ | 319.2 ± 26.8 (14) | 151.7 ± 19.9 (5) | 322.7 |
|  | 426.7 ± 28.1 (10) | 246.8 ± 25.8 (6) | 470.3 |
|  | 494.7 ± 44.0 ( 6) | 338.8 ± 13.4 (5) | 554.4 |
| $K^+$ | 8.2 ± 1.7 ( 6) | 124.6 ± 18.2 (5) | 8.6 |
|  | 12.1 ± 1.5 (12) | 185.1 ± 6.0 (6) | 10.2 |
|  | 18.2 ± 4.8 ( 5) | 183.6 ± 3.4 (6) | 12.0 |
| $Cl^-$ | 366.0 ± 45.0 ( 7) | 198.8 ± 15.5 (5) | 396.0 |
|  | 498.1 ± 49.3 ( 9) | 245.7 ± 31.1 (6) | 576.2 |
|  | 524.8 ± 48.0 ( 8) | 350.6 ± 40.5 (6) | 680.3 |

The values for sodium efflux are given in Table 3.   $^{22}$Na efflux rate constants
increased from 3.7 $h^{-1}$ in DSW to 5.3 $h^{-1}$ and 5.9 $h^{-1}$ in CSW and SW respectively.
Thus efflux rates range from 0.397 mEq Na $mg^{-1}$ $h^{-1}$ in DSW to 0.641 mEq Na $mg^{-1}$

$h^{-1}$ and 0.849 mEq Na $mg^{-1}$ $h^{-1}$ in SW and CSW respectively.

Table 3.    Sodium fluxes in L. mediterranea acclimated to different sea water
            concentrations.    Mean $\pm$ S.D., number of observations in brackets.
            Diffusive effluxes are calculated on the basis of the Goldman
            equations.

| SEA WATER ($mEq\ Na\ l^{-1}$) | INFLUX | EFFLUX | CALCULATED EFFLUXES |
|---|---|---|---|
| | ($mEq\ Na^{+}mg^{-1}h^{-1}$) | | |
| 322.7 (DSW) | 0.232 $\pm$ 0.100 (6) | 0.397 $\pm$ 0.037 (5) | - |
| 470.3  (SW) | 0.351 $\pm$ 0.040 (10) | 0.641 $\pm$ 0.113 (4) | 0.374 |
| 554.4 (CSW) | 0.632 $\pm$ 0.080 (7) | 0.849 $\pm$ 0.122 (7) | 0.568 |

The values for the sodium fluxes are one order of magnitude higher than those
previously given for sodium exchange rates in brackish and oceanic crustaceans
(13).    The sodium influx rates are high, but substantially smaller than efflux
rates, ranging from 0.232 to 0.632 mEq $mg^{-1}h^{-1}$ in DSW and CSW respectively.
Asymetric potentials between haemolymph and sea water (negative sign in reference to haemolymph) in the salinities investigated are slightly more negative
in DSW (-1.93 $\pm$ 0.6 mV) and more negative in CSW and SW (-3.30 and -2.95)
(Table 4).    Potentials measured in mysids which have not reached steady-state
concentrations in the body after transfer from SW to DSW have more marked
negative potentials (-13.91 mV $\pm$ 1.2 in 11 measurements) stabilizing after half
an hour to equilbrium potentials of -1.91 mV.    This fact suggested that
potential difference could be used as one indication of acclimation of animals
to new osmotic concentrations.

Equilibrium potentials calculated by the conventional Nernst equation (1):

$$E = \frac{RT}{z\,F} \ln Co/Ci$$ for sodium and chloride ions did not show any substantial

differences from the measured potentials.    The differences measured potentials
in CSW (-3.3mV) and $E_{Na}$ (+2.9 mV) and $E_{Cl}$ (-6.5 mV) is not marked, and is too
small to explain active extrusion of $Cl^{-}$ or $Na^{+}$ from the animals into sea water.
(Table 4).

Table 4.    Measured potentials (signs are given with reference to hemolymph)
            and calculated equilibrium potentials in L. mediterranea.

| SEA WATER CONCENTRATION (%) | EQUILIBRIUM POTENTIALS (mV) | | | MEASURED POTENTIALS (mV) |
|---|---|---|---|---|
| | $E_{Na}$ | $E_{Cl}$ | $E_{K}$ | |
| 70 (DSW) | +0.28 | -1.99 | + 1.20 | - 1.93 $\pm$ 0.60 (11) |
| 100 ( SW) | +2.45 | -3.67 | - 4.31 | - 2.95 $\pm$ 0.50 (10) |
| 120 (CSW) | +2.87 | -6.55 | -10.50 | - 3.30 $\pm$ 0.60 ( 9) |

The ratio of choloride to sodium conductance calculated by experimentally
determined potentials and calculated equilbrium potentials could be an indication of the relative permeabilities of the gills to sodium and chloride ions:

$$\frac{P_{Cl}}{P_{Na}} = \frac{E_{Na} - PD}{pD - E_{Cl}}$$

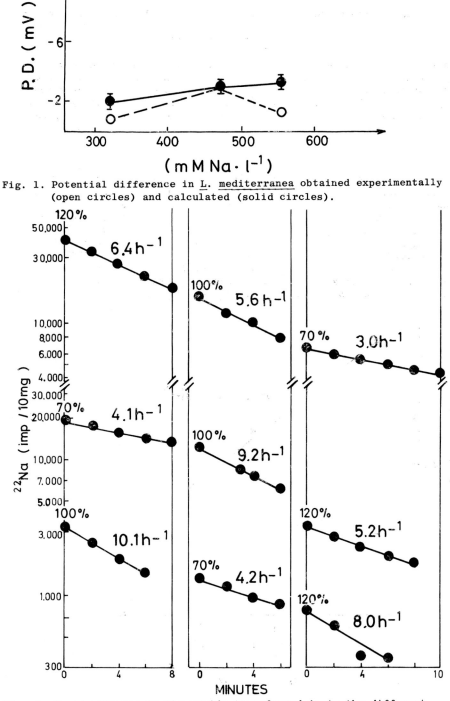

Fig. 1. Potential difference in L. mediterranea obtained experimentally
(open circles) and calculated (solid circles).

Fig. 2. Rapid effluxes in the mysids transferred in to the different
salinities.

From this equation the permeability coefficients $(P_{Na}, P_{Cl})$ are found to be:

$$P_{Na} \quad : \quad P_{Cl} \quad = \quad 1 \quad : \quad 0.72$$

The results confirm reduced chloride permeabilities, as has been shown previously for numerous marine and brackish crustacea and fish.    When the permeability coefficient is substituted in the Goldman equation, as described in
detail previously (5), the potentials in DSW and CSW may be readily calculated.
Experimentally obtained and predicted potentials agree well indicating that
membrane permeability does not change during the course of acclimation to various
salinities (Fig. 1).

In many Crustacea living in the sea, renal losses of sodium and chloride are
small relative to the total flux through the gills (14).    That mysids have a
slower sodium exchange rate at lower salinities might be explained by the well
known exchange diffusion (17) or simple diffusion phenomena (15).    The effect
is shown in Fig. 2 and needs further clarification.    The temperature coefficient $(Q_{10})$ for sodium efflux between 15 and 25$^{o}$C was 1.73, and the activation
energy was 8.9 kcal mole$^{-1}$.    The activation coefficient for free diffusion of
tritiated water in water, or sodium in water is 4.6 kcal mole$^{-1}$ (16).    The
activation energy of sodium measured on one artificial resin (8 to 12 kcal
mole$^{-1}$) is explained by simple diffusion and the value agrees well with the
activation energy for the mysid L. mediterranea (Fig. 3)

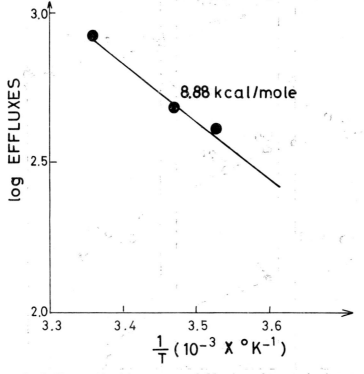

Fig. 3. Sodium activation energy following changes in temperatures

in L. mediterranea.  On horizontal axis are reciprocal values of

absolute temperature ($^{o}$K).  On vertical axis logarithms of effluxes.

## DISCUSSION

The purpose of this study was to investigate sodium kinetics and their inter-
dependence with different salinities and temperatures.   Sodium and chloride
in the haemolymph are isoionic to DSW, and hypoionic regulation of sodium and
chloride ions occurred in SW and CSW.   Under this condition the measured
influx of sodium from the medium is almost entirely due to passive diffusion
and the values are substantially lower than the efflux rate.   Assuming strictly
passive fluxes of sodium in DSW (70% SW), we calculated diffusive fluxes in SW
and CSW (120% SW), by means of a modified Goldman equation (5, 18, 22).
Calculated sodium fluxes are not substantially different from Na influxes,
which are no doubt diffusive.   Also, the differences between measured and
calculated sodium equilibrium potentials ($E_{Na}$) in SW and CSW are small, and
most probably not enough to explain a net efflux of sodium, although in steady-
state conditions total influx and efflux must be equal.   The apparently faster
effluxes might be explained rather by the fact that at this high concentration,
during a loading [22]Na from inside is exchanged with [23]Na from outside.
Exchange diffusion operating on a 1:1 basis for the results obtained would not
be a true reflection of the sodium effluxes.

Relative permeabilities for sodium are higher than for chloride in accordance
with many observations previously obtained on crustacea (5,14,15) and fishes
(17,18).   To verify the hypothesis of no change in the membrane permeabilities
of mysids to sodium in different salinities, we calculated potentials by method
of Goldman (5,14,18).   The results suggested electro-neutrality, as previously
noted in Palaemonetes, and calculated values are in the range of potentials
already obtained experimentally.

No effect of amiloride (Merck Co.), an inhibitor of sodium active transport,
in concentrations of $10^{-3}$M on influxes was obtained.   Activation energy for
sodium in L. mediterranea acclimated to sea water at the different temperatures
is 8.9 kcal mole $^{-1}$, a similar value having been already obtained on the artificially produced resin (8 - 12 kcal mole$^{-1}$).   In flounders with the active
sodium efflux acclimated to fresh water, the stimulation of active processes
by the addition of 10 mM KCl, caused an increase of sodium activation energy
from 10 to 28.8 kcal mole$^{-1}$ (21).   The facts concerning sodium active transport phenomena in mysids acclimated to different salinities suggest support
for simple diffusion and exchange diffusion.   The bathypelagic mysid
Gnathophausia ingens moves large volumes of sea water through its gills, and
might efficiently exchange a relatively large amount of oxygen between sea
water and the internal medium (8 ml / g wet weight/min) across the gills,
whose diffusion distance amounts to 1.5 - 2.5 um (19).   As described by
Shuskina (20) standard metabolic processes in mysids are substantially higher
than in other Crustacea.   The exceedingly high speed of water exchange through
the gills, which probably are not so strictly specialised for ionic transport
as gills in other Crustacea (3), and the relatively large gill surface and
thin membrane barriers might play an important role not only for the oxygen
diffusion (22), but also as a stimulating factor for ion transport through the
membrane without additional expenditure of energy.   The relatively high
permeability for sodium and also chloride may make L. mediterranea unable to
show a higher tolerance to different salinities.

## ACKNOWLEDGEMENTS

The author wishes to thank the self management local community of interest in

Yugoslavia for financial support, and to thank Drs H Barnes and D S McLusky for language correction, and Helen Thomson for typing the manuscript.

REFERENCES

(1)     GROSS, W., 1957.    An analyses of response to osmotic stress in
        selected decapod crustacea.    Biol. Bull. (Woods Hole) 112, 43-62.

(2)     FLORKIN, M., DUCHATEAU-BOSSON, G., JEUNIAUX, C. & SCHOFFENIELS, E.,
        1964.    Osmotic and ionic regulation in Eriocheir. Arch. Int.
        Physiol. Biochem. 72, 892-906.

(3)     KOCH, H. J., 1965.    Transcellular active transport of mineral ions by
        epithelial membranes of Arthropods. Arch. Biol. 76, 175-187.

(4)     LUCU, C., SIEBERS, D. & SPERLING, K. R., 1973.    Comparison of
        osmoregulation between Adriatic and North Sea Carcinus. Mar. Biol.
        22, 85-95.

(5)     LUCU, C., 1977.    Sodium kinetics in the shrimp, Palaemonetes pugio.
        II. Sodium fluxes and electrochemical potentials.    J. comp.
        Physiol. 115, 207-14.

(6)     SIMMONS, M. A. & KNIGHT, A. W., 1975.    Respiratory response of
        Neomysis intermedia (Crustacea : Mysidacea) to changes in salinity,
        temperature and season.    Comp. Biochem. Physiol. 50, 181-93.

(7)     McLUSKY, D. S. & HEARD, V. E. J., 1971.    Some effects of salinity  on
        the mysid Praunus flexuosus.    J. Mar. Biol. Ass. U.K. 51, 709-15.

(8)     BRAND, G. W. & BAYLY, I. A. E., 1971.    A comparative study of osmotic
        regulation in four species of calanoid copepod.    Comp. Biochem.
        Physiol. 38, 361-371.

(9)     GILFILLAN, E. 1972.    Reactiones of Euphauia pacifica Hansen (Crustacea)
        from oceanic, mixed oceanic-coastal and coastal waters of British
        Columbia to experimental changes in temperature and salinity.
        J. Exp. Mar. Biol. Ecol. 10, 29-40.

(10)    JUKIC, S., 1975.    Trawl fishing grounds in the central Adriatic (In
        Croatian).    Acta Adriatica 17, 1-86.

(11)    TIEGS, D. W. & MANTON, S. M. 1958.    The evolution of the Arthropoda.
        Biol. Rev. 33, 255-337.

(12)    WILSON, W. J., 1970.    Osmoregulation in isopods.    Biol. Bull. 138,
        96-108.

(13)    LOCKWOOD, A. P. M. & INMAN, C. B. E., 1973.    The blood volume of
        some amphipod crustaceans in relation to the salinity of the
        environment they inhabit.    Comp. Biochem. Physiol. 44, 935-41.

(14)    BALDWIN, G. F. & KIRSCHNER, L. B., 1976.    Sodium and chloride
        regulation in Uca adapted to 175% sea water.    Physiol. Zool. 49,
        158-171.

(15) SMITH, P. G., 1969. The ionic relations of Artemia salina (L.) II Fluxes of sodium, chloride and water. J. Exp. Biol. 51, 739-57.

(16) STEIN, W. D., 1967. The movement of molecule across cell membranes. In Theoretical and Experimental Biology Vol. 6, Academic Press.

(17) MOTAIS, R., ROMEU, F. G., & METZ, J., 1966. Exchange diffusion effect and euryhalinity in Teleosts. J. Gen. Physiol. 50, 391-421.

(18) KIRSCHNER, L. B., GREENWALD, L., & SANDRES, M., 1974. On the mechanism of sodium extrusion across the irrigated gill of sea water adapted rainbow trout (Salmo gairdnerii). J. Gen. Physiol. 64, 148-65.

(19) BELMAN, B. W. & CHILDRESS, J. J., 1976. Circulatory adaptations to the oxygen minimum layer in the bathypelagic mysid Gnathophausia ingens. Biol. Bull. (Woods Hole) 150, 15-37.

(20) SHUSHKINA, E. A., KUZMICHEVA, V. I. & OSTAPENKO, L. A., 1971. Energetic equivalents of body mass, respiration and caloricity of the Japan Sea mysids. (In Russ.). Okeanologia, 6, 1065-74.

(21) MAETZ, J., & EVANS, D. H. 1972. Effects of temperature on branchial sodium exchange and extrusion mechanisms in the seawater adapted flounder Platichtys flesus L. J. Exp. Biol. 54, 565-85.

(22) BURGGREN, W. W., McMAHON, B. R. & COSTERTON, J. W., 1974. Branchial water-and blood flow patterns and the structure of the gill of the crayfish Procambarus clarkii. Canad. J. Zool. 52, 1511-18.

# OSMOREGULATION OF THE EURYHALINE CHINESE CRAB *ERIOCHEIR SINENSIS*. IONIC TRANSPORTS ACROSS ISOLATED PERFUSED GILLS AS RELATED TO THE SALINITY OF THE ENVIRONMENT

**André Péqueux\* and Raymond Gilles**

*University of Liège, Laboratory of Animal Physiology, 22, quai Van Beneden, 4020 Liege, Belgium*

## ABSTRACT

Ionic distribution has been studied at the level of intact gills of euryhaline crabs *Eriocheir sinensis* adapted to fresh and sea waters. Transepithelial potential changes and ionic transports occuring during salinity changes across isolated perfused gills are discussed in relation to the crab osmoregulation. Changes in the activity of the $(Na^++K^+)$ATPase are also considered.

## INTRODUCTION

It is well known that the euryhaline chinese crab *Eriocheir sinensis* is capable of blood hyperosmotic regulation in diluted media although its blood remains close to isosmoticity with the surrounding medium in sea water (réf. 1 and 2).

Early works of Koch *et al.* (3) have established that the gills may be considered as playing the major part in the blood osmotic regulation occuring in diluted media. Since that time, information about the physiology of the gills and ionic movements they perform have remained scanty.

The purpose of the present work is to provide information on the ionic distribution at the level of intact gills of animals adapted to fresh water (FW) and sea water (SW). Ionic transport and transepithelial potential variations occuring during salinity changes across isolated perfused gills from FW-adapted crabs have been more specially investigated and changes in the activity of the $(Na^++K^+)$ATPase bound to the $Na^+$ pumping have also been considered.

## MATERIAL AND METHODS

Experiments were performed on isolated intact and perfused gills from chinese crabs *E.sinensis* adapted to FW and to SW respectively containing 0.63 and 474 mEq $Na^+$/l, 0.07 and 11 mEq $K^+$/l, 1.07 and 518 mEq $Cl^-$/l.

---

\* Chargé de Recherches du Fonds National de la Recherche Scientifique.

## Perfusion of isolated gills

Gills were cut off at their base and immediately flushed with
isotonic saline in order to avoid blood coagulation.
Polyethylene catheters were introduced in the afferent and effe-
rent blood vessels and they were gently fastened by means of a
neoprene-plexiglass clamp. The afferent catheter was then connected to a reservoir kept 15-20 cm higher than the gill preparation.
This gives a pressure inside the gill which is in agreement with
data of the literature (réf.4). Oxygen was continuously bubbled
through the incubation medium.

Transepithelial potential difference was measured by means
of two calomel electrodes (Radiometer K 400) respectively dipped
in the incubation medium and in the perfusate and connected to a
Keithley electrometer (Keithley Instruments 602).

## Incubation solution

So-called isotonic saline contained 240 mM NaCl, 5 mM KCl, 5 mM
$MgCl_2$, 12.5 mM $CaCl_2$, adjusted at pH 7.6 with borate buffer.

SW saline was twice more concentrated and a so-called artificial
fresh water (FW) was achieved by diluting "isotonic saline" 250
times while keeping the same pH value and buffer concentration.
Artificial SW was prepared by adding NaCl to FW up to the concentration of 500 mM.

## $Na^+$, $K^+$ and $Cl^-$ measurements

The isolated gills were blotted on filter paper, weighed and dried
at constant weight in an oven at 110°C for dry weight measurements.
The tissues were then digested for 48h in 4 ml HNO3 0.1 N. Tissue
ionic concentrations were calculated from the measurements of the
ion content in the digestion medium. $Na^+$ and $K^+$ determinations
were done by flame photometry. $Cl^-$ content was measured with a
Buchler-cotlove chloridometer. Extracellular space was estimated
by the 1% Inulin method.

## $^{22}Na^+$ fluxes measurements

$^{22}Na^+$ (0.25 µ curies/ml) was added in the medium bathing one side
of the epithelium and its appearance on the other side was measured
in 0.25 ml samples as a function of the incubation time. Radioactivity was determined by means of a γ scintillator Philips PW 4025/10.

## $(Na^+ + K^+)$ ATPase determinations

The membrane ATPase extracts were prepared from isolated gills
according to the method previously described (réf.5). The total
ATPase activity was determined to be maximum in presence of 4 mM
ATP, 5 mM $MgCl_2$, 100 mM NaCl, 25 mM KCl, 0.25 mM EGTA, Tris buffer
25 mM (réf.6). After incubation at 22°C for 30 min., the reaction
was stopped by adding 0.2 ml trichloroacetic acid 50%. Inorganic
phosphate and protein content were respectively determined by the

method of Fiske and Subbarow (7) and the method of Lowry *et al.*
(8). (Na$^+$+K$^+$)ATPase activity was calculated as the difference
between activity obtained with and without Na$^+$ and K$^+$ in the
medium. Activity was expressed in $\mu$ MPi/mg membrane proteins x h.

### RESULTS AND DISCUSSION

Tissue   as well as intracellular ionic and water contents have
been measured in non-incubated gills from crabs adapted to FW
and SW. The data of Table 1 shows important differences between
the three anterior gill  pairs (so-called "anterior gills") and
the three following ones (so-called "posterior gills").
The difference in Na$^+$ and Cl$^-$ content  are more specially marked
in FW adapted crabs. These results might indicate that the capa-
bility of the anterior gills to control their Na$^+$ content is less
than that of the posterior gills. On the contrary, both types
of gills would be able to control their Cl$^-$ content. It can nevertheless be concluded that both types of gills are not physiologically equivalent, at least when considering their ionic regulation
at the cellular level.   Such a difference, already suggested by
Koch in an early work of 1954, prompted us to undertake a study of
the ionic intracellular distribution and ionic movements in isolated perfused gills. The preparation we have been able to set up
for that purpose seems to remain in good shape at least during
150 minutes of perfusion; there is indeed no significant change
in the H$_2$O or K$^+$ content during that time (Table 2). Moreover, the
potential difference (PD) arising between the perfusate and the
bathing medium remains quite constant for more than five hours provided that oxygen is continuously supplied.

The PD arising when there is no concentration gradient across the
epithelium shows polarities of opposite signs in anterior and
posterior gills (Table 3). The PD is reversibly abolished by N$_2$
suggesting that it is related to the oxydative metabolism. This
is furthermore supported by the irreversible fall occuring when
dinitrophenol is added to the perfusion or to the incubation media.

The part played by the Na$^+$ and Cl$^-$ active transport mechanisms in
the establishment of the PD has been tested by using specific
pharmacodynamic agents like *ouabain* and *acetazolamide* (diamox).
Diamox at the concentration of 1.5 mg/ml abolishes the PD in all
cases whatever the gill type and the application side considered.
On the contrary, *ouabain* $10^{-4}$M only affects the PD of posterior
gills when applied on the outside. According to these results, the
anterior and the posterior gills of FW crabs would pump Cl$^-$ ions
and that activity would be responsable for the maintenance of a
part of the PD. On the other hand, the posterior gills only would
pump Na$^+$ ions at least partly by means of an ouabain-sensitive mechanism  working at the external side of the epithelium. This last
conclusion is supported by flux   experiments using radioactive
tracers. Results quoted in Table 4 indeed show a net Na$^+$ influx
against the concentration gradient at the level of the posterior
gills while a Na$^+$ leak occurs in the anterior ones. The fluxes fall
to negligible  values when posterior gills are kept in artificial
SW and perfused by SW saline.

A. Pequeux and R. Gilles

TABLE 1 : Extracellular space (ECS) and ionic
distribution at the level of gills of
crabs adapted to FW and SW.

| (a) µEq/gWW (b) mEq/l (c) g/gWW | ECS | IONS Na$^+$ | K$^+$ | Cl$^-$ | WATER |
|---|---|---|---|---|---|
| **GILLS** Anterior | | | | | |
| TISSULAR | | 137,6±4,5 (a) N=18 | 49,2±1,6 (a) N=18 | 119,1±3,4 (a) N=18 | 0,8004±0,0032 (c) N=18 |
| ECS ◄ Ext. Int. | 18,6±1,3 N=14 31,8±1,1 N=12 | | | | |
| CELLULAR | | 178,2 (b) | 160,6 (b) | 119,4 (b) | |
| Posterior | | | | | |
| TISSULAR | | 106,1±3,1 (a) N=18 | 74,7±1,4 (a) N=18 | 82,1±3,4 (a) N=18 | 0,7934±0,0040 (c) N=18 |
| ECS ◄ Ext. Int. | 11,6±0,7 N=18 18,7±0,4 N=12 | | | | |
| CELLULAR | | 113,2 (b) | 148,5 (b) | 66,1 (b) | |
| **BLOOD** **F.W.** | | 265,5±6,5 (b) N=8 0,63 (b) | 5,9±0,2 (b) N=8 0,07 (b) | 261,6±5,6 (b) N=8 1,07 (b) | |

| | ECS | Na$^+$ | K$^+$ | Cl$^-$ | WATER |
|---|---|---|---|---|---|
| **GILLS** Anterior | | | | | |
| TISSULAR | | 301,9±4,1 (a) N=18 | 61,0±2,4 (a) N=18 | 229,3±6,2 (a) N=18 | 0,7335±0,0068 (c) N=18 |
| ECS ◄ Ext. Int. | 11,1±1,0 N=14 27,7±1,3 N=11 | | | | |
| CELLULAR | | 326,7 (b) | 166,2 (b) | 128,0 (b) | |
| Posterior | | | | | |
| TISSULAR | | 209,6±4,1 (a) N=18 | 83,9±1,3 (a) N=18 | 204,9±5,1 (a) N=18 | 0,7744±0,0052 (c) N=18 |
| ECS ◄ Ext. Int. | 8,4±0,5 N=18 21,9±1,2 N=6 | | | | |
| CELLULAR | | 156,2 (b) | 181,9 (b) | 148,9 (b) | |
| **BLOOD** **S.W.** | | 492,7±6,2 (b) N=5 474 (b) | 8,5±0,4 (b) N=5 11 (b) | 468,7±9,9 (b) N=5 518 (b) | |

Exchanges are much higher in anterior gills but do not result in a net $Na^+$ flux.

TABLE 2 : Tissue $K^+$ and water content of anterior (Ant) and posterior (Post) gills perfused with and incubated in isotonic saline.

|  | $K^+$ μEq/g WW | $H_2O$ g/g WW |
|---|---|---|
| **Ant** | | |
| 30 min | 51.2 | 0.7818 |
| 150 min | 55.8 | 0.7793 |
| **Post** | | |
| 30 min | 96.4 | 0.7997 |
| 150 min | 95.1 | 0.7947 |

TABLE 3 : PD across perfused gill epithelium (in mV). Inside medium : isotonic saline (240 $mEqNa^+$/l). Outside medium: artificial FW + NaCl up to concentrations quoted in the first column. Sign refers to the inside medium.

| $Na^+$ out mEq/l | Ant. Gills | Post. Gills |
|---|---|---|
| 1 | − 49.4 ± 3.6 (n=5) | − 11.1 ± 5.2 (n=4) |
| 10 | − 32.4 ± 5.9 (n=5) | − 25.1 ± 8.7 (n=4) |
| 25 | − 11.1 ± 6.6 (n=7) | − 23.9 ± 4.4 (n=4) |
| 100 | − 1.7 ± 4.8 (n=7) | − 27.0 ± 2.3 (n=4) |
| 240 | + 21.9 ± 2.5 (n=9) | − 11.5 ± 1.8 (n=12) |
| 500 | + 19.6 ± 2.1 (n=7) | − 7.5 ± 4.3 (n=4) |

The fact that our results show a net movement of $Na^+$ out of the gills when they are placed in a FW medium does not necessarily mean that the crab _in vivo_ is unable to achieve its salt blood balance. As a matter of fact, ions can be provided to the animal by means other than active transport through the gills. On the other hand, the total net movement of $Na^+$ in the gills of the animals will be dependent on the total area of the anterior and posterior gills. It may thus well be that _in vivo_ the salt blood balance can be achieved only by ionic transport at the gill level.

TABLE 4 : Radiosodium fluxes across isolated perfused gills. Fluxes results are expressed as $\mu$ EqNa$^+$/g WW x h.

| (Na$^+$) (mEq/l) | | | Influx | Efflux |
|---|---|---|---|---|
| Environment | Perfusate | | | |
| 0.96 | 240 | Ant.G. | 5.46 | 112.92 |
| | | Post.G. | 21.75 | n.s. (1) |
| 10 | 240 | Ant.G. | 73.89 | 101.83 |
| | | Post.G. | 141.89 | n.s. |
| 500 | 500 | Ant.G. | 625.59 | 637.99 |
| | | Post.G. | n.s. | n.s. |

(1) not significant.

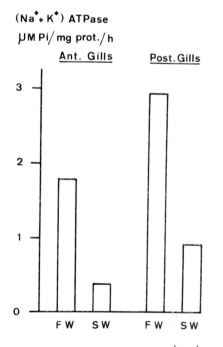

Fig.1. Specific (Na$^+$+K$^+$)ATPase activities in gills from FW and SW crabs.

The idea of an active transport of Na$^+$ located in the posterior gills and working essentially in diluted media is in agreement with data on the activity of the mitochondrial (Na$^+$+K$^+$)ATPase (ATP phosphohydrolase, E.N.3.6.1.3) extracted from both anterior and posterior gills. According to Fig.1., the specific enzyme activity is indeed much higher in the posterior gills of FW crabs than in the anterior ones. Moreover, adaptation to SW is accompanied by an important decrease in activity, supporting thus the idea that the Na$^+$ pumping is reduced in SW. This is consistent with the fact that the blood Na$^+$ concentration remains close to that of the surrounding medium when the crabs are acclimated to SW.

Part of this work has been aided by a grant 2.4511.76 from the F.R.F.C. to one of us (R.G.)

REFERENCES

(1)  Schoffeniels, E. & Gilles, R., 1970.  Osmoregulation in aquatic arthropods. In M.Florkin and B.T.Scheer (Eds). Chemical Zoology, V, pp.255-286. Academic Press, New York.

(2)  Gilles, R., 1975.  Mechanisms of ion and osmoregulation. In Marine Ecology (Kinne, O., Ed), II, Part I, Physiological Mechanisms, pp. 259-347. Wiley, New York.

(3)  Koch, H.J., Evans, J. & Schicks, E., 1954. The active absorption of ions by the isolated gills of the crab E.sinensis (M.Edw). Mededel.Vl.Acad.Wet.Kl.Wet., XVI, 5, 3-16.

(4)  Belman, B.W., 1976.  New observations on blood pressure in marine crustacea. J.Exp.Zool., 196, 71-78.

(5)  Péqueux, A., 1976.  Polarization variations induced by high hydrostatic pressures in the isolated frog skin as related to the effects on passive ionic permeability and active Na$^+$ transport. J.Exp.Biol., 64, 587-602.

(6)  Péqueux, A. & Gilles, R., 1977.  Osmoregulation of the chinese crab E.sinensis as related to the activity of the (Na$^+$+K$^+$)ATPase. Arch.Int.Physiol.Biochim., 85, 426-428.

(7)  Fiske, C.H. & Subbarow, Y., 1925. The colorimetric determination of phosphorus. J.Biol.Chem., 66, 375-400.

(8)  Lowry, O.H., Rosebrough, N.J., Farr, A.L. & Randall, R.J., 1951. Protein measurement with the folin phenol reagent. J.Biol.Chem., 193, 265-275.

# GUANINE AND PERMEABILITY IN SWIMBLADDERS OF SLOPE-DWELLING FISH

## Lindsay G. Ross* and John D.M. Gordon**

*Biology Department, Stirling University, Stirling, FK9 4LA, Scotland
**Scottish Marine Biological Association, Dunstaffnage Marine Research Laboratory, P.O. Box 3, Oban, Argyll, Scotland

## ABSTRACT

Fish possessing swimbladders and living at depth will experience high $pO_2$ differences across the swimbladder wall, with potential loss of gas and therefore loss of buoyancy. A major factor in reduction of gas loss is the presence of large quantities of guanine crystals in the tissues of the swimbladder. These crystals effectively reduce the surface area available for diffusion and also increase the path length.

Samples of swimbladder wall have been assayed for guanine content in a number of species caught by bottom-trawl from "R.R.S. Challenger". The study area was the Hebridean Terrace ($56^{o}$N-$57^{o}$N, $9^{o}$-$11^{o}$ W) which ranges in depth from 500 to 2000 m. An attempt has been made to assess the relationship between guanine content and observed depth distribution of the species studied.

## INTRODUCTION

Many species of fish use the swimbladder as a hydrostatic organ, thereby attaining neutral buoyancy. Demersal and bathybenthic species possessing swimbladders have been observed to be neutrally buoyant at depth (see Marshall, 1965) and it is known that their swimbladder gas is mainly oxygen (Kanwisher and Ebeling, 1957). The percentage of oxygen increases with depth in most fish (Scholander and Van Dam, 1953) and so the partial pressure of oxygen in slope-dwelling demersal species will be extremely high. Since diffusion of gas through a tissue increases with increasing partial pressure difference across the tissue (Krogh, 1919) maintenance of a gas-filled swimbladder will be metabolically expensive unless the swimbladder has a low oxygen permeability.

---

* Present address : Unit of Aquatic Pathobiology, University of Stirling, FK9 4LA, Scotland.

It has been known for some time that the swimbladder walls of
certain species have a low oxygen permeability (Bohr, 1894;
Scholander, 1954) and recently direct measurements have confirmed
this view (Kutchai and Steen, 1971; Denton et al, 1972; Lapennas
and Schmidt-Nielsen, 1977).   Scholander (1954) proposed that the
inclusion of solid materials in a tissue would reduce the rate of
passage of gases and Denton et al (1972) suggested that guanine
crystals present in the swimbladder wall provided a physical basis
for the observed low gas permeabilities.   These crystals are
very densely arranged in layers, thereby reducing the surface area
available for diffusion and lengthening considerably the diffusion
path

Marshall (1965, 1972) has shown that the number of retia mirabilia
and the length of their capillaries increases with depth of
occurrence in deep-sea fishes.   It thus seemed reasonable that
guanine content of the swimbladder could increase in a similar
manner in order to minimise gas loss and energy expenditure.   The
opportunity was taken to use time on "R.R.S. Challenger" to
investigate guanine levels in the swimbladder walls of selected
deep-sea fish.


## MATERIALS AND METHODS

The depth distribution of the species used in this work were
compiled from a series of 25 standard bottom trawl stations and
3 single-warp trawl stations.   These were carried out during a
major study of the biology and depth distribution of slope-
dwelling fish being conducted by the Scottish Marine Biological
Association.   This provided trawl caught material from a
consistent sampling area of the Hebridean Terrace ($56^\circ$-$57^\circ$N, $9^\circ$-
$11^\circ$W) and a depth range of 460 to 2000 m.

The location of the crystal layer in the swimbladder wall is of
interest.   Denton et al (1972) described crystals in the tunica
externa of *Conger conger* (L), and Lapennas and Schmidt-Nielsen
(1977) decided that the layer was in the sub-mucosa.   The
crystals can be located by interference microscopy (Denton and
Land, 1965) in fresh material.   In this study the swimbladder
wall of selected animals was separated into tunica interna,
tunica externa and serosa and viewed by plane-polarised light
microscopy aboard ship.

Samples for assay of purine content were taken by punch biopsy
using a cork borer and were transferred to tubes for frozen
storage.   In one series of experiments the tissues were sampled
by weight, and in this case the tubes were pre-weighed, stored
frozen after sampling and were reweighed in the laboratory ashore.

Purine content was determined by an enzyme assay technique
(Schuster, 1955; Nicol and Van Baalen, 1968).   The samples were
digested in 3 $cm^3$ of 0.1 N NaOH for about 72 h, centrifuged and
a 0.25 $cm^3$ aliquot withdrawn.   This was added to Tris buffer
pH 8.1 to a final volume of 3$cm^3$.   Small amounts of xanthine

oxidase (10 μl) and guanase (15 μl) were added, and the change
in optical density after each addition was monitored at 290 nm.
These changes were compared with those from a 50 μg xanthine/
50 μg guanine/cm$^3$ standard solution.

### RESULTS

The results of crystal location by polarised light microscopy of
separated swimbladder layers from seven anacanthines, and one
other species of interest, are shown in Table 1.    The crystals
most frequently occur as needles between 40 and 100 μm in length
and from 0.5 to 3.0 μm wide.    Plate-like stacks were found in
some fish, notably *Coryphaenoides rupestris*, and these were
hexagonal crystals of approximate dimensions 35 x 125 μm.

TABLE 1 The location of purine crystals in the
component layers of fish swimbladders.   Birefringence
denoted by +, no birefringence denoted by 0.

| Species | SEROSA | TUNICA EXTERNA | TUNICA INTERNA |
|---|---|---|---|
| *Pollachius virens* | 0 | 0 | +++ |
| *Molva dypterygia* | 0 | 0 | +++ |
| *Coryphaenoides rupestris* | 0 | + | ++ |
| *Nezumia aequalis* | 0 | 0 | ++ |
| *Lepidion eques* | 0 | + | ++ |
| *Halargyreus johnsonii* | 0 | 0 | ++ |
| *Mora moro* | 0 | 0 | + |
| *Synaphobranchus kaupi* | 0 | +++ | + |

The pooled depth data from the trawls is shown in Table 2 together
with the results of total purine assays.   Assay results are
expressed as μg/cm$^2$ or μg/mg as appropriate.

TABLE 2 The purine content of the swimbladder wall
and the depths of occurrence of various fish

| Species | DEPTH RANGE | MEAN DEPTH | PURINE $\mu g/cm^2$ | PURINE $\mu g/mg$ |
|---|---|---|---|---|
| Salmo trutta | 0-15 | 8 | 24 (2) | - |
| Scardinius erythropthalmus | 0-5 | 2 | 14 (2) | - |
| Cerastoscopelus maderensis | 0-650 | 300 | 73 (6) | - |
| *Coryphaenoides rupestris | 540-1750 | 1125 | 393 (4) | 5.0 (13) |
| *Nezumia aequalis | 670-1070 | 865 | 217 (3) | 10.6 (10) |
| *Trachyrhynchus murrayi | 960-1500 | 1230 | - | 13.0 (10) |
| *Coelorhynchus caelorhynchus | <460-760 | 630 | - | 6.2 (5) |
| *Coelorhynchus occa | 960-2000 | 1480 | - | 7.0 (5) |
| *Malacocephalus laevis | <460-540 | 500 | - | 6.2 (2) |
| *Chalinura mediterranea | 1240-2000+ | 1620 | - | 9.9 (4) |
| Pollachius virens | 0-200 | 100 | 47 (5) | - |
| *Molva dypterygia | 480-1050 | 770 | 275 (3) | - |
| *Brosme brosme | <460-1020 | 750 | 236 (2) | 1.1 (2) |
| *Micromesistius poutassou | 200-550 | 350 | 195 (3) | - |
| Merluccius merluccius | 400-800 | 500 | 292 (1) | - |
| *Lepidion eques | <460-1280 | 870 | 466 (7) | 3.9 (11) |

contd/...

| Species | DEPTH RANGE | MEAN DEPTH | PURINE $\mu g/cm^2$ | PURINE $\mu g/mg$ |
|---|---|---|---|---|
| *Halargyreus johnsonii | 540-1270 | 908 | 253 (2) | 10.5 (8) |
| *Mora moro | 650-1050 | 850 | 314 (2) | - |
| *Synaphobranchus kaupi | 500-3000+ | 1750 | 1097 (2) | 19.5 (5) |

\* = Fish caught by "Challenger".

Figures in parentheses denote number of determinations.

Figure 1 shows the depth distribution of some of the most common slope species. *Molva dypterygia*, *Brosme brosme* and *Mora moro* have not been included as they were less common and their distribution appeared to vary seasonally. *Micromesistius poutassou* is a pelagic fish which is taken only occasionally in the bottom trawl and the depth information on this species in Table 2 has been supplemented by data from echo-traces. *Synaphobranchus kaupi* occurred in small numbers at all depths and has been taken in Agassiz trawls down to 3000m close to the study area. The remaining species in Table 2 are not slope-dwelling but have been included because of their shallower habit.

The purine content of the swimbladder of these fish is plotted against mean depth of occurrence in Fig. 2 and Fig. 3. In both plots a positive correlation of purine content with depth is clearly discernable. The correlation coefficient of mean depth against total purine, by weight, is 0.63 (n=11) and is significant at the 2% level. The correlation coefficient of mean depth against total purine, by biopsy, is 0.899 (n=14) and is significant at the 0.1% level. It can be seen that there is a strong trend for the swimbladder to contain more deposited purines as the mean depth of the species increases. The regressed data are shown as broken lines.

## DISCUSSION

From the information gained during the seasonal trawling study it has been possible to determine the depth ranges of a number of demersal species. These distributions probably apply fairly strictly to the study area as there is some evidence that vertical range is latitude dependent. The study of purine content of the swimbladders of these fish is thus particularly relevant as the mean depths of occurrence have been determined simultaneously in most cases.

In the seven anacanthines studied the purine crystals were located in the tunica interna and this confirmed the observations of Lapennas and Schmidt-Nielsen (1977). In the apodan, *Synaphobranchus kaupi*, dense crystals were found in the tunica externa

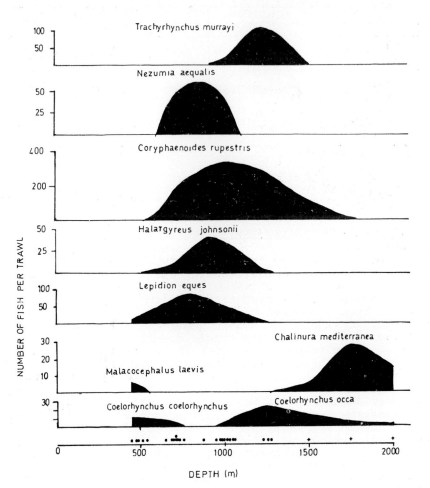

Fig. 1. The depth distribution of some of the most common slope-dwelling species. The mean depths of the trawls are also shown.

● = standard otter trawl
+ = single warp trawl

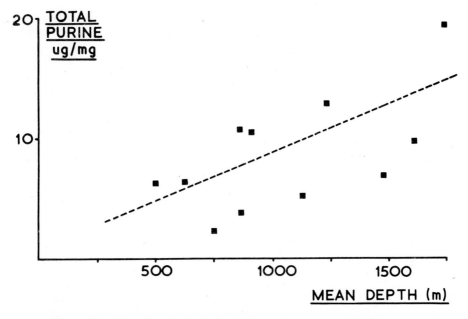

Fig. 2.   Graph of total purine content of the
swimbladder wall, determined by weight, against
mean depth of occurrence.

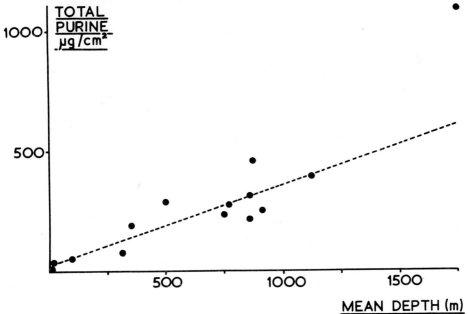

Fig. 3.   Graph of total purine content of the
swimbladder wall, determined by biopsy, against
mean depth of occurrence.

and it may be that the layers of the bladder separate differently in these fish leaving the submucosa attached to the outer layer.

It can be seen that there is a strong trend for the bladder to contain more purines as the depth of the living space increases and this is good supporting evidence for the theoretical predictions concerning the inclusion of impermeable crystals in tissues. The relationship is not a perfect functional one, however, and accordingly the regressed data have been indicated as dotted lines. Several factors contribute to randomise the points. The fish are always damaged in trawls, and the damage may be due to physical abrasion or foaming of the tissue on decompression. There will probably be little improvement of the data until these influences can be removed or quantified.

Recent trials with the single-warp trawl have shown that *Synaphobranchus kaupi* is present in hauls to at least 4000m. The mean depth of this species can consequently be revised to about 2000m which makes an improvement to both graphs. This trawl is convenient to use and does not catch elasmobranchs, with a consequent improvement in the condition of trawled teleosts. The advent of single-warp trawling techniques has significantly increased the depth range which could be covered in a continuation of this study and it is hoped to extend the series at some point in the future.

## ACKNOWLEDGEMENTS

One of us, L.G. Ross, wishes to acknowledge N.E.R.C. research studentship.

## LITERATURE CITED

Bohr, C., (1894). The influence of vagus section on gas disengagement in the air-bladder of fishes. Journal of Physiology, London, 15, 494-500.

Denton, E.J. & Land, M.F., (1967). Optical properties of the lamellae causing interference colours in animal reflectors. Journal of Physiology., London, 191, 23-24p.

Denton, E.J., Liddicoat, J.D. & Taylor, D.W. (1972). The permeability to gases of the swimbladder of the conger eel (*Conger conger*). Journal of the Marine Biological Association of the United Kingdom, 52, 727-746.

Kanwisher, J. & Ebeling, A., (1957). Composition of swimbladder gas in deep-sea fish. Deep-sea Research, 4, 211-217.

Krogh, A. (1919). The rate of diffusion of gases through animal tissues with some remarks on the coefficient of invasion. Journal of Physiology., London, 52, 391-408.

Kutchai, H. & Steen, J.B. (1971).    The permeability of the swimbladder.   Comparative Biochemistry and Physiology, 39A, 39A, 119-123.

Lapennas, G.N. & Schmidt-Nielsen, K. (1977).    Swimbladder permeability to oxygen.   Journal of Experimental Biology., 67, 175-196.

Marshall, N.B. (1965).    Systematic and biological studies of the Macrourid fishes (Anacanthini - Teleostii).   Deep-Sea Research, 12, 299-322.

Marshall, N.B. (1972).    Swimbladder organisation and depth ranges of deep-sea teleosts.   Symposia of the Society for Experimental Biology, 26, 261-272.

Nicol, J.A.C. & Van Baalen, C. (1968).    Studies on the reflecting layers of fishes.   Contributions on Marine Science, University of Texas, 13, 65-88.

Scholander, P.F. (1954).    Secretion of gases against high pressure in the swimbladder of deep-sea fishes.   II. The rete mirabile.   Biological Bulletins of The Marine Biological Laboratory, Woods Hole, 107, 260-277.

Scholander, P.F. & Van Dam.L., (1953).    Composition of the swimbladder gas in deep-sea fishes.   Biological Bulletins of the Marine Biological Laboratory, Woods Hole, 104, 75-86.

Schuster, L. (1955).    Guanase.   In Methods in Enzymology. 2, 480-482 (Ed. S.P. Colowick and N.O. Kaplan) New York & London, Academic Press.

# STRUCTURE AND FUNCTION OF CHLORIDE CELLS IN THE GILLS OF *ANGUILLA ANGUILLA*

**J.R. Sargent, B.J.S. Pirie, A.J. Thomson and S.G. George**

*N.E.R.C. Institute of Marine Biochemistry, Aberdeen AB1 3RA, Scotland.*

ABSTRACT

Gills of yellow eels in fresh water contain relatively few chloride cells distributed on both primary and secondary filaments. Seawater gills contain many chloride cells located solely on primary filaments. The incidence of chloride cell - chloride cell contacts is, therefore, much higher in seawater than in freshwater gills. The internal structures of chloride cells from freshwater and seawater gills are generally very similar, both cells being especially characterised by an extensive smooth tubular system (STS), that is derived from basal and lateral infoldings of plasma membranes, and numerous mitochondria. No internal differences were found between chloride cells that could account for the inwards and outwards pumping of NaCl across freshwater and seawater gills respectively. Intercellular spaces were particularly prominent between adjacent chloride cells, i.e. in seawater gills, and specialisation appears to occur at the short junctional region near the apical membranes of the cells, where a swollen area is commonly found between two short, ostensibly tight junctions. We consider that these areas are junctions through which NaCl passes outwards across the gills into seawater. To account for current ultrastructural, biochemical and physiological data we propose the following mechanism for NaCl pumping in seawater gills. The high density of NaCl pumps on the STS of adjacent chloride cells generates a particularly high concentration of NaCl in the intercellular spaces. NaCl moves outwards from these spaces into seawater through ion permeable junctions by diffusion aided by hydrostatic pressure stemming from arterial blood flow.

## INTRODUCTION

Chloride cells have long been implicated in pumping salt inwards across teleost gills in freshwater and outwards across gills in seawater. These cells are characterised by numerous mitochondria and an extensive STS that is derived from basal and lateral infoldings of the plasma membrane and contains a high density of $(Na^++K^+)$-dependent ATPase (1-11). The enzyme in chloride cells from eel gills, in both freshwater and seawater is indistinguishable from the enzyme in numerous mammalian and non-mammalian tissues (12,13). That is, at a cell membrane level, the enzyme pumps NaCl in the same direction in both freshwater and seawater chloride cells.

The inwards pumping of NaCl through chloride cells in freshwater gills is readily understood by analogy with the situation in amphibian skin (14,15).

The involvement of chloride cells in the outwards pumping of NaCl across
seawater gills has not so far been satisfactorily explained.    Recent
microscopical evidence has emphasised the importance of specialised junctions
between adjacent chloride cells, in both seawater eel gills (C. Sardet and
J. Maetz, personal communications) and in the avian salt gland (16).    The
present electron microscopic data confirm and extend our knowledge of the
structure of chloride cells in teleost gills.    The present paper is
concerned mainly with re-interpreting structural data to propose a new model
of salt pumping outwards across the seawater gill that is consistent with
current physiological and biochemical data.

### MATERIALS AND METHODS

The common eel migrates naturally from freshwater to seawater when fully
developed at a late stage in its life history.    Thus, yellow eels mature
sexually to silver eels in freshwater and it is the silver eel that migrates
to the sea to reproduce.    The eels studied here were yellow eels caught in
freshwater rivers and lochs in the summer, and also silver eels caught during
their late autumnal run to the sea.    The latter were adapted to full strength
seawater in the aquarium for at least 4 weeks with no mortalities whatsoever.
Mortalities of up to 50% occurred when yellow eels were transferred from
freshwater to seawater.    Therefore, unless otherwise stated the freshwater
and seawater eels studied here were the yellow and silver forms respectively.
Sources and characteristics of these fish have already been described (17).
Conventional light and electron microscopic methods used have already been
published in detail (18,19,20).

### OBSERVATIONS

A.    Light Microscopy
Findings are summarised in Fig. 1 where chloride cells stain black.

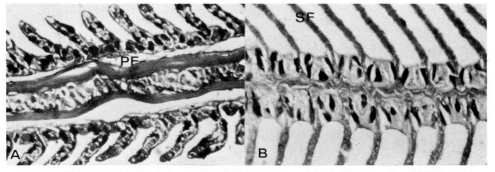

Fig. 1.    Gills stained with osmium tetroxide - zinc iodide (18). Chloride
cells are black.    A yellow eels, freshwater;  B silver eels, seawater.
Magnification   x 200

The yellow eel in freshwater has chloride cells on both primary and
secondary gill filaments (Fig.1A).    The silver eel in seawater has additional
chloride cells and these are located solely on the primary gill filaments
(Fig.1B).    It follows that the incidence of chloride cell-chloride cell
contacts is much greater in seawater than in freshwater gills.

B.  Electron Microscopy.

Figure 2 shows a typical chloride cell from the secondary gill filaments of a yellow eel in freshwater.    The cell is in contact with both blood and freshwater (spans the epithelium) and is presumably osmoregulating.    Cells from the primary filaments of yellow eels in freshwater were indistinguishable from the cell in Fig.2.    These freshwater chloride cells are rounded

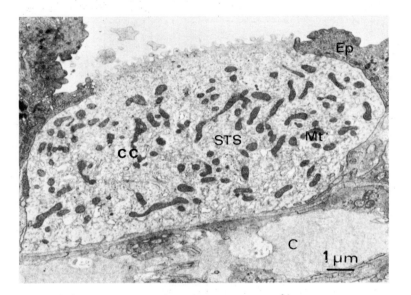

Fig. 2.  A chloride cell from the gills of a yellow eel in freshwater.
Tissue was fixed in formaldehide - glutaraldehyde, post-fixed in osmium tetroxide and stained with lead citrate - uranyl acetate (19,20).

and have a convex apical membrane.    Their numerous mitochondria and extensive STS are distributed rather randomly throughout the cytoplasm.    The apical membrane has numerous short microvilli and immediately underlying it is a mesh of microfilaments;  microtubules can also be seen in this area (Fig.3).    Cell to cell adhesion areas (desmosomes) occur frequently between chloride cells and adjacent respiratory epithelial cells.

Figure Legends.
The following abbreviations are used:  Am apical membrane;  C capillary; CC chloride cell;  D desmosome;  Ep epithelial cell;  Mf microfilament;  Mt mitochondria;  N nucleus;  Pm plasma membrane;  PF primary filament;  SF secondary filament;  STS smooth tubular system;  S swelling;  V vesicle.

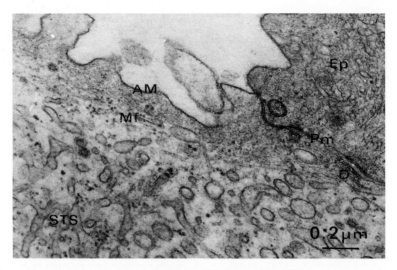

Fig. 3.  Apical region of a chloride cell from the gills of a yellow eel in freshwater.

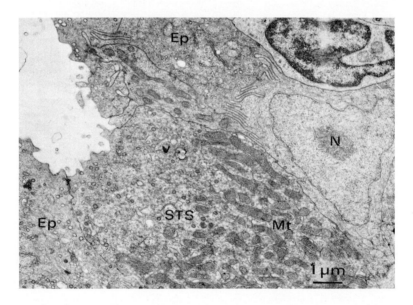

Fig. 4.  A Chloride cell from the gills of a silver eel in seawater.
Figure 4 shows a chloride cell spanning the primary gill filament of a silver eel in seawater.  The numerous mitochondria and their associated STS tend to be concentrated towards the serosal (basal) side of the cell.  The apical region underlying the concave apical membrane contains numerous vesicles.  Closer examination of this area shows that the vesicles have "fuzzy" contents suggestive of macromolecular contents (Fig.5).  The vesicles have membranes

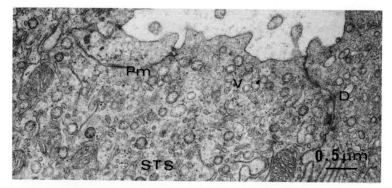

Fig. 5.  Apical region of a chloride cell from a silver eel in seawater.

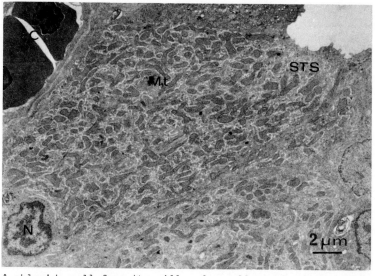

Fig. 6.  A chloride cell from the gills of a yellow eel adapted to seawater.

that are both thicker and stain more darkly than the membranes of the STS.
It has been suggested (21, 5) that apical vesicles are involved in
transporting NaCl outwards into seawater through chloride cells.   However,
Fig. 6 shows that apical vesicles are not at all prominent in chloride cells
from the primary filaments of a yellow eel successfully adapted to seawater.
We conclude that chloride cells can successfully osmoregulate in seawater
without containing apical vesicles.

Repeated examination of the apical regions of chloride cells from silver eels
in seawater failed to show fusion of apical vesicles with the apical membrane
and in no case were profiles suggestive of exocytosis observed (Figs.5,7B).
In contrast profiles strongly suggestive of exocytosis were commonly observed
in respiratory epithelial cells in both freshwater (Fig.2) and seawater (Fig.
7A).   The role of these vesicles and their contents is not known at present
for either chloride cells or respiratory epithelial cells.

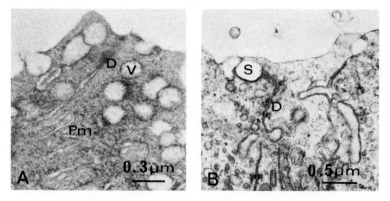

Fig. 7.  Apical regions of A, a respiratory epithelial cell and B, a chloride cell, both from a silver eel in seawater.

Areas of the apical membranes of chloride cells from silver eels in seawater that initially appeared as invaginations were invariably found on closer examination to be associated with areas of contact between adjacent chloride cells (Fig. 7B).   Such areas frequently consisted of a swollen area sited between two short, ostensibly tight cell junctions (Fig. 7B).   Boundaries between adjacent chloride cells were particularly clear below these junctions; spaces between chloride cells could frequently be traced continuously from the blood capillary close up to the junctional complex near the apical membranes of the cells.

Figure 8 shows clearly that the STS of chloride cells from silver eels in seawater is largely derived from infoldings of the plasma membranes both basally, facing the blood capillary, and laterally, facing adjacent chloride cells.   Similar infoldings were also seen in chloride cells from freshwater eels.

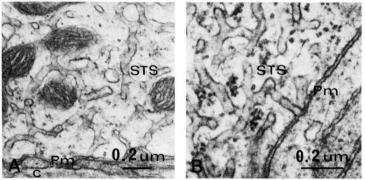

Fig. 8.  Plasma membrane infoldings in a chloride cell from a silver eel in seawater.  A, the basal region;  B, the lateral region.

DISCUSSION

The present work confirms what is well established for the structure of the gills of freshwater and seawater teleosts (1-11).   Adaptation from fresh-water to seawater is accompanied by a proliferation of chloride cells

resulting in an enhanced level of the sodium pump enzyme, $(Na^+ + K^+)$-
dependent ATPase, in gills.    The elevated level of the enzyme accounts for
the fact that more salt is pumped across the gills in seawater than in
freshwater (5).    It does not account for the fact that salt is pumped
outwards in seawater.    The structural evidence here is inconsistent with
the proposition that NaCl is transported outwards across chloride cells in
vesicles that bud off from the STS and discharge their contents by
exocytosis at the apical membranes (21, 5).    Thus, apical vesicles are not
at all obvious in chloride cells from the gills of yellow eels successfully
adapted to seawater (Fig. 6).    It has been shown recently that apical
vesicles in chloride cells from the salt glands of the marine turtle and
*Squalus acanthias* are deficient in $(Na^+ + K^+)$-dependent ATPase (10,11).
This finding is inconsistent with apical vesicles being derived generally
from the STS; it is also inconsistent with the vesicles being able to
create or to maintain high salt concentrations in their interiors.

The salient features of sodium pumping in chloride cells appear to us as
follows.    The $(Na^+ + K^+)$-dependent ATPases in freshwater and seawater
chloride cells are indistinguishable (12) and therefore they pump NaCl in
the same direction across the membranes of the STS in freshwater and
seawater.    The STS is positioned in the same location in freshwater and
seawater chloride cells.    It follows that NaCl is pumped in the same
direction, basally and laterally, in freshwater and seawater chloride cells.
We emphasise here a simple but important conclusion from the present
observations, namely that because there are more chloride cells in seawater
gills and because the cells are located there solely on primary filaments,
then it is certain that there are many more chloride cell - chloride cell
contacts in seawater than in freshwater gills.    Intercellular spaces
between adjacent chloride cells are immediately adjacent to a particularly
high concentration of sodium pumps and will inevitably contain a particularly
high concentration of NaCl.    These intercellular spaces, moreover, are
specialised in two respects.    First, they are continuous from the blood
capillary close up to the apical membranes.    The ease with which the
intercellular spaces between chloride cells can be penetrated by compounds
such as horse radish peroxidase and lanthanum salts is well established
(4,6,7).    Second, the junctional complex between adjacent chloride cells
appears specialised (Fig.7B) in that it consists of a swollen area sited
between two short, ostensibly tight junctions.    Such swollen areas are
characteristically found between "tight junctions" (zonulae occludens or
"punctuate kisses") that characterise "leaky" epithelia and are considered
to be a major route of ion permeation through such epithelia (22,23,24).
The "leakiness" of seawater gills to salt and water is particularly
pronounced and thoroughly documented (5).    In fact recent electron
microscopic studies using freeze etching have established that the "tight
junctions" between adjacent chloride cells in both seawater eel gills (C.
Sardet and J. Maetz, personal communications) and avian salt gland (16) are
single stranded and, therefore, probably highly permeable to salt.

We propose (Fig.9) simply that the very high density of sodium pumps
immediately facing the spaces between adjacent chloride cells produces a
concentration of NaCl in those spaces greater than in seawater.    A small
but finite diffusion of NaCl then occurs outwards through the ion permeable
junctions between chloride cells.    The bulk of NaCl in the intercellular
space will inevitably diffuse towards the serosal fluid proper and be
recycled back into the spaces through the chloride cells.    Thus a small

net outwards transport of NaCl will occur in the presence of a very large
exchange of NaCl across the gill epithelium, precisely what is found *in
vivo* (5).

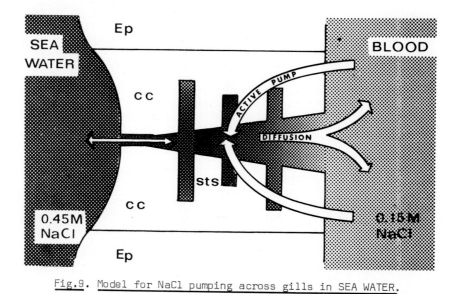

Fig.9. Model for NaCl pumping across gills in SEA WATER.

The existence of high concentrations of NaCl between adjacent chloride cells
in the avian salt gland has also been proposed recently by Ellis et al.,(16).

These authors suggest that the salt gland initially secretes an isotonic
saline into an area of its lumen lined by "secretory" rather than chloride
cells.   The isotonic fluid moves through the lumen into an area lined with
chloride cells where water is considered to move backwards through a standing
gradient of NaCl sited between adjacent chloride cells.   A hypertonic saline
is finally produced.   Backwards movement of water between adjacent chloride
cells in seawater gills is equally possible.   Indeed a role for chloride
cells in "pumping" water backwards across seawater gills has already been
proposed on independent grounds (25).   Production of an isotonic saline,
however, requires either outwardly directed sodium pumps, whose existence has
not been demonstrated in seawater gills, or saline filtration through
intercellular junctions.   A mechanism capable of driving isotonic saline
through such junctions is equally capable of expelling a hypertonic saline.
In this context it is noteworthy that hydrostatic pressure, applied serosally,
is capable of driving saline solution across numerous epithelia (26,27,28)
including the gills of seawater teleosts (29).   Evidence exists that, under
these conditions, salt moves across seawater gills by the intercellular
route (29).   It is possible, therefore, that NaCl moves outwards through
junctions between chloride cells not only down its diffusion gradient but
also under the influence of outwardly directed hydrostatic pressure stemming
from arterial blood flow through the gills.

In conclusion we propose that salt pumping in the gills of seawater teleosts
stems basically from an unusually high concentration of sodium pumps
delivering a very high concentration of NaCl into a specialised space

between adjacent chloride cells that is essentially "open" to seawater. The concentrations of NaCl in the space and the extent to which NaCl and water movements are determined by diffusive or hydrostatic forces remain to be tested.

REFERENCES

(1) Keys, A.B. & Willmer, E.N., 1932. "Chloride secreting cells" in the gills of fishes, with special reference to common eel. J. Physiol., 76, 368-378.

(2) Ogawa, M., 1962. Chloride cells in common Japanese eel, *Anguilla japonica*. Sci. Rept. Saitama Univ., 4, 131-137.

(3) Shirai, N. & Utida, S., 1970. Development and degeneration of the chloride cell during seawater and freshwater adaptation of the Japanese eel, *Anguilla japonica*. Z. Zellforsch. 103, 247-264.

(4) Conte, F.P., 1969. Salt secretion. In Fish Physiology. Ed. W.S.Hoar and D.J. Randall Vol. I, 241-292. Academic Press.

(5) Maetz, J., 1974. Aspects of adaptation to hypo- and hyper-osmotic environments. In Biochemical and Biophysical Perspectives in Marine Biology. Ed. D.C. Malins and J.R. Sargent Vol. 1, 1-167. Academic Press.

(6) Martin, B.J. & Philpott, C.W., 1973. The adaptive response of the salt glands of adult mallard ducks to a salt water regime: an ultrastructural and tracer study. J. Exp. Zool. 186, 111-122.

(7) Martin, B.J. & Philpott, C.W., 1974. The biochemical nature of the cell periphery of the salt gland secretory cells of fresh and salt water adapted mallard ducks. Cell Tiss. Res. 150, 193-211.

(8) Kamiya, M., 1972. Sodium-potassium activated adenosine triphosphatase in isolated chloride cells from eel gills. Comp. Biochem. Physiol. 43B, 611-617.

(9) Sargent, J.R., Thomson, A.J. & Bornancin, M., 1975. Activities and localisation of succinic dehydrogenase and Na$^+$/K$^+$-activated adenosine triphosphatase in the gills of freshwater and seawater eels. Comp. Biochem. Physiol. 51B, 75-79.

(10) Ellis, R.A. & Goertemiller, C.C., 1976. Scanning electron microscopy of intercellular channels and the localisation of ouabain-sensitive p-nitrophenyl phosphatase activity in the salt secreting lacrymal glands of the marine turtle, *Chelonia mydas*. Cytobiologie 13, 1-12.

(11) Goertemiller, C.C. & Ellis, R.A., 1976. Localisation of ouabain-sensitive potassium-dependent nitrophenyl phosphatase in the rectal gland of the spiny dogfish, *Squalus acanthias*. Cell Tiss. Res. 175, 101-112.

(12) Sargent, J.R. & Thomson, A.J., 1974. The nature and properties of the inducible sodium-plus-potassium ion-dependent adenosine triphosphatase in the gills of eels adapted to freshwater and seawater. Biochem. J. 144, 69-75.

(13) Bell, M.V., Tondeur, F. & Sargent, J.R., 1977. The activation of sodium-plus-potassium ion-dependent adenosine triphosphatase from marine teleost gills by univalent cations. Biochem. J. 163, 185-187.

(14) Ussing, H., 1958. Ionic movements in cell membranes in relation to the activity of the nervous system. Proc. 4th. Intern. Congr. Biochem. Vienna 3, 1-17. Pergammon Press.

(15) Farquhar, M.G. & Palade, G.E., 1966. Adenosine triphosphatase localisation in amphibian epidermis. J. Cell Biol. 30, 359-379.

(16)   Ellis, R. A., Goertemiller, C.C. & Stetson, D.L., 1977. Significance
       of extensive "leaky" cell junctions in the avian salt gland.
       Nature, 268, 555-556.

(17)   Thomson, A.J. & Sargent, J.R., 1977. Changes in the levels of chloride
       cells and (Na$^+$+K$^+$)-dependent ATPase in the gills of yellow and
       silver eels adapting to seawater. J. Exp. Zool. 200, 33-40.

(18)   Garcia-Romeu, F. & Masoni, A., 1970. Sur la mise en evidence des
       cellules chlorure de la branchie des poissons.   Arch. D'Anat.
       Microscop. Morphol. Exper. 59, 289-294.

(19)   Weakley, B.S., 1972. A beginners handbook in biological electron
       microscopy, p.209.  Churchill Livingstone.

(20)   George, S.G., Pirie, B.J.S. & Coombs, T.L., 1976. The kinetics of
       accumulation and excretion of ferric hydroxide in *Mytilus edulis*
       *(L.).* and its distribution in the tissues.  J. Exp. Mar. Biol. Ecol.
       23, 71-84.

(21)   Shirai, N., 1972. Electron microscope localisation of sodium ions and
       adenosine triphosphatase in chloride cells of the Japanese eel,
       *Anguilla japonica.* Fac. Sci. Univ. Tokyo Ser. IV. 12, 385-403.

(22)   Moreno, J.H. & Diamond, J.M., 1975. Cation permeation mechanisms and
       cation selectivity in "tight junctions" of gallbladder epithelium.
       In Membranes. Ed. by G. Eisenman Vol. 3, 388-403. Marcel Dekker,
       Inc.

(23)   Fromter, E. & Diamond, J.M., 1972. Route of passive ion permeation in
       epithelia. Nature New Biology. 235, 9-13.

(24)   Sacklin, H. & Boulpaep, E.L., 1975. Models for coupling salt and
       water transport. J. Gen. Physiol. 66, 671-733.

(25)   Motais, R. & Garcia-Romeu, F., 1972. Transport mechanisms in the
       teleost gill and amphibian skin. Ann. Rev. Physiol. 34, 141-176.

(26)   House, C.R., 1974. Water transport in cells and tissues. Monographs
       of The Physiological Society 24,  398-407. E. Arnold Ltd.

(27)   Boulpaep, E.L., 1972. Permeability changes of the proximal tubule of
       *Necturus* during salt loading. Amer. J. Physiol. 222, 517-531.

(28)   Grandchamp, A. & Boulpaep, E.L., 1974. Pressure control of sodium
       reabsorption and intercellular backflux across proximal kidney
       tubule. J. Clin. Invest. 54, 69-82.

(29)   Girard, J.-P., Sardet, C., Maetz, J., Thomson, A.J. & Sargent, J.R.,
       1977. Effet de l'ouabaine sur les branchies de truite adaptée à
       l'eau de mer. Proc. Inter. Union Physiol. Sciences XIII Abstr. No.
       778.

# PHYSIOLOGY AND THE CHEMICAL ENVIRONMENT

# PHYSIOLOGY OF DENITRIFYING BACTERIA FROM TIDAL MUDFLATS IN THE RIVER TAY

**G.M. Dunn, R.A. Herbert and C.M. Brown**

*Department of Biological Sciences, University of Dundee*

## INTRODUCTION

In many marine environments the supply of nitrogen is a potential limiting factor for primary productivity. While much attention has been focussed on the uptake and subsequent fate of nitrogen in phytoplankton, (see for example Morris, 1974) considerably less effort has been devoted to a study of the organisms involved in the recycling of this nutrient. This recycling is carried out predominantly by bacteria which, although comprising only a fraction of the total biomass, are solely responsible for some processes involved in the nitrogen cycle (Fig. 1). One such process is denitrification, and the isolation and physiology of some of the bacteria involved are the subjects of this study.

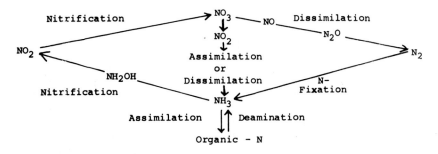

Fig. 1. An outline of the nitrogen cycle

Denitrification may result in a nett loss of nitrogen from an ecosystem. Strictly it concerns the reduction of nitrate ($NO_3^-$) and/or nitrite ($NO_2^-$) to gaseous products, although the term is often used to describe any process involving the dissimilatory reduction of $NO_3^-$ and $NO_2^-$. This process, which enables facultatively anaerobic bacteria to respire anaerobically using $NO_3^-$ as a terminal electron ($e^-$) acceptor (Fig. 2), is energetically superior to fermentative metabolism and is a common property of chemosynthetic bacteria (Payne, 1973). In addition, $NO_3^-$ dissimilation may lead to the reduction of $NO_2^-$ to ammonia ($NH_4^+$) (Fig. 3). This process, catalysed by a nitrite reductase has three postulated roles; it may be a detoxification mechanism removing $NO_2^-$ (Kemp and Atkinson, 1966), it may act as an $e^-$ sink since the reduction of $NO_2^-$ to $NH_4^+$ is a 6e$^-$ change (J.A. Cole pers. comm.), and finally it conserves the nitrogen in the readily assimilated form of $NH_4^+$. The process, therefore, can act as a means of conserving both energy and nitrogen.

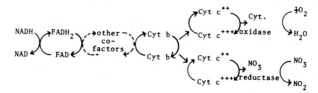

Fig. 2. Oxygen and nitrate as terminal e⁻ acceptors

This paper describes the effects of oxygen tension and salt concentrations on denitrifying bacteria isolated from the Tay estuary.

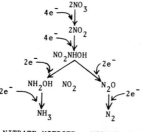

NITRATE NITRITE        NITRATE REDUCTION
REDUCTION          DENITRIFICATION

Fig. 3. Pathways of dissimilatory reduction of nitrate

## Study Area

The Tay is a relatively unpolluted river flowing into the North Sea east of Dundee. The study area was Kingoodie Bay, a tidal region of mud flats lying 16 km from the river mouth. Due to the large freshwater flow, salinities at Kingoodie never exceeded 21.6°/oo at high water (table 1). The water column contained up to ten times more $NO_3^-$ than $NH_4^+$, while the reverse was true in sediments. $NO_2^-$ was never detected in significant concentrations in water or sediment.

TABLE 1   Some nutritional characteristics of the Tay estuary at Kingoodie

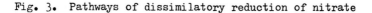

|  | Water | | | Sediment | | |
|---|---|---|---|---|---|---|
|  | *Maximum | Minimum | Mean | *Maximum | Minimum | Mean |
| $NO_3$ | 137 | 22 | 54 | 0.35 | 0.05 | 0.21 |
| $NH_4^+$ | 19.5 | 2.5 | 7.6 | 4.89 | 0.30 | 1.16 |
| Salinity | 21.6 | 2.0 | 11.9 | nd | nd | nd |
| Temperature | 18.0 | 3.5 | 9.0 | nd | nd | nd |

* Values obtained by sampling at monthly intervals between December 1975 and June 1977
° µg at $NL^{-1}$ water, µg at N g dry weight⁻¹ sediment, ⁺ °/oo, nd not determined

## Isolation of Bacteria

Denitrifying bacteria were isolated using chemostat enrichments (Jannasch, 1967) in the medium of Brown et al (1977) modified by the inclusion of glycerol as carbon source and containing $KNO_3$ in addition to $NH_4Cl$. Carbon-limited conditions were employed since an earlier study (Herbert, 1975) had shown that Kingoodie Bay sediments contained low total carbon levels and have low C:N ratios. Enrichments were carried out at three salt regimes; freshwater, 0.2M NaCl and 0.4M NaCl. The inoculum was 25 g sediments suspended in 500 $cm^3$ sterile saline of appropriate concentration which was used to fill a 500 $cm^3$ capacity chemostat. The dilution rate was 0.035 $hr^{-1}$ and the temperature 15°. Enrichments were run aerobically for 7 days (to select against obligate anaerobes), and then anaerobically (flushed with $N_2$) for a further 7 days. These conditions were designed to select for bacteria able to utilise nitrate as terminal $e^-$ acceptor. Bacteria were isolated and identified by conventional methods and checked for their ability to reduce $NO_3^-$ anaerobically.

In the absence of added NaCl Escherichia coli was dominant, at 0.2M NaCl two Klebsiella spp were isolated, while at 0.4M NaCl an unidentified coliform bacterium was dominant. This predominance of coliform bacteria contrasts with an earlier study (Herbert, 1974), but may be accounted for by the recent inflow of sewage at Kingoodie. It was of interest, however, to note that coliform organisms competed successfully with other bacteria for a limiting carbon source even in the presence of 0.4M NaCl and at a temperature of 15°C.

All these isolates reduced $NO_3^-$ to $NO_2^-$ anaerobically but not aerobically. Further work was carried out with Klebsiella K312 obtained from the 0.2M NaCl enrichment.

## Physiology of nitrate reduction

The aims of these experiments were firstly to determine the extent to which $NO_3^-$ availability contributed to anaerobic growth, secondly the products of $NO_3^-$ reduction and finally to correlate information in (1) and (2) with the synthesis of nitrate reductase (NR) and nitrite reductase (NiR). The particular environmental factors studied were the nature and concentration of the nitrogen source(s), the presence or absence of oxygen and the salinity.

The bacterium, a Klebsiella sp (K312) was grown in chemostat culture in the medium of Evans et al (1970) with glycerol as carbon source (modified by lowering the concentrations of all components by 50%), at a dilution rate of 0.1 $hr^{-1}$, at 15° and at a controlled pH of 7.8. All experiments were performed at a constant growth rate (0.1 $hr^{-1}$) under carbon- or nitrogen-limitation with $NH_4^+$, $NO_3^-$, or $NH_4^+ + NO_3^-$ in the medium and in the presence or absence of air and NaCl as detailed in tables 2-5. For the estimation of enzyme activities cultures were collected directly from the chemostat and harvested by centrifugation. The spent medium was retained and analysed for $NO_3^-$, $NO_2^-$ and $NH_4^+$ by methods listed previously (Brown et al 1972). Cell extracts were prepared by passage of cell pastes through a French pressure cell after which cell debris was removed by centrifugation. The supernatant obtained was centrifuged at 100,000 g for 1 hr to yield a supernatant (S) and pellet (P) for enzyme assay. NR was assayed by the method of Lowe & Evans (1964) and NiR by the method of Cole et al (1974). Bacterial populations were estimated as a viable cell count by plating on to Oxoid tryptone soya agar followed by incubation at 23° for 48 hrs.

TABLE 2  Bacterium K312 grown in a chemostat under carbon-limitation in a glycerol/$NH_4^+$ medium.  No nitrate present. D 0.1 hr$^{-1}$, 15°.

| Culture | Cell Count | $NO_3^-$ reductase* | | $NO_2^-$ reductase* | |
|---|---|---|---|---|---|
| | | S | P | S | P |
| Aerobic, no NaCl | $8.9 \times 10^9$ | 13.5 | 28.6 | nd | nd |
| Anaerobic, no NaCl | $5.4 \times 10^8$ | 11.7 | 44.7 | nd | nd |
| Aerobic, 0.2M NaCl | $1.6 \times 10^9$ | 10.8 | 16.4 | nd | nd |
| Anaerobic 0.2M NaCl | $6.7 \times 10^7$ | 15.9 | 35.0 | nd | nd |

* nmole/min/mg protein,  S soluble activity,  P particulate activity, nd not detected.

When grown under carbon-limitation with $NH_4^+$ (table 2) the bacterial population densities achieved aerobically were much higher than those anaerobically reflecting the absence of an alternative terminal e$^-$ acceptor.  Low levels of NR were detected in cell extracts but no NiR.  In contrast when $NO_3^-$ was substituted for $NH_4^+$ then the aerobic and anaerobic population densities were similar for a particular NaCl concentration indicating the anaerobic role of $NO_3^-$ as e$^-$ acceptor (table 3).  In addition while NR activity of aerobic

TABLE 3  Bacterium K312 grown in a chemostat under carbon-limitation in a glycerol/$NO_3^-$ medium.  D 0.1 hr$^{-1}$, 15°.

| Culture | Cell Count | $NO_3^-$ reductase* | | $NO_2^-$ reductase* | |
|---|---|---|---|---|---|
| | | S | P | S | P |
| Aerobic, no NaCl | $1.3 \times 10^9$ | 54.1 | 38.6 | nd | nd |
| Anaerobic, no NaCl | $1.3 \times 10^9$ | 500.1 | 2750.6 | nd | nd |
| Aerobic, 0.2M NaCl | $2.0 \times 10^8$ | 13.1 | 21.6 | nd | nd |
| Anaerobic, 0.2M NaCl | $1.8 \times 10^8$ | 496.6 | 1041.5 | nd | nd |

Symbols as table 2.

cultures were similar to those grown aerobically on $NH_4^+$, anaerobic cultures had very high NR activities especially in the particulate cell fraction.  This indicated that a dissimilatory NR was synthesised anaerobically and that the bulk of this enzyme was membrane bound.  No NiR activity was recorded however and the analysis of spent media showed that anaerobic cultures utilised more $NO_3^-$ than those grown aerobically and that this $NO_3^-$ utilisation could be accounted for by the production of $NO_2^-$ and small quantities of $NH_4^+$.

TABLE 4  Bacterium K312 grown in a chemostat under nitrogen-limitation in a glycerol/$NO_3^-$ medium.  D 0.1 hr$^{-1}$, 15°.

| Culture | Cell Count | $NO_3^-$ reductase* | | $NO_2^-$ reductase* | |
|---|---|---|---|---|---|
| | | S | P | S | P |
| Aerobic, no NaCl | $3.7 \times 10^9$ | 36.0 | 20.8 | nd | nd |
| Anaerobic, no NaCl | $9.7 \times 10^8$ | 2706.8 | 2828.6 | 1382 | nd |

Symbols as table 2.

Nitrogen-limited cultures might be expected to conserve nitrogen to a maximum extent. Aerobic cultures contained only low NR and no detectable NiR activity and spent medium analysis showed only low $NO_3^-$ and $NH_4^+$ levels present (table 4). Anaerobic cultures, however, had a markedly lower population density and these organisms contained high levels of soluble and particulate NR, and soluble NiR. These enzyme levels correlated well with the presence of significant quantities of both $NO_2^-$ and $NH_4^+$ in spent media.

In carbon-limited cultures containing both $NO_3^-$ and $NH_4^+$ then spent medium analysis showed both nitrogen sources to be utilised aerobically and anaerobically. This was confirmed using $^{15}N$ enriched $NO_3$. $NO_3$ utilisation, however, was stimulated anaerobically with the production of $NO_2$ and an increase in the $NH_4^+$ level in the spent media (relative to aerobic cultures). The activities of both NR and NiR were high anaerobically (table 5).

TABLE 5  Bacterium K312 grown in a chemostat under carbon-limitation in a glycerol/$NH_4^+$/$NO_3^-$ medium.  D 0.1 hr$-1$, 15°.

| Culture | Cell Count | $NO_3^-$ reductase* | | $NO_2^-$ reductase* | |
|---|---|---|---|---|---|
| | | S | P | S | P |
| Aerobic, no NaCl | $2.8 \times 10^9$ | 8.4 | 48.9 | nd | nd |
| Anaerobic, no NaCl | $7.8 \times 10^8$ | 1276.7 | 3781.6 | 1300 | nd |
| Aerobic, 0.2M NaCl | $4.5 \times 10^8$ | 23.3 | 11.2 | nd | nd |
| Anaerobic, 0.2M NaCl | $1.3 \times 10^8$ | 301.5 | 1512.1 | 499 | nd |

Symbols as table 2.

It is evident from the results in tables 2-5 that the presence of $NO_3^-$ under anaerobic conditions results in the synthesis of NR. The synthesis of NiR in nitrogen-limited anaerobic cultures may be to conserve the limiting substrate while utilising $NO_2^-$ as e$^-$ acceptor. The utilisation of $NO_3^-$ and $NH_4^+$ simultaneously indicates that at the concentrations used $NH_4^+$ did not repress $NO_3$ assimilation. It is difficult to account physiologically for the presence of NiR and tentative evidence of the reduction of $NO_2^-$ to $NH_4^+$ in the presence of medium $NO_3^-$ and $NH_4^+$. These results do indicate however, that in the Kingoodie sediments such reduction is likely to occur accounting in part for the relatively high $NH_4^+$ levels present. The synthesis of NR and NiR at appreciable levels only anaerobically and the synthesis of these enzymes in the presence of $NH_4^+$ is firm evidence for their dissimilatory function.

The principle effect of NaCl in these experiments was to lower the population density. This may reflect an increased utilisation of carbon source for osmoregulation in the presence of 0.2M NaCl.

CONCLUSIONS

Kingoodie bay sediments contain high levels of $NH_4^+$ relative to those of $NO_3^-$ throughout the year.

Denitrifying bacteria may be isolated readily from these sediments.

Chemostat enrichments showed that at 15° and the presence of 0.4M NaCl coliform bacteria are able to compete successfully for glycerol as limiting carbon source anaerobically.

The presence of $NO_3^-$ enables high culture densities to be maintained anaerobically due to its role as $e^-$ acceptor.

The dissimilatory reduction of $NO_3^-$ correlates with the synthesis of NR and in some instances NiR.

The products of dissimilatory reduction of $NO_3^-$ are $NO_2^-$ and $NH_4^+$.

## ACKNOWLEDGEMENTS

This work was supported in part by grant GR3/2729 from NERC. We are grateful to Dr J.A. Cole, for useful discussions.

## REFERENCES

Brown, C.M., Macdonald-Brown, D.S. and Stanley, S.O., 1972. Inorganic nitrogen metabolism in marine bacteria: nitrogen assimilation in some marine pseudomonads. Journal of the Marine Biological Association of the United Kingdom, 52, 793-804.

Brown, C.M., Ellwood, D.C. and Hunter, J.R., 1977. Growth of bacteria at surfaces: influence of nutrient limitation. FEMS Microbiology Letters, 1, 163-166.

Cole, J.A., Coleman, K.J., Compton, B.E., Kavanagh, B.M. and Keevil, C.M., 1974. Nitrite and ammonia assimilation by anaerobic continuous cultures of Escherichia coli. Journal of General Microbiology, 85, 11-22.

Evans, C.G.T., Herbert, D. and Tempest, D.W., 1970. The continuous cultivation of microorganisms. 2 Construction of a chemostat. In Methods in Microbiology, 2 (Ed. J.R. Norris and D.W. Ribbons). Academic Press.

Herbert, R.A., 1974. A preliminary study of the effects of salinity on the bacterial flora of the Tay estuary. Proceedings of the Royal Society of Edinburgh (B), 75, 138-144.

Herbert, R.A., 1975. Heterotrophic nitrogen fixation in shallow estuarine sediments. Journal of Experimental Marine Biology and Ecology, 18, 215-225.

Jannasch, H.W., 1967. Enrichments of aquatic bacteria in continuous culture. Archiv für Mikrobiologie, 59, 165-173.

Kemp, J.D. and Atkinson, D.E., 1966. Nitrite reductase of Escherichia coli specific for reduced nicotinamide adenine dinucleotide. Journal of Bacteriology, 92, 628-638.

Lowe, R.H. and Evans, H.J., 1964. Preparation and some properties of a soluble nitrate reductase from Rhizobium japonicum. Biochim. Biophys. Acta, 85, 377-389.

Morris, I., 1974. Nitrogen assimilation and protein synthesis. In Algal Physiology and Biochemistry (Ed. W.D.P. Stewart) Blackwell Scientific Publications.

# C/N ET CONTROLE DE LA PHYSIOLOGIE DES CULTURES DE PHYTOPLANCTON

**Jeanne Moal, Jean-François Samain et Jean-René Le Coz**

*Centre Océanologique de Bretagne-B.P. 337-29273 Brest Cédex, France*

## ABSTRACT

Nutrients can be used for induction of carbohydrate or protein metabolism of three unicellular algae, their chemical variations measured by C/N ratio. The C/N determination and evolution can be used as a control for growth phase and satured conditions. Cultures of routine production have been tested by such a method. The results are discussed.

## INTRODUCTION

Si dans des conditions de milieux identiques, les différentes espèces d'algues présentent des compositions chimiques voisines (Réf. 1), (Réf. 2), de nombreux travaux ont fait apparaître la sensibilité de ce matériel aux modifications du milieu. En particulier, la composition chimique des algues varie selon les concentrations de sels nutritifs (Réf. 3) ou la phase de croissance (Réf. 4), (Réf. 5). Ces modifications se traduisent surtout au niveau des glucides et des protéines (Réf. 6), (Réf. 7). Afin d'obtenir une nourriture vivante de composition choisie pour l'alimentation des Artemia, Copépodes et larves en expérimentation, nous avons testé la capacité d'adaptation de trois espèces d'algues unicellulaires in vitro : *Tetraselmis suecica, Phaeodactylum tricornutum, Monochrysis lutheri*. La situation du phytoplancton dans la chaîne alimentaire lui confère une place importante dans les mécanismes des tranferts énergétiques. Si pour la production secondaire, l'importance de la concentration du phytoplancton, de sa composition spécifique, de sa taille est connue, l'incidence de sa qualité chimique reste peu analysée. Pourtant les critères de qualité des algues vivantes sont primordiaux pour la réussite des élevages utilisant celles-ci comme source de nourriture : qualité bactériologique (Réf. 8) et valeur nutritive.

## MATERIEL ET METHODES

La maintenance des cultures est assurée dans des ballons en pyrex de 20 1 préalablement stérilisés à l'autoclave. Le milieu de culture standard (Réf. 9, tableau 2) est stérilisé par filtration sur filtre Millipore de 0,2 μ. La salle d'élevage est thermostatée à 20°, sous éclairage continu, et l'aération des cultures est assurée par bullage d'air comprimé enrichi en $CO_2$ (Réf. 10). Un quart de la culture est quotidiennement renouvelé, en substituant stérilement 5 1 de culture par 5 1 de solution nutritive.

Plusieurs paramètres permettant de suivre l'évolution de la culture, ont été analysés sur des prélèvements journaliers. <u>Une numération cellulaire</u> est effectuée au microscope inversé Reichert en utilisant une cellule de Malassez.

La composition en carbone et azote a été mesurée sur l'analyseur C.H.N.
Hewlett Packard. Un volume connu de la culture est recueilli sur filtre en
fibre de verre Whatman GF/C de 25 mm. Les nitrates et les phosphates ont été
déterminés à l'autoanalyseur Technicon, sur le surnageant des cultures après
centrifugation, selon la méthode Tréguer et Le Corre (11).

Pour les dosages de protéines, carbohydrates totaux, sucres réducteurs, un
volume connu de la culture est centrifugé, le surnageant éliminé et le culot
repris dans un volume d'eau distillée, dix fois inférieur à celui de départ.
Cette solution est aussitôt broyée aux ultra-sons pour l'extraction des composants cellulaires. Le dosage des protéines est effectué sur le surnageant du
broyat après centrifugation, selon la méthode de Lowry, adaptée au technicon
par Samain et Boucher (12). Sur le broyat total, les carbohydrates totaux ont
été mesurés selon la méthode de Dubois (13), adaptée au phytoplancton par
Charra Mallara (14), et les sucres réducteurs selon la méthode colorimétrique
de Willstätter (15) à l'acide 3,5 dinitrosalicylique. L'amidon est dosé par
le réactif iodo-ioduré après trois extractions du broyat dans du tampon phosphate pH 6,8 (Réf. 16).

RESULTATS

Expression de la composition chimique. Les travaux de Parsons et al (1) ont
montré la possibilité d'exprimer les variations de la composition chimique de
diverses algues unicellulaires par l'analyse des valeurs relatives du carbone,
de l'azote et du phosphore. Dans un premier temps, nous avons cherché à exprimer les variations des composants cellulaires par le C/N, dont la détermination peut être envisagée en routine. Les mesures de quelques composés cellulaires tels que carbohydrates totaux, protéines, amidon, acides aminés ont été
effectuées parallèlement à des mesures d'azote et de carbone sur des ballons
de production de Tetraselmis, Phaeodactylum et Monochrysis. La corrélation
entre le C/N et le rapport carbohydrates/protéines est positive et significative au seuil de 5% (r = 0,98). L'existence de cette corrélation permettra
l'utilisation du C/N en tant qu'expression globale des variations relatives
des carbohydrates et des protéines.

Orientation du métabolisme de Tetraselmis. Les grandes variations du C/N, en
relation avec le rapport carbohydrates/protéines sont à rapprocher des résultats obtenus par Antia (6), Myklestad (4) qui ont souligné l'importance des
quantités et qualités des sels nutritifs présents sur la composition chimique
des algues, en particulier sur leur teneur en carbohydrates et en protéines.
Dans cette optique, l'influence des variations de concentrations des sels nutritifs sur le C/N de Tetraselmis a été recherchée.

Six cultures continues de Tetraselmis ont été effectuées en présence de concentrations de sels nutritifs de 0,5 ; 1 ; 2,5 ; 5 ; 10 et 50 fois les teneurs
de la solution standard. La concentration en vitamines n'a pas été modifiée.
L'évolution du C/N pendant 10 jours est présentée dans la figure (1). Trois
niveaux moyens se distinguent couvrant une gamme de C/N allant de 5 à 20. Le
niveau inférieur est obtenu dès la concentration 2,5 caractérisant alors un
phénomène de saturation (fig. 2). Contrairement aux observations effectuées
sur les cultures non saturées (milieux 0,5 et 1) les valeurs de C/N sont sta-
bles et faibles dans les conditions saturées, traduisant une physiologie mieux
établie. L'analyse journalière des nitrates et phosphates montre que les milieux 0,5 et 1 sont épuisés en 24h et qu'une accumulation progressive des sels
se produit dans les milieux 5 et 10, confirmant le caractère saturant de ces
conditions ; le milieu 2,5 étant à la limite du phénomène d'accumulation (fig.3)

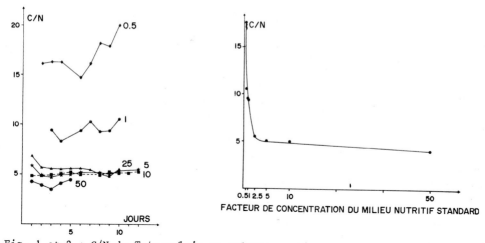

Fig. 1 et 2 : C/N de *Tetraselmis* en culture continue, aux concentrations 0,5 -
1 - 2,5 - 5 - 10 - 50 du milieu nutritif standard.

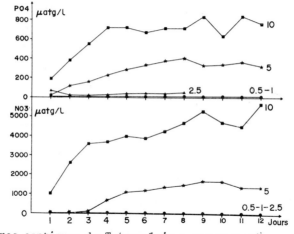

Fig. 3 : Cultures continues de *Tetraselmis* : concentrations résiduelles des
nitrates et des phosphates aux concentrations 0,5 - 1 - 2,5 - 5 - 10 - 50 du
milieu nutritif standard.

Par contre, le milieu 50 est devenu rapidement limitant pour la croissance ;
les cellules se sont rapidement décolorées et enkystées sous l'effet probable
des concentrations excessives en sels.

La modification progressive du C/N à travers les différents niveaux observés
peut être suivie sur les cultures 1, 5 et 10 dont l'enrichissement journalier
est supprimé. La concentration cellulaire, les concentrations de nitrates et
phosphates ainsi que le rapport C/N ont été contrôlés pendant 15 jours. La
phase exponentielle de croissance est d'autant plus longue et la concentration cellulaire élevée que la concentration initiale en sels était importante
(fig. 4). Le C/N augmente dès que la concentration en sels devient inférieure
au niveau de saturation et varie dans la gamme de 5 à 15.

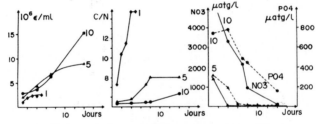

Fig. 4 : Cultures de *Tetraselmis* en milieu non renouvelé : concentration cellulaire, C/N, sels nutritifs pour trois concentrations initiales.

La composition chimique des cellules phytoplanctoniques des milieux 0,5 ; 1 et
2,5 a été analysée sur une dizaine de jours. Les résultats exprimés en µg/10⁶
cellules sont rassemblés dans le tableau 1. La composition chimique des cultures continues 0,5 et 1 est très semblable. La culture 2,5 se distingue par
des teneurs faibles en carbohydrates et en amidon, des teneurs supérieures en
azote, en protéines et en acides aminés. L'augmentation des carbohydrates dans
les milieux 0,5 et 1 est principalement liée à celle de l'amidon dont la proportion passe de 15 à 35%.

|  | C | N | C/N | Carbohy-drates | Protéines | Acides aminés | Amidon |
|---|---|---|---|---|---|---|---|
| Milieu 0,5 | 82 | 7,4 | 11,1 | 72,8 | 28,1 | 5,7 | 24,1 |
| Milieu 1 | 83,1 | 8,8 | 9,5 | 69,3 | 31,7 | 11 | 24,8 |
| Milieu 2,5 | 99,5 | 18,2 | 5,5 | 22,2 | 54,1 | 14 | 3,4 |

Tableau 1 : Composition chimique de *Tetraselmis* (µg/10⁶ cellules) aux concentrations 0,5 ; 1 ; 2,5 du milieu nutritif standard.

Variabilité comparée du C/N de *Tetraselmis, Phaeodactylum* et *Monochrysis*.
L'évolution du C/N en relation avec l'épuisement en sels a été étudiée sur
trois cultures en phase exponentielle : *Tetraselmis, Phaeodactylum* et *Monochrysis,* dont les milieux ne sont plus renouvelés. La variabilité intraspé-
cifique du C/N est aussi importante chez les trois espèces. Cependant, et bien
que les milieux nutritifs soient identiques au départ, les courbes de croissance sont très différentes (fig. 5).

Contrôle des cultures.: Les résultats précédents permettent de mettre en évidence l'extrême sensibilité de la composition chimique des cellules phytoplanctoniques aux variations de milieu. Le rapport C/N fournit une information
suffisante pour détecter ces modifications de composition. Il a donc été
mesuré systématiquement sur des cultures de routine effectuées au laboratoire
de production d'algues du COB. Trois espèces, destinées à l'alimentation des
larves de poissons, des Artemia et du zooplancton en expérimentation, y sont
cultivées.

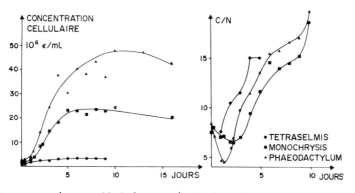

Fig. 5 : Concentrations cellulaires, C/N de 3 espèces phytoplanctoniques en
milieu nutritif standard non renouvelé.

Les valeurs moyennes du C/N et des principaux composés cellulaires, ont été
déterminées.La cinétique d'évolution du rapport carbone sur azote en réponse
à l'épuisement provoqué du milieu nutritif a été suivie afin de déterminer
l'influence d'éventuelles fluctuations du milieu sur la stabilité des cultures. Les valeurs du C/N des trois espèces sont soumises à une forte dispersion. *Monochrysis* présente une valeur de C/N moyen (8,6 ± 0,6) significativement plus basse que les deux autres espèces *Tetraselmis* (12,4 ±1,1),
*Phaeodactylum* (11,8 ± 0,9). Sa composition élevée en protéines et faible en
carbohydrates confirme cette donnée (tableau 2). Par contre, si *Tetraselmis*
ne se distingue pas de *Phaeodactylum* par son C/N, elle a une teneur significativement plus élevée en carbohydrates. L'analyse des glucides ne révèle de
l'amidon que pour *Tetraselmis* (43%). Des sucres réducteurs n'ont été décelés
que chez *Phaeodactylum* (23%). A l'absence de renouvellement du milieu pendant
deux jours, on observe une réponse très différente du C/N des trois espèces
(fig. 6). La variation du C/N est très rapide pour *Tetraselmis* et *Phaeodactylum*. Par contre *Monochrysis* semble peu affectée. L'analyse des concentrations finales en sels pendant cette période montre que seule cette espèce
n'a pas épuisé le milieu nutritif.

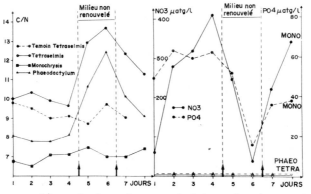

Fig. 6 : Culture continue de 3 espèces : cinétique de réponse du C/N et des
concentrations de NO3 et PO4 à un non renouvellement du milieu (jours 5 et 6)

|  | Protéines Carbone | Carbohydrates Carbone | Protéines Azote | Carbohydrates Azote |
|---|---|---|---|---|
| *Monochrysis* | 0,52 | 0,57 | 4,36 | 4,8 |
| *Phaeodactylum* | 0,36 | 0,87 | 4,27 | 10,3 |
| *Tetraselmis* | 0,36 | 1,46 | 4,3 | 17,6 |

Tableau 2 : Composition chimique des trois espèces phytoplanctoniques dans le milieu standard.

## DISCUSSION

La grande variabilité du C/N en réponse à des modifications du milieu et la corrélation positive entre le C/N et le rapport carbohydrates/protéines suggèrent des adaptations du métabolisme. Ces résultats montrent qu'il est possible d'orienter la composition chimique des trois cultures de phytoplancton étudiées en modifiant la concentration en sels nutritifs dans le milieu.

L'enrichissement du milieu en sels nutritifs se traduit par une diminution du rapport C/N jusqu'à un seuil minimum ($\simeq$ 5) à partir duquel les sels s'accumulent et le C/N reste stable. L'abaissement du C/N correspond surtout à une augmentation d'azote (tableau 1). En effet, bien que les carbohydrates diminuent et les protéines et acides aminés augmentent, le bilan carboné reste identique. Les protéines et acides aminés bien que plus abondants, ont cependant une participation moindre dans l'azote total des cellules ; l'augmentation d'autres composés azotés tels que les acides nucléiques ou les sels minéraux ($NH_4$ - $NO_3$) pourrait expliquer ce résultat. L'enrichissement d'acides nucléiques devrait conduire à des multiplications plus rapides. Ceci n'apparaît pas dans les cultures 0,5 ; 1 et 2,5 qui ont le même taux de croissance. Il s'agit donc probablement d'une accumulation de sels azotés dans les cellules végétales, ce qui confirme les résultats de Conover (7).

L'influence de l'épuisement des sels se répercute sur les phases de la croissance cellulaire ainsi que sur le C/N (fig. 4 et 5). Une concentration saturante en sels favorise le maintien en phase exponentielle et une faible valeur du C/N ; à l'épuisement progressif du milieu correspond l'amorce de la phase stationnaire et l'évolution du C/N vers des valeurs élevées. Le C/N peut être un bon indicateur des phases de croissance d'une culture phytoplanctonique et de ce fait permet d'en effectuer le contrôle. Les variations du C/N durant les phases de croissance confirment les données signalées par Myklestad (4), Skoglund (17) selon lesquels des cultures jeunes en phase exponentielle possèdent peu de carbohydrates par rapport à des cellules en phase stationnaire. Des études, in vivo, effectuées par Le Masson (18) en Atlantique aboutissent aux mêmes conclusions : des eaux jeunes et riches possèdent un C/N plus bas que des eaux anciennes et pauvres.

L'ensemble des résultats permet de confirmer que les variations intraspécifiques du C/N sont plus importantes que les variations interspécifiques et qu'il est possible de contrôler l'état physiologique des cultures par la mesure des valeurs moyennes du C/N et la vitesse de réponse de cet indice à l'absence d'apport de sels nutritifs. Cette vitesse permet de juger de la saturation des conditions du milieu. La richesse des algues en carbohydrates et en

protéines est orientable par intervention soit sur la composition du milieu
en sels nutritifs, soit sur le protocole de renouvellement des milieux de
culture. Dans le choix de la culture continue ou discontinue, l'expérimen-
tateur doit tenir compte de la différence de qualité chimique qui peut en
résulter. Le contrôle d'une culture discontinue (fig. 5) permet d'enregistrer
des C/N pouvant varier sur toute la gamme (5 à 20). Une telle culture permet
d'obtenir à la demande des algues de qualité chimique variée.

La réponse du C/N aux modifications de sels nutritifs varie selon les espèces.
Pour des conditions de milieux semblables, la composition chimique et le C/N
peuvent être différents (tableau 2, fig. 6). De plus, la présence d'amidon
chez *Tetraselmis*, même aux fortes teneurs en sels, ou de sucres réducteurs
seulement chez *Phaeodactylum*, paraît correspondre à une spécificité des algues
quant à la synthèse de leurs glucides.

Dans les cultures de routine du laboratoire de production d'algues, la valeur
du C/N pour les espèces *Tetraselmis* et *Phaeodactylum*, varie entre 8 et 13 ;
l'augmentation de ce rapport est rapide à l'absence de renouvellement de
milieu. Ces caractéristiques traduisent des conditions limitantes et la possibilité d'un vieillissement rapide de la culture en cas de déséquilibre des
sels nutritifs. Cette valeur de C/N est supérieure à celle que l'on a obtenu
pour *Tetraselmis* dans les mêmes conditions de milieu en culture continue
(C/N = 9,5) (tableau 1). Ceci est expliqué par le protocole de production de
routine au cours duquel aucun renouvellement de milieu n'est effectué pendant
le week-end ce qui induit des augmentations périodiques de C/N. Associée à
des conditions limitantes de milieu nutritif, cette technique fournit une
production variable en qualité chimique, orientée principalement sur des algues en phase préstationnaire, riches en carbohydrates et de faibles teneurs
protéiques. La culture de *Monochrysis*, dans les mêmes conditions, a un C/N
moyen inférieur (≈ 8) qui varie lentement à l'absence de renouvellement de
milieu. Ce comportement traduit des conditions proches de la saturation en
sels, une fin de phase exponentielle confirmée par une teneur protéique plus
importante et des carbohydrates en quantité plus faible.

### REMERCIEMENTS

Nous remercions pour leur active collaboration et leurs conseils : J.P. FLASSCH
J.C. ALEXANDRE, G. SALAUN, P.Y. GUENOLÉ, du laboratoire de production d'algues
du C.O.B., qui ont pris en charge la réalisation des cultures.

### REFERENCES

(1) PARSONS, T.R., STEPHENS, K., STRICKLAND, J.D.H., 1961. On the chemical
composition of eleven species of marine phytoplankters. Journal of Fisheries Research Board of Canada, 18, 1001-1016.

(2) RICKETTS, T.R., 1966. On the chemical composition of some unicellular
algae. Phytochemistry, 5, 67-76.

(3) HOBSON, L.A., PARISER, R.J., 1971. The effect of inorganic nitrogen on
macromolecular synthesis by *Thalassiosira fluviatilis* Hustedt and *Cyclo-
tella nana* Hustedt grown in batch culture. Journal of experimental marine
biology and ecology, 6, 71-78.

(4) MYKLESTAD, S., HAUG, A., 1972. Production of carbohydrates by the marine diatom *Chaetoceros affinis var Willei* (gran) Hustedt. Journal of experimental marine biology and ecology, 9, 125-136.

(5) BERLAND, B.R., BONIN, D.J., DAUMAS, R.A., LABORDE, P.L., MAESTRINI, S.Y., 1970. Variations du comportement physiologique de l'algue *Monallantus salina* en culture. Marine Biology, 7, 82-92.

(6) ANTIA, N.J., MC ALLISTER, C.D., PARSONS, T.R., STEPHENS, K., STRICKLAND, J. D.H., 1963. Further measurements of primary production using a large volume plastic sphere. Limnology and Oceanography, 8, 166-183.

(7) CONOVER, S.A.M., 1975. Partitioning of nitrogen and carbon in cultures of the marine diatom *Thalassiosira fluviatilis* supplied with nitrate, ammonium or urea. Marine Biology, 32, 231-246.

(8) LUCAS, A., PRIEUR, D., 1974. Le contrôle bactérien des élevages de larves de bivalves. Colloque sur l'Aquaculture. Actes et Colloques, n° 1, 1-24, CNEXO Ed.

(9) WALNE, P.R., 1966. Experiments in the large scale culture of the larvae of *Ostrea edulis* (L.). Fishery investigations, London, Ser 2, 25 (4), 1-53.

(10) FLASSCH, J.P., NORMANT, Y., 1974. Mise en place d'une unité de production d'algues au Centre Océanologique de Bretagne : premiers résultats. Colloque sur l'Aquaculture. Actes et Colloques, n° 1, 25-19, CNEXO Ed.

(11) LE CORRE, P., TREGUER, P., 1976. Contribution à l'étude de la matière organique dissoute et des sels nutritifs dans l'eau de mer. Thèse doctorat ès-Sciences, Université de Bretagne Occidentale.

(12) SAMAIN, J.F., BOUCHER, J., 1974. Dosage automatique de l'amylase et des protéines du zooplancton. Annales de l'Institut Océanographique, Paris, 50, 199-205.

(13) DUBOIS, M., GILLES, K.A., HAMILTON, J.K., REBERS, P.A., SMITH, F., 1956. Colorimetric method for determination of sugars and related substances. Analytical Chemistry, 28, 350-356.

(14) MALARA, G., CHARRA, R., 1972. Dosage des glucides particulaires du phytoplancton selon la méthode de Dubois. Notes de travail n° 6. Université de Paris VI. Station Zoologique de Villefranche-sur-Mer.

(15) WILLSTATTER, R., WALDSCHMIDT-LEITZ, E., HESSE, A.R.F., 1923. Z. Physiologie Chem., 126, 143.

(16) MARTIN, A.G., 1976. Etude de la matière organique particulaire. Thèse 3ème cycle. Université de Bretagne Occidentale.

(17) SKOGLUND, L., JENSEN, A., 1976. Studies of N. limited growth of diatoms in dialysis culture. Journal of experimental marine biology and ecology, 21, 169-178.

(18) LE MASSON, L., CREMOUX, J.L., MONTEL, Y., 1977. Analyse des rapports C/N/P du seston dans la partie orientale de l'Atlantique équatorial. Marine Chemistry, 5, 171-181.

# CONTRIBUTION TO STUDIES ON THE EFFECT OF ECTOCRINE SUBSTANCES ON THE DEVELOPMENT OF MARINE INVERTEBRATES. ABSORPTION OF LABELLED (14C or 3H) DISSOLVED ORGANIC SUBSTANCES BY THE EGGS AND LARVAE OF *EUPHAUSIA KROHNII*

**Jean-François Pavillon**

*Laboratoire de Physiologie des êtres marins, Institut Océanographique, 75000 Paris, France*

## ABSTRACT

[*]8 amino acids of the L series, 4 vitamins and a fatty acid have been tested in a dissolved state, in filtered sea water, which had been submitted to ultra violet and was free from organic substances, for 5 hours on eggs at an advanced stage of development and on larvae of *Euphausia krohnii* until the calyptopis I stage.

Absorption and utilisation in metabolism by the eggs and larvae, at concentrations resembling those existing in sea water, seem probable. Judging from the results, the egg appears to need less amino acids than the larva. Absorption of riboflavin increases with time, that of cobalamin and pyridoxin is weak for the egg and significant for the larva. Little palmitic acid is absorbed by the egg.

## INTRODUCTION

Studies made by Stephens and Schinske (ref. 17), Stephens (Ref. 12, 13, 14, 15, 16), Provasoli et al. (Ref. 11), Hernandorena (Ref. 5), Dezert (Ref. 2), Fevrier et al. (Ref. 4), Pavillon (Ref. 8, 9, 10) have shown the absorption by marine animals of a great number of dissolved organic molecules, possibly of ectocrine origin, and their role in certain metabolic functions.

These substances, eliminated by living animals, either by excretion or diffusion through the tissues, do indeed modify at a given place and time the mean characteristics of the dissolved organic substratum and can affect reproduction (incintive or inhibitory action), growth (by favouring or retarding development), nutrition (setting-off or inhibition of alimentary behaviour), survival (tolerance towards high concentrations, presence or absence of essentiel factors) and they intervene generally in the behaviour of the species and its evolution.

Knowledge on the nature and amounts of organic substances intervening in the metabolism of living animals, at the first stage of development, will be fundamental in the control of aquacultural breeding. Experiments carried out on the eggs and larvae of *Euphausia krohni* aimed at determining the nature and amounts of simple dissolved organic molecules, present in the oceans at concentrations from $10^{-3}$ to about 10 microg. $1^{-1}$. The use of labelled 14C or 3H organic molecules enabled us to detect quantities to the order of picog. $1^{-1}$.

---

[*] glycine, alanine, serine, cysteine, aspartic acid, glutamic acid, methionine, tyrosine, thiamin, riboflavin, pyridoxin, cobalamin, palmitic acid.

## METHOD

The eggs of *Euphausia krohnii* were collected with a WP2 plankton net, 25 to
50m deep during the month of July 1976 and part of August, in Villefranche-sur-
Mer at point B of the station. The eggs collected can be distinguished easily
in the plankton mass. More or less 500 microm. in diameter, they are made up
of a vitelline membrane, a perivitelline space approximately equal to the egg
radius and a double external membrane. The development stages chosen for the
experiment were the later ones when the nauplius appendices are visible.

Once sorted 50 of these eggs are distributed into cristallizers of
50 cl capacity containing 50 ml of sea water with an added labelled substance.
The sea water was previously filtered on a 0.45 microm. membrane, thus treated
with ultra violet rays according to the method of Manny et al. (6) in an apparatus for the combustion of dissolved organic matter. The environment thus
treated, cleared of all dissolved organic matter and rich in mineral salts,
proves particularly unfavourable to the growth of the pluteus, used as a biological test according to Bougis's (I) method Fig. I.

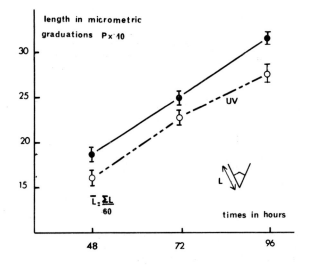

Figure 1.    Growth of <u>Arbacia lixula</u> pluteus in natural sea
             water (——) and in ultra-violet treated sea water
             (--).

The cristallizers are placed in the dark in a 20°C thermostat bath and covered
with aluminium paper. The eggs are collected every hour, placed on a 100 microm.
mesh sieve and thoroughly rinsed in clean sea water. They are then collected
on a filter paper (Whatman n°1), washed several times and submitted to combustion before being put into the scintillation counter. To do this, filters are
placed in small cellulose cones filled with monocrystalline cellulose powder,
in order to help combustion, and brought to a high temperature in an oven
(Packard, Tri-carb 306). The burnt tissues are transformed into water and car-
bonic gas and trapped in appropriate solvents and scintillants. When a radioactive substance labelled with 14C or 3H has been absorbed or adsorbed by tissues

it is retrieved after combustion in the form of 3H water or 14 CO2. The addition of a scintillant follows automatically (monophase for the 3H water, carbosorb and permafluor for the 14 CO2).

The advantage of this treatment is that a homogenous solution is obtained for scintillation counting. The yield is 99% $\pm$ 1%. However direct exposure of membranes to detection by scintillation gives approximate results owing to the impossibility of measuring autoabsorption, due to the filter and animals, above all in the case of low energy radioelements such as 3H (Emx 3H = 18 Kev, Emx 14C = 165 Kev. For example with *Artemia salina*cysts, the results obtained vary between 1 to 10 for 3 H.

As regards larvae, conditions are the same as for eggs at the start of the experiment, but eggs are distributed in lots of 50 into as many crystallizers. The labelled organic substances are added 24 hours after the beginning of the experiment, i.e. at the nauplius stage. 100% of the eggs are seen to hatch. Sampling is done 5 days out of 6, every 24 hours. The first sample is taken 24 hours after the substance is introduced. Stage Nauplius I and II are over. The calyptopis stage appear, in our experimental conditions, approximately three days after the experiment has begun. On the fifth and sixth day, mortality is high and may reach 100% in certain crystallizers.

### RESULTS

8, 14C amino acids of the L. series : glycine, alanine, serine, cysteine, aspartic acid, glutamic acid, methionine, tyrosine, 4 vitamins : thiamin, riboflavin (both 14C), pyridoxin, cobalamin (both 3H), and a fatty acid 14C palmitic acid, which have all been tested in a dissolved state.

### Eggs

The results obtained are included in table I and given in equivalent masses in picogr. On the whole, the quantities absorbed or retained are low as regards amino acids. The maximum quantities absorbed are respectively 62 pg. for aspartic acid, 74 pg. for glycine, 38 pg. for methionine and 310 pg. for serine. With vitamins mass values are higher for riboflavin than for thiamine. Riboflavin is absorbed the most. With palmitic acid the maximum absorbed quantities is 146 pg.

### Larvae

The results obtained are included in table 2. For larvae, at the nauplius I and II, metanauplius, calyptopis I stages, the absorption values are much higher for certain amino acids than for vitamins (with the exception of riboflavin). The highest values observed do not depend upon the development stage, but vary according to the kind of amino acid considered. Thus for aspartic acid the highest value is observed on the first day of sampling, 1 196 pg. i.e. at the nauplius I, II, and metanauplius stages, and then decreases. As for glycine, the highest value is observed on the third day of the experiment. As for vitamins, riboflavin is absorbed in important quantities : $43.10^3$ pg. on the third day. Cabalamin is absorbed in low amounts. With palmitic acid, the amount absorbed is very high on the first day : 4 105 pg.

|              | I          | 2          | 3          | 4          | 5          |
|--------------|------------|------------|------------|------------|------------|
| 14C glycine  | 43 ± 13    | 74 ± 17    | 54 ± 15    | 49 ± 14    | 73 ± 17    |
| alanine      | 23 ± 10    | 32 ± 11    | 23 ± 9     | 26 ± 10    | 22 ± 9     |
| serine       | 310 ± 35   | 210 ± 29   | 100 ± 20   | 113 ± 21   | 57 ± 15    |
| cysteine     | 17 ± 8     | 10 ± 6     | 16 ± 8     | 23 ± 10    | 27 ± 10    |
| aspartic a.  | 20 ± 9     | 24 ± 10    | 62 ± 16    | 29 ± 11    | 21 ± 9     |
| glutamic a.  | 42 ± 13    | 11 ± 7     | 21 ± 9     | 39 ± 12    | 62 ± 16    |
| methionine   | 88 ± 19    | 29 ± 11    | 48 ± 14    | 34 ± 12    | 45 ± 13    |
| tyrosine     | 13 ± 7     | 9 ± 6      | 22 ± 9     | 13 ± 7     | 13 ± 7     |
| 14C thiamin  | 231 ± 30   | 435 ± 42   | 503 ± 45   | 871 ± 59   | 671 ± 52   |
| riboflavin   | 369 ± 38   | 453 ± 43   | 514 ± 45   | 351 ± 37   | 1051 ± 65  |
| 3H cobalamin | 0.0        | 0.0        | 0.0        | 2 ± 2      | 12 ± 7     |
| pyridoxin    | 0.0        | 0.0        | 0.0        | 0.0        | 0.0        |
| 14C palmitic a. | 135 ± 23 | 67 ± 16    | 131 ± 23   | 59 ± 15    | 146 ± 24   |

TABLE 1   Results of absorption of dissolved organic substances during 5 hours by the eggs (N=50) of *Euphausia krohnii* in pg.

|              | I         | 2         | 3         | 4        | 5         | 6         |
|--------------|-----------|-----------|-----------|----------|-----------|-----------|
| 14C glycine  | 491+44    | 4234+130  | 5126+143  | —        | 4361+132  | 2471+88   |
| alanine      | 203+28    | 185+27    | 171+26    | 257+32   | —         | 227+30    |
| serine       | 422+41    | —         | 1043+64   | 1354+74  | 630+50    | 378+39    |
| cysteine     | 191+28    | 929+61    | 893+60    | 818+57   | —         | 942+61    |
| aspartic a.  | 1196+69   | 1207+69   | 255+32    | 224+30   | —         | 204+29    |
| glutamic a.  | 375+89    | 528+41    | 676+52    | 518+45   | —         | 385+39    |
| methionine   | 5370+146  | 6087+156  | —         | 8316+182 | 5588+149  | 3374+116  |
| tyrosine     | 471+43    | —         | 532+46    | 316+35   | 694+53    | 564+47    |
| 14C thiamin  | 1090+66   | 760+55    | 1260+70   | 2144+91  | —         | 940+61    |
| riboflavin   | $27.10^3$+328 | $17.10^3$+261 | $43.10^3$+415 | $27.10^3$+328 | — | $20.10^3$+283 |
| 3H cobalamin | 138+23    | 177+27    | 335+37    | 409+40   | —         | 445+42    |
| pyridoxin    | 9+6       | 10+6      | 18+8      | 22+9     | —         | 39+12     |
| 14C palmitic a. | 4105+128 | 3481+118 | 1853+86   | —        | 3078+111  | 2980+109  |

TABLE 2   Results of absorption of dissolved organic substances, during 6 days, by the larvae (nauplius, metanauplius, calyptopis I) of *Euphausia krohnii*.in pg., ( — no sample).

DISCUSSION

The absorption and utilization by eggs and larvae of dissolved amino acids and certain vitamins, at concentrations compatible with those existing in sea water seem likely and agree with results obtained with *Artemia salina* and *Arbacia lixula*. The needs of the egg are different than at the swimming stages when the energy loss increases. The absorption of vitamins is high, whatever the development stage. Cobalamin is slightly or even not at all absorbed by eggs, whereas it is absorbed at the later larval stages. Its contribution to the survival of *Artemia salina* larvae has already been shown by Hernandorena(Ref.5). As has been established the settlement in bathymetric layers of the eggs and larvae of *Euphausia* may correspond to stages of development and to the appearance of particular dissolved organic substances. Certain substances being more abundant in the upper layers where phyto- and zooplankton proliferate, appear in time and space in accordance with the biological cycles of the different species. Other substances intervening in growth, which are photosensitive, seem abundant at night only, riboflavin for instance, excretion of which by phytoplankton and copepods has been shown by Momzikoff(Ref. 7). These substances absorbed by organisms could be the primary food supply for the animal at the larval stage, before the whole digestive system is fully developed, compensating energy losses, promoting growth and ensuring survival. These experiments do not suffice to prove a direct effect of dissolved organic matter on the growth of *Euphausia krohnii* larvae but this is a first step.

REFERENCES

(1)  P. Bougis, Utilisation des pluteus en écologie expérimentale, Helgoländer Wiss. Meeresunters 15, 59-68 (1968).

(2)  C. Dezere, Rôle de l'isoxanthoptérine sur le développement de l'oeuf d'oursin *Arbacia lixula*, Bull. Mus. Nat. Hist. Natur., 2, 39, n°3, II, 588-594 (1967).

(3)  A. Fevrier et M. Barbier, Molécules organiques dissoutes dans l'eau de mer: utilisation de l'acide palmitique, de l'alcool cétylique et du dotriacontane par les invertébrés marins, J. Exp. Mar. Biol. Ecol., 25, 123-129 (1976).

(4)  A. Fevrier, M. Barbier et A. Salliot, Molécules organiques dissoutes dans l'eau de mer : capture par les invertébrés marins (acide palmitique, alcool cétylique, dotriocontane), C.R.Hebd. Séance, Acad. Sco. Paris, 281 série D, 239-241 (1975).

(5)  A. Hernandorena, Mise en évidence de l'action de la vitamine B12 sur la survie d'*Artemia salina*, Bull. Mus. Nat. Hist. Nat. 2°sem. T 35, n° 5, 507-514 (1963).

(6)  B.A. Manny, M.C. Miller, and R.G. Wetzel, Ultraviolet combustion of dis-
     solved organic nitrogen compounds in lakewaters, Limnology and
     Oceanography, V. 16 (I), 71-85 (1971).

(7)  A. Momzikoff, Substances fluorescentes des eaux de mer (ptérines
     et flavines ) et des planctons marins        Essai d'inter-
     prétation écologique. Thèse de doctorat, Université Pierre et Marie
     Curie, Paris, France,  (1977).

(8)  J.F. Pavillon, Action de quelques substances organiques dissoutes, sup-
     posées ectocrines, sur la cinétique du développement de l'oeuf et
     à la croissance de la larve d'un invertébré marin : Arbacia
     lixula (Linné), Thèse de doctorat en océanographie biologique,
     Université de Paris VI, France, 184 pp. (1975).

(9)  J.F. Pavillon, Action de trois substances supposées ectocrines (ribofla-
     vines, acide glutamique, glycine) sur la cinétique du développement
     de l'oeuf et la croissance de la larve de deux espèces d'échinides,
     Arbacia lixula et  Paracentrotus lividus, Marine Biology, 34, 67-75
     (1976).

(10) J.F. Pavillon, Etude de l'absorption de substances organiques dissoutes
     pouvant être ectocrines, marquées au 14C ou au 3H par les oeufs et
     les larves d'Artemia salina et d'Arbacia lixula,  Compte rendu de
     la réunion du GABIM - Endoume 18-19 nov.1976. Edit.du CNRS (1977).

(11) L. Provasoli, D.E. Conklin, A.S. D'Agostino, Factors inducing fertility
     in aseptic Crustacea, Helgolander, Wiss. Meeresunters, 2, 443-454
     (1970).

(12) G.C. Stephens, Uptake of organic material by aquatic invertebrates II.
     Accumulation of amino acids by the bamboo worms Clymenella torqueta,
     Comp. Biochem. Physiol. 10, 191-202 (1963 a).

(13)           -, Uptake of organic material by aquatic invertebrates II.
     Uptake of glycine by brackish water annelids, Biol. Bull. Mar.
     biol. Lab., Woods Hole, 126, 150-162 (1963 b).

(14)           -, Dissolved organic materials as a nutritional source for
     marine and estuarine invertebrates, In : Estuaries, Ed. by G.H.
     Lauff, Washington, D.C.: American Association for the Advancement of
     Science (Publs Am. Ass. Advmt Sci. N° 83), 367-373 (1967).

(15)           -, Dissolved organic matter as a potential source of nutrition
     for marine organisms, Am. Zool. V. 8, 95-106 (1968).

(16)           -, Amino acids accumulation and assimilation in marine organisms,
     In , Symposium on nitrogen metabolism and the Environment, Ed. by
     Campbell, J.W. and L. Goldstein, Academic Press, N.Y., 155-184 (1972).

(17) G.C. Stephens and R.A. Schinske, Uptake of amino acids by marine inver-
     tebrates, Limnol. Oceanog. 6, 175-181 (1961).

# THE EXTRACTION OF SPECIFIC PROTEINS FOR THE SIMULTANEOUS ECTODERMAL ABSORPTION OF CHARGED AND NEUTRAL AMINO ACIDS BY *ANEMONIA SULCATA* (COELENTERATA, ANTHOZOA)

**Dietrich Schlichter**

*Zoological Institute, University of Cologne, 5000 Koeln, FRG*

## ABSTRACT

Anemones posses distinct uptake systems for the absorption of
neutral, acidic and basic amino acids. The uptake systems for
acidic and basic amino acids seem to be highly specific. Neutral
amino acids are absorbed either by a single system with broad
specificity or by several systems with overlapping specificity.
It was possible to separate by means of gel filtration and
electrophoresis those proteins which specifically bind amino
acids. The molecular weights of these proteins are larger than
3o ooo. Although the systems for the uptake of charged and neutral amino acids are different as far as their specificity is
concerned, the isoelectrical points of the extracted proteins
are similar.

## INTRODUCTION

The structure and physiology of sea anemones is well adapted to
the uptake of amino acids and carbohydrates from sea water. The
absorbing external surface is greatly enlarged by tentacles and
an ectodermal microvilli fuzz. The uptake process is energy-
dependent. Absorption can even take place against gradients of
up to $1:1o^6$. Moreover calculations indicate that anemones gain
an energetic net profit by this kind of nutrition (Ref. 1).

In the sea the various kinds of DOM (dissolved organic material)
are present in different amounts. Specific uptake systems for the
different substances working simultaneously would utilize the
available dissolved nutrition to a high degree. Thus the anemones would be supplied most effectively with e. g. the distinct
classes of amino acids (basic, acidic and neutral with an either
polar of nonpolar side chain). The uptake would be independent of
the concentration of the potential nourishment in the water at
any given time. In contrast to this argument one or only a few
rather unspecific systems would lead to a similar result. In this
case the accumulation of only one amino acid would also be avoided. The more concentrated amino acids would be taken up at a
high rate but other amino acids of lower concentration would be
absorbed too.
In this paper the terms "uptake or absorption" include all those
mechanisms which lead to the incorporation of amino acids due to
the binding and translocation of molecules from the ambient water
into the ectodermal cells.
The first part of this paper deals with experiments concerning the
specificity of amino acid uptake systems. As far as these invest-

155

igations are concerned it is necessary to make certain restrict-
ions: Single inhibitor/substrate combinations are helpful to determine the specific properties of the uptake systems. Unfortunately these studies do not provide very much information as to
how these systems might function in a highly complex environment
like the sea.
The second part of this paper deals with investigations concerning the biochemical equivalent to the inhibition experiments. By
means of gel filtration and electrophoresis it was possible to
extract proteins which specifically bind amino acids.

## MATERIALS AND METHODS

### Animals and their Maintainance

The sea anemones, Anemonia sulcata, were collected on the coast
of the Normandy (France). They were kept in artificial sea water
(Tropic Marin Neu). Salinity: 3o-32 ‰; temperature in the storage
tanks: 15° C; illumination: light:dark = 14:1o h; the experiments
were carried out at 21-23° C. At this temperature the anemones
were conditioned for 5 days.

### Experimental Procedures Concerning Inhibition Experiments

In order to evaluate the absorption capacity of the anemones for
amino acids, the concentration of tritium labelled amino acids
in the incubation medium (25o ml of ventilated and sterilized
artifical sea water) was measured. The sea water contained
streptomycin in order to exclude any microbial influence. The
radioactive amino acids were purchased from Amersham-Buchler.
First of all the rate of uptake was measured for a single $^3$H-
amino acid (L-configuration). The concentration to which the
anemones were subjected ranged from 8-8o nmol $l^{-1}$. After measuring the "standard absorption", the uptake of the same $^3$H-amino
acid was determined for the same anemone but now in combination
with a different unlabelled amino acid (L-configuration) of the
same or of an other class at a much higher concentration (5oo
$\mu$mol $l^{-1}$).

### Experimental Procedures Concerning the Extraction of Proteins

Tentacles (in average 5oo mg dry weight) were amputated and washed several times in sterilized sea water. Then they were incubated in sterilized sea water containing a $^{14}$C amino acid (1 $\mu$mol
$l^{-1}$) for 2 min. After this 2 min pulse-label the tentacle tissue
was immediately washed in an ice cooled buffer (6 M urea, o.o5 M
Tris/HCl pH 8.4) and homogenized (Potter-Elvejhem). After additional sonification the material was centrifuged for 6o min at
2o ooo rpm. All preparation steps were carried out at 4° C.

### Preparation of the soluble protein fractions. Gel filtration: Co-
lumns (4o x 2.o cm, 9o x 2 cm) were packed with Bio-Gel P 1o,
P 15o A 5m and equilibrated with the same buffer as mentioned
above. 1 - 2 ml of the supernatant (concentrated by ultrafiltration) were applied to the columns and eluted with same buffer.
Fractions containing the highest radioactivity were put together
(batches 1, 2) and concentrated by means of ultrafiltration (Ami-

con membrane UMO5). The protein content was determined by the
method of Schaffner and Weissmann (2), with bovine serum albumine
as the standard.
Electrophoresis: SDS-gel electrophoresis (slab gels) was performed according to Brewer et al. (3), isoelectric focusing (rod
gels) according to Finlayson and Chrambach (4). After electrophoresis the gels were either immediatly frozen or fixed in cold
12.5 % TCA. The gels were sectioned into 1.1 mm slices. The radio-
acticity was measured according to Tishler and Epstein (5). The
isoelectrical points of the separated proteins were established
by introducing 8 proteins (pH 4.4. - 1o.65, purchased from Serva)
which served as markers.

## RESULTS AND THEIR DISCUSSION

### Inhibition Experiments

Mutual effect on the uptake of amino acids belonging to the same
class. If the concentration of the competing amino acid e. g.
valine was increased, the uptake of the substrate e. g. $^{3}$H-leu-
cine steadily decreased, Fig. 1. If the anemones were left in the
incubation medium for e. g. 24 h the concentration of the labelled amino acid reached that of the standard absorption, Fig. 2.

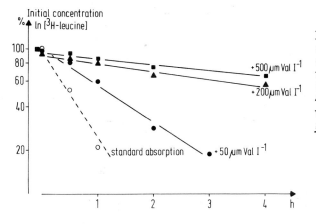

Fig. 1. The effect
of increasing valine
concentrations on the
uptake of $^{3}$H-leucine
(initialconcentration
4o nmol l$^{-1}$) from
water by Anemonia
sulcata.

These experiments give qualitative evidence that the uptake-and/
or the translocation centers were only saturated at high substrate
concentrations which in general not occur in the biotope. A decrease of e. g. leucine was still measurable although the concentration level of valine was 1o ooo times higher. Similar results as demonstrated for the combination $^{3}$H-leucine/valine
(both neutral apolar amino acids) were also obtained from corresponding combinations such as: $^{3}$H-leucine/isoleucine; $^{3}$H-serine/
threonine (neutral polar); $^{3}$H-glutamic acid/aspartic acid (acidic). The experiments show that the uptake of amino acids belonging to the same class is reciprocally influenced. Proline
and cystine seem to play an exception to the rule. Thus under
natural conditions, the uptake seems to be regulated by the

actual concentration in the sea. Those amino acids in high concentration will be absorbed to a larger extent. After incorporation
the consumption is surely regulated by mechanisms according to
the physiological state of the individual cells.

Mutual effect on the uptake of amino acids belonging to different
classes. 1) The effect of neutral amino acids (including histidine which exhibits a basic tendency) on the uptake of charged
amino acids: The uptake of basic amino acids was inhibited, wher-
as the effect on the absorption of acidic amino acids was variable: most caused no inhibition others showed a weak inhibitory
effect (e. g. serine, tyrosine). 2) The effect of acidic amino
acids on the uptake of neutral or basic amino acids: Their uptake was not inhibited. 3) The effect of basic amino acids on the
uptake of neutral or acidic amino acids: The absorption of neutral amino acids was influenced by different degrees: The uptake
of e. g. alanine and phenylalanine was largely inhibited, while
the absorption of e. g. leucine and methionine was only slightly
affected. The uptake of acidic amino acids was not influenced at
all (Fig. 2).

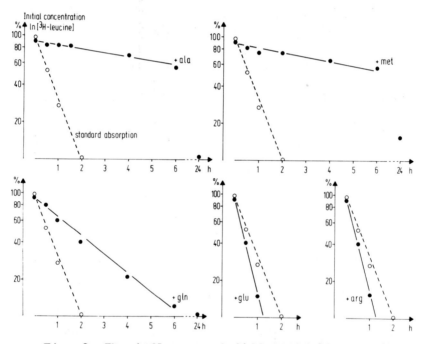

Fig. 2. The influence of different classes of
amino acids (5oo µmol $l^{-1}$) on the uptake of $^3$H-
leucine (25 nmol $l^{-1}$).

The experiments indicate that anemones possess at least three
distinct uptake systems for amino acids with different specificity. The absorption system for acidic amino acids is highly specific followed by systems for the uptake of basic and neutral amino

acids with less specificity. Any kind of neutral amino acids
with either a polar, nonpolar, aliphatic, aromatic or hetero-
cyclic side chain seems to be absorbed by one unspecific system
or by several systems with overlapping affinities. These results
are in accordance with investigations of e. g. Bamford and
Stewart (6), investigating the absorption of amino acids by
Arenicola marina; experiments of Siebers (7) who studied the
uptake of amino acids by Enchytraeus albidus and Nereis
diversicolor or with experiments of Pappas and Read (8) who
investigated the uptake of amino acids by cestodes. The latter
characterised different uptake systems for acidic, basic and
neutral amino acids in cestodes. In addtition they demonstrated
that the absorption of neutral amino acids takes place through
at least 3 different systems with poorer specificity.
The specificity of the amino acid uptake is not quite as selective as might be expected. The reduced specificity of the receptors, especially for neutral amino acids, may be quite logical.
The reasons for this assumption are already described for the
absorption of amino acids by cestodes (Ref. 8). The broad specificity prevents the accumulation of the most predominant amino
acid in the sea water in the amino acid pool of the anemone. On
the other hand several highly specific systems would lead to the
same result. The synthesis of only a few uptake systems may have
advantages with respect to the energy required to produce these
systems compared to the synthesis of 1o very specific uptake systems.

Investigations of van Pilsum et al. (9) indicate that the anne-
lide  Glycera dibranchiata even took up substances which it could
not metabolize. This fact could indicate that a large amount of
DOM (regarding quality, not quantity) is best utilized by uptake
systems with restricted specificity. Consequently a large spectrum of substances is automatically absorbed including non-use-
ful ones too.

The results of the inhibition experiments lead to the assumption
that specific proteins (receptors) are responsible for the amino
acid uptake. This consideration was the basis for the following
biochemical investigations.

## Extraction of Proteins Specifically Binding Amino Acids

Gel filtration. Figure 3 gives evidence that after the extraction
of soluble proteins $^{14}C$-amino acids are still attached to them.
More than 9o % of the $^{14}$C-amino acids of batch 1 are precipitable
(12.5 % cold TCA) together with proteins. The same can be shown
by ultrafiltration of batch 1. Only an insignificant increase of
radioactivity was detectable in the ultrafiltrate. In experiments
using a solution of 1 % SDS in o.8 M NaCl for protein extraction
the $^{14}$C-amino acids do not elute together with proteins of the
size mentioned above. If the proteins of batch 1 - isolated as
described in materials and methods - were treated with SDS,
instead of TCA less than 1o % of the $^{14}$C-amino acids remained
attached. Thus most of the $^{14}$C-amino acids are not covalently

bound. In addition to this the SDS experiments show that in fact
after the pulse label of 2 min $^{14}$C-amino acids are neither
significantly incorporated into macromolecules nor bound to

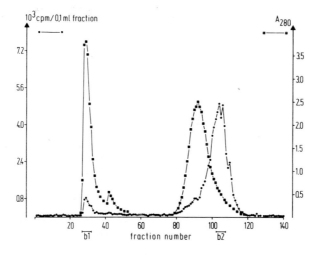

Fig. 3. Gel filtration (Biogel P 15o) of
tentacle proteins after a 2 min pulse label
with $^{14}$C-leucine. The radioactivity of batch
1 (b 1) was coprecipitable with protein; batch
2 (b 2) contains free $^{14}$C-leucine. Column:
4o x 2.o cm, buffer: 6 M urea, o.o5 M Tris/HCl
pH 8.4; flowrate: 9 ml h$^{-1}$; fraction volume:
1.4 ml.

t-RNA. In that case treatment with SDS should not liberate $^{14}$C-
amino acids.

The radioactivity of batch 2 is due to free or associated $^{14}$C-
amino acids. The high content of free $^{14}$C-amino acids indicates
that although the tentacle tissue was carefully washed several
times before homogenization, the conditions for protein extraction were not satifactory; most $^{14}$C-amino acids seem to dissoci-
ate during the isolation process.

Control experiments –to test whether the $^{14}$C-amino acids are
specifically bound or loosely attached– with bovine serum albumine (BSA) show in the case of leucine, glutamic acid and lysine
that these amino acids are not co-precipitable with BSA; in contrast to tyrosine which is bound by BSA.


Gel electrophoresis. SDS-gel electrophoresis: The separation of
the proteins of batch 1 showed 6 distinct proteins. Their molecular weight ranged from 3o ooo – 8o ooo (monomers), as indicated
by the marker proteins. The disadvantage of SDS-gel electrophoresis was that it is impossible to correalate the radioactivity of

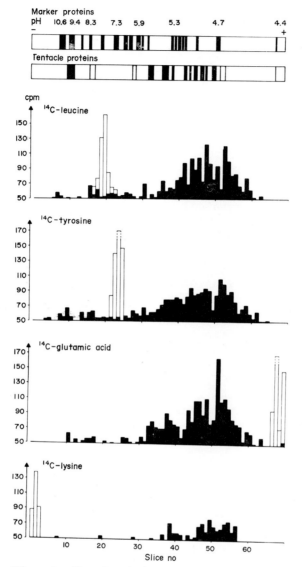

Fig. 4. Isoelectric focusing of protein
of batch 1, after concentrating it by
ultrafiltration; excluding molecules with
a molecular weight of larger than 500. Black
columns: Radioactivity in gels containing
[14]C-amino acids and proteins. White columns:
Radioactivity of free [14]C-amino acids after
isoelectric focusing under the same conditions.

the substrate with a specific protein in the gels, because SDS
treatment breaks up the substrate/protein complex.

Isoelectric focusing in polyacrylamid gels: The visible results
of the electrophoretic migration are 15 bands, 9 more compared
with SDS-gels. This does not imply that more distinct proteins
are detectable by this technique. Isoelectric focusing always
produce more protein bands (compare the "8" marker proteins).
The isoelectric points of the different proteins ranged from
pH 9.4 and 4.4. The great majority have IPs between pH 5.8 and
4.6.

Important results concerning the specific binding of $^{14}$C-amino
acids were expected from the determination and localization
of the radioactivity in gels by isoelectric focusing. In the
gels proteins were separated. Before separation the tentacle
tissue had been pulse labelled either with $^{14}$C-leucine, $^{14}$C-
tyrosine, $^{14}$C-glutamic acid or $^{14}$C-lysine.

As already discussed for SDS-gels, the amino acids are not
covalently bound. This seems to be the main reason why the
separation by isoelectric focusing does not yield satisfying
results (Fig. 4). During polymerisation and under the influence
of the electric field a large amount of $^{14}$C-amino acid/protein
complex probably dissociated thus liberating the $^{14}$C-amino acids
which then either contaminate the gels or migrate to their IP's.
Therefore the highly radioactive regions of the gels did not
exclusively contain the $^{14}$C-amino acid/protein complex. To
specify regions of $^{14}$C-amino acid/protein complexes, control
experiments with free $^{14}$C-amino acids were carried out (white
columns in Fig. 4). After substraction of the back ground
radioactivity, $^{14}$C-amino acids, bound to protein, were found to
band in a similar IP-region. The binding proteins for the amino
acids mentioned above have similar IP's, according to the separation method used.

The results of gel filtration and electrophoresis experiments
could also be discussed as follows: It is possible that not
the proteins which specifically bind amino acids were extracted
but also protein(s) which translocate the attached amino acids
across the membrane. The carrier protein could transport all
amino acids, independent of their charge or structure. Thus
the first step of the uptake, the attachment of amino acids
to specific receptors could go undetected in the experiments
dealt with so far.

Acknowledgements: The author is indepted to Miss H. Krisch for
skilful technical assistance. These investigations were supported
by the Deutsche Forschungsgemeinschaft.

## REFERENCES

(1) Schlichter, D., 1973. Ernährungsphysiologische und ökolo-
    gische Aspekte der Aufnahme in Meerwasser gelöster
    Aminosäuren durch Anemonia sulcata (Coelenterata,
    Anthozoa). Oecologia (Berlin) 11, 315-35o.

(2) Schaffner, W. & Weissmann C., 1973. A rapid, sensitive and
    specific method for the determination of protein in
    dilute solution. Analytical Biochemistry 56, 5o2-514.

(3) Brewer, J. M., Pesce, A. J. & Ashworth, R. B., 1977. Experi-
    mentelle Methoden in der Biochemie. 362 pp. G. Fischer
    Stuttgart, New York.

(4) Finlayson, G. R. & Chrambach, A., 1971. Isoelectric focusing
    in polyacrylamid gel and its preparative application.
    Analytical Biochemistry 4o, 291-311.

(5) Tishler, P. V. & Epstein, C. J., 1968. A convenient method
    of preparing polyacrylamid gels for liquid scintillation
    spectrometry. Analytical Biochemistry 22, 89-98

(6) Bamford, D. R. & Stewart, M., 1973. Absorption of neutral
    amino acids by the gut of Arenicola marina. Journal of
    Comparative Physiology 82, 291-3o4

(7) Siebers, D., 1976. Absorption of neutral and basic amino
    acids across the body surface of two annelid species.
    Helgoländer wissenschaftliche Meeresuntersuchungen 28,
    456-466.

(8) Pappas, P. W. & Read, C. P., 1975. Parasitological Review:
    Membrane transport in helminth parasites. Experimental
    Parasitology 37, 469-53o.

(9) Van Pilsum, J. F., Taylor, D. & Bans, L., 1975, Studies on
    the uptake of creatine from sea water by the marine
    annelid, Glycera dibranchiata. Comparative Biochemistry
    and Physiology 51 A, 611-617.

# THE UPTAKE AND UTILIZATION OF DISSOLVED AMINO ACIDS BY THE BIVALVE *MYA ARENARIA* (L.)

## Michael G. Stewart

*Department of Biology, The Open University, Milton Keynes, MK7 6AA, England*

ABSTRACT

Studies in vivo and in vitro were undertaken to investigate the uptake of dissolved amino acids by the bivalve Mya arenaria. Absorption occurs primarily via the ectodermal tissues, in particular the gills, and there is little loss of amino acid from the gills to the surrounding medium. The absorbed amino acid can be metabolized or incorporated into the animal. Evidence is presented for the presence of transport systems for neutral, basic and acidic amino acids on the gills and these have been characterized in terms of their transport constant (Kt) and the maximum velocity of uptake (Vmax). Although it appears that the animal has a capacity for amino acid uptake in excess of the normal environmental concentrations, the results of the present work demonstrate that in common with several other marine invertebrates, Mya has an ability for skin digestion, and it is suggested that this could provide an additional source of amino acids for absorption via the gill transport mechanisms.

INTRODUCTION

Since Stephens & Schinske (1961) reinvestigated Putter's theories (1909) on the utilization of dissolved organic matter (D.O.M.) by aquatic animals, a wealth of literature has appeared documenting the ubiquitous ability of soft-bodied marine invertebrates to absorb dissolved nutrients, primarily via their ectodermal tissues. Reviews by Stephens (1972), and Southward & Southward (1972) have emphasised the important supplemental role of this source of nutrition to many of these animals.

Bivalve molluscs, by virtue of the high rate of water flow through their mantle cavity, are an attractive group in which to study the uptake of D.O.M. and in the mussel Mytilus edulis (Pequignat, 1973) and in the estuarine clam Rangia cuneata (Anderson & Bedford, 1973) it has been shown that the gills are primarily responsible for the removal of amino acids from solution. For an accurate determination of the kinetic characteristics of amino acid absorption by bivalve gill tissue it is necessary to utilize an in vitro gill preparation, and this approach has been followed in the soft-shell clam Mya arenaria by Stewart & Bamford (1975), the Californian coastal mussel, Mytilus californianus by Wright et al. (1975) and in the horse mussel Modiolus modiolus by McCrea (1976). The present work reports the results of a more detailed investigation in vitro, but also in vivo, on the absorption and utilization of amino acids by Mya arenaria, and considers preliminary evidence that in this animal extracellular digestion within the mantle cavity could provide an additional source of nutrients for absorption via the carrier mediated processes on the gills.

### METHODS

Specimens of Mya arenaria, (25-110 mm shell length) were collected from the intertidal region of Belfast Lough and transferred to the marine aquarium of the Zoology Department. These were kept in tanks containing 20l of aerated sea water at a temperature of $10^{\circ}$C and salinity 34-36$^{\circ}$/oo. The water was changed daily and animals were allowed an acclimatization period of at least 48h before an experiment.

For experiments in vivo animals (2 per dish) of 25-35 mm shell length were placed in 750 ml of instant ocean (Griffin & George, Birmingham) of salinity 34$^{\circ}$/oo and pH 7.8, containing 0.01 mM L-phenylalanine labelled with $^{14}$C (0.01 μCi/ml) Antibiotics (streptomycin sulphate 1gm/l and penicillin G 200,000 units/l) were added to inhibit bacterial growth. At 10 min, 30 min, 60 min, 3h, 9.5h, 18h, 24, 3 days and 7 days after the start of the experiment animals were removed and the total $^{14}$C remaining in the instant ocean was measured. The animals were opened and divided into several tissue portions, gills, mantle, siphon, foot, adductor muscles, digestive glands and gonad (including the gut). The tissues were rinsed in sea water, were weighed, and placed in 5 volumes of 80% ethanol (EtOH) overnight to extract the tissue fluids, and a 0.5 ml sample of this was spread on planchettes and counted in a Nuclear Chicago gas flow counter for determination of the soluble $^{14}$C L-phenylalanine in the tissues. The tissues were dried to constant weight at $90^{\circ}$C and the dry weight obtained. To determine the amount of L-phenylalanine bound to the tissue the ethanol extracted tissue was digested in 30% KOH and the $^{14}$C present was counted.

Experiments in vitro were carried out on isolated gill tissue. Animals were taken from the tanks immediately before an experiment and the gills were excised and cut into segments approximately 10 mm x 10 mm. These were routinely preincubated for 30 min in artificial sea water (ASW). For each incubation two segments of gill were placed in 10 ml ASW in open flasks containing a known concentration of substrate labelled with $^{14}$C (0.01 - 0.04 μCi/ml). Incubation temperature was $10^{\circ}$C. The procedure for preparation of the gill segments, composition of the ASW medium, and weighing, sampling and counting procedures were similar to those reported in previous papers (Stewart & Bamford, 1975; Bamford & James, 1972). Uptake of amino acids into the tissues was expressed in μ moles/g EtOH dry wt/unit time) and the tissue fluid/ medium concentration ratios (C.R.) were also calculated for each experiment. Results are given $\pm$ standard error of the mean (S.E.M.).

In a number of experiments following incubation of gill tissue in L-phenyl-alanine, L-lysine and L-aspartate, the integrity of the absorbed amino acid was checked using ascending one- and two- dimensional paper chromatography as described previously (Stewart & Bamford, 1975).

Samples of sea and interstitial water were collected from the locality in which the clams were obtained and analysed for amino acid content on a Technicon Amino Acid autoanalyser. Details of this procedure have been given previously (Stewart, 1975).

Electrophoretic analysis was carried out on samples which were obtained from
mantle cavity fluid, and by wiping the surfaces of the branchial epithelium
(gills, siphon, mantle and foot) with a piece of Whatman No. 3 filter paper,
approximately 3 mm x 3 mm in size.  Mantle cavity fluid was collected by
tapping the shell and exposed mantle of the animals: this caused them to
expel mantle fluid via the siphon, or via the pedal gape.  When mantle fluid
and wipings of mantle epithelium were collected from animals on the shore, to
limit enzyme denaturation samples were placed in vials and frozen in vacuum
flasks containing solid $CO_2$.  Tissue extract samples (obtained from washed
and blotted tissue by extraction in an equal volume of phenoxyethanol –
phosphate – sucrose solution), together with the mantle fluid and branchial
epithelium wipes, were analysed by horizontal starch gel electrophoresis and
afterwards the gels were stained to show leucine aminopeptidase (LAP), non-
specific esterases (NSE) and acid phosphatase (AcP).  Details of electrophoretic and enzyme staining procedures have been given elsewhere (Stewart,
1975).

RESULTS

Absorption and Utilization of Amino Acid : in vivo studies

The data from experiments in which the absorption in vivo of 0.01 mM $^{14}C$
L-phenylalanine was examined are shown in Figs. 1 and 2, and Table 1.

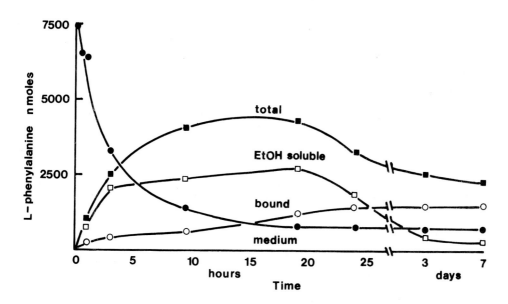

Fig. 1.    Incubation in vivo of Mya arenaria in instant ocean containing 0.01
mM L-phenylalanine, for various periods of time.  Each point is the mean of at
least 3 replicates.   (●) L-phenylalanine remaining in medium, (■) total uptake
per animal (EtOH soluble + bound), (□) total EtOH soluble L-phenylalanine
uptake, (O) total tissue bound L-phenylalanine,

In Fig. 1 it can be seen that the L-phenylalanine in the medium is rapidly
removed, until approximately 750 n moles remain after 18h.  This time
corresponds to that at which the maximum L-phenylalanine quantity - 4300 n
moles (EtOH soluble + bound) is found in the animals.  The amount in the
animals declines after this time falling to 2500 n moles after 7 days.  It
can be noted that while the EtOH soluble $^{14}$C L-phenylalanine initially forms
the larger portion of the total $^{14}$C found in the tissues, the bound portion
increases to become the major portion after 24h.  When the $^{14}$C L-phenylalanine
taken up by the animals at the various time intervals is added to that
measured remaining in the medium it is noted that a portion is unaccounted
for (Table 1) and since antibiotics were present, it must be assumed that
this represents the percentage metabolized by the animal and lost as $^{14}CO_2$.
This percentage increases from 22% in 3h to almost 60% of the total present
initially by the end of one week.

TABLE 1    In vivo incubation of Mya arenaria in 750 ml of instant
ocean containing 0.01 mM $^{14}$C L-phenylalanine for periods of up to
one week at a temperature of $10^{o}$C, showing the portion of amino
acid presumed metabolized by the animal.

| Time | 10min | 30min | 60min | 3h | 9.5h | 18h | 24h | 3days | 7days |
|------|-------|-------|-------|----|------|-----|-----|-------|-------|
| % missing presumed metabolized | – | – | – | 22 | 27 | 30 | 48 | 56 | 59 |

When the percentage of the $^{14}$C total taken up at time intervals 10 min, 60
min, 24h and 7 days, by the various tissue portions is shown (Fig. 2) it can
be seen that the major part of the $^{14}$C L-phenylalanine absorbed is found in
the ectodermal tissues which are normally in contact with the contents of the
mantle cavity particularly, in the earlier time intervals, in the gills.  At
these times the gonad tissue portion which includes the gut has relatively
little $^{14}$C material present.

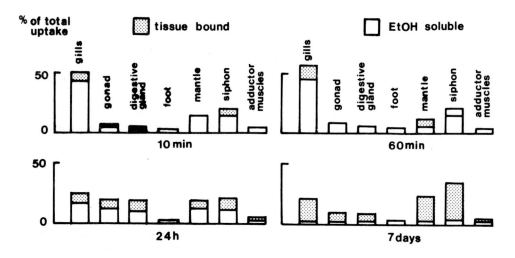

Fig. 2.    Percentage of total uptake in different tissue portions of Mya after
in vivo incubation in 0.01 mM L-phenylalanine for various periods of time.

These results demonstrate the ability of the clam to absorb and metabolize an amino acid and strongly suggest that this is mainly due to the involvement of the ectodermal tissues.


## In Vitro Studies

Absorption of amino acids against a chemical concentration difference. The viability of the isolated gill preparation of Mya arenaria was established earlier (Stewart & Bamford, 1975). In preliminary experiments the ability of gill segments to absorb the neutral amino acids L-phenylalanine and α-amino-isobutyrate (α-AIB), the basic amino acid L-lysine and the acidic amino acid L-aspartate, from low substrate concentrations, was measured in 30 min incubations. The results presented in Table 2 demonstrate an absorption of all four amino acids against a chemical concentration difference, and chromatographic analysis of the tissue extracts showed that of the absorbed amino acids, 84% of the L-phenylalanine, 89% of the L-lysine and 76% of the L-aspartate were located in positions on the chromatograms corresponding to the original $^{14}$C labels. These results argue strongly that an active transport mechanism exists for the absorption of neutral, basic and acidic amino acids in Mya gill.

TABLE 2   The absorption of α-AIB, L-phenylalanine, L-lysine or L-aspartate by gill segments in 30 min incubations at a temperature of $10^{\circ}$C. Each result is the mean of at least 4 replicates expressed $\pm$ S.E.M.

| Amino acid | Initial concn (mM) | C.R. | Uptake (μmoles/g EtOH dry wt) |
|---|---|---|---|
| α-AIB | 0.2 | 2.45 ± 0.32 | 5.10 ± 0.78 |
| L-phenylalanine | 0.2 | 4.81 ± 0.55 | 9.68 ± 0.86 |
| L-lysine | 0.2 | 2.38 ± 0.54 | 4.81 ± 0.33 |
| L-aspartate | 0.005 | 2.91 ± 0.10 | 0.07 ± 0.01 |

Net flux of amino acid in Mya gill tissue. Leakage, or efflux, of accumulated $^{14}$C labelled amino acid from gill tissue was measured following incubation of gill segments in 0.05 mM $^{14}$C α-AIB for 60 min, the results are shown in Table 3.

TABLE 3   Release of $^{14}$C α-AIB by Mya gill segments following 60 min incubation in 0.05 mM $^{14}$C α-AIB, and re-incubation in either ASW, or 5 mM α-AIB. Each result is the mean of 4 replicates expressed ± S.E.M.

| Re-incubation media | C.R. | Uptake (μ moles/ g/EtOH dry wt) | α-AIB appearing in medium as % of that taken up time (min) | | | |
|---|---|---|---|---|---|---|
| | | | 5 | 10 | 30 | 60 |
| None - control | 7.29 ± 0.29 | 3.43 ± 0.09 | – | – | – | – |
| ASW | 7.35 ± 0.35 | 3.14 ± 0.28 | 0.24 | 0.22 | 0.20 | 0.25 |
| 5 mM α-AIB | 9.18 ± 0.92 | 4.18 ± 0.51 | 0.33 | 0.28 | 0.60 | 0.24 |

These results clearly demonstrate that there is little leakage of accumulated amino acid to the ambient medium, and also that external amino acid concentration has little effect on efflux at the concentration tested since no increase in $^{14}$C α-AIB was recorded in the re-incubation medium when 5 mM α-AIB was present, a concentration much higher than that in the tissues (α-AIB is not found in the free amino acid pool of Mya, and the only α-AIB present in the tissues is that from the $^{14}$C labelled α-AIB absorbed in the initial 60 min incubation).

Kinetic studies. In order to determine the kinetic characteristics of trans-port of α-AIB, L-lysine and L-aspartate, uptake of these amino acids was measured as a function of concentration in 5 min incubations (concentration range 0.0025 to 0.1 mM for α-AIB and L-lysine, and 0.0005 to 0.1 mM for aspartate). The results shown in Fig. 3 indicate that all 3 amino acids are absorbed by mediated transport systems, absorption being essentially non-linear over the concentration range employed.

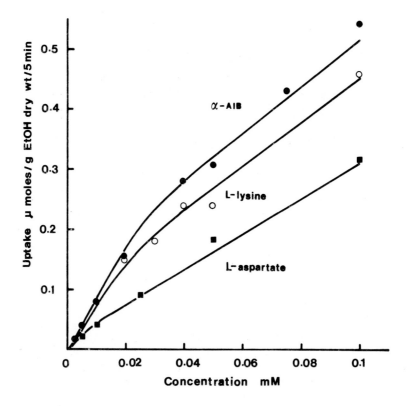

Fig. 3. Absorption of α-AIB (●), L-lysine (o), and L-aspartate (■) by gill segments as a function of the initial medium concentration. Each point is the mean of at least 6 determinations.

A linear transformation of the data on the curvilinear portion of each graph was effected by means of a Hofstee plot (Hofstee, 1960) in which V (the velocity of uptake) is plotted against V/S (S = substrate concentration). The Kt (transport constant) and Vmax values (max velocity of uptake) derived from these plots are shown in Table 4.

TABLE 4    Values of Kt and Vmax for α-AIB, L-lysine and L-aspartate absorption by Mya gill segments, obtained from Hofstee plots of the data in Fig. 3.

| Amino acid | Kt (mM) | Vmax (μ moles/g EtOH dry wt/5 min) |
|---|---|---|
| α-AIB | 0.122 | 1.085 |
| L-lysine | 0.040 | 0.456 |
| L-aspartate | 0.009 | 0.058 |

## Amino Acid Analysis of Sea and Intersitial Water

Sea water and intersitial water samples were collected in August (1974) and February (1975), and analysed for amino acid content. The results are presented in Table 5.

TABLE 5    Amino acid analysis of sea and interstitial water samples from Belfast Lough. The amino acid content is given in μ moles. The results are the average of duplicate amino acid determinations of two samples.

| Amino acid concentration μ moles | aspartate | threonine | serine | glutamic | glycine | alanine | valine | isoleucine | leucine | tyrosine | phenyl-alanine | Total μ moles |
|---|---|---|---|---|---|---|---|---|---|---|---|---|
| Sea water | 0.1 | 0.1 | 0.1 | + | 0.2 | 0.5 | + | + | + | + | + | 1.0 |
| Interstitial water | 0.2 | 0.2 | 0.2 | 0.1 | 0.2 | 0.8 | 0.2 | 0.1 | 0.2 | + | 0.1 | 2.3 |

Also present in trace amounts (+) in both sea water and interstitial water samples were cysteine, methionine, lysine, histidine, arginine and proline.

The quantities of amino acid present are very low and near the limit of resolution of the technique used to identify them: for the surface water sample a total of 1.0 μ moles were present and for the interstitial water sample the total was 2.3 μ moles. The amino acid present in highest concentration in each case was alanine. The amino acid levels measured in the sea water sample are within the range measured for the Irish Sea by Riley & Segar (1970).

## Starch-Gel Electrophoresis

Electrophoretic examination was made of samples of wipings of the gills, the mantle, foot, siphon, of mantle cavity fluid drained from the animals, and of tissue extracts from mantle and gill. A positive reaction was obtained for

LAP and NSE in all the samples, and mantle fluid and gill wipe samples gave a
weak positive reaction for AcP.  The experiment was repeated four times,
similar results being obtained in all cases.  The zymograms of all the sample
extracts (including the tissue extracts) contained 3 similar bands of LAP
activity and 2 similar bands of NSE activity.  Only one band appeared in the
sample containing AcP.  Electrophoretic analysis of sea water samples failed
to show any enzyme activity present.

In further experiments, to determine if enzyme activity in the mantle cavity
fluid increases with the length of time the shell is closed down, a comparison
was made of the LAP and NSE activity in samples of gill wipings and mantle
fluid collected from animals on the shore, from animals immediately on return
from the shore to the Zoology Department, and from animals kept in or out of
sea water tanks in the laboratory for various periods of time.  The enzyme
activity in these samples is shown in Table 6.

TABLE 6     Enzyme activity of tissue samples and mantle fluid taken
from animals on the shore or from animals maintained in the
laboratory in or out of water for various periods of time.  Enzyme
analysis as described in the methods section.  Key to enzyme
concentration:  ++ strongly present:  + present:  - absent.

| Sample | How collected | time animal out of water (h) | Gill wipe LAP | Gill wipe NSE | Mantle fluid LAP | Mantle fluid NSE |
|--------|---------------|------------------------------|------|-----|------|------|
| A | From animal on shore | 0 | ++ | + | + | +/- |
| B | From animal on return to laboratory from shore | 2 | ++ | ++ | ++ | + |
| C | As B | 18 | ++ | ++ | ++ | ++ |
| D | As B, but in tank in laboratory for 1 week | 0 | ++ | ++ | +/- | +/- |
| E | As D | 2 | ++ | ++ | ++/+ | + |

These preliminary results suggest that the enzyme activity in the mantle
fluid does increase with the length of time the animal is closed down, but
that the enzyme activity on the gill and mantle surfaces appears to remain
relatively constant.


DISCUSSION

The present series of experiments in vivo and in vitro demonstrate that Mya
arenaria has the ability to absorb amino acids, primarily via the well
developed carrier systems present on the gills.  This evidence supports the
findings of Stephens & Schniske (1961), Pequignat (1973) and Anderson &
Bedford (1973), that bivalves can take up amino acids directly from sea water.
Additionally the in vivo experiments showed that the animals appeared to have
the ability to metabolize L-phenylalanine, and also that they could incorporate
it, or a labelled metabolite, in their body tissues.

The experiments in which uptake by isolated gill tissue of examples of neutral (L-phenylalanine and α-AIB), basic (L-lysine) and acidic (L-aspartate) amino acids was examined, demonstrated the presence of an active process for the absorption of these three classes of amino acids, and the flux experiments with α-AIB showed that there is little loss of amino acid from the gills to the surrounding medium. That the uptake process was carrier mediated for α-AIB, L-lysine and L-aspartate was confirmed when the absorption of these substrates over a range of concentrations was shown to be non-linear and could be described in terms of Michaelis-Menten kinetics, with the parameters Kt (transport constant) and Vmax (maximum velocity of uptake) being determined for each amino acid. The Vmax of the three classes of amino acids showed marked differences, with that of the neutral > basic > acidic. These results are similar to those recorded in amino acid transport studies with the intestine of the lugworm Arenicola marina (Bamford & Stewart, 1973) and in the gut of the sea urchin Echinus esculentus (James, 1974).

In addition the findings that in Mya gill neutral, basic and acidic amino acids are actively absorbed is in agreement with the transport studies in lugworm intestine and sea urchin gut, and also in the tapeworm Hymenolepis diminuta (Read et al., 1963) and in mammalian intestine (Schultz et al., 1970). In all these cases the three classes of amino acids were actively absorbed by distinct carrier mediated process. Although the present report has not dealt with the interaction of the 3 classes of amino acids, it appears that 3 separate sites do exist for their absorption in Mya gill (Stewart, 1975).

A comparison of the Kt values for absorption of the neutral, basic and acidic amino acids by gill, with the amino acid concentrations measured in sea and interstitial water (Table 5) shows that the Kt values are of several orders of magnitude higher, even though the interstitial water samples were collected from the deposits in which Mya were buried. Since it might be expected that the Kt values for amino acid absorption by a marine organism would be related to the free amino acid concentrations in its normal environment (Stephens, 1972), these findings require explanation. It is known that the presence of an unstirred water layer at the mammalian intestinal mucosa can artificially increase Kt values (Wilson & Dietschy, 1974) and if this is present at the gill membrane, Kt values might be similarly elevated. However, in isolated gill tissue the beating of the cilia make this possibility unlikely.

Another explanation may be that in the present work no allowance has been made for the presence in the gills of an extracellular compartment, and in the isolated gill of the mussel Mytilus californianus Wright & Stephens (1977) have demonstrated that this can account for 66% of the total radio-activity present in the tissue 10 min after incubation in cycloleucine of concentration 5 mM. These two authors argue that if no correction was made for the extracellular space the rate of cycloleucine uptake by Mytilus would be overestimated by 350%. However in the present study only data from the lower portion of the V vs S graph (substrate concentration < 0.05 mM) were used in drawing the Hofstee plots from which the Kt and Vmax values for uptake of the amino acids were calculated, and the extracellular space makes relatively little contribution to uptake from these amino acid concentrations. It would therefore seem unreasonable to argue that the estimations of Kt and Vmax for amino acid uptake by Mya gill are inaccurate.

An alternative possibility is that an additional source of amino acids is made available to the gill carrier mechanisms by digestion of material within the mantle cavity. The presence of hydrolytic enzymes including α-amylase, chymotrypsin and trypsin has been demonstrated in the mantle cavity of _Mytilus edulis_ (Pequignat, 1973) and it is also known that the body surfaces of the sea stars _Asterias_ and _Henricia_ and the urchin _Echinocardium cordatum_ have a digestive capacity (Pequignat, 1972). Zottoli & Carriker (1974) have demonstrated the external release of proteases by stationary burrow dwelling polychaetes which keeps the burrow clear of fouling organisms, but which has been suggested to cause extra-organismic breakdown of proteins to amino acids, with subsequent absorption of the resultant amino acids through the skin. In the purple urchin _Paracentrotus lividus_ de Burgh (1975) has demonstrated that the spines have a digestive capacity, and McCrea (1976) has demonstrated the presence of α-amylase, leucine aminopeptidase, non-specific esterases, and acid and alkaline phosphatases in gill mucus and mantle fluid of _Modiolus modiolus_. In _Mya_ the presence of three enzymes or groups of enzymes, acid phosphatase, non-specific esterases and leucine aminopeptidase was demonstrated on the gill surfaces and the results of the experiments in which the animals were taken out of water closed down (with the mantle cavity sealed) for varying periods of time suggested that these could even be secreted to the mantle cavity fluid. No specific function is assigned to these enzymes in the present study, and the preliminary nature of this work precludes any serious estimation being made of the value of digestion within the mantle cavity of _Mya_. Nonetheless one might speculate that extra-alimentary extracellular digestion could be of importance to animals like _Mya_ living in areas rich in decaying organic matter, in providing a source of amino acids, additional to dissolved free amino acids, for absorption via the ectodermal carrier mediated processes.

While the work reported here clearly demonstrates the ability of _Mya_ both to absorb and utilize D.O.M., it is difficult to estimate the importance of this source of nutrients in the animals energy budget. A comparison of the quantity of the amino acid absorbed, with that necessary to support to the observed oxygen consumption, is of little value in animals like _Mya_ which spend much of their time in anaerobic environments and have been described as facultative anaerobes (Hochachka & Mustafa, 1973). In addition the actual amounts of nutrients absorbed may depend not only on the freely available D.O.M., but also on that which can be made available through skin digestion. Only when all these factors have been fully elucidated will it be possible to realistically assess the value of ectodermal nutrient absorption pathways to the nutrition of marine invertebrates.

## ACKNOWLEDGEMENTS

This work was carried out during the tenure of a post-graduate studentship in the Department of Zoology, Queens University, Belfast. Grateful thanks are expressed to Dr. D.R. Bamford for advice and constructive criticism and to Dr. A. Ferguson for advice on electrophoretic procedures.

## REFERENCES

Anderson, J.W., & Bedford, W.B., 1973. Physiological response of the estuarine clam _Rangia cuneata_ to salinity. _Biological Bulletin of the marine biological laboratory_, Woods Hole, 144 (2), 229-247.

Bamford, D.R., & James, D.W., 1972.  An in vitro study of amino acid and
  sugar absorption in the gut of Echinus esculentus.  Comparative Biochemistry
  and Physiology, 42A, 579-590.

Bamford, D.R., & Stewart, M.G., 1973.  Absorption of charged amino acids by
  the intestine of Arenicola marina.  Comparative Biochemistry and Physiology,
  46A, 537-547.

deBurgh, M.E., 1975.  Aspects of the absorption of dissolved nutrients by
  spines of Paracentrotus lividus (Lamarck).  Ph.D. Thesis, University of
  Dublin.

Hochachka, P.W. & Mustafa, T., 1973.  Enzymes in facultative anaerobiosis of
  molluscs. I - malic enzymes of oyster adductor muscle - Comparative
  Physiology and Biochemistry, 54B, 625-637.

Hofstee, B.H.J., 1960.  Non-logarithmic linear titration curves.  Science.
  N.Y. 131, 39.

James, D.W., 1974.  Amino acid absorption through the gut of the regular
  echinoid, Echinus esculentus L.  Ph.D. Thesis, The Queen's University of
  Belfast.

McCrea, S.R., 1976.  Comparative studies of amino acid absorption in bivalve
  gill in relation to environmental factors.  Ph.D. Thesis, The Queen's
  University of Belfast.

Pequignat, E., 1972.  Some new data on skin-digestion and absorption in
  urchins and sea starts (Asterias and Henricia), Marine Biology, 12, 28-41.

Pequignat, E., 1973.  A kinetic and autoradiographic study of the direct
  assimilation of amino acids and glucose by organs of the mussel Mytilus
  edulis.  Marine Biology, 19, 227-244.

Putter, A., 1909.  Die Ernahrung der Wassertiere and der Stoffhaushalt der
  Gewasser.  Fisher, Jena.

Read, C.P., Rothman, A.H., & Simmons, J.E. (Jnr.)., 1963).  Studies on
  membrane transport with special reference to parasite-host integration.
  Annals of the New York Academy of Science, 113, 154-205.

Riley, J.P., & Segar, D.A., 1970.  The seasonal variation of the free
  combined dissolved amino acids in the Irish sea.  Journal of the Marine
  Biological Association of the United Kingdom, 50, 713-720.

Schultz, S.G., Yu-Tu, L., Alvarez, O.U. & Curran, P.F., 1970.  Dicarboxylic
  amino acid influx across brush border of rabbit ileum.  The Journal of
  General Physiology, 56, 621-639.

Southward, A.J., & Southward, E.C., 1972.  Observations on the role of
  dissolved organic compounds in the nutrition of benthic invertebrates.
  III Uptake in relation to organic content of the habitat.  Sarsia, 50,
  29-46.

Stephens, G.C., & Schinske, R.A., 1961.  Uptake of amino acids by marine
  invertebrates.  Limnology and Oceanography, 6, 175-181.

Stephens, G.C. 1972.  Amino acid accumulation and assimilation in marine
   organisms.  in: Symposium on nitrogen metabolism and the environment.
   (Ed. J.W. Cambell and L. Goldstein), Academic Press, New York, 155-174.

Stewart, M.G., 1975.  Studies of amino acid absorption by tissues of the
   bivalve mollusc Mya arenaria.  Ph.D. Thesis, The Queen's University of
   Belfast.

Stewart, M.G., & Bamford, D.R. 1975.  Kinetics of alanine uptake by the
   gills of the soft shelled clam Mya arenaria.  Comparative Biochemistry and
   Physiology, 52A, 67-74.

Wilson, F.A., & Dietschy, J.M., 1974.  The intestinal unstirred layer:  its
   surface area and effect on active transport kinetics.  Biochemica et
   Biophysica Acta, 363, 112-126.

Wright, S.H., Johnson, T.L., & Crowe, J.H. 1975.  Transport of amino acids
   by isolated gills of the mussel, Mytilus californianus.  Journal of
   Experimental Biology, 62, 313-325.

Wright, S.H., & Stephens, G.C., 1977.  Characteristics of influx and net
   flux of amino acids in Mytilus californianus.  Biological Bulletin of
   the marine biological laboratory, Woods Hole, 152 (2), 295-310.

Zottoli, R.A., & Carriker, M.R., 1974.  External release of protease by
   stationary burrow-dwelling polychactes.  Journal of marine Research, 32,
   331-342.

# HEAVY METALS AND POLLUTION

# MECHANISMS OF IMMOBILIZATION AND DETOXICATION OF METALS IN MARINE ORGANISMS

**Thomas L. Coombs and Stephen G. George**

*Institute of Marine Biochemistry, Aberdeen, Scotland*

## ABSTRACT

Current concepts of metal metabolism have been reviewed with a view to understanding the factors that influence the uptake, storage and elimination of essential and pollutant trace metals in aquatic organisms.   Examples from our own studies on estuarine molluscs exposed to heavy metals have been used to illustrate these factors.   When metal uptake was combined with electron microscope studies, a novel storage and detoxication mechanism was revealed, where formation of vesicles within the cell enclose the metal within a membrane.   This prevents contact of excess metal with vital constituents and effectively detoxifies it until eliminated or passed on to other tissues, as required.   The generality of this mechanism has been established.

## INTRODUCTION

The hazards of heavy metal pollution in the aquatic environment have focussed attention on the presence of metals in marine and freshwater organisms.   While there is abundant chemical data, essential for monitoring changes in metal composition of key species, detailed knowledge of the metabolism of both essential and trace metals in aquatic organisms is sparse.   Understanding the factors that influence the uptake, storage and elimination of metals will be essential for developing predictive models, which will greatly assist in the structuring of realistic pollution control programmes.   In this paper we shall review the current concepts of metal metabolism and report on a novel mechanism for metal uptake and storage, which appears to have a widespread occurrence, illustrating the various aspects with examples from our own studies on estuarine shellfish.

## MODEL SYSTEMS

The basic step in any metal metabolic pathway, and the one where our knowledge is most lacking, is transport of the metal ion across a cellular or organelle membrane.   Some of the possible ways that this may be visualized are schematized in the Figure below.   These have been largely developed from extensive studies on the transport of $Na^+$, $K^+$ and other monovalent cations in association with osmoregulation and mitochondrial $H^+$ transport.   Figure I(a) illustrates the 'Pore' theory, where ions are transported down a potential gradient through the pore, whose geometry may confer some cation specificity. The second pathway involves a carrier, which complexes with some degree of specificity with a metal ion, neutralizing the charge on the ion and conferring hydrophobicity to the complex in order to allow penetration of the

179

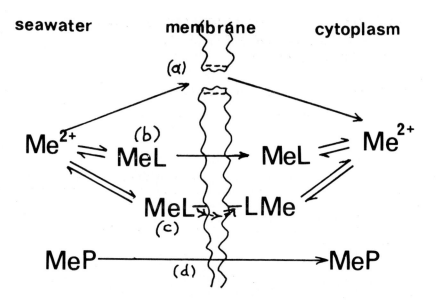

Fig. 1.   Mechanisms for metal ion transport across a
membrane
L represents a naturally occurring ligand and
P represents a pollutant with metal complexing
properties.

phospholipid membrane bilayer, Fig. I(b).    The cyclic ether ionophores are
good examples of these type of carriers (Ref. I).    The pathway of Fig. I(c),
may be considered as a more specialized case of carrier-mediated transport,
where the complexing ligand is attached to the membrane.    Complexation with
a suitable metal ion, induces a conformational change in the membrane which
allows the complex to flip-over into the cytoplasm.    The antibiotic
Gramicidin acts as a pore former, while the antibiotics Valinomycin and
Nonactin are carriers (Ref.I).    When other than monovalent cations are
considered, there is much less experimental data available and this relates
mainly to calcium and magnesium.

It can be seen that a pollutant metal can interfere with any of these
processes by competing with an essential metal and gain entry into the cell
for attack on vital intercellular systems.    Such competitive action at the
same time may induce a deficiency of the displaced functional metal ion.
This possibility will be missed, when pollution studies concentrate solely on
chemical analysis of the metal under consideration and neglects to measure
the other naturally occurring elements.    Organic pollutants, which possess
complexing groups can also affect metal ion transport by preferentially
complexing the metal and possibly altering its normal pathway, as illustrated
by Fig. I(d).    This in turn may result in either an excess or a deficiency
within the cell.    Experimental procedures need to be devised to examine all
of these aspects in aquatic systems.

## BIOLOGICAL EXAMPLES

Thus the chemical form of the metal presented to the cell, i.e. its biological availability, may have a profound effect on its transport.   It is generally agreed that metal ions in seawater are not present as free hydrated ions but are multi-complexed to inorganic and organic ligands, while the situation in freshwater is not as complex (Ref.2).    Changes in salinity will therefore have the potential to change metal uptake, as has been shown by ourselves and many others (Refs.3,4).    Naturally occurring or synthetic complexing agents also can modify metal uptake.   As an example of this the uptake of lead by *Mytilus edulis* [L.] has been followed (Ref.5).    The lead at 0.Ippm in seawater was added as nitrate or was firstly complexed with citrate, humic and alginic acids or pectin.   The uptake curves are illustrated in Fig. 2.    For lead as nitrate, all of the tissues have absorbed the metal, with the highest concentration being found in the kidney (300 µg/g dry wt. tissue).    When the lead was complexed with citrate a 3-4 fold increase in both the rate of

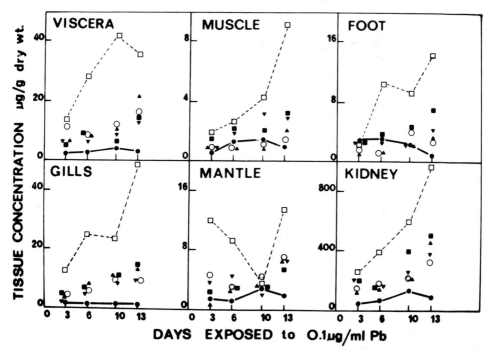

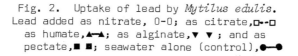

Fig. 2.   Uptake of lead by *Mytilus edulis*.
Lead added as nitrate, O-O; as citrate,□--□
as humate,▲—▲; as alginate,▼ ▼ ; and as
pectate,■ ■; seawater alone (control),●—●

accumulation and the final tissue concentrations is seen.   The high molecular weight complexes humic and alginic acids and pectin however, are not as effective and produce at best a I.5-2 fold increase.

Thus complexation of the lead can significantly increase the absorption without changing the tissue distribution. We have found a different situation for the uptake of cadmium and iron by *Mytilus*. For cadmium both low and high molecular weight complexes gave an equal increase in the rate of absorption (Ref. 6). For iron, depending on the type of complex used, either an increase or a decrease was obtained and changes in the tissue distributions were observed (Ref. 7). Our experiments with cadmium uptake by *Mytilus* gills *in vitro* gave results that are in accord with a process of facilitated diffusion (Scheme I(b), i.e. carrier assisted (Ref. 8). Whether the carrier is a metallothionien-like polypeptide secreted from the cell, as occurs with citrate or the ferrichromes in plant cell exudates, is a question that awaits further investigation.

## FINE STRUCTURE STUDIES: *MYTILUS*

Electron microscopic investigation of tissues can assist in delineating uptake mechanisms. We have applied this technique to the uptake of lead and iron by *Mytilus*. These fine structure studies were combined with X-ray microprobe analysis for the *in situ* identification of metals at the subcellular level and revealed the presence of small electron-dense granular particles within membrane-bound vesicles, suggestive of concentrated metal, in cells of gills, viscera and kidney. The analyses confirmed the presence of lead and iron within these vesicles and examples are shown in the electron micrographs in Fig. 3. (Refs. 5,9). The metal, which in the case of iron is normally present as particulate hydrated ferric oxide, is taken up by a process of endocytosis i.e. engulfment of the metal by the epithelial cell membrane, which then pinches off to form the membrane-bound vesicle inside the cell. With the help of $^{59}$Fe pulse labelling, we have deduced that after endocytosis the vesicle, after fusing with a lysosome in some cases, migrates to the basal end of the cell and is then excreted by a reverse process of exocytosis into the circulating fluid. Here in turn the metal is reabsorbed by the circulating amoebocytes by a similar endocytosis for subsequent transfer to the kidney and other tissues for storage and eventual excretion (Ref.9). By this means *Mytilus* can tolerate the extremely high concentrations of lead and iron within the tissues, isolating the potentially toxic metal within a membrane, thereby immobilizing and detoxifying it. Such a mechanism for metal ion transport represents a new system differing from any of those described earlier.

## FINE STRUCTURE STUDIES: *OSTREA*

We have also investigated the mechanisms for the detoxication of zinc and copper in *Ostrea edulis L.* (Ref.10). 'Green Sick' oysters from Cornwall with elevated zinc and copper concentrations in their tissues were used. The combined electron microscope and microprobe studies revealed structural compartmentation of the zinc and copper in separate, distinct granular amoebocytes Fig.3. The metals are immobilized as with *Mytilus* in membrane limited vesicles within the amoebocytes, but each metal is associated with a different chemical compound, zinc with phosphorus and copper with sulphur. In *Ostrea* these vesicles are *not* found in the tissue cells but only in the amoebocytes, which can penetrate all of the tissues and are found mostly in the mantle and gills. In *Mytilus*, however, vesicles containing iron, lead and zinc are found in specific tissue cells, principally in the kidney as well as in amoebocytes.

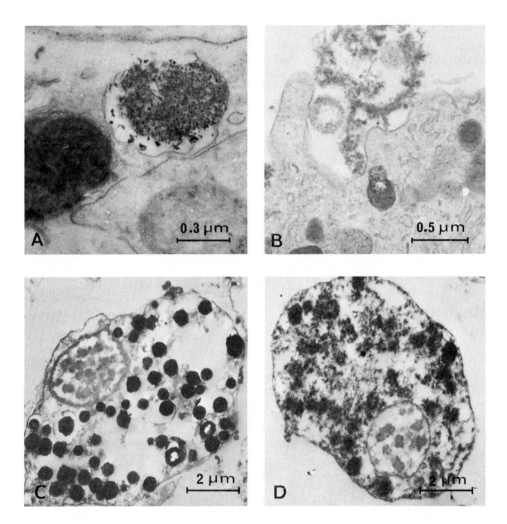

Fig. 3.  Electron micrographs of *Mytilus edulis* and *Ostrea edulis*
tissues exposed to heavy metals showing metal containing
vesicles.  (A) lead in *Mytilus* kidney; (B) *Mytilus* amoebocyte
endocytosing particles of ferritin, an iron containing protein.
(C) zinc containing vesicles in amoebocyte in *Ostrea* mantle.
(D) copper containing vesicles in amoebocyte in *Ostrea* mantle.

## GENERALITY OF METAL STORAGE IN VESICLES OR GRANULES

Stimulated by these findings, a search for other examples was carried out and
has been proved to be most successful.  For example, storage of copper and
iron by a copper tolerant species of the freshwater isopod, *Asellus meridianus*
occurs in the hepatopancreas in two types of vesicle.  One type contains zinc
only in a granular form and the second contains copper only in a smooth
unstructured form. The copper is also associated with sulphur within the
vesicle (Ref.11).  Zinc and copper granules are also found in the viscera of
the barnacle, *Balanus balonoides*, (Ref.12), and calcium is stored in a
granular form in a host of organisms both terrestrial and aquatic (Ref.13).
An extensive list has now been compiled, which contains examples from many
phyla.  This is presented in Table I.  While not claiming to be
comprehensive, the list does contain a wide spectrum of species ranging from
protozoa to man and indicates that this mechanism is indeed a general
phenomenum for polyvalent cation transport.  There are exceptions however, for
in our studies on cadmium uptake in *Mytilus* and *Ostrea*, we have been unable so
far to detect any localized storage of this metal in vesicles.  Instead there
appears to be a more generalized spread throughout the cytoplasm.
Detoxication and storage in this case is by complexation to thionein in the
cytoplasm and could represent a different immobilization mechanism.

The dominance of calcium in Table I suggests that the other metals may be
sharing a common metabolic pathway that was originally evolved for the control
of excess calcium associated with shell formation, muscle contraction, nerve
stimulation, mitochondrial function and exocrine secretion (Ref.14).  If this
is the case then metal pollutants could exert their sublethal effects at any
of these loci.  In support of this hypothesis there is the well established
competitive action between calcium and heavy metals shown in freshwater
toxicity studies, in metal uptake studies in plants grown in metal contaminated
soils and in induced metal deficiency studies in animals (Ref.15).  Organic
compounds that interfere with this type of endocytosis by reaction with the
membrane system will also represent another type of pollutant requiring
further studies.

Some knowledge of the chemical form in which the metals are stored inside the
vesicle is available.  It has been shown that calcium is associated with
carbonate and phosphate (Ref.15), zinc with phosphorous, copper with sulphur
and vanadium with sulphuric acid (Refs.11,12,16).  Whether the metals are
associated with simple inorganic anions or more complex organic molecules is
not known.  Since active concentration processes normally use energy from
ATP,it is a simple hypothesis to suggest that the phosphorous that is found
inside the vesicles may have originated from ATP.  Whether an ATP-metal
complex is directly associated with an endocytosis mechanism is not known,
although ATP-metal complexes have been demonstrated to have a high stability
(Ref.17).  Experiments designed to isolate intact metal containing vesicles
may give answers to some if not all of the questions posed above.

## ACKNOWLEDGEMENTS

We gratefully acknowledge the technical assistance of Mr.B.J.S. Pirie and Mrs.
A. Cheyne and the continuing advice and support of the Director of The
Institute of Marine Biochemistry, Dr P.T. Grant.  Part of the studies reported
above have been supported under Contract No. 086/087-74-7-ENX U.K. of the
EEC. Environmental Research Programme.

TABLE I   Occurence of Metals in Granules or Vesicles

| PHYLUM | ORDER | SPECIES | TISSUE | METAL | REF. |
|---|---|---|---|---|---|
| PROTOZOA | Gymnosomatida | Proroden | - | Ca | 13 |
| COELENTERATA | Scleractinia | Renilla | scleroblasts | Ca | 13 |
|  | Semaeostomae | Aurelia | statoliths | Ca | 13 |
| PLATYHELMINTHS | Cyclophyllidea | Taenia | - | Ca | 13 |
| ANNELIDA | Polychaeta | Nereis | epidermis nephridia | Cu,Pb | 4 |
| MOLLUSCA | Pulmonata | Helix | hepatopancreas | Ca,Zn,Cu | 13 |
|  |  | Biomphalaria | leuocytes | Cu | 4 |
|  | Gastropoda | Littorina | hepatopancreas | Ca | 13 |
|  | Bivalvia | Anodonta | hepatopancreas mantle,kidney | Ca,Mn,Zn | 18 |
|  |  | Mytilus | gills, gut, kidney | Fe,Pb,Zn | 5,9 |
|  |  | Pecten | kidney, gut | Cu,Zn,Mn | 4 |
|  |  | Mercenaria | gills, kidney, gut, mantle | Fe | 26 |
|  |  | Macrocallista | mantle | Au | 4 |
|  |  | Ostrea | amoebocytes | Zn,Cu | 10 |
| ARTHROPODA | Cirripedia | Balanus | hepatopancreas | Zn,Cu | 12 |
|  | Lepidoptera | Bombyx | mid-gut | Ca | 13 |
|  | Ensifera | Gryllus | malphigian tubule | Ca | 13 |
|  | Isopoda | Asellus | hepatopancreas | Zn,Cu,Pb | 11 |
|  |  | Ligia | hepatopancreas | Cu,Zn | 19 |
|  |  | Sphaeroma | hepatopancreas | Cu | 19 |
|  | Decapoda | Calinectes | hepatopancreas | Cu,Ca | 15 |
|  |  | Procambarus | hepatopancreas | Cu,Fe | 4 |
|  |  | Crangon | hepatopancreas | Cu | 4 |
| CHORDATA | Ascidiacea | Ciona | vanadocytes | V | 16 |
|  | Anacanthini | Gadus | pancreas | Zn | 20 |
|  | Heterosomata | Pleuronectes | pancreas | Zn | 20 |
|  | Cyclostomata | Myxini | pancreas | Zn | 20 |
|  | Primates | Homo sapiens | pancreas,liver | Zn,Cu,Ca | 20,21 |
|  | Rodentia | Rattus | liver,kidney | Ca,Pb,Hg | 14,22,27 |
| PLANTA |  | Zea mays | - | Pb | 23 |
|  |  | Nymphaea | - | Ca | 24 |
|  | Alga | Stigeoclonium | - | Pb | 25 |

REFERENCES

(1)  Chance, B. & Montal, M., 1971.  Ion-translocation in energy conserving
     membrane systems.  In Current Topics in Membrane and Transport (Eds.
     F. Bronner and A.Kleinzeller), Vol. 2 pp 99-156, New York, Academic
     Press.
(2)  Millero, F.J., 1975.  The physical chemistry of estuaries.  In Marine
     Chemistry of the Coastal Environment. (Ed. T. Church), pp 25-55,
     Washington, D.C., American Chemical Society Advanced Chemical Series.
(3)  George, S.G., Carpene, E. & Coombs, T.L., 1977.  Effect of salinity on
     the uptake of cadmium by the common mussel.  Proc. 12th Eur. mar. biol.
     Symp.
(4)  Bryan, G.W., 1976.  Some aspects of heavy metal tolerance in aquatic
     organisms.  In Effects of Pollutants on Aquatic Organisms. (Ed. A.P.M.
     Lockwood), pp 7-34, Cambridge, Cambridge University Press.
(5)  Coombs, T.L., 1977.  Uptake and storage mechanisms in marine organisms.
     Proc. Analy. Div. Chem. Soc., 14, 218-221.
(6)  George, S.G. & Coombs, T.L., 1977.  The effect of chelating agents on the
     uptake and accumulation of cadmium by *Mytilus edulis*.  Marine Biology,
     39, 261-268.
(7)  George, S.G. & Coombs, T.L., 1977.  Effects of high stability iron
     complexes on the kinetics of iron accumulation and excretion in
     *Mytilus edulis (L.)*.  J. exp. mar. Biol. Ecol., 28,      (in the press).
(8)  George, S.G. & Carpene, E.,  Unpublished results in preparation.
(9)  George, S.G., Pirie, B.J.S. & Coombs, T.L., 1976.  The kinetics of
     accumulation and excretion of ferric hydroxide in *Mytilus edulis (L.)*.
     and its distribution in the tissues.  J. exp. mar. Biol. Ecol., 23,
     71-84.
(10) George, S.G. & Coombs, T.L., 1977.  Detoxication of metals by marine
     bivalves:  an ultrastructural study of the compartmentation of copper
     and zinc in the oyster, *Ostrea edulis (L.)*.  Marine Biology, (in the
     press).
(11) Brown, B., Zoology Department, Newcastle-on-Tyne University.  Personal
     communication.
(12) Walker, G., 1977.  "Copper" granules in the barnacle, *Balanus balanoides*.
     Marine Biology, 39, 343-349.
(13) Simkiss, K., 1976.  Intracellular and extracellular routes in
     biomineralization.  In Calcium in Biological Systems. (Ed. J.C.
     Duncan), pp 423-444.  Cambridge, Cambridge University Press.
(14) Carafoli, E., Clementi, F., Drabikowski, W. & Margreth, A. 1975.
     Calcium Transport in Contraction and Secretion.  588 pp. New York,
     Elsevier.
(15) Coombs, T.L., 1972.  The distribution of zinc in the oyster, *Ostrea
     edulis*, and its relation to enzymic activity and to other metals.
     Marine Biology, 12,  170-178.
(16) Carlisle, D.B., 1968.  Vanadium and other metals in ascidians.  Proc.
     Royal Soc. London,  B171, 31-42.
(17) Coombs, T.L., 1974.  The nature of the zinc and copper complexes in the
     oyster, *Ostrea edulis*.  Marine Biology,  28, 1-10.
(18) Harrison, F.L., 1969.  Accumulation and distribution of $^{54}$Mn and $^{65}$Zn in
     freshwater clams.  In Radioecology, (Eds. D.J. Nelson & F.C. Evans).
     Proceedings of the Second National Symposium, USAEC-CONF-670503.,
     pp 198-200.  Springfield, Virginia, U.S. Commerce Department.

(19) Wieser, W., 1968.  Aspects of nutrition and the metabolism of copper in isopods.  American Zoologist,  8, 495-506.

(20) Grant, P.T. & Coombs, T.L., 1970.  Proinsulin, a biosynthetic precursor of insulin.  Essays in Biochemistry,  6, 69-92.

(21) Goldfischer, S., 1965.  The localization of copper in the pericanalicular granules (lysosomes) of liver in Wilson's disease (hepatolenticular degeneration).  Amer. J. Path., 46, 977-984.

(22) Fowler, B., Brown, H.W., Lucier, G.W. & Beard, M.E., 1974.  Mercury uptake by renal lysosomes of rats ingesting methyl mercury hydroxide. Arch. Path., 98, 297-301.

(23) Malone, C., Koeppe, D.E. & Miller, R.J., 1974.  Localization of lead accumulated by corn plants.  Plant Phys., 53, 388-394.

(24) Arnott, H.J. & Pautard, F.G.E., 1970.  Calcification in plants.  In Biological Calcification.  (Ed. H. Schraer), pp 375-446.  Amsterdam, North Holland.

(25) Silverberg, B.A., 1975.  Ultrastructural localization of lead in Stigeoclonium tenue.  Phycologia,  14, 265-274.

(26) Fowler, B.A., Wolfe, D.A. & Hettler, W.F., 1975.  Mercury and iron uptake in mantle epithelial cells of Quahog clams (Mercenaria mercenaria) exposed to mercury.  J. Fish. Res. Bd. Canada,  32, 1767-1775.

(27) Walton, J.R., 1973.  Granules containing lead in isolated mitochondria. Nature London, 243, 100-101.

# THE EFFECT OF SALINITY ON THE UPTAKE
# OF CADMIUM BY THE COMMON MUSSEL,
# *MYTILUS EDULIS* (L.)

## Stephen G. George, Emilio Carpene* and Thomas L. Coombs

*Institute of Marine Biochemistry, St. Fittick's Road, Aberdeen, Scotland*

## ABSTRACT

The effect of salinity and osmolarity on cadmium uptake by *Mytilus edulis* (L.)
has been studied.    Cadmium accumulation *in vivo* and influx *in vitro* is
increased by dilution of sea water or decreased osmolarity.   The influx is
dependent upon the osmolarity and the relationship between cation uptake and
cellular volume may be similar to the phenomenon observed in mitochondria.

## INTRODUCTION

Many marine invertebrates, including the common mussel, *Mytilus edulis*,
accumulate heavy metals such as Cd, Cu, Zn and Pb and can tolerate very high
tissue levels without apparent signs of toxicity.   Although the concentrations
of these heavy metals are low in most waters, run off from metalliferous rocks
and human activity can cause locally high concentrations.   The occurrence of
high metal concentrations in animals from these areas has been the subject of
numerous surveys (see eg. Refs. 1,2).

Cadmium is one of the more toxic heavy metals to man and its accumulation
from sea water by the common mussel has been measured in a number of studies
(Refs. 3,4,5,6).   The effects of various environmental factors on the net
accumulation have been studied, largely to establish the validity of the
mussel as an indicator of pollution and therefore these studies represent
observations and have not established the mechanism of cadmium absorption.
These studies include the effects of temperature (Refs. 3,5), addition of
zinc (Refs. 3,4,5) lead and copper (Ref.4), the presence of organic metal
chelating agents (Ref.6) and salinity (Refs. 4,5).

Recent experiments carried out in this laboratory have established a possible
mechanism for cadmium absorption (George and Carpene, in preparation) and in
the present paper the effects of altered salinity on the uptake of cadmium by
the mussel have been studied.

## METHODS AND MATERIALS

Mature specimens of *Mytilus edulis* were collected from Montrose Basin,
Kincardineshire.   The mussels were maintained in a sea water aquarium at
$10^{0}$C (salinity 33 ‰) and allowed to acclimate for at least 10 days before

---

* present address, Institute Biochem. F.M.Vet., Bologna, Italy.

189

an experiment.   Cadmium solutions were prepared in 0.45$\mu$m Millipore[R]-filtered sea water from $^{109}CdCl_2$ (Radiochemical Centre Ltd., Amersham, Bucks, England) and unlabelled carrier.

*In vivo* accumulation experiments were carried out with batches of 15 mussels maintained in polythene tanks containing 2l. of aerated,filtered sea water with 100$\mu$g/l. cadmium chloride at different salinities.   Reduction of salinity was obtained by dilution with distilled water.   At intervals of three days, faeces were removed, the water was changed and three animals were removed for analysis.   The soft tissues were removed, blotted and dry weights obtained by air drying for three days at 95$^{o}$C in tared glass counting vials. Radioactive cadmium was measured with a Packard Model 5210 crystal scintillation counter, the counts being corrected for background and radioactive decay.

*In vitro* uptake experiments were carried out using isolated gills.   The shell valves were prised apart and the adductor mussels severed.   Each gill segment consisting of two lamellae, joined at the top by mantle tissue, from three animals, was transferred to flasks containing 10ml filtered sea water and radioactively labelled $CdCl_2$ (0.1$\mu$g/ml) at 15$^{o}$C, under an atmosphere of oxygen. Gill tissue was either removed immediately for controls, or after 6 min. incubation in a shaking water bath, blotted by a standardised procedure, weighed to obtain the wet tissue weight and then the radioactive cadmium was measured.   Cadmium uptake by the incubated tissues was corrected by subtraction of the control values.   The salinity of the incubation medium was reduced by dilution and in certain experiments the osmolarity was adjusted by addition of varying amounts of sucrose.   Osmolarities were measured with an Advance Model 3D freezing point depression osmometer.

### RESULTS

### Effect of Salinity on Cadmium Accumulation *in vivo*.

Accumulation of cadmium by mussels exposed to 0.1$\mu$g/ml $CdCl_2$ in sea water of different salinities was followed over 15 days and the results are plotted in Fig. 1.

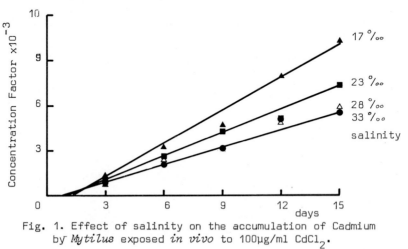

Fig. 1. Effect of salinity on the accumulation of Cadmium by *Mytilus* exposed *in vivo* to 100$\mu$g/ml $CdCl_2$.

In all experiments uptake in the total soft tissues is approximately linear
with time.   Higher cadmium concentrations are found at lower salinities.
Analysis of variance shows that there is no significant difference between
regression lines for 28 ‰ and 33 ‰ S and those for 23 ‰ and 17 ‰S are
significantly different.   In 50% sea water (s.w.) the rate of accumulation
is approximately 2-fold greater than in 100% s.w.   Mussels either non-
acclimated or acclimated to 17 ‰ S for 10 days before the experiment did not
show any significant difference in their accumulation of cadmium when
maintained in 17 ‰ S s.w.

## Effect of Salinity on Cadmium Uptake by Mussel Gills *in vitro*.

Uptake of cadmium by isolated gills incubated in media of different salinities
containing 0.1µg/ml $CdCl_2$ was measured and the results are plotted in Fig. 2.

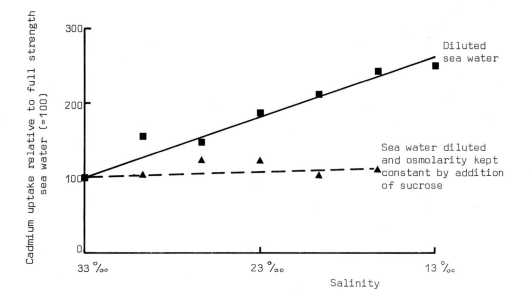

Fig. 2.   Effect of salinity on Cadmium uptake by isolated
*Mytilus* gills incubated *in vitro* with 0.1µg/ml $CdCl_2$.

The uptake of cadmium is greater at lower salinities, the uptake in 60% s.w.
being about 2-fold greater than in 100% s.w.   The increased uptake represents
an increase in the rate of cadmium uptake and not necessarily in the final
steady state concentration of cadmium since the incubation time was short and
steady state conditions are not attained until 30-60min. incubation.   The 100%
s.w. used in these experiments has an osmolarity of 1010 mOsm.   The uptake of
cadmium by gills incubated in media with reduced salinities to which sucrose
was added to maintain the osmolarity at 1010 mOsm was measured and the results
are also plotted in Fig. 2.   There is no increase in the uptake of cadmium in
a reduced salinity medium under these conditions.   Table 1 shows the results
of an experiment in which the salinity was kept constant at 8 ‰ S and the
osmolarity was increased by addition of sucrose.

TABLE 1.   Effect of varying Osmolarity on Cadmium uptake *in vitro*.

| Osmolarity, mOsm. | 250 | 625 | 900 | 1010 | 1430 | 1650 |
|---|---|---|---|---|---|---|
| Cadmium uptake, µg/g wet wt. tissue. | 0.27 | 0.2 | 0.14 | 0.13 | 0.12 | 0.115 |

Gills were incubated in media containing 0.1µg/ml Cd for 6min. at 15$^{o}$C and cadmium uptake measured.

As the osmolarity is increased the uptake of cadmium by the gills decreases until the osmolarity of 100% s.w. (1010 mOsm) is reached when a further increase in osmolarity of the medium has no effect.

## DISCUSSION

Previous studies have indicated that environmental variables may affect the rates of heavy metal uptake in marine bivalve shellfish (Refs. 3,4,5). In the present study we have investigated more fully the effects of one variable, salinity, on the uptake of cadmium by the common mussel, *Mytilus edulis*.

An alteration in the salinity of the surrounding sea water has several physiological effects on euryhaline organisms, such as the mussel, which may affect the net uptake of metal ions.   *Mytilus* responds to a rapid decrease in salinity by closing its shell valves at about 50% s.w. However, if a low salinity is maintained, then the animal has to open them again to feed and respire aerobically.   It has been reported that the filtration rate is decreased at low salinities (Ref. 7) and therefore there will be less metal accumulated from particulates or in food and uptake from solution may be decreased if water filtration is limiting.   It has been shown experimentally in another marine bivalve, the oyster, that cadmium is mainly absorbed from solution and that only 10% could come from food present in the same water (Ref. 8).   The mussel regulates the ionic composition of its blood and in a dilute sea water environment it is isosmotic (Ref. 9).   Regulation is fairly rapid and takes about 4hr. to come to equilibrium when the animal is placed in 50% s.w. and about 4 days if the valves are propped open in 25% s.w.   In dilute sea water, water is taken up osmotically and the tissue water content increases.   However, the tissues do not behave as simple osmometers since the theoretical changes in ionic concentrations are not attained.

In agreement with the previous reports (Refs. 4,5) we have shown that mussels *in vivo* accumulate more cadmium in dilute sea water than in 100% s.w. Accumulation is linear with time under all salinity regimes studied (50% to 100% s.w.), thus demonstrating that it is an alteration in rate and not capacity of the system.   In another *in vitro* study we have evidence that uptake of cadmium by gills is by facilitated diffusion, that there is no free cadmium within the cell and it is complexed to a high molecular weight compound (George & Carpene, in prep.).   Uptake appears to be a passive process in that the rate is unaffected by addition of metabolic inhibitors.   Under the experimental conditions used in these *in vitro* experiments, we are studying the cadmium influx since the metal is firmly bound within the cell to a high molecular weight compound.   Using the same system to study the effects of salinity on the rate of cadmium uptake by gills we have shown that the rate increases with a decrease in salinity in the same manner as *in vivo*.   The experiments also show that this increase is due to the effect of osmolarity of the surrounding medium.   If the osmolarity is kept constant by the addition of sucrose and the salinity varied, the cadmium flux is unaltered.    If the salinity is kept constant and the osmolarity is varied, then the cadmium flux is altered.   However, there does not appear to be a direct proportionality between cadmium uptake and osmolarity and a further increase in osmolarity above 100% s.w. does not decrease the rate of cadmium uptake.   A similar situation is found in mitochondria which swell osmotically during the active uptake of $K^+$ and $Ca^{2+}$ ions (Ref.10) and therefore ionic concentration and volume are related.  Again the situation in mitochondria is complex and they do not behave as simple osmometers.  Since cadmium transport in *Mytilus* gill epithelium appears to occur by facilitated diffusion, the observed osmotic effects may be due to the increased ion fluxes or a physical effect of swelling of the cell membrane causing unmasking of a carrier or trans-membrane pore.  Further detailed experiments are required to fully elucidate the exact mechanism of these effects.

ACKNOWLEDGEMENT

We acknowledge the continued interest and help of Dr. P.T. Grant, the Director, Institute of Marine Biochemistry.

REFERENCES

(1)  Mullin,J.B. & Riley,J.P., 1956.  The occurrence of cadmium in sea water
     and in marine organisms and sediments.  J. mar. Res. 15, 103-114.
(2)  Peden,J.D.,Crothers,J.M., Waterfall,C.E. & Beasley, J.1973.  Heavy metals
     in Somerset marine organisms.  Mar. Pollut. Bull. 4, 7-9.
(3)  Fowler,S.W. & Benayoun, G. 1974.  Experimental studies on cadmium flux
     through marine biota.  Comparative studies of food and environmental
     contamination.  159-178. Vienna: International Atomic Energy Agency.
(4)  Philips,D.J.H.  1976.  The common mussel *Mytilus edulis* as an indicator
     of pollution by zinc, cadmium, lead and copper.1.Effects of
     environmental variables on uptake of metals.  Mar. Biol. 38, 59-69.
(5)  Jackim,E., Morrison,G. & Steele,R. 1977.  Effects of environmental
     factors on radiocadmium uptake by four species of marine bivalves.
     Mar.Biol. 40, 303-308.
(6)  George, S.G. & Coombs,T.L. 1977.  The effects of chelating agents on the
     uptake and accumulation of cadmium by *Mytilus edulis*.  Mar.Biol.  39,
     261-268.
(7)  Bøhle,B. 1972.  Effects of adaptation to reduced salinity of filtration
     activity and growth of mussels (*Mytilus edulis* L.)  J. exp.mar.Biol.
     Ecol. 10, 41-47.
(8)  Kerfoot,W.B. & Jacobs,S.A. 1974.  Cadmium accrual in a combined waste-
     water treatment-aquaculture system.  Proc. 1st. annual NSF trace
     contaminants conference. ed. Fulkerson.  Oak-Ridge National
     Laboratories, ORNL-NSF-EATC5, Oak Ridge, Tenn.
(9)  Robinson,J.D. 1964.  Osmotic and ionic regulation.  Physiology of the
     Mollusca. ed. Wilbur & Yonge.  Academic Press, New York.

# RESPONSE OF EMBRYOS OF THE AMERICAN OYSTER, *CRASSOSTREA VIRGINICA*, TO HEAVY METALS AT DIFFERENT TEMPERATURES

## John R. MacInnes and Anthony Calabrese

*National Marine Fisheries Service, Northeast Fisheries Center, Milford Laboratory, Milford, Connecticut, U.S.A.*

## ABSTRACT

The acute toxicity of four heavy metals (copper, mercury, silver, and zinc) added individually to embryos of the American oyster, Crassostrea virginica, in natural seawater was studied at 20, 25, and 30°C. The toxicity of copper-zinc and mercury-silver mixtures to oyster embryos at the above temperatures was also determined. All of these metals, added either individually or in combination, were less toxic at 25°C than at either 20 or 30°C, suggesting that oyster embryos are more susceptible to metal toxicity at either 20 or 30°C than at 25°C. Less than additive effects were observed at 20 and 25°C with mercury and silver in combination. Simple additive effects were noted at 30°C for the mercury-silver mixture and at 20, 25, and 30°C for the copper-zinc mixture.

## INTRODUCTION

In estuarine and coastal regions, discharges of chemical wastes generally occur as mixed effluents subject to fluctuating salinities and temperatures. Although numerous published studies report the toxicities of individual metal pollutants to various species of marine invertebrates under optimal environmental conditions (Wisely and Blick, 1967; Kobayashi, 1971; Eisler, 1973; Calabrese et al., 1973), only limited information is available on the biological effects of mixtures of metals (Gray and Ventilla, 1973; Benijts-Claus and Benijts, 1975), particularly environmental conditions conducive to stress.

We report here the toxicity of copper, zinc, mercury, and silver, both individually and in combination, for embryos of the American oyster, Crassostrea virginica, maintained at three different temperatures. The oyster embryo was chosen as the bioassay organism largely because of the ease of rearing this life stage in the laboratory and our familiarity with its environmental requirements (Loosanoff and Davis, 1963; Davis and Calabrese, 1964; Calabrese and Davis, 1966). Oyster embryos have also been shown to be more sensitive to metal pollutants than oysters at later life stages (Calabrese et al., 1977). The four metals, whose combined effects we report here, were chosen because of their known toxicities to oyster embryos at 25°C (Calabrese et al., 1973).

## MATERIALS AND METHODS

Adult oysters, obtained from Long Island Sound in the vicinity of New Haven,

195

Connecticut, were induced to spawn in the laboratory by thermal stimulation and the addition of sperm from one or more sacrificed males, as previously described by Loosanoff and Davis (1963). After the oysters began spawning, they were transferred to individual dishes. When spawning ceased, the eggs were fertilized and transferred to a five-liter container, where egg density was determined. To determine the effect of metals on survival and development of oyster embryos, 20,000 to 22,000 fertilized eggs were put into each of a series of 1-liter polypropylene beakers containing 1-µ filtered, ultra-violet-treated natural seawater (26 ± 1 o/oo salinity). Duplicate cultures were established for each of the test metal concentrations or combination of metals, and six untreated cultures served as controls. A minimum of six concentrations was used both for single and for combined metal tests.

The metals, tested as inorganic salts, were cupric chloride ($CuCl_2.2H_2O$), zinc chloride ($ZnCl_2$), silver nitrate ($AgNO_3$), and mercuric chloride ($HgCl_2$).

The pH levels in all test containers, with metal salts added, ranged from 7.4 to 8.0, a range determined as optimal for development of oyster embryos (Calabrese and Davis, 1966). Dissolved oxygen levels ranged from 100% saturation, or slightly supersaturated at the beginning of each test, to 90-100% saturation after 48 hours.

All tests were static and were initiated within 1 hour after the eggs were fertilized. They were terminated between 44-48 hours, when embryonic development to the straight-hinge larval stage was completed. To determine the effect of metal toxicity on embryonic development, the embryos that developed either normally or abnormally in each culture were collected on a 36-µ nylon screen. The larvae were then resuspended in seawater in a 250-ml graduated cylinder and, after thorough mixing, a 4-ml sample was removed and preserved in 5% buffered neutral formalin. The samples were examined under a compound microscope, and the embryos that had developed into either normal or abnormal larvae were counted.

The experimental results, expressed as net risk percentages, were calculated from the following equation formulated by Woelke (1972):

$$\text{Percent net risk} = \frac{\% \text{ treatment abnormal} - \% \text{ control abnormal}}{100 - \% \text{ control abnormal}} \times 100$$

The $EC_{50}$ values, which are the concentration of metal or metals causing 50% abnormal development of the test population, and their 95% confidence limits were determined from the straight-line graphic interpolation method of Litchfield and Wilcoxin (1949).

To determine $EC_{50}$'s for the individual metals, oyster embryos were exposed to a range of concentrations of silver, mercury, copper, and zinc, individually, at temperatures of 20, 25, and 30°C. To determine $EC_{50}$'s for combinations of metals, embryos were exposed to copper-zinc and silver-mercury mixtures at the same temperatures. For the mixtures, each metal was added at approximately 50% of its $EC_{50}$ as determined above, thus theoretically contributing equally to the toxicity of the mixture. In the copper-zinc mixture, that is, equitoxic solutions of copper and zinc were added as 1 Cu:10 Zn, because copper has a tenfold greater toxicity to oyster embryos than zinc. In the mercury-silver mixture, the ratio was 1:2 (Table 1).

TABLE 1   Concentrations of Heavy Metal Ions Added, as Inorganic
Salts, in Parts Per Billion to Natural Seawater Medium (26 ± 1 o/oo
Salinity)

---

### Individually

| Cupric chloride | Zinc chloride | Mercuric chloride | Silver nitrate |
|---|---|---|---|
| 5 | 50 | 8 | 10 |
| 10 | 100 | 10 | 20 |
| 15 | 150 | 12 | 25 |
| 20 | 200 | 14 | 30 |
| 25 | 250 | 16 | 35 |
| 35 | 350 | 20 | 50 |

### In combination

| Cupric chloride and zinc chloride | Mercuric chloride and silver nitrate |
|---|---|
| 5 + 50 | 6 + 12 |
| 10 + 100 | 8 + 16 |
| 15 + 150 | 10 + 20 |
| 20 + 200 | 12 + 24 |
| 25 + 250 | 14 + 28 |
| 30 + 300 | 16 + 32 |
| 35 + 350 | |

---

The toxicity of metal mixtures was determined by using the additive toxicity
index developed by Marking and Dawson (1975).  The necessary calculations for
the index are:

$$\frac{A_m}{A_i} + \frac{B_m}{B_i} = S$$

where A and B are chemicals, i and m are toxicities (the $EC_{50}$ values) of the
individual metals and the mixture, respectively, and S is the sum of the
biological activity.  To establish linearity and to assign a reference point
of zero for simple additive toxicity, Marking and Dawson (1975) calculated
the index as follows: additive index = $\frac{1}{S}$ - 1.0 for S < 1.0 (greater than
additive toxicity) or S (-1) + 1.0 for S > 1.0 (less than additive toxicity).
Additive indices of -, 0, and + indicate less than additive, additive, and
more than additive, respectively.  The significance of additive indices close
to zero was assessed by substituting values from the 95% confidence intervals
into the formula to determine whether the range of additive indices overlapped zero (simple additivity).

The results are based on four tests, each with metals individually and with
metals in combination.

RESULTS

The concentrations of heavy metals, both individually and in combination,
that caused 50% abnormal development at three different temperatures are
shown in Tables 2 and 3.  The toxicity of mercury, zinc, and copper was not
influenced by temperature, as indicated by overlapping of the 95% confidence
intervals of $EC_{50}$ values among three different temperatures.  Silver, however,
was significantly more toxic at 20 than at 25°C, as shown by the non-over-
lapping of their 95% confidence intervals.  Mercury and copper were the most
toxic metals, followed by silver and then zinc.

The toxic effect of the copper-zinc mixture was that of simple additivity at
each of the three temperatures used, as indicated by the 95% confidence intervals of the additive indices which overlapped zero (Table 3).  However,
there was a statistically significant less-than-additive effect for the
mercury-silver mixture at 20 and 25°C, but just a simple additive effect at
30°C (Table 2).

TABLE 2  Toxicity of Mercury and Silver (in Parts Per Billion),
Individually and in Combination, to Embryos of the American Oyster,
Crassostrea virginica, at Three Different Temperatures in Natural
Seawater (26 ± 1 o/oo Salinity)

| Metal | 48-hr $EC_{50}$ of metal salts | | |
|-------|---------|---------|---------|
|       | 20°C | 25°C | 30°C |
| *Individually* | | | |
| Hg | 11.4 (10.4-12.5)[1] | 12.6 (12.0-13.2) | 10.2 ( 7.9-13.5) |
| Ag | 24.2 (19.6-29.3) | 35.3 (30.8-40.4) | 32.2 (27.3-38.0) |
| *In combination* | | | |
| Hg | 9.2[2] ( 8.2- 9.9) | 11.2 ( 9.8-12.8) | 9.0 ( 7.2-11.2) |
| + | + | + | + |
| Ag | 18.4 (16.4-19.7) | 22.4 (19.6-25.6) | 18.0 (14.5-22.4) |
| *Additive index* | | | |
| Hg + Ag | -0.57 -0.96 to -0.22 (L.A.)[3] | -0.52 -0.90 to -0.23 (L.A.) | -0.44 -1.24 to +0.09 (S.A.)[4] |

[1] 95% confidence interval of $EC_{50}$ values; [2] Mercury and silver added at 1:2
ratio; [3] Significantly less than additive; [4] Simple additivity.

TABLE 3  Toxicity of Zinc and Copper (in Parts Per Billion), Individually and in Combination, to Embryos of the American Oyster, Crassostrea virginica, at Three Different Temperatures in Natural Seawater (26 $\pm$ 1 o/oo Salinity)

| Metal | 48-hr EC$_{50}$ of metal salts | | |
| --- | --- | --- | --- |
| | 20°C | 25°C | 30°C |
| Individually | | | |
| Zn | 205.7 (151.1-278.2)[1] | 324.5 (274.4-373.2) | 229.6 (108.9-489.9) |
| Cu | 15.1 ( 8.5- 26.7) | 18.7 ( 15.7- 23.0) | 18.3 ( 14.5- 23.1) |
| In combination | | | |
| Zn | 139.8[2] (109.7-178.2) | 156.3 (119.6-203.5) | 93.8 ( 56.6-155.2) |
| + | + | + | + |
| Cu | 14.0 ( 11.0- 17.8) | 15.6 ( 12.0- 20.3) | 9.4 ( 5.7- 15.5) |
| Additive index | | | |
| Zn + Cu | -0.61 -2.27 to +0.24 (S.A.)[3] | -0.32 -1.04 to +0.19 (S.A.) | +0.08 -1.49 to +1.76 (S.A.) |

[1] 95% confidence interval of EC$_{50}$ values; [2] Copper and zinc added at 1:10 ratio; [3] Simple additivity.

Temperature, of course, affected the dissolved oxygen levels in both experimental and control beakers; the levels decreased from 7.4 ppm at 20°C to 6.1 ppm at 30°C.

It must be remembered that the metal concentrations reported here are those added to the test solutions initially.  Effective concentrations of the test metals may be reduced by gaseous exchange, organism uptake, absorption to container walls, or sequestration by any chelating agents that may be present in the seawater (Portmann, 1970; Calabrese et al., 1973).


### DISCUSSION

The order of individual relative toxicities of the four metals (Hg>Cu>Ag>Zn) in this study was similar to that reported by others.  Calabrese et al. (1973), using artificial seawater, reported the toxicity of metals to C. virginica embryos to be Hg>Ag>Cu>Zn.  Calabrese and Nelson (1974) reported metal

toxicity to embryos of the hard clam, <u>Mercenaria</u> <u>mercenaria</u>, to be Hg>Ag>Zn.
Kobayashi (1971) found metal toxicity to be in the order of Hg>Cu>Zn for
embryos of the sea urchin, <u>Anthocidaris</u> <u>crassispina</u>.

Temperature alone had some effect on normal embryonic development of oysters.
In control cultures, only 2.3% of the embryos developed abnormally at 25°C,
whereas at 30 and 20°C there was 11.6% and 4.3% abnormal development, respectively.  Even though percent net risk values were corrected for abnor-
malities in controls, the influence of temperature on the toxicity of metals
was indicated by the different EC$_{50}$ values obtained at each of the test temperatures (Tables 2 and 3).  Whether the metals were added individually or
in combination, oyster embryos appeared to have greater resistance to metal
toxicity at 25°C than at either 20 or 30°C, although the increase in toxicity
was statistically significant only in the case of silver at 20°C.

The reason for the mercury-silver mixtures having a less than additive toxic
effect at 20 and 25°C was probably a loss of silver by precipitation when
combined with the chloride ions of mercury and of seawater.  That this mixture becomes simply additive at 30°C may be due to the increased solubility
and penetration of metals at higher temperatures.  It also indicates that
each of the two metals acted independently on the embryos.  The simple additivity of the copper-zinc mixtures showed that these two metals also acted
independently on the embryos.

The influence of temperature on chemical toxicity on aquatic organisms, as
discussed by Cairns <u>et al</u>. (1975), is complex.  Temperature alone may be a
lethal factor, and some toxicants may alter lethal thermal limits.  Thermal
effects on aquatic organisms include changes in osmoregulatory processes and
in enzyme activity.  Any toxicant that acts on enzymes involved in energy
metabolism or that causes a change in the rate of oxygen uptake, for instance
by blockage of respiratory gas exchange at the gills of fishes, may have its
effect potentiated by a temperature increase.  Higher temperatures generally
mean greater solubility of metal salts, as well as an increased rate of water
and solute movement across the cell membrane.  Any one or all of the above
factors may have contributed to the increase of the toxicity of mercury-
silver mixtures at 30°C observed here.  We have no explanation at this time
for the increased toxicity of silver at lower temperature (20°C).  Because
oxygen solubility decreases with increasing temperatures, one must also consider that any effect of temperature on metal toxicity may be partially
moderated by the availability of dissolved oxygen.


## ACKNOWLEDGEMENTS

We thank James E. Miller for providing technical assistance in this study
and Rita S. Riccio for her technical review and typing of this manuscript.


## REFERENCES

Benijts-Claus, C. & Benijts, F., 1975.  The effect of low lead and zinc con-
    centrations on the larval development of the mud-crab <u>Rhithropanopeus</u>
    <u>harrisii</u> Gould.  In <u>Sublethal Effects of Toxic Chemicals on Aquatic Ani-</u>
    <u>mals</u> (Ed. J.H. Koeman and J.J.T.W.A. Strik), pp. 43-52.  Amsterdam:
    Elsevier Press.

Cairns, J., Jr., Heath, A.G., & Parker, B.C., 1975. The effects of temperature upon the toxicity of chemicals to aquatic organisms. Hydrobiologia,
47, 135-171.

Calabrese, A., Collier, R.S., Nelson, D.A., & MacInnes, J.R., 1973. The toxicity of heavy metals to embryos of the American oyster Crassostrea virginica. Marine Biology, 18, 162-166.

Calabrese, A. & Davis, H.C., 1966. The pH tolerance of embryos and larvae of
Mercenaria mercenaria and Crassostrea virginica. Biological Bulletin,
Marine Biological Laboratory, Woods Hole, Mass., 131, 427-436.

Calabrese, A., MacInnes, J.R., Nelson, D.A., & Miller, J.E., 1977. Survival
and growth of bivalve larvae under heavy metal stress. Marine Biology,
41, 179-184.

Calabrese, A. & Nelson, D.A., 1974. Inhibition of embryonic development of
the hard clam, Mercenaria mercenaria, by heavy metals. Bulletin of Environmental Contamination and Toxicology, 11, 92-97.

Davis, H.C. & Calabrese, A., 1964. Combined effects of temperature and
salinity on development of eggs and growth of larvae of M. mercenaria and
C. virginica. Fishery Bulletin U.S., 63, 643-655.

Eisler, R., 1973. Annotated Bibliography on Biological Effects of Metal in
Aquatic Environments. 287pp. Washington, D.C.: U.S. Environmental Protection Agency Rep. R3-73-007. U.S. Government Printing Office.

Gray, J.S. & Ventilla, R.J., 1973. Growth rates of a sediment-living marine
protozoan as a toxicity indicator for heavy metals. Ambio, 2, 118-121.

Kobayashi, N., 1971. Fertilized sea urchin eggs as an indicating material
for marine pollution bioassay, preliminary experiments. Publications of
the Seto Marine Biological Laboratory, 18, 379-406.

Litchfield, J.T., Jr. & Wilcoxin, F., 1949. A simplified method of evalu-
ating dose-effect experiments. Journal of Pharmacology and Experimental
Therapeutics, 96, 99-113.

Loosanoff, V.L. & Davis, H.C., 1963. Rearing of bivalve mollusks. In
Advances in Marine Biology (Ed. F.S. Russell), Vol. 1, pp. 1-136.
London: Academic Press.

Marking, L.L. & Dawson, V.K., 1975. Method for assessment of toxicity or
efficacy of mixtures of chemicals. Investigations in Fish Control.
No. 67. 7pp. U.S. Department of the Interior, Fish and Wildlife Service.

Portmann, J.E., 1970. A discussion of the results of acute toxicity tests
with marine organisms, using a standard method. F.A.O. Technical Confer-
ence on Marine Pollution and its Effects on Living Resources and Fishing.
FIR:MP/70/E-31, 1-13.

Wisely, B. & Blick, R.A.P., 1967. Mortality of marine invertebrate larvae
in mercury, copper, and zinc solutions. Australian Journal of Marine
and Freshwater Research, 18, 63-72.

Woelke, C.E., 1972.  Development of a receiving water quality bioassay criterion based upon the 48-hour Pacific oyster (Crassostrea gigas) embryo. Washington Department of Fisheries Technical Report 9, 93pp.

# THE IMPACT OF POLLUTION ON THE INTERTIDAL FAUNA OF THE ESTUARINE FIRTH OF FORTH

**D.S. McLusky, M. Elliott and J. Warnes**

*Dept. of Biology, University of Stirling, Stirling, Scotland*

ABSTRACT

The impact of domestic and industrial effluents on the inter-tidal fauna of the estuarine Firth of Forth will be reviewed and discussed.   Upstream of Alloa a marked oxygen sag occurs, and the fauna consists predominantly of oligochaetes.   Below Alloa the Forth increases in volume, and due largely to dilution, water quality improves.   Below Kincardine Bridge the Forth is up to 5 km wide at high water, and at low water large intertidal mud-flats are exposed.   Large populations of macrofauna occur, prin-cipally <u>Hydrobia ulvae</u>, <u>Nereis diversicolor</u>, <u>Macoma balthica</u> and <u>Cerastoderma edule</u>, which are fed on by major populations of Shelduck and wading birds.   This area also receives the effluent from the petro-chemical complex at Grangemouth, Longannet power station, coal-mines, and domestic waste.   The impact of these effluents is often marked near to their point of discharge, but despite this the biomass and productivity of the intertidal fauna is high overall.

INTRODUCTION

The Firth of Forth may be conveniently divided into three sections, the narrow part between Stirling and Kincardine Bridge which is dominated by river flow derived principally from the River Teith and only shows a marked increase in salinity below Alloa, the wider estuarine part between the Kincardine and Queensferry Bridges which is bordered by extensive intertidal mudflat areas, and the broadest part below the Queensferry bridges which is virtually open sea.   This present paper is concerned solely with the estuarine Forth, which is to the west of the Queensferry bridges.   The quality of water in this area, and its hydrography have been studied by Collett (1) and Stout (2).   An introduction to the intertidal fauna of the area has been given by McLusky <u>et al</u>. (3).   This paper is a review of the impact of pollution on the intertidal fauna, and has been

compiled from data collected for several unpublished reports and
theses.

## STIRLING-KINCARDINE BRIDGE

The narrow part of the tidal estuary from Stirling to Kincardine
Bridge is 28 km in length.   Conditions at Stirling are dominated
by land-water river flow from the Teith, Forth and Allan,
averaging 44.5 $m^3s^{-1}$.   At Stirling the Forth receives the
partially treated domestic sewage effluent from Stirling and
nearby towns, at Cambus the Forth has received in the past a
large volume of effluent from a large whisky distillery, and
near Alloa it receives domestic effluent from Alloa and Clack-
mannan District.   The effect of these effluents on water quality
produces an oxygen deficit approaching 9g $m^{-3}$ at principal spring
tides, and 7g $m^{-3}$ at principal neap tides, in the vicinity of
Alloa (Ref. 2).   The salinity of the water at Alloa ranges from
virtually fresh water at low water, up to 17‰ salinity at
highest water.   Below Alloa the salinity increases to a range
at Kincardine Bridge of 4 to 25‰, as the oxygen deficity
decreases markedly.

The fauna from Stirling to Alloa has been found to be dominated
by large populations of oligochaete worms (principally Tubifex
tubifex O.F. Muller and Limnodrilus hoffmeisteri Claparede) which
occur in densities up to 2400/$m^2$ in the Cambus area.   Also
present are substantial numbers of nematode worms.   Below Alloa,
the oligochaetes are still a principal component, but the species
composition changes to Tubifex costatus (Claparede) and Peloscolex benedeni Udekem.   Nematode worms remain present, but are
joined by increasing numbers of invertebrate macrofauna.   First
to appear below Alloa are Corophium volutator (Pallas) and Nereis
diversicolor O.F. Muller up to 700 and 3000 $m^{-2}$ respectively.
Next occurs Hydrobia ulvae (Pennant) in densities of up to
2000 $m^{-2}$, followed by Macoma balthica (L.) at up to 400 $m^{-2}$.
Finally at Kincardine Bridge and below have been recorded Mytilus
edulis L., Mya arenaria L. Carcinus maenas (L.) and Littorina
littorea (l.) and Littorina saxatilis (Olivi).

## KINCARDINE BRIDGE TO QUEENSFERRY BRIDGES

Below Kincardine Bridge the estuarine Forth increases markedly
in width, the salinity increases until it is almost that of seawater at Queensferry at all states of the tide, and the oxygen
deficit continues to decrease.   The major potentially polluting
influences in this area are industrial.   The large Longannet
power station, which is the most powerful in Europe, and its
smaller neighbour at Kincardine utilise the estuary water for
cooling purposes, and have a total circulatory capacity of

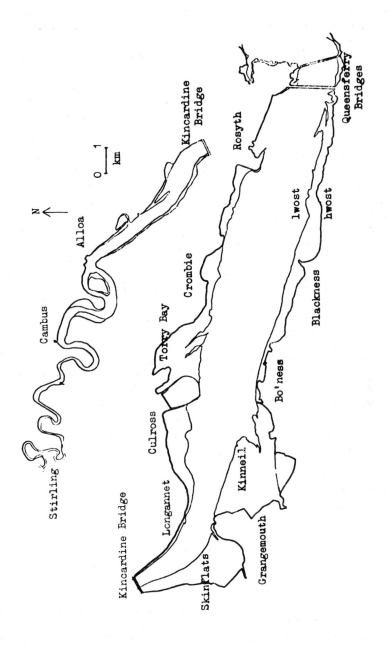

Figure 1.     The estuarine Firth of Forth, with place-names as indicated in the text.

123 $m^3$ $s^{-1}$.    The water temperature increase has been found not
to exceed 2.5°C (Ref. 1).    The Grangemouth petro-chemical
complex appears to have a discharge of 20 - 25 t/day of BOD,
which produces an oxygen deficit of 1.5 g $m^{-3}$ (Ref. 2).    In
addition domestic effluent (variously treated) and industrial
waste (largely paper mill origin), enters the Forth in the
vicinity of Grangemouth from the rivers Carron and Avon.    Further down domestic effluent from Bo'ness, Dunfermline and
smaller towns enters the Forth, as well as waste water from
mine workings.

The intertidal areas of this part of the Forth consists of
three major areas, Skinflats and Kinneil on the south shore,
respectively west and east of Grangemouth Docks, and Torry Bay
on the north shore.    Additionally smaller intertidal areas
occur at Culross, Crombie and around Blackness.    The fauna of
Skinflats is dominated by Hydrobia ulvae and Nereis diversicolor.
These species occur in large numbers, forming an attractive
diet for many birds, including Shelduck (Ref. 4) and wading birds.
Preliminary estimates by Warnes of the biomass and productivity
indicate a mean biomass for Hydrobia at Skinflats of 4.7 g flesh
dry weight $m^{-2}$, and an annual production of 6.4 g $m^{-2}$.    It
appears that Hydrobia has a life span of 2 years on the Forth
with an overall Production/Biomass ratio of 1.36 (P/B:0 group
4.08;   I group 1.90;   II group 0.033).    Nereis diversicolor is
abundant at Skinflats, with densities up to 1200 $m^{-2}$, Corophium
volutator occurs in numbers up to 3000 $m^{-2}$ in several areas, and
oligochaetes occur widely (mean 20000 $m^{-2}$).    Macoma balthica
is the only bivalve in significant numbers (up to 1000 $m^{-2}$).
Cerastoderma edule was found in one area prior to the winter of
1976/77, however following a period of lower interstitial
salinity (17% ) no more Cerastoderma have been observed.

The fauna of Torry Bay has been studied by Elliott (5), who has
shown that the annual production of intertidal macrofauna is
approximately 10 g flesh dry weight $m^{-2}$.    The principal element
in this production is Hydrobia ulvae with a production of 5.99 g
flesh $m^{-2}$ $yr,^{-1}$ derived from an annual mean biomass of 3.576 g
flesh $m^{-2}$.    Bivalves constitute a major element in the annual
production with Macoma .balthica producing 1.365 g flesh $m^{-2}$ yr-1
from an annual mean biomass of 2.328 g flesh $m^{-2}$, Cerastoderma
edule (L.)  producing 1.21 g flesh $m^{-2}$ $yr^{-1}$, from an annual mean
biomass of 0.995 g flesh $m^{-2}$ and Mya arenaria production of
0.801 g flesh $m^{-2}$ $yr^{-1}$ from a mean biomass of 0.287 g flesh $m^{-2}$.
He has also shown the presence of a population of Retusa obtusa
(Montagu) (annual production 0.143 g flesh $m^{-2}$ yr-1, mean biomass
0.042 g flesh $m^{-2}$) which has been proven to prey upon the Hydrobia population.

Overall he has shown that the populations of Cerastoderma, Mya, Hydrobia, are faring well in comparison with other populations elsewhere in Europe, however the P/B ratio (production/biomass) of Macoma is very low, and only comparable to that from deep water populations in the Baltic Sea.   The slow growth rate of Macoma in the Forth was commented on by McLusky and Allan (6), and further work by Elliott has confirmed this, without being able to identify any normal environmental parameter which may be responsible.   Heavy metal levels have been studied, and although they are at relatively high levels in the fauna and sediments of the Forth, the levels are generally within the ranges of concentration not regarded as abnormal by Bryan and Hummerstone (7);   (except for cadmium which is present in the Torry Bay Macoma at $108 \pm 27$ ppm, in comparison to up to 0.85 ppm noted by Bryan and Hummerstone).   No firm conclusions can be drawn as yet but it might appear that certain heavy metals are thus implicated in the reduced productivity of the Macoma population.

The Kinneil area has been studied by a series of intensive surveys over the period 1975-1977.   Transect lines $\frac{1}{2}$ km apart have been sampled with samples collected at 100 m intervals. The area is bounded to the west by Grangemouth docks, and to the east by Kinneil coal mine and Bo'ness.   The large mudflat area is bisected by the small River Avon, and is backed by a large reclamation area on which is situated the Grangemouth petro-chemical complex.   The petro-chemical complex discharges industrial effluent via two principal discharge points, and domestic effluent enters the area at a further two discharge points.   Macoma balthica has been found in the surveys in the central and eastern parts of the area, with populations up to 1600 m$^{-2}$.   Cerastoderma edule appeared in the same area in summer 1975, and populations of up to 2000 m$^{-2}$ at several stations have persisted since then.   Hydrobia ulvae has been found at most stations, with densities up to 48,000 m$^{-2}$.   Hydrobia is however absent from near the outfall and track of the refinery effluent, and from the area adjacent to the chemicals outfall. Nereis diversicolor and Nephthys hombergi Lamarck have been found extensively in the outer and eastern parts of the area, along with occasional specimens of Corophium volutator, Mytilus edulis and Mya arenaria.   Oligochaete worms (principally Peloscolex benedeni) have been found widely distributed in the area, with maximum abundance (up to 60,000 m$^{-2}$) near to the mouth of the Avon, and towards Grangemouth Docks.   Areas further out on the mudflat, and eastwards, which are inhabited by bivalves etc., having fewer oligochaetes, and areas immediately adjacent to the petro-chemical discharges being devoid of oligochaetes.

On the basis of these results four categories of faunistic
diversity are proposed for this area:

1.  "Abiotic".    No visible life at all.

2.  "Grossly polluted".    In these areas only oligochaeta are
    found, in reduced abundance.    Hydrobia is generally absent,
    although occasional scattered individuals may be found,
    which could have been carried in by the preceding tide.

3.  "Polluted".    Oligochaetes are abundant, and form the
    dominant fauna.    Other species may be present in reduced
    numbers, especially Hydrobia.

4.  "Largely unpolluted".    Macoma, Cerastoderma, Nereis,
    Nephthys, and Hydrobia, present and often abundant.
    Oligochaetes reduced in abundance.

Wharfe (8, 9) has studied the impact of a refinery in Southern
England, and Wharfe (10) has reviewed the classification of the
impact of pollution in terms of community studies.    The results
of the present study in the Kinneil area give further confirm-
ation of the value of community studies as a method of assessing
the impact of pollution on an intertidal estuarine mud-flat.
The four categories proposed for this Kinneil area accord well
with those of Wharfe, who additionally suggested "relatively
healthy", a category never completely reached in this particular
area of the Forth, although it does occur further downstream.

Applying these categories to the intertidal communities at
Kinneil, it is found that the "abiotic" and "grossly polluted"
conditions occur in the immediate vicinity of the two major
petro-chemical effluents.    Within approximately 300 m conditions
improve and should be classified as "polluted".    These polluted
conditions, with abundant oligochaetes, but a reduced represent-
ation of other macrofauna, occur in the Kinneil area at the
western end towards Grange-burn and Grangemouth docks, and at
upper shore areas to the west of the River Avon.    The outer part
of the mudflats, and the eastern part towards Bo'ness support
a diverse and abundant macrofauna which attracts many feeding
birds to the area.

### DISCUSSION

It can be seen from the results presented that the Forth has
suffered in the past, and continues to be affected by extensive
industrial and domestic pollution.    However the upper part of
the estuary now receives a considerably reduced input of effluent,
and over the coming years the oxygen deficit at Alloa should

become less pronounced.    Further downstream three major intertidal areas have been identified.    Skinflats, the outer part
of Kinneil, and Torry Bay support diverse and abundant populations of macrofauna, notably <u>Hydrobia ulvae</u> and <u>Macoma balthica</u>.
The annual production of these areas, where measured, is
approximately 10 g flesh dry weight m$^{-2}$, which is comparable
with other North European estuaries.    Warwick and Price (11)
estimated the annual production of macrofauna in a Lynher
estuarine mud-flat as 13.2 g flesh dry weight m$^{-2}$, whilst Wolff
and de Wolf (12  ) estimate the comparable annual macrofaunal
production from the Grevelingen estuary as 39.8 - 32.7 g m$^{-2}$
year$^{-1}$.    The preliminary estimate from the Forth is thus similar
to that from the Lynher, but rather lower than that from the
Grevelingen estuary.    Overall it can be seen that large areas
of the mudflats of the Forth are quite productive, however this
productivity is markedly impaired in the vicinity of certain
effluent discharge points where community changes indicate
polluted or sometimes grossly polluted conditions.

## ACKNOWLEDGEMENTS

This study has been financed by the University of Stirling, the
Nature Conservancy Council and British Petroleum.    The assistance of student helpers is gratefully acknowledged.

## REFERENCES

(1)    COLLETT, W.F. 1971.    The quality of the Forth estuary (1).
       Proceedings of the Royal Society of Edinburgh, 71,
       137-141

(2)    STOUT, H.P., 1976.    Prediction of oxygen deficits associ-
       ated with effluent inputs to the Forth estuary.
       Proceedings of the Institution of Civil Engineers, 61,
       351-366.

(3)    McLUSKY, D.S., BRYANT, D., ELLIOTT, M., TEARE, M. & MOFFAT,
       G., 1976.    Intertidal fauna of the industrialized Forth
       estuary,    Marine Pollution Bulletin, 7, 48-51.

(4)    BRYANT, D.B. & LENG, J.W., 1975.    Feeding distribution and
       behaviour of Shelduck Tadorna tadorna in relation to
       food supply.    Wildfowl, 27, 20-30.

(5)    ELLIOTT, M.E., 1977.    Studies on the production ecology of
       several mollusc species in the estuarine Firth of Forth.
       Ph.D. Thesis, University of Stirling.

(6)    McLUSKY, D.S. & ALLAN, D.G., 1976.    Aspects of the biology
       of Macoma balthica (L.) from the estuarine Firth of
       Forth.    Journal of Molluscan Studies, 42, 31-45.

(7)    BRYAN, G.W. & HUMMERSTONE, L.G., 1977.    Indicators of
       heavy-metal contamination in the Looe estuary (Cornwall)
       with particular regard to silver and lead.    Journal of

the Marine Biological Association of the United
Kingdom, 57, 75-92.

(8)  WHARFE, J.R., 1975.   A study of the intertidal macrofauna
around the B.P. Refinery (Kent) Limited.   Environmental
Pollution, 9, 1-12.

(9)  WHARFE, J.R., 1977.   An ecological survey of the benthic
invertebrate macrofauna of the lower Medway estuary.
Journal of Animal Ecology, 46, 93-113.

(10) WHARFE, J.R., 1976.   Characterization of benthic types in
the lower Medway estuary.   Marine Pollution Bulletin,
7, 170-2.

(11) WARWICK, R.M. & PRICE, R., 1975.   Macrofauna production
in an estuarine mud-flat.   Journal of the Marine
Biological Association of the United Kingdom, 55, 1-18.

(12) WOLFF, W.J. & de WOLF, L., 1977.   Biomass and production
of zoobenthos in the Grevelingen estuary, The Netherlands
Estuarine and Coastal Marine Science, 5, 1-24.

# LEAD TRANSPORT IN THE COMMON MUSSEL
## *MYTILUS EDULIS*

**Meinhard Schulz-Baldes**

*Institut für Meeresforschung, 2850 Bremerhaven, Germany*

ABSTRACT

In the course of establishing mussels as monitoring organisms for heavy metal pollution the kinetics of lead uptake into the soft parts of Mytilus edulis have been studied. The differences in organ specific uptake rates reflect the pathway of lead into and within the animal. Lead is taken up at gills and viscera, distributed by the blood and finally stored in membrane bound vesicles within excretory cells of the kidney as demonstrated by electron microscopy and x-ray-microanalysis.

INTRODUCTION

Marine molluscs accumulate trace metals from seawater. Mussels and oysters as sessile and ubiquitious organisms are being used more and more as indicators of heavy metal pollution ( Refs. 1, 6, 7, 10 ). The data of a "mussel watch" in terms of chemical concentrations have to be interpreted on a biological basis. The influence of environmental parameters ( salinity, temperature, presence of natural chelators and suspended material, quantitative and qualitative changes in food ) has to be considered as well as internal physiological cycles during the year ( storage of reserve material, production of sperms and eggs ). The influence of these factors has to be evaluated on the basis of metal distribution and metabolism within the animal. The present study is concerned with uptake kinetics during the first hours of lead exposure and the subsequent distribution among different organs of Mytilus edulis.

MATERIAL AND METHODS

Mussels Mytilus edulis were collected from nautical buoys in the southern German Bight and maintained in aerated polythene containers at a constant

211

temperature of 12 $^\circ$C. The seawater ( 33 ‰ ) was changed every third day and the animals were fed a suspension of _Dunaliella marina_. Lead was administered as dissolved lead chloride from a stock solution. Analytical procedures for flameless atomic absorption spectroscopy have been described earlier ( Ref. 9 ). For electron microscopy _Mytilus_ was fixed in 0.1 M phosphate buffered ( pH 7.4 ) 2.5 % glutaraldehyde, partly postfixed in 1 % osmium tetroxide, dehydrated in a graded alcohol series and embedded in Durcupan. Ultrathin sections, either stained by uranyl acetate and lead citrate or unstained, were examined in a Zeiss EM 9 or a Philipps EM 301 with attached EDAX-707 x-ray-microanalyzer.

## RESULTS

During the first hours of lead exposure, the uptake into the total softbody of _Mytilus edulis_ occured in two phases ( Fig. 1 a,b ). The curves can be interpreted ( Refs. 5, 8 ) as a sequential system of two single compartments. The first phase follows an exponential time function ( Fig. 1 b ) indicating a reversible exchange of lead until time $t_o$ :

$$C/M = k_i^I/k_o^I \left( 1 - e^{-k_o^I \cdot t} \right) \tag{1}$$

where C/M = concentration factor = $\dfrac{\text{lead in tissue ( mg/kg d.w. )}}{\text{lead in medium ( mg/l )}}$ , $k_i^I$ = inward flux constant of phase I ( 1/hours ), $k_o^I$ = outward flux constant of phase I ( 1/hours ) and t = time ( hours ).

$k_o^I$ is obtained graphically ( slope of straight line in Fig. 1 b, upper part ), $k_i^I$ is calculated at equilibrium conditions of phase I using equation ( 1 ). Phase II is described by a linear function with irreversible uptake ( $k_i^{II}$ = slope of straight line in Fig. 1 a, $k_o^{II}$ = 0 ) :

$$C/M = K + k_i^{II} \cdot t \tag{2}$$

where K = constant and $k_i^{II}$ = inward flux constant of phase II ( 1/hours ).

The curves of separate uptake into different organs do not allow a definite explanation for this general uptake pattern. There was a tendency for a slower uptake into the kidney during the first 50 hours ( Fig. 2 a ), whereas gills and blood showed a more rapid uptake during this time interval ( Fig. 2 b ), compared with the uptake during the following days. The absolute figures of uptake rates for kidney, gills, blood, viscera and adductor muscle were in the ratio of 64 : 6 : 5 : 3 : 1.

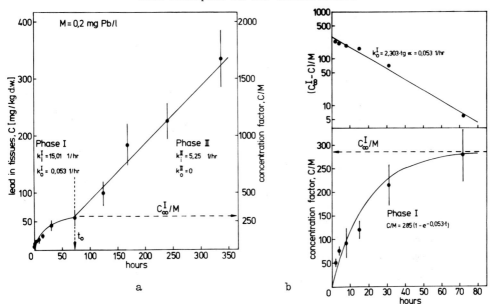

Fig. 1 a,b. <u>Mytilus edulis</u>. Lead uptake into total softbody from 0.2 mg Pb/l.
Each symbol represents mean lead concentrations of 10 animals $\pm$ 1 standard
deviation. a.) two phase model, phase I : $t < t_o$, phase II : $t \geqslant t_o$. b.) uptake
during phase I with graphical determination of $k_o^I$.

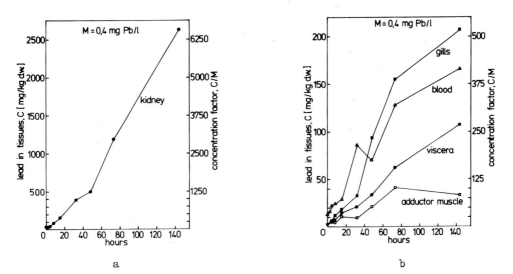

Fig. 2 a,b. <u>Mytilus edulis</u>. Lead uptake into individual organs from 0.4 mg Pb/l.
Each point represents the mean of 5 analyses. a.) uptake into the kidney. b.)
uptake into gills, blood, viscera and adductor muscle. Notice different scales.

Table 1. Mytilus edulis. Distribution of lead in different organs two days after injection of 100 µg Pb. Given are lead concentrations ( conc. ) and lead contents ( cont. ).

| injected organ | blood | gills | | foot | | kidney | | mantle | | add. muscle | | viscera | | remainder | | Σ |
|---|---|---|---|---|---|---|---|---|---|---|---|---|---|---|---|---|
| | conc. mg/l | conc. mg/kg | cont. µg | conc. mg/kg | cont. µg | conc. mg/kg | cont. µg | conc. mg/kg | cont. µg | conc. mg/kg | cont. µg | conc. mg/kg | cont. µg | conc. mg/kg | cont. µg | cont. µg |
| control | | | | | | | | | | | | | | | | |
| no.1 | 0,1 | 2,3 | 0,2 | 2,4 | 0,3 | 17,3 | 1,5 | 2,7 | 1,1 | 3,1 | 0,2 | 10,2 | 1,3 | 2,7 | 0,7 | 5,2 |
| no.2 | 0,1 | 5,0 | 0,4 | 2,0 | 0,2 | 38,6 | 2,2 | 3,6 | 0,9 | 3,3 | 0,2 | 2,9 | 0,3 | 3,4 | 0,5 | 4,7 |
| foot | | | | | | | | | | | | | | | | |
| no.3 | 1,0 | 23,3 | 2,1 | 275,0 | 39,3 | 120,4 | 9,8 | 10,8 | 4,8 | 14,4 | 1,0 | 45,8 | 5,8 | 175,4 | 35,0 | 97,8 |
| no.4 | 0,8 | 64,8 | 7,8 | 247,3 | 24,6 | 109,7 | 10,1 | 19,8 | 6,5 | 12,5 | 0,9 | 61,8 | 4,5 | 56,2 | 12,4 | 66,8 |
| muscle | | | | | | | | | | | | | | | | |
| no.5 | 0,5 | 30,8 | 2,8 | 5,7 | 0,5 | 163,7 | 10,7 | 10,4 | 1,4 | 196,6 | 10,0 | 21,5 | 1,1 | 65,1 | 9,3 | 35,8 |
| no.6 | 0,4 | 40,0 | 3,6 | 8,5 | 0,8 | 267,0 | 17,4 | 43,4 | 10,7 | 454,5 | 31,2 | 17,5 | 1,2 | 85,8 | 13,5 | 78,4 |
| mantle | | | | | | | | | | | | | | | | |
| no.7 | 0,4 | 38,8 | 3,6 | 2,3 | 0,3 | 182,6 | 15,0 | 38,4 | 11,3 | 7,3 | 0,5 | 24,2 | 2,5 | 52,1 | 8,7 | 41,9 |
| no.8 | 0,3 | 41,0 | 3,3 | 4,4 | 0,4 | 58,1 | 3,7 | 42,8 | 9,4 | 8,2 | 0,3 | 12,3 | 0,8 | 41,7 | 5,6 | 23,5 |
| viscera | | | | | | | | | | | | | | | | |
| no.9 | 6,2 | 25,8 | 2,0 | 6,1 | 1,0 | 108,2 | 6,4 | 6,5 | 1,3 | 8,5 | 0,7 | 193,4 | 19,7 | 109,4 | 9,9 | 41,0 |
| no.10 | 2,5 | 46,3 | 3,7 | 17,4 | 1,2 | 125,6 | 8,7 | 22,8 | 7,4 | 8,9 | 0,5 | 243,0 | 23,5 | 101,1 | 13,2 | 58,2 |

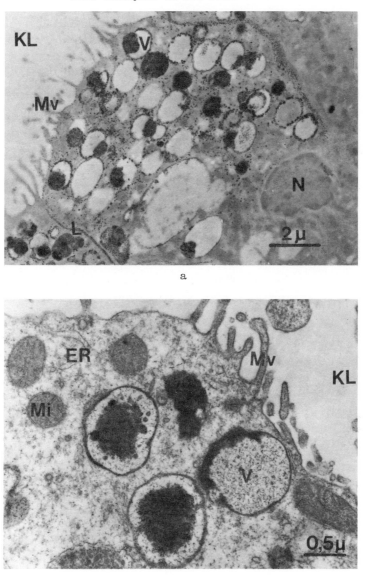

a

b

Fig. 3 a,b. <u>Mytilus</u> <u>edulis</u>. EM micrographs of lead granules in kidney excretory cells. ER = endoplasmic reticulum, KL = kidney lumen, L = lateral cell membrane, Mi = mitochondria, Mv = microvilli, N = nucleus, V = vesicle with lead granule. a.) unstained section of specimen fixed only by glutaraldehyde. b.) stained section of specimen fixed by glutaraldehyde and osmium tetroxide.

The extremely high values for the lead accumulation in the kidney find an explanation on EM micrographs. Even on unstained sections of excretory cells ( Fig. 3 a ) electron dense granules were evident. Lead was stored as a phosphorus and sulfur rich complex in membrane bound vesicles, i.e. in an extracellular compartment ( Fig. 3 b ). The uptake into the cells appears to occur by pinocytosis from the kidney lumen, especially at the cell apex rich in microvilli. However there was always a marked precipitation along the lateral cell membranes, sometimes even on the cell membranes of the basal labyrinth. The localization and identification of lead, phosphorus and sulfur on ultrathin sections was carried out by x-ray-microanalysis in transmission mode ( TEM ) and by x-ray-mapping in scanning-transmission mode ( STEM ).

### DISCUSSION

A two phase model has been described by Mason, Cho & Anderson ( 5 ) studying mercury uptake in Crassostrea virginica. This uptake pattern can probably be established for more metals and organisms, but was not found in published experiments when the first measurements have been carried out one or two days after the start of the experiment. Thus changes during the first hours may have been overlooked. A linear increase of the concentration factor during artificial metal exposure has been often reported for bivalve molluscs ( Refs. 3, 4, 11 ). However, as the concentration factor should reach a maximum value at equilibrium conditions, this apparently linear relationship has to be viewed as initial part of an exponential relationship. The time to reach equilibrium seems to be a metal specific value. In most cases it is a very slow process, Crassostrea virginica continues to take up cadmium from 5 µg/l after more than 10 months ( Ref. 13 ). The immediate uptake into gills and blood and the somewhat slower start of uptake into the kidney are taken as an indication for the internal transport routes of lead. It appears that the rate limiting step is not the uptake into the animal at the gill surface, but the transport within the animal to the kidney followed by uptake into the excretory cells and the formation of granules.

Such granules have been described by George, Pirie & Coombs ( 3 ) in various parts of Mytilus edulis after exposure to ferric hydroxide and by Fowler, Wolfe & Hettler ( 2 ) in mantle epithelial cells of Mercenaria mercenaria exposed to mercury. Walker ( 12 ) reported copper and zinc granules from another invertebrate, the barnacle Balanus balanoides. The formation of lead granules in ex-

cretory cells of Mytilus edulis implies a change in the chemical species, from
ionic to a complexed particulate form. The cell membrane of the excretory cells
is proposed as site of complex formation since the pericardial fluid, i.e. the
ultrafiltrate of the blood, has a high concentration of soluble lead. This
fluid is transported via the reno-pericardial canal into the kidney lumen. At
the surface of the excretory cells uptake occurs by pinocytosis, then the lead
is stored in membrane bound vesicles. This immobilisation of lead in a chemical
inert form outside the cytoplasm might be an internal detoxification process
as described by Walker ( 12 ) for Balanus. Cells loaded with lead granules
are either ejected as a whole or the apical part of the cell containing most
of the granules is pinched off as reported by George, Pirie & Coombs ( 3 ).
The lead leaves the mussel in a particulate form directly with the urine or
after uptake into amoebocytes.

## ACKNOWLEDGEMENTS

The research was supported by a grant from the Deutsche Forschungsgemeinschaft.
Frau I. Neuendorff provided excellent technical assistance.

## REFERENCES

( 1 )  Chow, T.J., Snyder, H.G. & Snyder, C.B., 1976. Mussels ( Mytilus ) as
           an indicator of lead pollution. The Science of the Total Environment,
           6, 55 - 63.

( 2 )  Fowler, B.A., Wolfe, D.A. & Hettler, W.F., 1975. Mercury and iron uptake
           by cytosomes in the mantle epithelial cells of quahog clams ( Merce-
           naria mercenaria ) exposed to mercury. Journal of the Fishery Research
           Board of Canada, 32, 1767 - 1775.

( 3 )  George, S.G., Pirie, B.J.S. & Coombs, T.L., 1976. The kinetics of accu-
           mulation and excretion of ferric hydroxide in Mytilus edulis (L.)
           and its distribution in the tissues. Journal of experimental marine
           Biology and Ecology, 23, 71 - 84.

( 4 )  George, S.G. & Coombs, T.L., 1977. The effects of chelating agents on
           the uptake and accumulation of cadmium by Mytilus edulis. Marine
           Biology, 39, 261 - 268.

( 5 )  Mason, J.W., Cho, J.H. & Anderson, A.C., 1976. Uptake and loss of inor-
           ganic mercury in the eastern oyster ( Crassostrea virginica ).
           Archives of Environmental Contamination and Toxicology, 4, 361 - 376.

( 6 )  Phillips, D.J.H., 1976. The common mussel Mytilus edulis as an indicator
       of pollution by zinc, cadmium, lead and copper. I. Effects of en-
       vironmental variables on uptake of metals. Marine Biology, 38, 59 -
       70.

( 7 )  Philipps, D.J.H., 1976. The common mussel Mytilus edulis as an indicator
       of pollution by zinc, cadmium, lead and copper. II. Relationship of
       metals in the mussel to those discharged by industry. Marine Biology,
       38, 71 - 80.

( 8 )  Ružić, I., 1972. Two-compartment model of radionuclide accumulation into
       marine organisms. I. Accumulation from a medium of constant activity.
       Marine Biology, 15, 105 - 112.

( 9 )  Schulz-Baldes, M., 1972. Toxizität und Anreicherung von Blei bei der
       Miesmuschel Mytilus edulis im Laborexperiment. Marine Biology, 16,
       226 - 229.

( 10 ) Schulz-Baldes, M., 1973. Die Miesmuschel Mytilus edulis als Indikator
       für die Bleikonzentration im Weserästuar und in der Deutschen Bucht.
       Marine Biology, 21, 98 - 102.

( 11 ) Schulz-Baldes, M., 1974. Lead uptake from sea water and food, and lead
       loss in the common mussel Mytilus edulis. Marine Biology, 25, 177 -
       193.

( 12 ) Walker, G., 1977. "Copper" granules in the barnacle Balanus balanoides.
       Marine Biology, 39, 343 - 349.

( 13 ) Zarroogian, G.E. & Cheer, S., 1976. Accumulation of cadmium by the
       American oyster, Crassostrea virginica. Nature, London, 261, 408 -
       410.

# INTERSPECIFIC DIFFERENCES IN TOLERANCE OF *EURYTEMORA AFFINIS* AND *ACARTIA TONSA* FROM AN ESTUARINE ANOXIC BASIN TO LOW DISSOLVED OXYGEN AND HYDROGEN SULFIDE

**Sandra L. Vargo\* and Akella N. Sastry**

*Graduate School of Oceanography, University of Rhode Island, Kingston, Rhode Island 02881*

## ABSTRACT

The Pettaquamscutt River, Rhode Island, USA, is an estuarine anoxic basin. *Acartia tonsa* is the numerically dominant summer copepod species and *Eurytemora affinis* the winter-spring dominant. These two species have similar abilities to tolerate low dissolved oxygen concentrations ($1/LD_{50}$ = 1.18 - 2.40), but *E. affinis* is more tolerant of hydrogen sulfide ($LD_{50}$ = 12 uM - 44 uM) than *A. tonsa* ($LD_{50}$ = 2 uM - 11 uM). Acclimation temperature and salinity affect the tolerance of *E. affinis* to low oxygen concentrations but not to hydrogen sulfide. Acclimation temperature and salinity does not affect the low dissolved oxygen tolerance of *A. tonsa* but salinity affects its hydrogen sulfide tolerance. Comparing survival times of 50% of the animals exposed to hydrogen sulfide, *E. affinis* lasts twice as long as *A. tonsa* at three to four times the concentration. There is no correlation in either species of points of maximum tolerance to low dissolved oxygen concentrations and hydrogen sulfide. This implies different mechanisms of adaptation to the two stresses. The field distributions of the two species agree well with the laboratory response, although both exhibit a lower tolerance to hydrogen sulfide in the laboratory than would be expected.

## INTRODUCTION

Anoxic basins occur world-wide and may be seasonal (Norwegian fjords) or permanent (Black Sea). Formation of a strong halocline in temperate regions or a thermocline in tropical regions combined with a high sill prevents exchange with the upper waters (1). Organic material sinks to depth where biological respiration uses up oxygen at a faster rate than it is renewed. After aerobic bacteria deplete the oxygen supply, sulfate-reducing bacteria, using sulfate as a hydrogen receptor, produce hydrogen sulfide (2).

The Pettaquamscutt River is a Rhode Island estuary consisting of two anoxic basins and a long shallow channel connecting these to Narragansett Bay. The lower basin is the more saline of the two and is the area concerned in this investigation. The maximum depth is 20 m with a sill at about 1 m from the surface. The basin is anoxic below 5m year-round and according to Gaines and Pilson (3) hydrogen sulfide concentrations are 4.5 mM at 12.5 m compared to a maximum of 300 uM for the Black Sea. Although temperature and salinity vary

---

\*Present address: Chesapeake Biological Laboratory, University of Maryland, Solomons, Maryland 20688

seasonally and the level of the anoxic layer changes, due to the strong halocline, the waters in the basin seldom turn over, although thermal stratifica-
tion disappears in the fall and the spring.  Thus the zooplankton community
is exposed to a variety of environmental changes over its vertical distribution which it must either escape, adapt to or succumb.

Research on the low dissolved oxygen tolerance of zooplankton has been largely
confined to animals from the oxygen minimum layer.  *Calanus finmarchicus* and
*Acartia clausi* from the Black Sea have tolerance limits of 0.2 ml $O_2$/L and
0.12 - 0.17 ml $O_2$/L respectively (4).  *Gnathophausia ingens* from the oxygen
minimum layer tolerated 0.14 - 0.26 ml $O_2$/L for long periods (5).  In field
studies, Bull (6) found *Eurytemora hirundoides* at 0% oxygen concentrations
with hydrogen sulfide present and Sewell and Fage (7) found copepods in the
oxygen minimum layer at a concentration of 0.325 ml $O_2$/L.  Although low oxygen
concentration may limit vertical distribution of some species separating
assemblages of animals, copepods occur at oxygen concentrations as low as
0.09 - 0.15 ml $O_2$/L (8) and have been observed aggregating at the oxygen-
hydrogen sulfide interface in lakes (9).

Beadle (10) and von Brand (11) have reviewed the physiological responses of
aquatic invertebrates to low dissolved oxygen, but most previous work concerns
benthic or parasitic organisms and neglects the interaction of hydrogen sulfide and low dissolved oxygen.  Studies of the combined hydrogen sulfide and
low dissolved oxygen stress are confined to benthic species (12)(13)(14).
Generally there are great interspecific differences in tolerance depending on
the habitat of the species.

The aim of this investigation was to relate the effects of hydrogen sulfide
and low dissolved oxygen at various temperature and salinity combinations to
the vertical and seasonal changes in the zooplankton community of the Pettaquamscutt River.  An experimental laboratory approach combined with field
sampling is used.

### METHODS

Field sampling indicated that in the Pettaquamscutt the two numerically dominant copepod species were *E. affinis* (21 - 114/L) in the spring and *A. tonsa*
(4 - 10/L) in the summer.  Field animals were collected for experiments and
held in culture.  A multi-factorial approach was used to clarify the effect
of hydrogen sulfide and low dissolved oxygen on these two species at different
temperature and salinity combinations.  An experimental matrix of three temperatures and four salinities was used.  The animals were acclimated to the
temperature-salinity combination but were stressed acutely with hydrogen sulfide or low dissolved oxygen.  A range of five concentrations was used to
determine an $LD_{50}$ value for each of these stresses.  Response was monitored
at intervals over a two-hour exposure.  An animal was counted dead if it became immobile and sank to the bottom of the flask.  This is realistic, as in
the natural environment once this happens the animal would encounter progressively higher hydrogen sulfide or lower dissolved oxygen concentrations.  At
the end of the test the water in each flask was analyzed for hydrogen sulfide
(15) or oxygen (16), and the animals held 24 hours to assess delayed effects.
Female copepods were kept at least one week and the number of eggs, nauplii,
and copepodites produced noted.  $LD_{50}$ values were calculated from the percent
mortalities by the graphical method (17) or using the probit analysis program
available in Statpack, the IBM prepared statistical programs.  Only the 30
minute $LD_{50}$ values will be discussed here as after this time the number of

animals responding changed little.  Correlation coefficients and the relative importance of temperature and salinity were determined using stepwise regression and equation (1) as the statistical model.

(1)   $LD_{50}$ or $1/LD_{50} = b_1x_1 + b_2x_2 + b_3x_3 + b_4x_4 + b_5x_5$

$LD_{50}$ or $1/LD_{50}$ was the dependent variable and temperature $^\circ C$ ($x_1$), salinity o/oo ($x_2$), temperature-squared ($x_3$), salinity-squared ($x_4$), and temperature times salinity ($x_5$) were the independent variables.  A response surface was fitted using the methods reviewed in Alderice (18).  Because absence of oxygen not its presence is the stress factor, $LD_{50}$ values for low dissolved oxygen are analyzed as $1/LD_{50}$.  Therefore, as the graphical presentation increases, tolerance increases.  Tolerance to hydrogen sulfide is directly related to concentration and is analyzed directly.

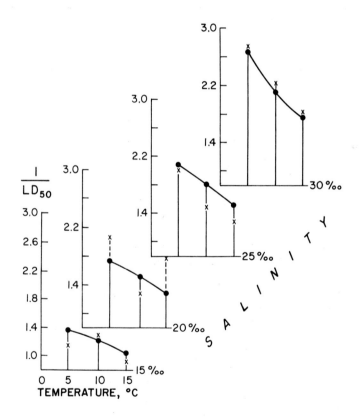

Fig. 1  Response surface to low dissolved oxygen calculated for *E. affinis* males, 30 min. exposure.  The regression equation is $1/LD_{50} = 0.084$ ($x_2$) $- 0.0023$ ($x_5$) $+ 0.28$, $r^2 = 0.86$.  Computed points are represented by (●) and observed by (x).

## RESULTS AND DISCUSSION

*E. affinis* is a low temperature euryhaline form.  Differences in response to
low dissolved oxygen due to sex are apparent.  For the males regression analysis indicated salinity is the most important variable with the temperature-
salinity interaction the only other significant variable (p > .01).  As temperature decreases and salinity increases, tolerance to low dissolved oxygen
increases (Fig. 1).  The maximum observed tolerance was 2.50 at 5°C and
30 o/oo.  For females temperature was the most important variable, then salinity, then temperature squared (Fig. 2).  The temperature-salinity interaction
was not significant.  However, again as temperature decreased and salinity
increased, tolerance increased but reached a maximum of 2.50 at 5°C at a lower
salinity (25 o/oo) than males.  Overall males exhibited the expected response
with their highest tolerance at 5°C, 25-30 o/oo and lowest at 10-15°C and
15 o/oo.  The response of females is more variable but they exhibit the same
increase at low temperatures but overall were less tolerant than the males.
The females were ovigerous at the time and energy requirements for reproduction may account for the difference.  In addition as the females are about 50%
larger than the males, their decreased surface to volume ratio and hence
lower rate of diffusion across their body surface may also be a factor.

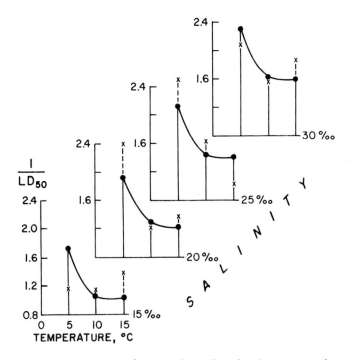

Fig. 2  Response surface to low dissolved oxygen calculated for *E. affinis* females, 30 min. exposure.  The regression equation is $1/LD_{50} = 0.038\ (x_2) - 0.33\ (x_1) +
0.013\ (x_3) + 2.49$, $r^2 = 0.76$.  Computed points are repre-
sented by (●) and observed by (x).

In contrast, very little of the variability in hydrogen sulfide tolerance could be accounted for by temperature and salinity. Maximum tolerance to hydrogen sulfide was 47 uM at 5°C and 25 o/oo for males and 60 uM at 5°C and 15°C and 15 o/oo for females. There was no correlation between low dissolved oxygen tolerance and hydrogen sulfide tolerance. Comparing laboratory results to field distribution, *E. affinis* occurred at much higher levels of sulfide (994 uM) than expected from laboratory results. The salinity and temperature at this concentration ranged from 6.5 - 9°C and 24-25 o/oo corresponding well to high levels tolerated at 5°C and 10°C under experimental conditions.

*A. tonsa* which prefers higher temperatures and salinities (19) was tested for low dissolved oxygen tolerance in the same manner as *E. affinis* and the same statistical model used in analyzing the results. Temperature and salinity did not account for the variability in response. There was no significant difference due to sex. Neglecting variability with temperature and salinity *A. tonsa* and *E. affinis* have low oxygen tolerances of the same magnitude varying from 0.25 - 0.98 ml $O_2L$ for *A. tonsa* and 0.4 - 0.98 ml $O_2L$ for *E. affinis*. These are somewhat higher concentrations than tolerance limits found for zooplankton from the oxygen minimum layer reflecting differing capacities for physiological adaptation.

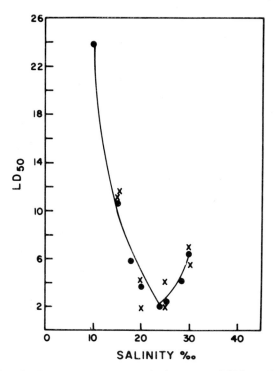

Fig. 3 Response curve to hydrogen sulfide calculated for *A. tonsa* males, 30 min. exposure. The regression equation is $LD_{50} = -5.34\ (x_2) + 0.11\ (x_4) + 65.65$, $r^2 = 0.95$. The computed points are represented by (●) and observed by (x).

However, temperature and salinity account for much of the variability in hydrogen sulfide tolerance in *A. tonsa* (Figs. 3 & 4). Little difference in response due to sex was noted. In both, salinity and salinity squared were the most important variables. Tolerance was at a minimum at salinities of 24-25 o/oo for males and 20 o/oo for females. Maximum observed tolerance was 11.5 uM for males at 15 o/oo and 16 uM for females at 30 o/oo. Again no correlation was found between tolerance to low oxygen and hydrogen sulfide. There was no delayed mortality or effect on hatching of eggs from females exposed to either low dissolved oxygen or hydrogen sulfide in either species.

Comparing the responses of the two species their low oxygen tolerance is about the same, but *A. tonsa* has a much lower tolerance to hydrogen sulfide than *E. affinis*. The survival time of 50% of the *A. tonsa* when exposed to hydrogen sulfide decreases sharply to less than 10 min. at 10 - 20 uM hydrogen sulfide while *E. affinis* tolerates 30 - 50 uM hydrogen sulfide for 20 - 40 min. The tolerance of *A. tonsa* is linked to salinity and increases at lower salinities indicating differential permeability is not a factor in tolerance as it increases with reduced salinity. The lack of correlation between maximum tolerance to low dissolved oxygen and hydrogen sulfide in both species indicates the organisms meet these two stresses differently. They may both compensate for reduced oxygen by the same means, such as reduction of oxygen requirements or changing uptake rates. However, *A. tonsa* lacks an effective

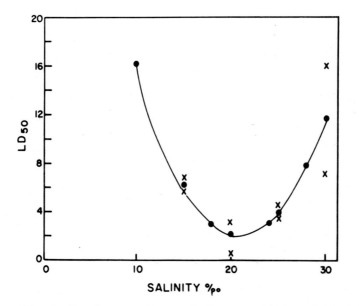

Fig. 4 Response surface to hydrogen sulfide calculated for *A. tonsa* females, 30 min. exposure. The regression equation is $LD_{50} = 0.12\ (x_4) - 4.97\ (x_2) + 53.97$, $r^2 = 0.84$. The computed points are represented by (●) and the observed by (x).

mechanism for hydrogen sulfide tolerance.  One possibility is that *E. affinis* has the ability to switch to anaerobic glycolysis and *A. tonsa* does not. Theede, *et. al.* (12) has hypothesized that anaerobic glycolysis, which does not involve the cytochrome system, is not subject to sulfide inhibition.

Comparing the responses of the two species in the field, *A. tonsa* disappears at lower sulfide levels than *E. affinis*.  It does not occur at sulfide concentrations of more than 579 uM and does not often penetrate below the 5 uM isopleth.  Temperature at this depth is about 18°C with a salinity of 23 o/oo at which the hydrogen sulfide tolerance of *A. tonsa* is at a minimum as shown by the experimental study.  Therefore, their field distribution can be in part explained by the physiological responses of the two species although they tolerate higher concentration of hydrogen sulfide than in the laboratory. Whether this is due to shorter periods spent at higher hydrogen sulfide concentrations, changes in permeability to sulfide under culture conditions or some other factor requires further investigation by *in situ* exposure of both species in the natural vertical sulfide gradient.

### REFERENCES

(1)  Richards, F.A., 1965.  Anoxic basins and fjords.  In Chemical Oceanography (eds. J.P. Riley and F. Skirrow), p. 611-644.  New York, N.Y.: Academic Press.

(2)  Hutchinson, G.E., 1957.  The sulfur cycle in lake waters.  In Treatise on Limnology, p. 753-787.  New York, N.Y.:  John Wiley and Sons.

(3)  Gaines, A.G., Jr. and Pilson, M.E.Q., 1972.  Anoxic waters in the Pettaquamscutt River.  Limnology and Oceanography, 17, p. 42-49.

(4)  Nikitine, W.M. and Malm, E., 1934.  L'influence de l'oxygene des ions hydrogene et de l'acide carbonique sur la distribution verticale du plankton de la mer Noire.  Annales de Institut Oceanographique de Monaco, 14, p. 137-171.

(5)  Childress, J.J., 1968.  Oxygen minimum layer:  vertical distribution of the mysid *Gnathophausia ingens*.  Science, 160, p. 1242-1243.

(6)  Bull, H.O., 1931.  Resistance of *Eurytemora hirundoides* Nordquist, a brackish water copepod to oxygen depletion.  Nature, 127, p. 406-407.

(7)  Sewell, P.B. and Fage, L., 1948.  Minimum oxygen layer in the ocean. Nature, 162, p. 949.

(8)  Vinogradov, M.E. and Voronina, N.M., 1961.  Influence of the oxygen deficit on the distribution of plankton in the Arabian Sea.  Deep Sea Research 9, p. 523-530.

(9)  Sorokin, Y.I., 1965.  On the trophic role of chemosynthesis and bacterial biosynthesis in water bodies.  In Primary Productivity in Aquatic Environments (ed. C.R. Goldman) p. 189-205.  Berkeley:  University of California Press.

(10)  Beadle, L.C., 1961.  Adaptations of some aquatic animals to low oxygen levels and to anaerobic conditions.  Symposium, Society for Experimental Biology, 15, p. 120-131.

(11)   von Brand, T., 1946. Anaerobiosis in Invertebrates (ed. B.J. Leyet), 328 pp. Biodynamica Monograph No. 4 Normandy, Missouri.

(12)   Theede, H., Ponat, A., Hiroki, K. and Schlieper, C., 1969. Studies on the resistance of marine bottom invertebrates to oxygen deficiency and hydrogen sulfide. Marine Biology (Berlin), 2, p. 325-337.

(13)   Wieser, W. and Kanwisher, J., 1959. Respiration and anaerobic survival in some seaweed-inhabiting invertebrates. Biological Bulletin, 117, p. 594-600.

(14)   Fenchel, T., 1969. The ecology of marine microbenthos. Ophelia, 6. p. 1-183.

(15)   Cline, J.D., 1969. Spectrophotometric determination of hydrogen sulfide in natural waters. Limnology and Oceanography, 14, p. 454-458.

(16)   Carritt, D.E. and Carpenter, J.H., 1966. Comparison and evaluation of currently employed modification of the Winkler method for determining dissolved oxygen in seawater: a NASCO report. Journal of Marine Research, 24, p. 286-318.

(17)   Goldstein, A., 1964. Biostatistics: An Introductory Text. 272 pp. New York, N.Y.: MacMillan Co.

(18)   Alderice, D.F., 1972. Factor combinations. In Marine Ecology V 1, Pt. 3 (ed. O. Kinne) p. 1659-1722. New York, N.Y.: Wiley-Interscience.

(19)   Jeffries, H.P., 1962. Succession of two *Acartia* species in estuaries. Limnology and Oceanography, 7, p. 354-364.

**BEHAVIOUR**

# INTRASPECIFIC ORGANISATION IN PARROT FISH

**Robin W. Bruce**

*Department of Zoology, The University, Glasgow, U.K.*

## ABSTRACT

Observations on 6. species of parrot fishes (family Scaridae) were undertaken at Aldabra Atoll in the Indian Ocean. An account of site attachment and intraspecific organisation of both colour phases of these species is given. The results are compared with the descriptions of habits of other labroid fishes from other areas.

## INTRODUCTION

The tropical labroid fishes (wrasses and parrot fishes) have a behavioural repertoire which even for coral reef fishes is extremely wide. The basic units of the social organisation of these abundant and conspicuous species need to be known if any attempt at understanding reef fish communities is desired. The labroids have been the focus of attention, both in the Caribbean and at the Great Barrier Reef, where the habits and life histories of several species have been described and attempts have been made to relate sexual inversion (protogynous hermaphroditism) to the colour polymorphism and dualistic mating systems that most species show (1,2,3,4,5,6,7).

## MATERIAL AND METHODS

Aldabra is an elevated limestone atoll about 750 km from the East African coast in position 9°24'S, 46°20'E (8). Results presented are based on 5 months' recording, between April and August 1976, while snorkelling at one site on the shallow subtidal reef slope off Ile Picard, due west of the research station. Before commencing this study several hundred hours had been spent at this site during the previous 6 months and the area had been partially mapped. The following 6 species of parrot fish were studied: Scarus frenatus Lacepède, S. lepidus Jenyns, S. scaber C. & V., S. psittacus (Forskal), S. sordidus Forskal and S. viridifucatus (Smith). The taxonomy of many parrot fishes is uncertain at present and the above nomenclature is tentative. Each species has 2 colour phases in adult life, an initial phase and a terminal phase, hereafter referred to as IP and TP. The IPs are small adult individuals which are drably coloured (dull brown, reddish brown or pale yellow). The TPs are large males which are brightly coloured, brilliant

229

blue-green usually being the most dominant colour.    All 6
species show full sexual dichromatism,  i.e. some colouration
elements are present only in the TPs (5).    Elsewhere TPs have
been shown to be always male and have developed from IP individuals, which can either by ♂ or ♀, i.e. TPs have arisen by
colour change or colour change and sex change (1,6).    Therefore
there are two types of males in a population, primary (gono-
choristic) males and secondary males (derived from female
individuals).    Such a population is termed diandric;  in some
species only secondary males are present (monandry) (9).    It is
assumed that these schemes exist for Aldabran scarids, although
to date, insufficient material has been collected to be certain
of the exact sexual nature of the populations.    All 6 species
are common diurnal herbivores in the shallow waters around
Aldabra.

The identification of fish as individuals is crucial to this
study.    This was achieved by close examination of individuals
for scars, blemishes, fin irregularities and other distinguish-
ing characteristics.    Note was made of the individual markings,
then the fish was followed for 30 min, the area covered by the
fish being also noted.    The location was either marked on a map
or a buoy marker was used to identify the site.    This site was
then re-checked on subsequent occasions for the presence of that
fish.    A fish present at the same location on 3 separate but
not consecutive days is here described as showing site
attachment.    The maximum known duration of site attachment is
also given.    Record was also made of whether the fish was
solitary or in a group with respect to conspecifics.    If TPs
and IPs were present at one location the degree of overlap in
their respective ranges was noted and is here described as total
(a TP covering exactly the same area as an IP or group of IPs)
or partial (a TP and an IP or group of IPs overlapping at part
of their respective ranges.    A total of 20 hr observations were
made on each species, 10 on TPs and 10 on IPs.    During this
time the fish was followed and all interactions between the
observed fish and conspecifics noted including any spawning
behaviour.    When possible the identity of the other fish
involved in the interaction was also noted.    A potential
interaction was defined as occurring when two fish were within
one metre of each other, at this distance it was assumed that
each was aware of the others' presence.    A potential interaction could result in no action by either party, a mild
displacement or a violent encounter.    Note was made of which
fish won the encounter (if there was a winner).    Other aspects
of the behaviour of species are described as they arise in the
text.    A fish showing site attachment and defence of an area by
violent interactions is referred to as being territorial.

## RESULTS

Table 1 gives details of site attachment and territory sizes of
the 6 species.    An account of behaviour by species follows:
S. psittacus.    Individuals of this species, 6 of each phase,
showed no evidence of site attachment.    During a 30-min observation period these individuals would cover many hundreds of

TABLE 1   Site Attachment and Territory Sizes

| A | B | C | D | E |
|---|---|---|---|---|
| S. sordidus TP | 5 | 3 | 94 | 40-90 |
| S. sordidus IP | 11 | 8 | 22 | 50-100 |
| S. psittacus TP | 6 | 0 | 0 | - |
| S. psittacus IP | 6 | 0 | 0 | - |
| S. lepidus TP | 4 | 4 | 143 | 250-350 |
| S. lepidus IP | 8 | 8 | 128 | 250-350 |
| S. scaber TP | 2 | 2 | 114 | 200-300 |
| S. scaber IP | 2 | 2 | 52 | 40-90 |
| S. frenatus TP | 2 | 2 | 78 | 300-600 |
| S. frenatus IP | 8 | 5 | 22 | 200-300 |
| S. viridifucatus TP | 1 | 1 | 65 | 1000 |
| S. viridifucatus IP | 5 | 5 | 49 | 200-300 |

Key to columns:  A, species and phase;  B, number of individuals
recognised;  C, number of individuals showing site attachment;
D, maximum known duration of site attachment;  E, territory size
in $m^2$.   Species are ranked in order of decreasing abundance.

metres with no regular cycle being noted.   Individuals could
not be found on subsequent days of observation.   No cohesive
groups of either or both phases formed during 20 hr observation.
Transient groups, of up to 6 individuals would form but, within
minutes the individuals would separate and the group would not
re-form.   During the total observation period no violent interactions were observed, even between TP individuals.   Mild
interactions did occur, however, and usually took the form of
one individual displacing another from a feeding site, the
aggressor would then commence to feed there.   None of the
individuals was seen to spawn, but spawning was often seen at
other times.   Both pair spawnings (involving a TP individual
and an IP individual) and group spawnings (involving several
IPs) were seen.   These spawnings were similar to reported
spawning observations for other scarid species (3,10,11).   At
spawning time, which was after the diurnal high tide, violent
TP:TP interactions were seen, the TPs sparring and chasing each
other.   TP fish appeared to defend small spawning territories
against the intrusions of other TP fish.   The sexually active
TP S. psittacus is very distinctively marked, having a very dark
purple head and lower rear flank, with a yellow flush along the
base of the dorsal fin.   At times other than spawning these TPs
are the dullest of 6 Scarus TPs studied, the overall colour is
dull green with feint purple triangle on the top of the head.

S. lepidus.   Four TPs and 8 IPs were individually recognised.
All interactions between TP individuals were violent and TPs
were always solitary.   All TPs and IPs showed site attachment.
The IPs were grouped, in groups of 3 and 4 and also 1 solitary
individual was also present.   The range of the IPs matched

exactly the range of a TP, the fourth TP individual was a small
specimen, lacking the caudal filaments characteristic of TPs of
this species.   No IPs were present in its territory.   Displacements occurred within the IP groups although no violent
interactions were seen in 10 hr observations.   Three violent
interactions between IPs were recorded when an intruding IP
entered the group's territory.   In each case the intruder was
chased out of the territory.   All TPs, with the exception of
the small individual with no tail filaments, showed a well
developed patrolling behaviour, travelling around their territories in a regular manner.   The territories were all longer
than broad (30 m x 10 m approx.) and the patrolling was timed
for 2 individuals (time taken for the TP to travel from one end
of the territory to the other).   The maximum period was 7 min
and the mode was 3 min.   During these patrols the TP would
aggressively chase individual IPs, but not chase the IP out of
the territory.   While performing this display the TP would arch
its back and close its caudal fin and scull rapidly with its
pectorals.   The IP would keep ahead of the TP and eventually
abruptly change direction.   The TP would then cease the display
and recommence patrolling.   On several occasions the IP would
take refuge in a crevice and again the TP would cease the
display.   There was no patrolling of the joint territory by the
IPs and no aggressive display by an IP directed at another IP
was observed.   Pair spawning was seen twice with recognised
individuals, both occupying the same ranges.   There was little
noticeable colour change in the TP when spawning.   Group
spawning was never seen.

S. frenatus.  Two TPs  and 8 IPs were individually recognised.
Both TPs were present at their respective sites for the duration of the observations.   Five of the 8 IPs were also present
throughout the study period.   The other 3 were seen on 2
occasions but on subsequent checking could not be found.   The
TPs were always solitary with respect to other TPs and all
interactions observed between TPs were violent.   The IPs were
in 3 groups of 2, 3 and 3 individuals.   There were size
differences between members of the group.   No violent
encounters were seen within the groups, but 18 violent
encounters were recorded directed at individuals not belonging
to the group under observation in 10 hr recording (14 were
directed at intruders of unknown origin and 4 at members of
neighbouring groups).   Displacements were, however, seen
within the group.   Violent encounters and displacements
occurred between TP and IP individuals but usually there was no
interaction (16 no interaction, 4 displacement, 3 violent).
The TPs showed no aggressive display towards IPs nor any
patrolling behaviour (see S. lepidus).   None of the recognised
individuals was seen to spawn.   Elsewhere on the reef front
pair spawnings between TPs and IPs were seen.   No group
spawning was recorded.   During spawning no colour change was
observed in the TPs but an intensification of the existing
colours occurred.   Overlap of the ranges of the TPs and the IP
groups was only partial.

S. viridifucatus.    This was the rarest of the 6 species studied.
Only 1 TP was individually identified and was present in its
range throughout the duration of the study.    The range was very
large (1,000 m²).    This individual reacted violently to con-
specific TPs in its range, although such encounters were rare
(3 in 10 hr).    The attacks were exceedingly violent, the
resident fish rushing at and chasing the intruder for 10's of
metres.    The IPs again showed group organisation with 2 groups
of 3 and 2 individuals being observed.    The members of the
groups showed site attachment and were present at their respective sites for the duration of the study.    Violent encounters
between IPs within the groups were not recorded although
displacements occurred.    Violent encounters occurred when
individuals entered the group's range and were usually chased
out by a group member.    The TP showed no patrolling of its
range, and no aggressive display towards the IPs was observed
(see S. lepidus).    Usually there was little contact between the
TP and the IPs and usually no interaction occurred, although
several displacements by the TP were seen.    The overlap of IPs
and TPs respective ranges was only partial, although the size of
the TP's range and lack of patrolling and interactions with
neighbours made assessment of respective territories inaccurate.
No spawning was seen.

S. scaber.    Two TPs were recognised and remained at their
respective sites throughout the observation period.    The TPs
were always solitary within their ranges and all interactions
with other TPs were violent.    The 2 recognised IPs were always
solitary and all interactions with other IPs were also always
violent.    The IPs were present at their respective sites
throughout the study.    As with S. frenatus and
S. viridifucatus there was little interaction between the TP and
IP and overlap of TP and IP ranges was only partial.    Accurate
assessment of ranges, however, was again difficult due to lack
of patrolling behaviour or regular interactions with neighbouring conspecifics.    Pair spawning, however, was observed
between an IP and a TP on two separate occasions, that had
partially overlapping ranges.    No colour change in the TP was
noted.    Group spawning was never seen.

S. sordidus.    This is the most common species at the site.
Five TPs and 11 IPs were recognised.    The TPs were always
solitary and showed site attachment.    Two, however, were not
present throughout the duration of the study (moved to new site?
predated?).    All interactions between TP individuals were
violent.    The IPs were in groups of 3,4 and 4.    The group of 3
individuals were at a site marked by a buoy, which was lost
during a storm.    The site attachment information is incomplete
for these 3 individuals.    The other groups were present at their
respective sites for the duration of observations on them.    The
members of a group reacted violently towards intruders, but not
to other members of the group.    Territorial boundaries could be
assessed accurately in this species due to the frequency of
interactions with neighbours or neighbouring groups.    The TPs
showed no aggressive display towards IPs, although violent
interactions were observed.    There was no patrolling behaviour

of the TP in its territory.    Possibly the small size of the
territories (40-90 m$^2$) precluded the need for patrolling.
Overlap of the TP and IP's ranges was partial.    Spawning was
not seen with recognised individuals but every day after the
diurnal high tide TPs would become sexually active, cease
feeding, intensify their colours and rise 2-3 metres above their
territories.    Here they would spar with neighbouring TPs, swim
in circles and bob-swim (cf. Barlow (11)) at passing IPs.    On
several occasions IPs were seen to leave their territories and
swim out to deeper water, passing on the way several TPs which
would display to them.    Pair spawning would occur with a TP
individual a considerable distance from the IP's range.    After
spawning the IP would return to its territory.    The recognised
IPs moved off singly into deep water at spawning time on several
occasions, but contact with the fish was always lost in water
12-15 m deep.    Usually the IP would return to its territory
within a few minutes.    No group spawning was seen.

### DISCUSSION

S. psittacus (both phases) are best described as roving solitary
foragers, forming temporary associations with a few TP and IP
individuals.    Violent interactions between TPs were only
observed at spawning time.    Both pair and group spawning were
observed in this species.    There was no site attachment, except
for TPs at spawning time.    This brief account is similar to
descriptions of the wrasses, Thalassoma lunare (L.) (4), and
T.bifasciatum (Bloch)(3,5,7,10) and the parrot fish S. fasciatus
C. & V. (1).    The temporary territoriality by the TPs at
spawning time has been described as leking (5,6,7).    The colour
change at spawning in the TP S. psittacus is noteworthy.
Spawning colouration bears no resemblance to non-spawning
colouration either in colour or pattern.

S. lepidus exists in groups of a TP plus a number of IPs.
Patrolling behaviour and aggressive display by the TP towards
IPs were noted for this species.    When observed, spawning
between marked individuals was within the group (little colour
or pattern change was noted in the TPs at spawning).    This is
similar to the description of Labroides dimidiatus C. & V. (4,
13), a species which is monochromatic.    The group organisation
is referred to as harem formation.    Robertson (13) showed that
in the harems of L. dimidiatus sex reversal was controlled
socially by the presence of the male fish.    Removal of the male
resulted in the top female changing sex.    However, the presence
of a small TP S. lepidus without IPs, at the Aldabra site
suggests that if sex change is controlled by the presence of a
TP in the group, it is not the only method of TP production in
S. lepidus.

S. sordidus has solitary territorial TPs and group territorial
IPs, but there is only partial overlap of the respective territories and observations on spawning indicate that IPs do not
spawn with the TP which is nearest.    This description does not
fit comfortably on any of the published accounts, although
"extra-haramic spawning" have been noted (5,6).    The above

observations suggest that harem structure does not exist in this
species, although both TPs and IPs are territorial.    This
situation is best described as discrete TP and IP territoriality.

The remaining 3 species all show discrete TP and IP territoriality, lack of patrolling behaviour or aggressive displays by
the TPs.    However, the low density of these species and
localised feeding made territorial boundaries difficult to
define and it is possible that with more detailed study overlap
of TP and IPs may be total.    It is interesting to note that
S. scaber IPs are territorial and solitary, unlike the group
territoriality shown by the other territorial IPs.    Whether
this is induced by low density,other environmental factors, or
is a species attribute remains to be discovered.

In their discussion of the mating patterns of the labroid
fishes of the Caribbean, Warner & Robertson describe all
labroids as being either leking or haremic in social organisation (5,6).    The present author thinks such categorisation is
premature and that a previous description of social organisation
in labroids, placing leking and harem formation at different
ends of a spectrum is much closer to the truth (4).    Any
comparative study of social systems of the labroids must contain
information on the permanence of the groups and the extent of
"extra-haremic spawnings" and "intra-haremic spawnings".    The
social organisation of one parrot fish (S. croicensis Bloch) has
been shown to be very labile (14) and the formation of schools
as a mechanism for circumventing the territoriality of competi-
tors is well documented (15).    Similarly, at Heron Island
S. sordidus and S. frenatus show no territoriality (1) unlike
the Aldabra individuals.    There is a need to know what factors
control the social organisation of the labroids at a given site
as well as description of the full range of social organisation
shown by these abundant and widespread reef fishes.

## ACKNOWLEDGEMENTS

I am indebted to the Leverhulme Trust and the University of
Glasgow for financial support, and to the Royal Society for
permission to work at their Aldabra Research Station.    I would
like to thank Mr P.S. Meadows and Dr G.W. Potts for encouragement and advice;   Dr J.E. Randall for giving much useful
information on nomenclature and to Dr D.R. Robertson for
introducing me to the labroids.

## REFERENCES

(1)   Choat, J.H. & Robertson, D.R., 1975.    Protogynous herma-
        phroditism in fishes of the family Scaridae.    In
        Intersexuality in the Animal Kingdom (Ed. R.Reinboth).
        Heidelberg:   Springer-Verlag.    263-283.

(2)   Reinboth, R., 1968.    Protogynie bei papageifischen
        (Scaridae).    Zeitschrift für Naturforschung, 23b,
        852-855.

(3)  Reinboth, R., 1973.   Dualistic reproductive behaviour in
         the protogynous wrasse <u>Thalassoma bifasciatum</u> and some
         observations on its day-night changeover.
         <u>Helgoländer wiss Meersunters</u>, 24, 174-191.

(4)  Robertson, D.R. & Choat, J.H., 1974.   Protogynous
         hermaphroditism and social systems in labrid fish.
         Proceedings of the Second International Coral Reefs
         Symposium, 1, 217-225.

(5)  Warner, R.R. & Robertson, D.R., 1977.   Sexual patterns in
         the labroid fishes of the western Caribbean.   I. The
         wrasses (Labridae).   <u>Smithsonian Contributions to
         Zoology</u> (In the Press).

(6)  Robertson, D.R. & Warner, R.R., 1977.   Sexual patterns in
         the labroid fishes of the western Caribbean.   II. The
         parrot fishes (Scaridae).   <u>Smithsonian Contributions
         to Zoology</u> (In the Press).

(7)  Warner, R.R., Robertson, D.R. & Leigh, E.G., 1975.   Sex
         change and sexual selection.   <u>Science</u>, 190, 633-638.

(8)  Stoddart, D.R., Taylor, J.D., Fosberg, F.R. & Farrow, G.E.,
         1971.   Geomorphology of Aldabra Atoll.
         <u>Philosophical Transactions of the Royal Society,
         London, B</u>, 260, 31-65.

(9)  Reinboth, R., 1967.   Biandric teleost species.   <u>General
         and Comparative Endocrinology</u>, 9, Abstract No. 146.

(10) Randall, J.E. & Randall, H.A., 1963.   The spawning and
         early development of the Atlantic parrot fish,
         <u>Sparisoma rubripinne</u> with notes on the other scarid
         and labrid fishes.   <u>Zoologica, New York</u>, 48, 49-60.

(11) Barlow, G.W., 1975.   On the sociobiology of four Puerto
         Rican parrot fishes (Scaridae).   <u>Marine Biology</u>, 33,
         281-293.

(12) Buckman, N.S. & Ogden, J.C., 1973.   Territorial behaviour
         of the striped parrot fish <u>Scarus croicensis</u> Bloch
         (Scaridae).   <u>Ecology</u>, 54, 1377-1382.

(13) Robertson, D.R., 1972.   Social control of sex reversal
         in a coral reef fish.   <u>Science</u>, 177, 1007-1009.

(14) Ogden, J.C. & Buckman, N.S., 1973.   Movements, foraging
         groups, and diurnal migrations of the striped parrot
         fish <u>Scarus croicensis</u> Bloch (Scaridae).   <u>Ecology</u>,
         54, 1377-1382.

(15) Robertson, D.R., Sweatman, H.P.A., Fletcher, E.A. &
         Cleland, M.G., 1976.   Schooling as a mechanism for
         circumventing the territoriality of competitors.
         <u>Ecology</u>, 57, 1208-1220.

# BALCIS ALBA (DA COSTA) - A 'TEMPORARY' ECTOPARASITE ON NEOPENTADACTYLA MIXTA ÖSTERGREN

**L. Cabioch\*, J.N.R. Grainger\*\*, B.F. Keegan\*\*\* and G. Könnecker\*\*\***

*\*Station Biologique de Roscoff, France*
*\*\*Zoology Dept., Trinity College, Dublin Ireland*
*\*\*\*Zoology Dept., University College Galway, Ireland*

ABSTRACT

Laboratory and *in situ* studies have shown that the prosobranch *Balcis alba* is a temporary ectoparasite on the boreal holothuroid *Neopentadactyla mixta*. This association is described in relation to aspects of the species' functional anatomy and ecology.

## INTRODUCTION

The eulimids are relatively unmodified prosobranch molluscs which are ectoparasitic on echinoderms. Two common species, *Balcis alba* (da Costa) and *Balcis devians* (Monterosato), are widely distributed in the eastern North Atlantic and in the Mediterranean, *B. devians* having been found on *Mesothuria intestinalis* (Ascanius), *Echinus esculentus* L. and *Strongylocentrotus dröbachiensis* (O.F. Müller), according to Pelseneer (1928), and on *Antedon bifida* (Pennant), according to Fretter (1955). *Balcis alba* had never been seen feeding, but, from its frequent occurrence with *Spatangus purpureus* O.F. Müller, it was suspected that this echinoid might be its host (viz. Fretter and Graham, 1962). Prompted by the co-occurrence of the prosobranch and *Neopentadactyla mixta* in the coastal waters of Brittany (where both species are relatively rare; viz. Cabioch, 1965) and of western Ireland, recent studies show that *B. alba* is a temporary ectoparasite on this boreal holothuroid.

## RESULTS

*Neopentadactyla mixta* populates coarse sand and gravel-type substrates, within the depth range 4-200m, and is known from Tromsø, Norway (Brun, 1964) to Arcachon, France (Koehler, 1921). *In situ* investigations now show this burrowing sea-cucumber to be more common than was suggested by earlier records. This may be due to the fact that the animal's escape response quickly takes it outside the digging range of many dredges and grabs. The cylindrical body, which is somewhat attenuated at the ends, can exceed 55 cm. in length and burrows by advancing its distended mid-section through the substrate. In large specimens, the podia tend to be crowded into this middle part of the body where they form up to six double rows.

Typically, *N. mixta* adopts a U-shaped posture within the deposit and, when feeding, the protruding anterior end bears a crown of arborescent tentacles which can have a spread of 100 to 140 cm$^2$. This holothuroid might best be described as an 'impingement' feeder (Bullivant, 1968), seston adherring to the 15 large mucus coated tentacles which are arranged peripherally around the

237

mouth.    These are placed deep within the pharynx, in random order.    Five
smaller tentacles, usually forming an inner circle around the mouth, also play
a role in the feeding process for as many as three of these structures have
been observed to follow a single large tentacle into the pharyngeal cavity.
The indications are that feeding is seasonal, the animal remaining dormant
during the cooler months of the year.    When active, the sea-cucumber exhibits
a diurnal feeding rhythm, retracting between 1-4 hours after sunrise, remaining
quiescent for 1-2 hs, and then re-emerging over a 4h. period (Könnecker and
Keegan, 1973).    On retraction, it may burrow to depths of more than 40 cm
within the substrate.

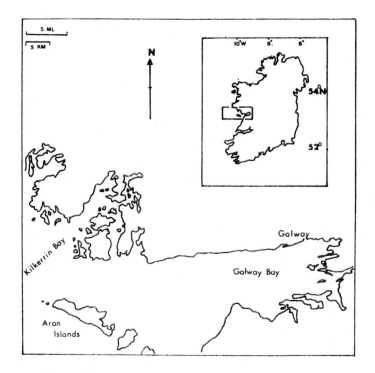

Fig. 1.    Location map of Kilkerrin Bay,
            Irish west coast.

*N. mixta*, in common with many echinoderms, is highly gregarious and may be
found in dense aggregations.    This phenomenon is extreme in parts of
Kilkerrin Bay, on the Irish west coast (Fig. 1), where densities of more than
200 individuals/m$^2$ are not unusual.    At one such location, the holothuroid
and *Balcis alba* dominate the macrobenthos to the exclusion of most other
species (Table 1, and Keegan, 1974) and may, between them, have a biomass in
excess of 500g. dry wt./m$^2$

## Table 1

Kilkerrin Bay – List of species'occurrences at 10 stations
(Quantitative suction-sampling;   sample size:   0.25 m$^2$/  45 cm.)

| Species | Station n | | | | | | | | | |
|---|---|---|---|---|---|---|---|---|---|---|
| | 1 | 2 | 3 | 4 | 5 | 6 | 7 | 8 | 9 | 10 |
| Neopentadactyla mixta | 18 | 20 | 9 | 16 | 5 | 10 | 14 | 10 | 16 | 5 |
| Balcis alba | 28 | 24 | 11 | 9 | 8 | 11 | 15 | 8 | 22 | 11 |
| Branchiostoma lanceolatum | - | 2 | - | - | 1 | - | - | - | - | - |
| Glycera alba | - | - | - | 2 | - | 2 | - | - | - | - |
| Nereis sp. | 2 | 1 | - | - | - | - | - | 1 | - | - |
| Echinocyamus pusillus | - | 2 | - | - | - | 1 | - | - | 1 | - |
| Luidia ciliaris | - | - | 1 | - | - | - | - | - | - | 1 |

Balcis alba moves about on a lanceolate foot which is small in relation to
the awl-shaped shell (max. size 19.5 mm, authors' experience).   Extremely
motile, it seemingly travels upon and within uncompacted coarse deposits
with equal ease.   In the Kilkerrin Bay area, these deposits are regularly
dislodged by strong tidal streams and it is possible that the copious amounts
of mucus secreted by the snail's pedal glands may help it to maintain its
position under such circumstances.   Balcis appears to be highly sensitive
to its environment, particularly to changes in light intensity.   The eyes
are large and are carried on a level with the bases of slender, pointed
tentacles.   This part of the body is not usually protruded but the eyes
are conspicuous through the shell.

Balcis has a long unarmed proboscis which is withdrawn into the haemocoele
when not in use.   The proboscis is acrembolic;   that is, on retraction it
turns completely outside in, beginning at the mouth.   At its inner end, it
passes into a narrower tube which is sharply demarcated from the true mouth.
Behind this, Fretter (1955) and Fretter and Graham (1962) identify an oral
tube, followed by a buccal cavity and a greatly elongated oesophagus.   The
proboscis can penetrate the body wall and pass deeply into its host.

In situ and laboratory studies, carried out during the summer period, revealed
the following about the association between the prosobranch and the holothuroid:

- B. alba mates during the summer months and, at this time, it
  displays a diurnal rhythmicity in its burrowing behaviour which
  parallels that of Neopentadactyla mixta.

- The snail moves randomly to the direction of current flow and may
  locate its host by sight.

- Some 30 to 100 seconds after making physical contact with the sea-cucumber, *Balcis* everts its proboscis and penetrates the body-wall. Penetration is attended by localised contraction of the body-wall around the point of entry.

- In the aquarium, the point of entry was not restricted to any part of the body surface. However, in the field, it is invariably located immediately below the tentacle crown. The snail connects to *N. mixta* solely with the proboscis; the foot does not appear to assist in making or in maintaining the attachment.

- Within the host's body cavity, the proboscis did not seek out a specific organ or tissue, and could be extended up to six times the length of the shell. It moves about actively and uses a pumping action to draw off the coelomic fluid, the rapid flow being clearly visible through its walls.

- Under experimental conditions, attachment was maintained for up to 30 hours.

- The prosobranch shows a marked preference for *Neopentadactyla mixta* and could only be induced to feed on another holothuroid, (*Cucumaria normani* Pace), after been starved for 12-14 days.

- Up to 6 snails were seen to feed simultaneously on a single aquarium-held holothuroid, apparently without doing it permanent damage.


DISCUSSION

The manner in which the prosobranch penetrates *N. mixta* has not been ascertained. When the proboscis is everted, the true mouth comes to lie at its tip and this, by muscular action, may pinch away the holothuroid's relatively tough skin. Fretter and Graham (1962) refer to the possibility (in *B. devians*) that the secretion of the pedal glands might produce some toxic or digestive effect on the tissues of the host. There is, of course, also the possibility that the proboscis itself may release some digesting secretion. Whatever the mode of penetration, the feeding link, once formed, cannot be disrupted easily and endures, at least for some time, after the holothuroid burrows into the substrate. It remains to be seen if the snail can locate and penetrate its host within the sediment.

Whilst no attempt has been made to measure the energy content of the sea-cucumber's body fluid, the long attachment time suggests that it is low. This raises the question of excretion-rate, on the part of the ectoparasite, which must be very fast to deal with the high fluid intake. Attempts to monitor this have, so far, proved unsuccessful. Could it be that the "clouds of secretion" liberated by *B. devians*, when feeding on *Antedon* (viz. Fretter, 1955), are largely the products of excretion?

The authors intend to further research the above and other aspects of this interesting association at a further time.    Particular attention will be given to the possibility that the association has a seasonal dimension related to the species' reproductive cycles.

## REFERENCES

Brun, E., 1964.    Echinodermata, Oslo (Univ. Press), 53pp. (Mimeogr.).

Bullivant, J.S., 1968.   A revised classification of suspension feeders. Tuatara, 16,   151-160.

Cabioch, L., 1965.   Notes sur la fauna marine benthique de Roscoff. Echinodermes.   Cahiers de Biologie Marine, 6, 265-268.

Fretter, V., 1955.   Observations on *Balcis devians* (Monterosato) and *Balcis alba* (Da Costa).   Proceedings of the Malacological Society of London, 31, 159-162.

Fretter, V. & Gramham, A.,   1962.   British Prosobranch Molluscs,   Their Functional Anatomy and Ecology.   Ray Society, London, 755.

Keegan, B.F., 1974.   The macrofauna of maerl substrates on the west coast of Ireland.   Cahiers de Biologie Marine, 15, 513-530.

Koehler, R., 1921.   Échinodermes.   Fauna de France, 1, 1-210.

Könnecker, G., & Keegan, B.F., 1973.   *In situ* behavioural studies on echinoderm aggregations Part I.   *Pseudocucumis mixta*.   Helgoländer wiss Meeresunters, 24, 157-162.

Pelseneer, P., 1928.   Les parasites des mollusques et les mollusques parasites.   Bulletin Société zoologique de France, 53, 158-189.

# THE MIGRATION OF PLAICE LARVAE
# *PLEURONECTES PLATESSA* INTO THE
# WESTERN WADDEN SEA

**F. Creutzberg, A.Th.G.W. Eltink and G.J. van Noort**

*Netherlands Institute for Sea Research, Texel, Netherlands*

## ABSTRACT

The question how in the Wadden Sea very small O-group plaice concentrate in
early spring, is the subject of the present study carried out in 1974, 1975
and 1977. Evidence was found that in March and April, through selective transport by tidal currents, a net inward movement of stage 4 and 5 larvae takes
place in the tidal inlets (e.g. the Marsdiep). This implies that the larvae
should respond to some stimuli by either swimming pelagically or by staying on
the bottom. In an experimental device (a circular tidal stream apparatus) it
became clear that feeding conditions act upon the swimming behaviour of the
larvae. Starvation releases pelagic swimming, whereas feeding induces the
metamorphosing larvae to lie on the bottom. This suggests that in the North
Sea the settling larvae are subjected to a shortage of adequate benthic food,
whereas the tidal flats of the Wadden Sea, where feeding conditions are very
favourable, act as a trap for settling larvae.

## INTRODUCTION

During last decades it became evident that coastal and inshore areas - the
Wadden Sea in particular - are essential as nursery grounds for plaice (Ref. 1,
2, 3, 4 and 5). The spawning areas, on the other hand, are found in open sea
(Ref. 6 and 7). One of the main spawning areas of the North Sea plaice is
located in the Southern Bight, 20-60 miles off the coast. It shifts north
easterly in the course of the spawning season (December-February).

As a consequence of north-easterly residual currents the eggs and larvae are
carried toward the latitude of the Wadden Sea. Simpson (6) arrived at an estimated average drift of 2.4 miles per day, varying between 0 and 5 miles per
day. Apart from a slight tendency to approach the continent off Texel island,
the eggs are drifted parallel with the coastline of Holland and Germany. Larvae
in early stages of development approximately show a similar course of drift
(Ref. 8). According to Simpson (6) the larvae will be distributed over a very
large area parallel to the continental coastline, but some 20-40 miles from it.

The question, therefore, arises how the large concentrations of O-group plaice
in the Wadden Sea in April and May should be explained. In the period between
the drift of early larval stages (1 and 2) and the arrival of very small O-
group plaice (stage 4 and 5) on the tidal flats of the Wadden Sea, an inshore
movement must have taken place.

In the present paper the attention will be limited to the actual inward movement from the North Sea into the Wadden Sea. From earlier work it is known

243

that elvers, *Anguilla vulgaris* (Ref. 9) as well as swimming crabs *Macropipus holsatus* (Ref. 10) use the tidal currents selectively for transport either inward or outward the Wadden Sea. Such a mechanism is also described for pink shrimp *Penaeus duorarum* in the Everglades, Florida, U.S.A.(Ref. 11). The question arises whether young plaice (larvae or metamorphosed larvae) migrate in the same way into the Wadden Sea. In the early spring of the years 1974, 1975 and 1977 series of oblique plankton hauls were made in or near the tidal inlet Marsdiep with an Isaacs-Kidd mid-water trawl during the ebb as well as during the flood. Significant differences in density of larvae between ebb and flood will provide evidence for a net transport in   a single direction. Additionally, the behaviour of larvae is studied in the laboratory in a circular tidal stream apparatus in order to detect possible stimuli which release either pelagic swimming (resulting in passive transport) or lying on the bottom.

## MATERIAL AND METHODS

### Field Methods

At selected stations, in or near the entrance of the Wadden Sea between Den Helder and Texel, series of oblique plankton hauls were made from an anchored or sailing vessel (R.V. "Aurelia" or R.V. "Ephyra") during the flood as well as during the ebb. The duration of the series (at most 3 days) varied with weather conditions and availability of vessels. In 1974 the stations were located in the Marsdiep (about 27 m depth) and a few miles inshore in the tidal gullies Texelstroom (about 28 m depth) and Malzwin (about 16 m depth). In 1975 all hauls were made in the Marsdiep and in 1977 in the Texelstroom.

The samples were taken with a modified Isaacs-Kidd midwater trawl (Ref. 12) with a mouth area of 7.29 $m^2$ and a length of 20 m. The net was made of polyamid plankton gauze (Monodur no. 1400; 1.4 mm aperture). For each oblique haul, lasting 15-25 minutes, the net was lowered in steps of 3-3½ m depth intervals (lasting 2-4 min each) and hauled in slowly again. Afterwards the maximum depth to which the net was lowered and the amount of water that passed through the net was measured. With the introduction of a net-sonde winch in 1977, the depth could be read on board during each haul immediately.

The larvae were preserved in 3% formalin and sorted into morphological stages as described by Ryland (13). All counts were converted into numbers per 10,000 $m^3$. The 95% confidence limits of the mean were calculated after a $y = \log(x+1)$ transformation of the converted counts (zero counts were present). For transformation back the formula

$$\log(\bar{x}+1) = \bar{y} \pm t.s_{\bar{y}} + 1.15\ s_y^2\ \frac{n-1}{n}$$

was used in order to obtain arithmetic values (the original scale) instead of the derived values (Ref. 14 and 15).

### Laboratory Experiments

In order to study the swimming behaviour of plaice larvae under conditions of tidal currents, a circular stream apparatus was used as described by Venema and Creutzberg (10). For each experiment 30 to 60 larvae were placed in the experimental circular channel. The current was kept constant at about 7 cm per sec. The movements of the larvae were recorded over periods of 10 minutes

simply by counting the individuals passing a vertical reference line, upstream
or downstream, either swimming pelagically or crawling on the bottom. The
counts were converted into number of larvae per 100 passing per minute; in
other words by assuming the presence of 100 larvae in the channel. During the
experiments, conditions, such as salinity, temperature and odour content
(water from tidal flats), were gradually changed through a system of a water
supply and an overflow. Special attention was paid to conditions which enhance
or reduce the tendency of pelagic downstream swimming or passive transport.

RESULTS

Plankton Surveys

Numbers of plaice larvae, collected in 23 series of oblique plankton hauls in
the tidal inlet of the Wadden Sea between Den Helder and Texel in the spring
of 1974, 1975 and 1977 are summarized for ebb and flood catches separately in
Table 1 and in Fig. 1. Most larvae were found in March and April. In nearly
all cases the larvae, present in the water column, were more abundant during
the flood than during the ebb tide. Apparently, from all larvae transported
into the Wadden Sea on the flood, only one third returned with the ebb tide.
In 12 series confidence limits for ebb and flood catches do not even overlap;
in some series, however, confidence limits are wide, mostly due to a shortage
of hauls.

When the results of the different years in question are compared, it appears
that the total number of larvae entering through the Marsdiep shows remarkable
differences, amounting to 53 million in 1974, 256 million in 1975 and 1033
million in 1977. These figures are rough estimates, derived from the differences between the ebb and flood catches (Fig. 1), from the fact that one $km^3$
of water flows in and out the Wadden Sea through the Marsdiep at each tide and
from the assumption of a uniform larval distribution in the tidal inlet. The
question arises, of course, whether these between-year differences of net
inward transport are reflected in the densities of 0-group plaice, occupying
the tidal flats in the months subsequent to the immigration. The mean density
of 0-group plaice on the Balgzand (a well studied area belonging to the tidal
basin of the Marsdiep) was, at peak values, about 25 per 1000 $m^2$ in 1974,
about 130 per 1000 $m^2$ in 1975 and at least 280 per 1000 $m^2$ in 1977 (unpublished
NIOZ data). The total numbers of 0-group plaice present on the Balgzand (50
$km^2$) at peak densities, therefore, would represent 2.36% (1974), 2.54% (1975)
and > 1.36% (1977) of the total amount of larvae immigrated through the Marsdiep. It should be noted that the total surface of the tidal basin covers 680
$km^2$ (13.6 x Balgzand) and that the total surface of its tidal flats covers
130 $km^2$ (2.6 x Balgzand) (Ref. 16). The time elapsing between the immigration
maximum and the appearance of peak densities on the Balgzand is in the order
of 35-45 days.

During the surveys all larvae were sorted into the developmental stages as
described by Ryland (13). Table 2 shows the composition of the larval population in the Marsdiep area in 1974, 1975 and 1977, as well as the percentage
of larvae washed back with the ebb after inward transportation on the flood.
In 1975 all larvae were measured and the mean length of each stage is also
given in this table. In Fig. 2 the mean numbers of larvae caught during ebb
and flood in 1975 and 1977 are shown for the larval stages separately. It is
clear that a shift from early to late stages takes place in the course of the
season. In 1974 the numbers of larvae caught were too small, and the duration
of the surveys in the season too short to present a comparable picture for

F. Creutzberg, A. Th. G. W. Eltink and G. J. van Noort

TABLE 1   Mean numbers of plaice larvae per 10,000 m$^3$ found in oblique hauls during ebb and flood tide with 95% confidence limits and numbers of hauls (n)

| date | Ebb catches numbers 10,000 m$^{-3}$ | | (n) | Flood catches numbers 10,000 m$^{-3}$ | | (n) |
|---|---|---|---|---|---|---|
| 28. ii.74 | 0 | ( 0-   1  ) | ( 6) | 1 | (  0-   3) | ( 4) |
| 4.iii.74 | 0 | – | ( 1) | 0 | – | ( 1) |
| 13.iii.74 | 9 | ( 0-546  ) | ( 3) | 15 | (  1-255) | ( 4) |
| 21.iii.74 | 0 | ( 0-  0.5) | (12) | 2 | (  1-  5) | ( 9) |
| 28.iii.74 | 3 | ( 0-  7  ) | ( 9) | 21 | ( 12- 50) | (13) |
| 4. iv.74 | 4 | ( 1-  8  ) | (11) | 14 | (  9- 22) | (10) |
| 10. iv.74 | 2 | ( 1-  5  ) | ( 8) | 6 | (  3- 14) | (12) |
| 27. ii.75 | 4 | ( 3-  6  ) | (19) | 10 | (  8- 14) | (19) |
| 6.iii.75 | 4 | ( 2-  6  ) | (21) | 9 | (  6- 15) | (17) |
| 20.iii.75 | 16 | (13- 21  ) | ( 8) | 65 | ( 32-139) | ( 7) |
| 26.iii.75 | 4 | ( 1-  8  ) | ( 8) | 6 | (  2- 13) | ( 2) |
| 3. iv.75 | 23 | ( 6- 90  ) | ( 3) | 49 | ( 12-211) | ( 4) |
| 10. iv.75 | 12 | ( 9- 17  ) | (18) | 30 | ( 24- 37) | (17) |
| 16. iv.75 | 5 | ( 3-  7  ) | ( 9) | 25 | ( 16- 38) | ( 8) |
| 24. iv.75 | 3 | ( 1-  6  ) | (15) | 20 | ( 15- 27) | (19) |
| 1.  v.75 | – | – | – | 28 | (  3-212) | ( 3) |
| 15.  v.75 | 10 | ( 6- 26  ) | (17) | 9 | (  3- 26) | (12) |
| 29.  v.75 | 11 | ( 4- 22  ) | (20) | 3 | (  1-  7) | (11) |
| 2.iii.77 | 86 | (48-153  ) | ( 5) | 170 | ( 80-371) | ( 5) |
| 10.iii.77 | 70 | (46-107  ) | (13) | 247 | (159-381) | (10) |
| 23.iii.77 | 61 | (29-110  ) | (10) | 109 | ( 59-219) | (12) |
| 29.iii.77 | 11 | ( 3- 32  ) | ( 9) | 148 | ( 81-240) | (10) |
| 25. iv.77 | 1 | ( 0-  9  ) | ( 3) | 28 | ( 10- 86) | ( 9) |

TABLE 2   Larval stages. Composition of the population, percentage of larvae washed back, and mean length in 1975

| stage | Occurrence (% of total) | | | | Return with ebb (% of flood) | | | | Mean length (1975) |
|---|---|---|---|---|---|---|---|---|---|
| | 1974 | 1975 | 1977 | mean | 1974 | 1975 | 1977 | mean | |
| 3 | 3.2 | 0.4 | 0 | 1.2 | – | – | – | – | 8.5 mm |
| 4a | 12.3 | 4.3 | 1.6 | 6.1 | 34.6 | 115.7 | 41.6 | 64.0 | 10.2 mm |
| 4b | 35.0 | 57.2 | 50.1 | 47.4 | 35.9 | 56.9 | 36.2 | 43.0 | 11.9 mm |
| 4b' | 38.5 | 16.9 | 21.0 | 25.5 | 36.6 | 27.1 | 40.7 | 34.8 | 12.8 mm |
| 5 | 10.9 | 21.2 | 27.2 | 19.8 | 5.4 | 22.8 | 21.5 | 16.6 | 14.3 mm |

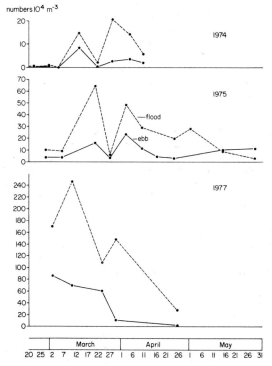

Fig. 1   Number of pelagic plaice larvae in the
Marsdiep area during ebb and flood

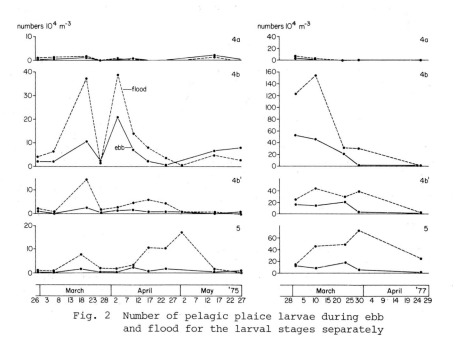

Fig. 2   Number of pelagic plaice larvae during ebb
and flood for the larval stages separately

that year. Figure 2 also shows that the clearest differences between ebb and
flood catches are found in stage 5 larvae. Table 2 demonstrates that the percentages of larvae transported back by the ebb are significantly lower in
stage 5 larvae than in earlier stages. In stages 4a, 4b and 4b' the three
years mean value suggests a possible trend of an increasing effectiveness of
the selective tidal transport with age, but the figures of the separate years
do not justify definite conclusions.

Since the oblique plankton hauls were made under varying conditions, such as
day and night, different phases of the tides and varying maximum depths to
which the midwater trawl was lowered, the effect of these conditions has been
studied on the 1975 material. In general, catches were lower during the day
than during the night: 75% in the ebb hauls and 85% in the flood hauls. The
high variability of the figures, however, did not justify the application of
a correction. No significant effect of the phase of the tide (ebb or flood,
each subdivided into 3 equal periods) could be demonstrated. The maximum depth
to which the midwater trawl was lowered, varying from about 10 to 27 m, did
not affect significantly the catches. In the strong and turbulent currents in
the tidal inlet, apparently, no vertical gradient of larval density was present. Through a shortage of observations an analysis of a possible interaction
between these different conditions is not possible.

Laboratory Experiments

The selective transport of plaice larvae by tidal currents, as demonstrated
above in the plankton surveys, implies that the larvae, under certain conditions, must swim pelagically (to be transported) and, under other conditions,
should stay on the bottom (to resist transport). Studies on the behaviour of
plaice larvae (Stage 4 and 5) in a circular stream apparatus are still in
progress. First results, however, will be briefly reported in the present
paper for a better understanding of the mechanism of retention of the plaice
larvae in the Wadden Sea.

With the intention to release adequate swimming behaviour in the circular
stream apparatus, with current velocities of about 7 cm per sec, ebb and flood
conditions were simulated. When the larvae were introduced into the experimental channel (30-60 individuals), they invariably stayed at the bottom lying
on one side. During the artificial ebb the larvae were subjected to decreasing
salinity (e.g. from $35.9^\circ/oo$ to $29.6^\circ/oo$), increasing temperature (e.g. from
$5.7^\circ C$ to $7.5^\circ C$; spring conditions), an increasing amount of water taken from
the tidal flats (smell of food) or a combination of these factors. The flood,
on the other hand, was simulated by increasing salinity, decreasing temperature and decreasing amount of "Wadden Sea odour" through a supply of sea
water, filtered over charcoal. These experiments, however, did not reveal any
behaviour in the larvae through which a possible inward migration into the
Wadden Sea might be explained. During none of the experiments a significant
positive or negative rheotaxis was observed, nor any tendency to swim in the
water column.

Surprising effects, however, were observed by changing feeding conditions.
Starvation clearly released pelagic swimming, whereas feeding induced the
metamorphosing larvae to lie on the bottom. This effect is shown in Fig. 3,
where counts of pelagically transported larvae, passing an arbitrary vertical
line in the course of an experiment, are given. As far as, during this experiment, larvae were found on the bottom, they clearly displayed a negative

rheotaxis (downstream crawling over the bottom) during the periods of starvation.

Tentatively the hypothesis may be advanced that in the North Sea metamorphosing and settling larvae are confronted with a shortage of adequate benthic
food. Indeed, the larvae caught pelagically in the Marsdiep with flood as
well as with ebb, were nearly all found with empty stomachs. Only in 3% of the
larvae some food particles were found in the stomach. On the tidal flats of
the Wadden Sea, on the other hand, newly-settled larvae have nearly all been
found with full stomachs, suggesting favourable feeding conditions. The tidal
flats, over which the larvae are spread out during flood, may therefore act
as a trap for settling larvae.

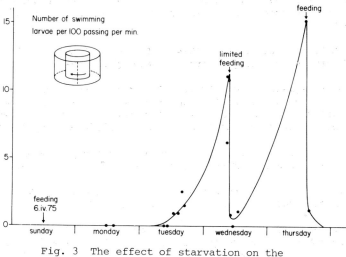

Fig. 3   The effect of starvation on the
swimming behaviour of plaice larvae

## DISCUSSION

The results obtained so far may readily explain the retention of plaice larvae
in the Wadden Sea once arrived in the tidal inlets. In one flood tide the
arrival on the tidal flats will be fairly sure. The feeding conditions on the
flats prevent the larvae from being transported back with the ebb. We are,
however, still unable to explain satisfactorily the movements from the open
sea towards the tidal inlets of the Wadden Sea. As stated earlier the eggs
and larvae are drifted parallel to the continental coastline some 20-40 miles
from it (Ref. 6 and 8). For the occupation of the nursery grounds, however,
a movement towards the coastline must take place. Two possible mechanisms,
probably reinforcing each other, may underly this onshore movement. (a) According to Harding and Talbot (8) metamorphosing stages of the plaice in the North
Sea spend long periods in water layers just above the sea bed, whereas Ramster,
Medler and Jones (17) mention a marked onshore residual drift at the bottom,
particularly off the Dutch coast. (b) The other possible mechanism is based
on the assumption that in the North Sea metamorphosing larvae (stage 4 and 5),
as the result of a shortage of suitable benthic food, still spend long periods
swimming pelagically, transported in any direction. Swimming activity, however,
may be reduced when larvae are subjected to offshore water movement, carrying
olfactory substances from coastal and inshore areas. A net onshore transport

of larvae could be the final result. In the circular tidal stream apparatus some indications were obtained that swimming activity of starving larvae decreases when the smell of food (extract of mussels and shrimps) is introduced. This study is still in progress.

## REFERENCES

(1)    Bückmann, A., 1934.    Über die Jungschollenbevölkerung der deutschen Wattenküste der Nordsee.    *Berichte der Deutschen wissenschaftlichen Kommission für Meeresforschung*, Neue Folge 7, 205-213.

(2)    Zijlstra, J.J., 1972.    On the importance of the Waddensea as a nursery area in relation to the conservation of the southern North Sea fishery resources.    *Symposia of the Zoological Society of London,* 29, 233-258.

(3)    Becker, H.B. & Postuma, K.H., 1974.    Enige voorlopige resultaten van vijf jaar "Waddenzee-project".    *Visserij* 27, 69-79.

(4)    Rauck, G. & Zijlstra, J.J., 1977.    On the nursery-aspects of the Waddensea for some commercial fish-species and possible long-term changes. *International Council for the Exploration of the Sea symposium on the changes in the North Sea fish stocks and their causes,* 36, 1-16.

(5)    Kuipers, B.R., 1977.    On the ecology of juvenile plaice on a tidal flat in the Wadden Sea.    *Netherlands Journal of Sea Research,* 11, 56-91.

(6)    Simpson, A.C., 1959.    The spawning of the plaice in the North Sea. *Fisheries Investigations, London,* Series 2 22, 1-111.

(7)    Bannister, R.C.A., Harding, D. & Lockwood, S.J., 1974.    Larval mortality and subsequent year-class strength in the plaice *(Pleuronectes platessa L.).*    In *The Early Life History of Fish* (Ed. J.H.S. Blaxter) 765 pp. Springer Verlag Berlin, Heidelberg, New York.

(8)    Harding, D. & Talbot, J.W., 1973.    Recent studies on the eggs and larvae of the plaice *(Pleuronectes platessa L.)* in the Southern Bight. *Rapport et procès-verbaux des réunions. Conseil permanent international pour l'exploration de la mer,* 164, 261-269.

(9)    Creutzberg, F., 1961.    On the orientation of migrating elvers *(Anguilla vulgaris* Turt.*)* in a tidal area.    *Netherlands Journal of Sea Research* 1, 257-338.

(10)    Venema, S.C. & Creutzberg, F., 1973.    Seasonal migration of the swimming crab *Macropipus holsatus* in an estuarine area controlled by tidal streams.    *Netherlands Journal of Sea Research,* 7, 94-102.

(11)    Hughes, D.A., 1969.    Responses to salinity change as a tidal transport mechanism of pink shrimp, *Penaeus duorarum. Biological Bulletin, Marine Biological Laboratory, Woods Hole, Mass.,* 136, 43-53.

(12)    Isaacs, J.D. & Kidd, L.W., 1953.    Isaacs-Kidd midwater trawl. Final report.    *Scripps Institution of Oceanography Ref.* 53-3, Oceanographic equipment report no. 1.

(13)  Ryland, J.S., 1966.    Observations on the development of larvae of the
      plaice, *Pleuronectes platessa* L., in aquaria.    *Journal du Conseil
      permanent international pour l'exploration de la mer*, 30, 177-195.

(14)  Elliott, J.M., 1973.    Some methods for the statistical analysis of
      samples of benthic invertebrates.    *Scientific publications, Fresh-
      water Biological Association* No. 25, 148 pp.

(15)  Becker, H.B. & Corten, A., 1974.    The precision of abundance estimates
      from young herring surveys in the North Sea.    *International Council
      for the Exploration of the Sea, Pelagic Fish (Northern) Committee*
      C.M. 1974/H:19, 6 pp.

(16)  Zimmerman, J.T.F., 1976.    Mixing and flushing of tidal embayments in
      the western Dutch Wadden Sea. Part I: Distribution of salinity and
      calculation of mixing time scales.    *Netherlands Journal of Sea
      Research*, 10, 149-191.

(17)  Ramster, J.W., Medler, K.J. & Jones, S.R., 1976.    Residual drift regimes
      in the Southern Bight of the North Sea during the Joint North Sea
      Data Acquisition Project of 1973 (JONSDAP 73).    *International Council
      for the Exploration of the Sea, Hydrography Committee*, C.M. 1976/C:5,
      9 pp.

# CRUSTACEAN LARVAL PHOTOTAXIS: POSSIBLE FUNCTIONAL SIGNIFICANCE

### Richard B. Forward, Jr. and Thomas W. Cronin

*Duke University Marine Laboratory, Beaufort, N.C., 06520 and Zoology Department, Duke University, Durham, N.C., 27706, U.S.A.*

## ABSTRACT

Light adapted larvae from the estuarine crab Rhithropanopeus harrisii show a positive phototaxis to moderate and high light intensities, but become negative at lower intensities. The pattern reverses upon dark adaptation. The negative phototaxis by light adapted larvae is speculated to participate in predator avoidance and/or diurnal vertical migration. Present evidence suggests that it is probably not involved in migration, since the light intensity level necessary for producing this behavior exceeds that which initiates negative phototaxis. In addition, estuarine light measurements indicate that the rate of intensity decrease at sunset may be slower than dark adaptation. Thus, it is predicted that the negative phototaxis probably functions primarily during predator avoidance in the higher light intensities, which occur near the surface of the water during the day.

## INTRODUCTION

Most larvae of benthic crustaceans show directional movements upon stimulation with a directional light source (phototaxis). The sign of phototaxis by larvae of the crab Rhithropanopeus harrisii depends upon light or dark adaptation and the light stimulus intensity. Following dark adaptation, larvae show negative phototaxis and/or reduced levels of positive phototaxis to high intensity light and become strongly positively phototactic to lower intensities (dark adapted phototactic pattern - DAPP). The pattern reverses upon light adaptation as the larvae show a positive response to high intensities, while a negative response is seen at lower intensities (light adapted phototactic pattern - LAPP)[1] (Foward, 1974; Forward and Costlow, 1974) This pattern is not unique to R. harrisii, as it is reported for six other brachyuran species (Forward, 1977; Herrnkind, 1968).

Forward (1974) originally hypothesized that the changes in phototaxis upon light and dark adaptation (LAPP and DAPP) could lead to a diurnal vertical migration pattern. An ascent is possible at dawn since the larvae lose the negative response after dark adaptation. The presence of negative phototaxis to low light levels after light adaptation, could lead to a descent from surface waters at sunset. However, recent work indicates that this negative phototaxis is part of a shadow response probably used for predator avoidance (Forward, 1976).

The present study experimentally investigated the hypothesis that the negative phototaxis to low light subsequent to light adaptation can in fact lead to a vertical descent at sunset. At least one of two events must occur for this to be true. First, the light intensity which evokes negative phototaxis must be sufficient for inducing the LAPP. If this does not occur, then secondly, subsequent to light adaptation, negative phototaxis should persist for at least the time that it would take naturally occurring light intensity to decrease from the level necessary for inducing the LAPP to the level for the negative response. The results presented indicate that the first situation does not occur and suggest that the second is unlikely. Thus the proposed hypothesis is not well supported.

## MATERIALS AND METHODS

Ovigerous specimens of Rhithropanopeus harrisii (Gould) were collected from the Neuse River in eastern North Carolina, U.S.A. All experiments were conducted with the first larval stage (Stage I zoea), which were reared as previously described (Forward, 1976). Two sets of experiments were conducted, in addition to field observations of light intensity changes at sunset. Approximately equal numbers of larvae from at least three separate females were tested in each experiment. To avoid complications due to biological rhythms in behavior, all experiments were begun four to six hours after the beginning of the light phase of the LD 12:12 cycle, on which larvae were reared.

The first series of experiments were designed to determine the minimum light intensity to which the larvae must be adapted before they will show the LAPP. A microscope-television system was used to observe larval behavior (for details see Forward, 1974b). The light stimulus source was a slide projector having a 300 W incandescent lamp interference filtered to 499 nm (Optics Technology; half band pass 14 nm) and intensity as measured with a radiometer (YSI, model 65) was controlled with neutral density filters.

The general procedure was to place larvae, previously exposed to room lights, in the experimental cuvette and vertically irradiate them from above, using the foregoing stimulus system (for vertical stimulation technique see Forward, 1976) for 30 min at various light intensity levels. This time was chosen because it is probably sufficient for light adaptation to occur (e.g., Hyatt, 1975; Waterman, 1961). Furthermore vertical stimulation was used to prevent long term excessive crowding near the light sources which occurs over time upon horizontal stimulation. Larvae were then stimulated horizontally with a range of light intensities. Responses were recorded on video tape and analyzed for positive and negative phototaxis as described previously (Forward 1974a).

The second series of experiments was designed to determine the length of time the LAPP persists after light adaptation. The procedure consisted of light adapting groups of 10 larvae to various light intensity levels for at least 30 min with the light stimulus system used in the previous experiments. The larvae were then transfered to the center section of a rectangular test chamber (2.5 x 3 x 15 cm) which was divided horizontally into 5 equal compartments. After 30 sec in darkness the larvae were stimulated continuously in a horizontal plane with light from a slide projector filtered to 500 nm with a thin film filter (half band pass 7 nm; Ditric Optics Co.) and set at various intensities by neutral density filters. At 1 min intervals the horizontal larval distribution was observed by turning on a fluorescent lamp mounted horizontally behind the test chamber and filtered to wavelengths longer than 600 nm with red cellophane (Dupont No. "K" 210 FCRD). Larvae in the section furthest from the light were considered to display negative phototaxis. The data presented from these experiments are the times until the maximum negative response occurred and until the response fell to 50% of this level. The latter is considered indicative of the length of time that negative phototaxis persisted.

The third portion of the study involved determinations of underwater light intensities at sunset. Since measurements of this type are very dependent upon climatic conditions and geographical location, the intent of this study was to obtain representative information on the rate of change in intensity. Measurements were made with a submarine photometer (Kahl Scientific Inst. Corp., Model # 268WA310) fitted with a cosine collector and filtered with a blue filter (Corning No. 4-72; peak wavelength 472 nm, half band pass 54 nm). The spectral range of the light measurement system duplicates that for R. harrisii (Forward and Costlow, 1974) and thus measures light, which the larvae would perceive. A deck cell similarly filtered was used to measure surface intensities. Measurements were made on evenings, which had few clouds on the horizon and, for comparison, in two areas within the Newport River Estuary, N.C. at different tidal phases where the larvae can occur. Intensities were measured every 10 minutes at the surface and specific intervals throughout the water column.

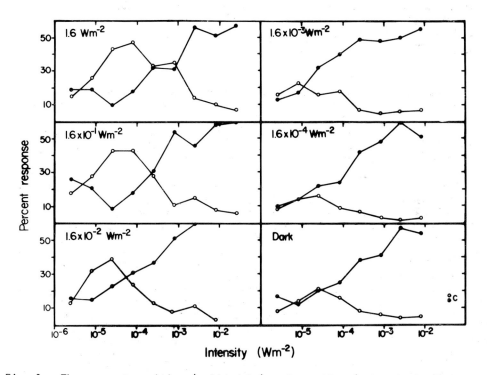

Fig. 1. The percent positive (solid dots) and negative (open circles) phototaxis (ordinate) after light adaptation to the intensities shown and stimulation with a range of intensities (abscissa). Dark control shows responses after 30 min in darkness. C-dot and C-opn circle in the dark figure are the respective control levels of swimming in the positive and negative phototactic directions with no stimulus present. (n=237). The average sample size for each plotted point is 60.

## RESULTS AND DISCUSSION

The levels of positive and negative phototaxis to various stimulus levels subsequent to adaptation at different light intensities is shown in Fig. 1. Light adaptation to intensities of $1.6 \times 10^{-2}$ $Wm^{-2}$ and greater induce a negative response to low intensities (approximate range $5 \times 10^{-5}$ to $10^{-3}$ $Wm^{-2}$) and a positive response to higher intensities. Table I shows the upper and lower threshold intensities for evoking the negative response and the approximate intensities which cause the maximum response upon adaptation to the three intensity levels. The range of intensities to which the larvae respond negatively shift to lower levels as the light adaptation level is lowered. Furthermore, there is a very slight (8%) reduction in the maximum negative response level as the adaptation intensity is reduced.

TABLE I.  Lower and upper threshold intensities and those which evoke the maximum negative phototactic response upon adaptation to various intensity levels as shown in Fig. 1.  Thresholds were determined as those intensities which evoke the lowest significant (at 5% level) percent response (27%).  The maximum response levels are estimated from the curves.  All intensities are in $Wm^{-2}$.

| Light adaptation intensity | Maximum response level (%) | Lower threshold | Maximum response intensity | Upper threshold |
|---|---|---|---|---|
| 1.6 | 47 | $8.5 \times 10^{-6}$ | $8 \times 10^{-5}$ | $1.3 \times 10^{-3}$ |
| $1.6 \times 10^{-1}$ | 43 | $7.0 \times 10^{-6}$ | $5 \times 10^{-5}$ | $2.7 \times 10^{-4}$ |
| $1.6 \times 10^{-2}$ | 39 | $6.0 \times 10^{-6}$ | $2.4 \times 10^{-5}$ | $6.5 \times 10^{-5}$ |

The negative response is absent both upon light adaptation to lower light intensities ($1.6 \times 10^{-3}$ and $1.6 \times 10^{-4}$ $Wm^{-2}$) and upon dark adaptation as the levels of negative phototaxis do not differ significantly (5% level) from the controls as indicated by determining a Z statistic for testing differences between two proportions (Walpole, 1974).  In addition, for these 3 cases (dark, $1.6 \times 10^{-3}$ and $1.6 \times 10^{-4}$ $Wm^{-2}$) the overall phototactic pattern is very similar.  This clearly indicates that intensities which evoke the negative response are too low for inducing the LAPP.

Therefore it is necessary to measure the length of time that the negative response persists after adaptation to various light levels.  Since the range of intensities to which the larvae respond negatively changes with the light adaptation intensity, two experimental series were initiated. First, larvae were light adapted to a range of light intensities which are sufficient for light-adaptation (4.7, $4.7 \times 10^{-2}$, $4.7 \times 10^{-3}$ $Wm^{-2}$) and then stimulated continuously with a constant light intensity ($4.8 \times 10^{-4}$ $Wm^{-2}$), which according to Fig. 1 evokes a negative repsonse.  As shown in Table II there is a decrease in both the length of time until the maximum response level and until a level at 50% of this value occurs as the adaptation intensity decreases.

In the second series of experiments the larvae were light adapted for at least 30 min to a constant light level ($4.7 \times 10^{-3}$ $Wm^{-2}$), then transferred to the test chamber and continuously stimulated with either of three intensities ($4.8 \times 10^{-4}$, $6.4 \times 10^{-5}$, $1.5 \times 10^{-5}$ $Wm^{-2}$), all of which evoke a negative response.  According to Fig. 1, this adaptation level was near the lowest, which induces the LAPP, and the lowest stimulus level ($1.5 \times 10^{-5}$ $Wm^{-2}$) was about the lowest level, which would induce a negative response.  As seen in Table II, both the time until a maximum negative response occurs and until 50%

Table II. Times to maximum negative phototaxis and to 50% of this level upon light adaptation to various intensities and then continuous stimulation with intensities which evoke the negative response. The mean (m) and standard deviation (SD) of the times are rounded off to the nearest minute. n is the number of determinations, each of which used 10 larvae. For comparison the length of time (min) that it would take surface intensities at site 1 and 2 (from Figs. 2 and 3) to decrease from the adaptation intensity to the stimulation levels are shown. Similar calculations are made for an initial adaptation level of $4.7 \times 10^{-3}$ as shown in Figs. 2 and 3.

| Light adaptation intensity ($Wm^{-2}$) | Stimulus intensity ($Wm^{-2}$) | n | Maximum response level | Time to maximum response level | | Time to 50% response level | | Time for surface intensity decrease | | Time for decrease from lowest adaptation intensity | |
|---|---|---|---|---|---|---|---|---|---|---|---|
| | | | | m | SD | m | SD | site 1 | site 2 | site 1 | site 2 |
| 4.7 | $4.8 \times 10^{-4}$ | 6 | 90% | 5 | 2 | 17 | 5 | 66 | 68 | | |
| $4.7 \times 10^{-2}$ | $4.8 \times 10^{-4}$ | 6 | 77% | 3 | 1 | 12 | 4 | 22 | 24 | | |
| $4.7 \times 10^{-3}$ | $4.8 \times 10^{-4}$ | 7 | 64% | 2 | 1 | 7 | 3 | 11 | 12 | 39 | 43 |
| $4.7 \times 10^{-3}$ | $6.4 \times 10^{-5}$ | 6 | 87% | 4 | 1 | 20 | 9 | 22 | 23 | 56 | 59 |
| $4.7 \times 10^{-3}$ | $1.5 \times 10^{-5}$ | 8 | 70% | 6 | 3 | 27 | 7 | 31 | 32 | 73 | 68 |

of this value is observed increase as the stimulus level decreases.

The results from these experiments support those shown in Fig. 1 by indicating that continuous stimulation with light intensities which evoke the negative response are not sufficient to continue this reponse. In addition, the observed variation in the maximum percentage of larvae showing the negative response (Table II) is consistent with the concept that upon adaptation to lower intensities, the range of intensities to which the larvae respond best is shifted to lower levels. Upon adaptation to 4.7, $4.7 \times 10^{-2}$ and $4.7 \times 10^{-3}$ $Wm^{-2}$, larvae are stimulated with $4.8 \times 10^{-4}$ $Wm^{-2}$, which according to Fig. 1 is an intensity that either evokes a maximal response or is above those which cause these high levels. In the 3 foregoing adaptation situations the maximum response level declines by 26% (Table II). The above concept can explain this variation because with lower adaptation intensity, the intensity which evokes the maximal response is shifted to levels below $4.8 \times 10^{-4}$ $Wm^{-2}$.

A second concept which is inferred from the variation in response times (Table II) is that subsequent to adaptation to light levels that cause the LAPP, the range of intensities that induce the negative response shifts to lower levels over time. This is perhaps most clearly indicated upon light adaptation at $4.7 \times 10^{-3}$ $Wm^{-2}$, which initially establishes an intensity range that evokes the negative response. That this range shifts over time to lower intensities is indicated by the fact that upon continuous stimulation with lower stimulus levels ($4.8 \times 10^{-4}$, $6.4 \times 10^{-5}$, $1.5 \times 10^{-5}$ $Wm^{-2}$), which do not induce the LAPP, the times to the maximum level and until 50% of this level are longer (Table II).

The times from the foregoing experiments are instructive when compared to the field situation at sunset. Figures 2 and 3 show the change in light intensity over time, which can be used to estimate the length of time that it would take for the light intensity to change from a level that causes the LAPP, to a level that can evoke the negative response. Even though light intensity decreases with depth, the rate of change in intensity over time is similar at all depths (Fig. 2, 3). The dashed lines shows the intensity decrease from about the lowest light level which induces the LAPP (e.g., $4.7 \times 10^{-3} Wm^{-2}$). Prior to the beginning of this curve the larvae would have been adapted to approximately this intensity for at least 30 min. The times shown in Table II are calculated from the beginning of the curve. The time it would take the light intensity to fall from this level to those which evoke the negative response at both measurement sites always exceeds the length of time that the responses persist (Table II). In fact, the time difference is so great that

it seems highly unlikely that a descent due to a negative phototaxis could
result under this situation.

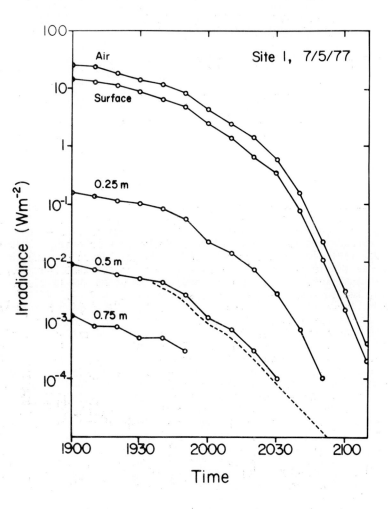

Fig. 2. Site 1 downward irradiance (ordinate) as measured at the surface
and various depths in the water column. Measurements were made throughout
low tide at different times (abscissa) at the end of the day. Sunset occurred
at 2025. The dashed curve is calculated from the measurements and approxi-
mates the situation in which a larva would be light adapted for at least 30
min to about $4.7 \times 10^{-3}$ Wm-2 and then experience the light intensity decline
at sunset.

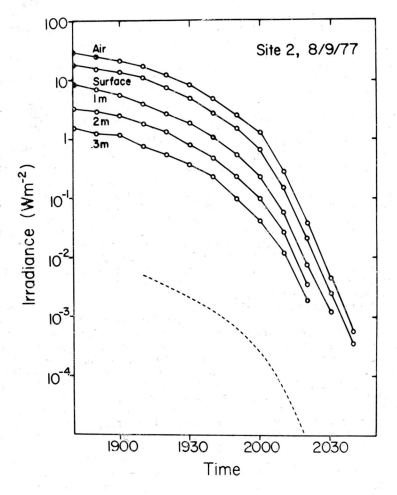

Fig. 3.  Site 2 downward irradiance is plotted as described for Fig. 2.
Light intensity measurements were made just after high tide.  Sunset occurred
at 2002.

Further consideration of Figs. 2 and 3 shows that the greatest rates of
change occur at times later than true sunset.  Thus, using the change in
surface intensities as representative of the most rapid changes, it is possible to determine the length of time that it would take the intensity to
decrease from the light adaptation level used for experiments shown in Table

II to the various stimulus levels. These calculated times always exceed the length of time that the negative response persists. Although this again indicates that the negative response will not occur, there are several problems with the foregoing comparison.

In this situation, we are comparing the length of time that the negative response persists upon an instantaneous intensity reduction (laboratory experiments) to times in the field for a continuous decrease from one intensity, through lower intensities which can induce the LAPP to a final lower level. For the comparison to be correct, it is necessary to assume that the larvae instantaneously adapt to different light intensities and that the negative phototactic response also adjusts rapidly. Even though crustacean photoreceptors can light-adapt quickly, the process does not occur instantaneously and requires several minutes (e.g., Waterman, 1961). Also, negative phototaxis represents a sensory-motor response and hence adjustments to different intensities may involve both sensory and motor changes, the time course of which is probably not instantaneous. This is somewhat supported by the fact that the negative response persists for some minutes after exposure to intensities which are too low to induce the LAPP (Table II). Thus the times measured in the laboratory represent the minimum time for the negative phototaxis to persist, and the true times in the field are probably longer. Since the difference between the field and laboratory times is in some cases not great, it is possible that a negative phototaxis could be evoked in the field. If this occurs, however, it probably only persists for a short amount of time.

In conclusion, it was initially stated that either of two events must occur for the negative phototaxis to low light intensities to result in a vertical descent by the larvae at sunset. First, it is clear that the LAPP is not induced upon adaptation to intensities which evoke the negative response. Secondly, the collected data indicate that underwater light intensities decrease too slowly to evoke the response. However, due to the experimental design and the physiology of crustacean phototaxis, it is difficult to rule out the possibility that the negative response will not persist long enough for the decline in light intensities at sunset to evoke the response.

Although more work is needed to resolve this matter, this study indicates that physiology of larval phototaxis is not well adapted to have the negative phototaxis participate in a descent at sunset. This suggests that it may primarily be involved in predatory avoidance (Forward, 1976) which would function near the surface during the day as a shadow response. Finally, although this study was confined to stage I zoeae, the physiology of photoresponsiveness is very similar for all four zoeal stages of R. harrisii (Forward and Costlow, 1974), which indicates that the results probably also apply to these other stages.

### ACKNOWLEDGEMENTS

This study was supported by Environmental Protection Agency Grant No. R-8038383-01-0. We thank Mrs. M. Forward and Mr. M. Latz for their technical assistance.

### LITERATURE CITED

Forward, R.B., Jr., 1974 a. Negative phototaxis in crustacean larvae: possible functional significance. Journal of Experimental Marine Biology and Ecology, 16, 11-17.

Forward, R.B., Jr., 1974 b. Phototaxis by the dinoflagellate Gymmodinium splendens Lebour. Journal of Protozoology, 21, 312-315.

Forward, R.B., Jr., 1977.  Occurrence of a shadow response among brachyuran
    larvae.  Marine Biology, 39, 331-341.
Forward, R.B., Jr., and Costlow, J.D., Jr., 1974.  The ontogeny of phototaxis
    by larvae of the crab Rhithropanopenus harrisii.  Marine Biology, 26, 27-
    33.
Herrnkind, W.F., 1968.  The breeding of Uca pugilator and mass rearing of the
    larvae with comments on the behavior of the larvae and early crab stages.
    Crustaceana (Suppl.), 2, 214-224.
Hyatt, G.W., 1975.  Physiological and behavioral evidence for color discrimi-
    nation by fiddler crabs (Brachyura, Ocypodidae, genus Uca).  In,
    Physiological Ecology of Estuarine Organisms.  (Ed. F.J. Vernberg).  U.
    of South Carolina Press. p. 333-365.
Walpole, R.E., 1974.  Introduction to Statistics.  New York.  The Macmillan
    Co.  pp. 340.
Waterman, T.H.  1961.  Light sensitivity and vision.  In, The Physiology
    of Crustacea (Ed. T.H. Waterman) Vol. II. p. 1-64.

# EMERGENCE TIMES OF THE INTERTIDAL MIDGE *CLUNIO MARINUS* (CHIRONOMIDAE) AT PLACES WITH ABNORMAL TIDES*

**Fred Heimbach**

*Physiological Ecology Section, Department of Zoology, University of Cologne, GFR*

## ABSTRACT

On the English Channel coast the tides move abnormally in the area of the Isle of Wight. On short sections of the coast the times of the low tides differ very much, and the semidiurnal tidal curves are deformed, so that in some places double high and low waters occur. The Clunio marinus imagines of the other European populations of the North Sea and Atlantic coasts emerge in a strong correlation to local spring low water at a time of day determined by the daily light-dark-cycle. Those of the Channel populations show a modified timing of emergence: they can emerge within a period of time about three times as long. Within this "gate" of emergence, also determined by the light-dark-cycle, temperature changes correëated with the exposure of the habitat by the tides, determine the actual time of emergence. This is a successful adaptation to the abnormal tidal conditions and the wide range of the intertidal habitat concerned in this area.

## INTRODUCTION

The marine midge Clunio marinus is one of the rare kinds of insects which adapted their life cycle in the midlittoral to tidal movements (Ref. 1). The pupae drift out of the tubes on the ground, where the larvae have pupated, to the water surface, where the extremely short-lived imagines emerge. After a short mating flight on the water surface the females lay their eggmasses down by the edge of the water on algae or similar substratum. The points at which the habitat is exposed to the laying of eggmasses are precisely determined by the semidiurnal and lunar tidal cycles. Only on three or four days during spring tides is the lower midlittoral exposed to the air for some hours. The eclosion of the imagines must be timed perfectly with these hours because of the shortness of their lives. Therefore, on the

---

*I wish to say thanks to Prof. Dr. D. Neumann for the guidance in this research, which is part of a doctoral thesis, and his aid with the field observations on the English coast. This work was supported financially by the Deutsche Forschungsgemeinschaft.

one hand, they emerge semilunar-periodically (semilunar rhythm of pupating) on three or four days about spring tides and, on the other hand, within a certain time of day about one to two hours before local spring low water (Ref. 1,2; Fig. 2a).

In the English Channel around the Isle of Wight the tides are distorted because of the special geographical position as the tidal waves comé in from the North Sea and the Atlantic Ocean. So e.g., within a distance of 2o km double low water and extremely long durations of high water with a rapid fall come about (Fig. 1), correpondingly the daily times of spring low water differ for several hours. According to this, the emergence times of the adjacent populations should differ for several hours, too. On the other hand, owing to the additional relatively great differences in tides from day to day one could assume somewhat altered times of eclosion. The daily emergence time then should be more flexibly determined and more in accordance with the actual tidal movements.

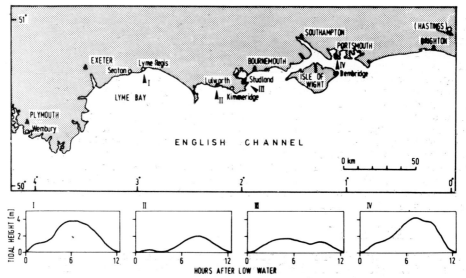

Fig. 1. Location of Clunio populations along the coast of South England (above) and the tidal curves during spring tides of four selected places (below). Circles: places of discovery of Clunio marinus, dots: places of populations examined in this paper.

## MATERIAL AND METHODS

A quantitative registration of the emergence time in nature was impossible because of the roughness of the sea. Therefore the main interest was to find if there were imagines emerging or new females which had not yet laid their eggmasses. The altitude of the tides at Studland could constantly be checked at marks on poles in the water. The times are given in CET.

For breeding experiments in the laboratory, eggmasses of Clunio were collected in Lulworth Cove, Studland and Bembridge in

October 1973 and April/May 1974, taken to Cologne and bred according to the method of Neumann (1). They were bred in fully air-conditioned rooms with a light-dark-cycle of 16 hrs light and 8 hrs darkness (= LD 16:8) or LD 12:12 at 1ooo to 25oo lux, 18° to 2o° C. The emerging midges were collected in an apparatus which was developed similar to that of Honegger's (3), which collects the midges in one-hour intervals. In the experiments with temperature pulses the water ran through an additional basin in which it could be warmed up or cooled down. In the experiments with semilunar emergence and temperature cycles the water ran from the experimental unit with the culture bowls into two basins where it could be warmed or cooled respectively. A valve directed the warm or cold water back into the experimental unit. Turbulences were created by a small motor combined with a vibrator mounted on the set up.

### RESULTS

## The Biotope

In contrast to the locations of Clunio so far known the larvae of the South English populations settle on the whole midlittoral. Bunches of small red algae which are the typical environment of Clunio were not only found at the usual level of the midlittoral because of the irregularity in the tides. At Studland they occur at all          levels because of the extremely long duration of high water. A density of almost 1ooo larvae per square metre, which is not rare  with Clunio, was observed at only a few places. It seems generally to be remarkably rarer than at other locations, which is probably due to the lack of fine sand.

## Emergence in Nature

As to the observations so far made the imagines of Clunio at Studland and Lulworth Cove do not emerge at certain, constant times of day as the populations so far known do (Ref. 4). In one night in Lulworth Cove the eclosion began before midnight and lasted until 1.3o o'clock (29/4/1975) and in an other night (11/5/1975) masses of midges were swarming at 2.3o o'clock and many copulations were observed, which indicates that females must have emerged immediately before. In Studland emerging midges or copulae could be detected from about 21 to 8 o'clock (Fig. 2b), but only rarely in daytime. Within these limits the actual timing of the eclosion of the pharate imagines was determined by the tides, so that midges from the same levels in the littoral emerged almost simultaneously, midges from different levels at corresponding different times. Along one level they emerged within one hour, the males clearly before the females. Figure 3 shows the beginning of the emergence from different levels of the littoral at two different days of the lunar cycle, in dependence on the actual tidal process. The two data found in the year before are added to the figure according to the tides in that night. The relation between the emergence time and the tides, however, seemed to be not always the same: whereas with falling water the eclosion began at a water depth of 1o to 2o cm above the substratum, in little depressions it occasionally did not begin until the connection to the sea was interrupted and the water had not sunk any more for a little while.

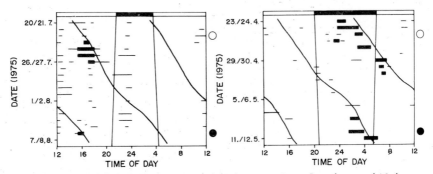

Fig. 2. Sketches of the times of eclosion within a semilunar cycle, observed with an intertidal population of Clunio marinus in Bergen/Western Norway (left) and one in Studland/South England (right). The thin lines indicate times of observation without eclosion, the thick ones with eclosion. The curved lines show the times of daily low water. The moonphases are represented on the right side of the sketches. Darkness from sunset to sunrise is plotted out black above.

The semilunar synchronisation of eclosion seems not to be as markedly expressed as with the populations of Clunio marinus known so far (Fig. 2). It is, however, not possible to give a quantitative account of the emerging midges because of the length of the daily period of eclosion, the continuous emergence of the midges from different littoral levels and the exposed position towards the rough sea.

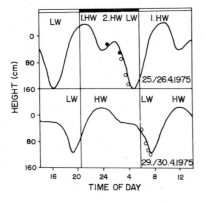

Fig. 3. Beginning of the eclosion of Clunio marinus at Studland from different levels of substratum in dependence on the actual tides on two different days of the lunar cycle (open circles). Black circles represent results of the year before (24/4/1974), according to the tidal movements in that night. Darkness from sunset to sunrise is plotted out black above. LW, HW = low, high water.

## Laboratory Experiments

The daily time of eclosion of the England stocks was, in the LD-cycles, almost two to three times as great as that of other Clunio stocks (Ref. 1). On an average the males emerged 1 to 1.5 hrs before the females. Position and shape of the peaks of emergence

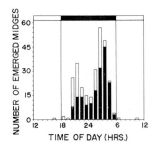

Fig. 4. Extension of the emergence time of
the Clunio marinus stock from Studland in
LD 12:12, shown by the result of an experiment with almost two peaks of emergence.
White part of columns = male, black = female.
Darkness is plotted out black above. Sum of
one culture bowl in three nights.

differed somewhat from one experiment to the other, sometimes distributions with almost two peaks came about (Fig. 4; compare also
Ref. 5). The position of the peaks of emergence fell roughly into
the hours of darkness in all examined LD-cycles. Each stock
showed nearly constant positions towards "light-off" (Fig. 5).

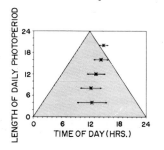

Fig. 5. Position of the daily times of
emergence of the Clunio marinus stock from
Studland in LD-cycles of different lengths
of light. Mean values and standard deviations are indicated. Females only, n = 112
to 329 each cycle. Dotted area = darkness.

The emergence times of the three examined stocks  lie about 3o min
to two hours before the mean time of spring low water under LD-
cycles corresponding to the natural ones in the season of eclosion.
The different emergence times, therefore, are genetically adapted
to the local tides (Table 1). But as there was a wide range of
eclosion to be observed in nature as well as in artificial LD-
cycles, within which range the midges emerged in dependence on
the actual tides, additional temperature pulses were given in the
tidal rhythm apart from the artificial LD-cycle. As a result of
this the imagines emerged within a considerably shorter period
at the time of the temperature pulses. The emergence time was
shifted within the LD-cycle according to the pulses, but it
remained within a certain "gate" which was similar to the entire
range of emergence at constant temperatures (Fig. 6).

Table 1 Comparison of the daily emergence times and the
spring low water times at the places of observation along
the South English coast.

| Location | Daily time of | |
| | spring low water | emergence at LD 12:12/ 16:8 (Mean values,females) |
| --- | --- | --- |
| Lulworth Cove | 23.3o – o.3o h | 23.28 / 1.2o h |
| Studland | 3.3o – 4.3o h | 1.53 / 2.47 h |
| Bembridge | 5.oo – 6.oo h | 3.22 / 5.o8 h |

The times are given in local time.

Under this constant condition the midges emerged mainly towards
the end of the "gate". Turbulences in a tidal rhythm, however,
according to the experiment concerning semilunar synchronisation,
did not yield any considerable shift of the daily peak of eclosion.

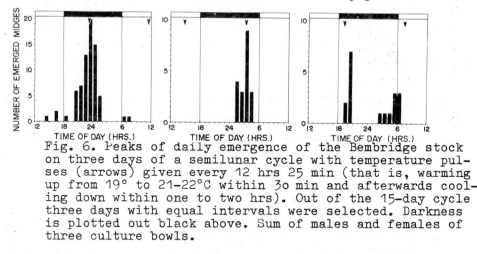

Fig. 6. Peaks of daily emergence of the Bembridge stock
on three days of a semilunar cycle with temperature pulses (arrows) given every 12 hrs 25 min (that is, warming
up from 19° to 21-22°C within 3o min and afterwards cooling down within one to two hrs). Out of the 15-day cycle
three days with equal intervals were selected. Darkness
is plotted out black above. Sum of males and females of
three culture bowls.

A semilunar rhythm of emergence could be achieved in an artificial
moonlight cycle as well as in a 15-day cycle with turbulences in
a tidal rhythm, just as it has been found at other Clunio stocks
(Ref. 1,6). Additionally a 15-day cycle with temperature cycles
in a tidal rhythm induced semilunar synchronisation in the English
Channel stocks (Fig. 7). A final interpretation of these experi-

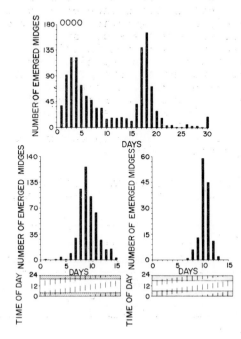

Fig. 7. Semilunar eclosion of the
Clunio marinus stock from Studland
in different zeitgeber cycles.
Above: artificial 3o-day moonlight
cycle with four nights dim light of
o.4 lux (circles).
Below left: artificial turbulence
cycle of 12 hrs 25 min with 6 hrs
turbulence each (indicated in the
frame below).
Below right: artificial temperature
cycle of 12 hrs 25 min with 6 hrs
warming up from 18° to 22° C (indicated in the frame below).
In every case the results of a few
cycles, males and females of three
culture bowls each, are stated.

ments concerning natural conditions cannot be given for the
time being with the present data.

### DISCUSSION

The imagines of the Clunio populations along the English Channel
coast emerge within a period three times as long as that of other
populations. Within this "gate" of emergence, synchronized by the
LD-cycle, temperature changes caused by the tidal movements determine the actual time of emergence. In constant temperatures and
LD-cycles similar to the natural ones the midges emerge towards
the end of the "gate", about 3o min to two hrs before the local
time of spring low water. This means that the emergence times of
the different populations are genetically adapted to the local
tidal conditions although their locations are in no greater distances to each other than 2o and 55 km. This is surprising in so
far as a more precise adaptation of the emergence time to spring
low water time could be superfluous because of the synchronizing
effect of the temperature changes. In contrast to other coasts,
substrata are appropriate for Clunio larvae also in the upper midlittoral, which is due to long inundation caused by the abnormal
tides. The wide "gate" of emergence and the tide-parallel emergence time therefore are a successful adaptation to the progressive exposure of the wide biotop covering the whole midlittoral. A smaller fraction of the imagines emerge also when
the water rises, when no safe laying of the eggmasses is secured
as the sea is almost always rough here. The restriction to a daily
emergence gate of a certain length is useful in so far as too
high a number of losses can thus be avoided.

The reliability of temperature changes in the water as time cues
is poor as there is no arrangement of layers of temperatures in
the rough sea. Accordingly, the temperature changes in the substratum will occur in most cases at the open air after the water has
fallen at a time when the imagines should no longer emerge. Hence
a timing of the eclosion at the next tidal phase is purposeful.
It is open to further examinations how far the emergence time is
programmed by one or more preceding temperature changes. It has
been proved for Arctic populations of Clunio that the emergence
time can be determined by temperature changes (Ref. 7). Here, one
finds an immediate eclosion following the rise of temperature
caused by the sinking of the warmer surface water during ebb tide
and a determination of the emergence time to roughly one tidal
cycle later (Ref. 8).

Although, as usual with Clunio, in the laboratory a semilunar
rhythm of eclosion could be induced (Ref. 6), in nature no strict
synchronisation of the reproduction time during spring tides
could be found. It does not seem to be of a special significance
here. However, no real quantitative data about semilunar eclosion
are known, and experiments with more than one zeitgeber cycles
or with corresponding abnormal rhythms have not been carried out.
One could assume that the synchronisation, which seems to be
weakly or not at all expressed, is due to the abnormal tidal
rhythms and, as a result, abnormal patterns of zeitgebers.

REFERENCES

(1) Neumann, D., 1966. Die lunare und tägliche Schlüpfperiodik
    der Mücke Clunio. Steuerung und Abstimmung auf die Ge-
    zeitenperiodik. Zeitschrift für vergleichende Physio-
    logie, 53, 1 - 61.

(2) Neumann, D., 1976. Adaptations of Chironomids to intertidal
    environments. Annual Review of Entomology, 21, 387-414.

(3) Honegger, H.-W., 1977. An automatic device for the investi-
    gation of the rhythmic emergence pattern of Clunio
    marinus. International Journal of Chronobiology (in the
    press).

(4) Heimbach, F., 1976. Semilunare und diurnale Schlüpfrhythmen
    südenglischer und norwegischer Clunio-Populationen
    (Diptera, Chironomidae). Doctoral thesis, University
    of Cologne, GFR.

(5) Welbers, G., 1972. Zeitliche Anpassung an periodisch wieder-
    kehrende Umweltbedingungen in Entwicklung und Verhalten
    von Tieren. Staatsexamensarbeit, Pädagogische Hochschule,
    Cologne, GFR.

(6) Neumann, D., 1976. Mechanismen für die zeitliche Anpassung
    von Verhaltens- und Entwicklungsleistungen an den Ge-
    zeitenzyklus. Verhandlungen der Deutschen Zoologischen
    Gesellschaft, 9-28.

(7) Pflüger, W. and Neumann, D., 1971. Die Steuerung einer ge-
    zeitenparallelen Schlüpfrhythmik nach dem Sanduhr-
    Prinzip. Oecologia (Berl.), 7, 262-266.

(8) Pflüger, W., 1973. Die Sanduhrsteuerung der gezeitensynchro-
    nen Schlüpfrhythmik der Mücke  Clunio marinus im ark-
    tischen Mittsommer. Oecologia (Berl.), 11, 113-150.

# DIURNAL VERTICAL MIGRATION AND ZOOPLANKTON-EPIBENTHOS RELATIONSHIPS IN A NORTH NORWEGIAN FJORD

**C.C.E. Hopkins and B. Gulliksen**

*Aquatic Biology Group, Institute of Biology and Geology, University of Tromso, P.O. Box 790, N-9001 Tromso, Norway*

## INTRODUCTION

The phenomenon of diurnal vertical migration was described about 25 years ago (1) as one of the greatest puzzles of pelagic natural history. Since then, studies have mainly concentrated on temperate and tropical areas but relatively little effort has been devoted to polar regions. However, the intense seasonal changes which occur in polar seas involving parameters (phytoplankton, light, etc.) that may influence migration patterns of zooplankton suggest that such studies should be most rewarding. These considerations prompted the development of a project designed to ellucidate the dynamics of vertical migration in Balsfjord, a north Norwegian fjord within the arctic circle. In addition, following a recommendation of the Norwegian Oceanographic Committee (2) it was decided that research should also be focused on plankton-benthos interactions. This paper describes some of the results of such work over ca. 24 hrs from 4-5 April 1977.

## MATERIAL AND METHODS

### Study area

Balsfjord is situated just south of Tromsø, and is ca. 40 km long. It has a sill at the entrance with a 35 m threshold depth. The fjord is divided into three basins, the middle one being the study area. The sampling station (69°21'N 19°06'E) was near Svartnes where the depth is 180-190 m and the bottom consists of fine mud.

### Hydrography

Temperature and salinity (T.S.) profiles were taken from 0-170 m with a Neil-Brown Instruments C.T.D. sonde at ca. 12.00, 18.00, and 24.00 hrs on 4 April, and at ca. 06.00 hrs on 5 April.

### Phytoplankton standing crop

Chlorophyll $a$ concentrations were examined using a Turner fluorometer coupled to a water pump and hose. Profiles were taken from 0-50 m at the same times as the T.S. profiles.

Light

The photosynthetically active radiation (400-700 nm) was measured using a Quantum sensor (microEinsteins m$^{-2}$sec$^{-1}$).  Incident radiation was measured continuously over the study period but sub-surface radiation was measured from 0 - ca. 40 m at about the same time as the T.S. and Chl.$a$ profiles.

Zooplankton sampling

The vertical distribution of zooplankton was investigated using a Longhurst-Hardy Plankton Recorder (LHPR) (3) fitted in a towing frame with a net of 0.5 m diameter and a filtering system of 500 $\mu$m.  Oblique hauls were made from near the bottom of the fjord to the surface.  Ship speed was 2.5 knots and the LHPR was hauled in at ca. 10 m min$^{-1}$ providing discrete samples at ca. 10 m depth intervals.  Hauls were taken at 13.10-13.27 hrs and 19.10-19.30 hrs on 4 April, and at 01.01-01.25 hrs and 07.26-07.40 hrs on 5 April.  Depth was monitored during the first two hauls with a Furuno net sonde but this was replaced by a Simrad Trawl Eye as it enabled the LHPR to be safely brought closer to the bottom.

Epibenthos sampling

Bottom samples were collected using a Beyer's epibenthic sledge fitted with a 0.5 m diameter, 500 $\mu$m mesh net (4).  The sledge was hauled along the bottom at ca. 1 knot, and the volume of water filtered was estimated from the distance travelled.  Hauls were taken at 14.00-14.14 hrs and 20.15-20.30 hrs on 4 April, and at 02.12-02.28 hrs and 07.57-08.11 hrs on 5 April.

RESULTS

Environmental background

T.S., density, sub-surface irradiance, and Chl.$a$ profiles are presented in Fig. 1.  Thermoclines were absent, but slight transients were often visible.  Salinity was generally stable as were $\sigma_t$ profiles.  Sub-surface radiation changes followed those of incident radiation (Fig. 2).  Chl.$a$ profiles showed some temporal changes but mean levels were generally constant from 0-30 m.  Primary production was also limited to the 0-30 m layer (H.-C. Eilertsen, pers. comm.).

Zooplankton distributions from the LHPR

The diurnal vertical migration of the copepod *Calanus finmarchicus* is shown in Fig. 3.  Females were most abundant whilst stage V's and males were more rare.  Stage V's showed some migration with most individuals going into the 0-50 m zone by 01.01 hrs before moving down by 07.26 hrs.  Females had a bimodal distribution at 13.10 hrs but the majority were at 0-30 m.  By 19.10 hrs numbers were evenly distributed from 0-140 m and at 01.01 hrs large numbers were found from 0-50 m.  A downward movement was evident by 07.26 hrs and many were found in deep waters.  Males showed no clear signs of vertical migration with maximum numbers usually found from 0-50 m.

The diurnal vertical distribution of the copepod *Metridia longa* is shown in Fig. 4.  Few males were found at 13.10 hrs but by 19.10 hrs many were found from 0-140 m.  The majority reached the surface by 01.01 hrs and reduced numbers were present towards the bottom, but numbers were lower at 0-20 m than in

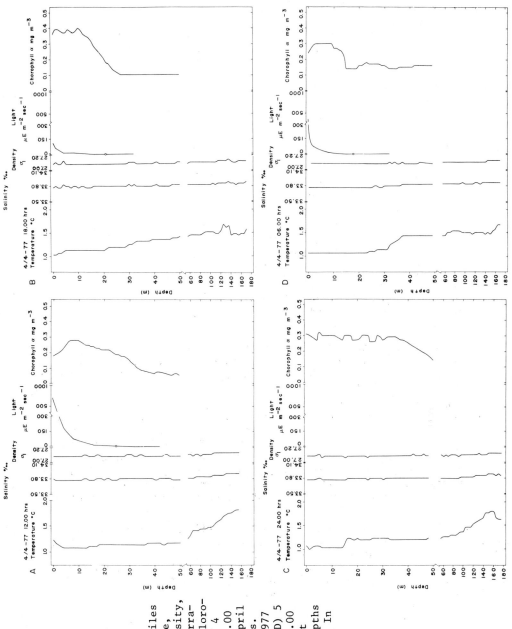

Fig. 1. Profiles of temperature, salinity, density, sub-surface irradiance and chlorophyll $a$. (A) 4 April 1977 12.00 hrs. (B) 4 April 1977 18.00 hrs. (C) 4 April 1977 24.00 hrs. (D) 5 April 1977 06.00 hrs. 1% light extinction depths are circled. In (C) light was < 1.0 uEm$^{-2}$.

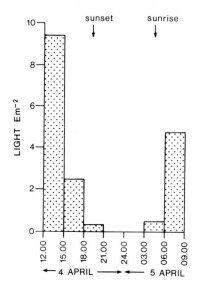

Fig. 2.  Histogram of incident radiation
(Em$^{-2}$) integrated over 3 hr periods.

the previous haul probably indicating that a descent had started.  By 07.26 hrs the majority were at 130-170 m.  Males showed the same pattern as females at 13.10 hrs.  By 01.01 hrs high numbers were found towards the surface and at 07.26 hrs the majority were down at 150-170 m.

The diurnal vertical distribution of the copepod *Pseudocalanus elongatus* is shown in Fig. 5.  Clear signs of migration were not seen in stage V's in the first three hauls but there were signs that a descent had occurred by 07.26 hrs. Females were found at 13.10 hrs in high numbers from 0-20 m, but signs of increasing numbers were also found below 110 m.  At 19.10 hrs large numbers were still present but the centre of distribution lay at ca. 70 m.  By 01.01 hrs maximum densities were at 0-40 m, and by 07.26 hrs a descent had begun.  Males were always scarce except at 01.01 hrs when greater numbers were found from 0-50 m.

The diurnal vertical distribution of the euphausiid *Thysanoessa raschii*, euphausiid eggs, the chaetognath *Sagitta elegans*, and total copepods are shown in Fig. 6.  *T. raschii* had a bimodal distribution at 13.10 hrs with concentrations at 0-20 m and 130-160 m.  At 19.10 hrs the surface group had consolidated and the deeper group had moved upwards.  At 01.01 hrs most *T. raschii* were found from 0-160 m but by 07.26 hrs a general descent had begun.  Euphausiid eggs showed no diurnal depth changes, with most eggs being found from 0-60 m.  *S. elegans* always showed a bimodal distribution having surface and deeper assemblages.  Some migration seems to have occurred and signs of a surface withdrawal were visible by 01.01 hrs.  Total copepods showed some migration, especially by 01.01 hrs when the majority were in the surface waters and at 07.26 hrs when a withdrawal was evident.  It is clear, however, that a high proportion were found from 0-30 m at 13.10 hrs.

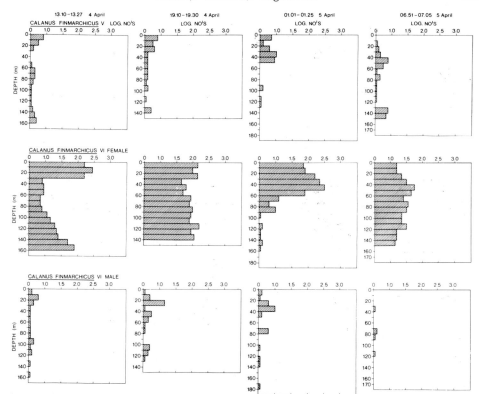

Fig. 3. Diurnal vertical distribution of *Calanus finmarchicus*. Abundance (log.nos.) standardised pr. 10 m³ water flow.

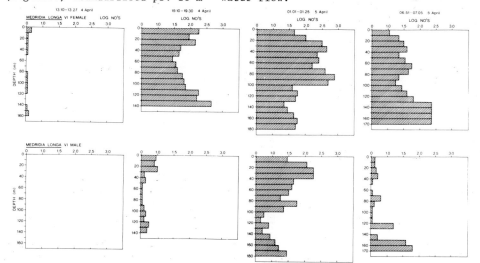

Fig. 4. Diurnal vertical distribution of *Metridia longa*. Abundance (log. nos.) standardised per 10 m³ water flow.

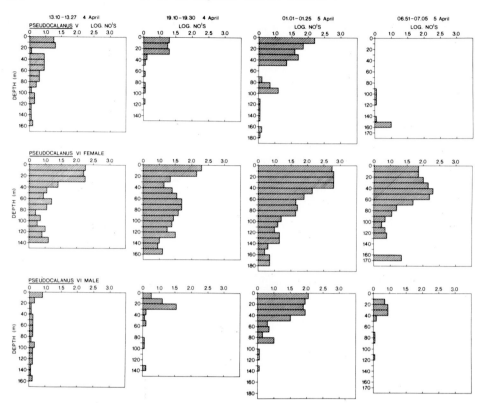

Fig. 5. Diurnal vertical distribution of *Pseudocalanus elongatus*. Abundance (log.nos.) standardised per 10 m$^3$ water flow.

Typically epibenthic or semi-epibenthic taxa were not found in LHPR hauls taken at 13.10 and 19.10 hrs. However, at 01.01 hrs the amphipod *Rhacotropis macropus* was found from 100-120 m and the mysid *Stilomysis grandis* was found from 60-70 m. At 07.26 hrs *S. grandis* was found from 140-150 m. Numbers were always low ($< 1.0/10$ m$^3$).

## Epibenthos distributions

Crustaceans and chaetognaths were the most abundant taxa found in the Beyer's epibenthic sledge (Table 1). Bivalves, polychaetes, and echinoderms (especially *Ctenodiscus crispatus*) were also relatively abundant. The numbers of individuals fluctuated from haul to haul. Calanoid copepods ($> 95\%$ *M. longa*) and *S. elegans* were most abundant in the morning haul (07.57 hrs) and least abundant after midnight (02.12 hrs). The decapod *Pandalus borealis* was found in greatest numbers in the morning haul (07.57 hrs). The amphipod *R. macropus* was abundant and had its greatest densities during the dark hours (20.15 hrs, 02.12 hrs). Euphausiids were only recorded at 14.00 hrs and 20.15 hrs.

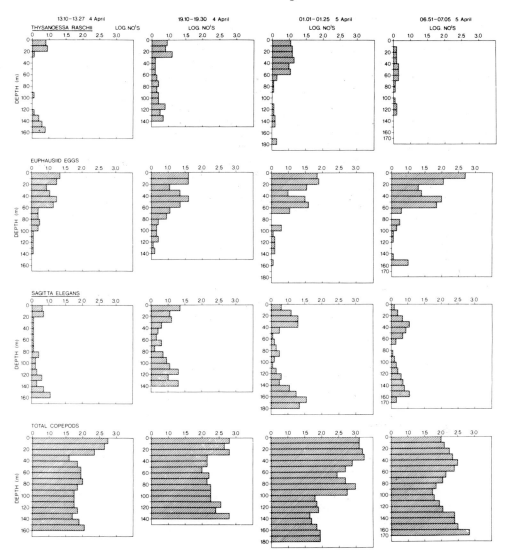

Fig. 6.  Diurnal vertical distribution of *Thysanoessa raschii*, euphausiid eggs, *Sagitta elegans*, and total copepods.  Abundance (log.nos.) standardised per 10 m³ water flow.

## DISCUSSION

4-5 April was a time of spring conditions in Balsfjord and T.S. profiles were indicative of a mixed water column. Incident light had changed from a 24 hr dark photoperiod of winter towards a more typical 12 hr light:12 hr dark photoperiod. Chl.$a$ had increased from low winter values and preliminary spring "bloom" conditions were developing from 0-30 m.

Most of the zooplankters showed a "text book" diurnal vertical migration (5) which involved a rise towards the surface in the evening from a deeper "day-depth", a withdrawal from the surface around midnight before eventually reaching a position by 06.00 hrs approaching the previous day-depth. Examples of a "dawn rise" were not evident, possibly because the LHPR sampling times did not closely coincide with sunrise. The pattern of migration reflected changes in incident and sub-surface irradiance, and supports the theory that the proximate simulus for vertical migration is the level of ambient illumination (6). Temperature and salinity, under the mixed hydrographic conditions, did not appear to constrain migration.

TABLE 1   Abundance of species/groups in samples collected with the Beyer's epibenthic sledge. Numbers are standardised for 10 $m^3$ of water flow.   + = present, ++ = several found, +++ = very numerous.

| Species/group | TIME | | | |
|---|---|---|---|---|
| | 1400-1414 | 2015-2030 | 0212-0228 | 0757-0811 |
| CRUSTACEA | | | | |
| *Copepoda calanoida* | 153.6 | 308.6 | 131.8 | 1935.3 |
| Mysidacea | | | | |
| *Stilomysis grandis* | 0.8 | 0.4 | 1.2 | 3.3 |
| *Erythrops serrata* | 8.1 | 4.7 | 20.7 | 2.0 |
| *Pseudomma truncatum* | 1.8 | 4.7 | 3.2 | 0.3 |
| Isopoda | | | | |
| Isopoda indet. | 1.8 | 0.3 | 1.5 | 0.3 |
| *Munnopsis typica* | 1.3 | | 1.0 | |
| Amphipoda | | | | |
| Amphipoda indet. | 0.2 | | | |
| *Arrhis phyllonyx* | 0.6 | 2.6 | 1.0 | 1.7 |
| *Halirages fulvocinctus* | 0.4 | | | 8.1 |
| *Rhachotropis macropus* | 27.5 | 134.2 | 138.2 | 45.4 |
| *Hyperia* sp. | 0.4 | | | |
| Euphausiacea | | | | |
| *Thysanoessa raschii* | 0.2 | 3.2 | | |
| Decapoda | | | | |
| *Pandalus borealis* | 0.9 | 0.1 | 0.3 | 1.3 |
| *Sabinea septemcarinatus* | 0.1 | 0.1 | 0.7 | 0.3 |
| CHAETOGNATHA | | | | |
| *Sagitta elegans* | 59.1 | 103.4 | 55.8 | 236.8 |
| MOLLUSCA | | | | |
| Bivalvia indet. | ++ | +++ | + | ++ |
| POLYCHAETA | | | | |
| Polychaeta indet. | +++ | + | | + |
| ECHINODERMATA | | | | |
| *Ctenodiscus crispatus* | +++ | + | | |
| *Ophiura* spp. | + | | | + |
| PISCES | | | | |
| *Lycodes* sp. | | | 0.1 | |

The scarcity of *M. longa* in the 13.10 hr haul was probably caused by the LHPR not being deployed close enough to the bottom to sample the whole population. This is supported by studies made with a 120 Khz echosounder (Hopkins, in prep.) which show that a concentrated zooplankton sound scattering layer, including abundant *M. longa*, was present at 13.10 hrs from 160 m to the bottom, at 19.10 hrs from 100-150 m, at 01.01 hrs from 0-50 m, and at 07.26 hrs from 140 m to the bottom.

On occasions a high proportion of zooplankters showed a bimodal depth distribution. The deeper assemblage found at 13.10 hrs is compatible with the concept of a deeper day-depth distribution. However, the presence also of a surface dwelling assemblage, especially visible at mid-day, appears to coincide with the 0-30 m layer of primary production. This is clear with *C. finmarchicus* at 13.10 hrs when densities from 0-30 m are ca. 20 times greater than in the 30-40 m layer. Some of these "photosynthetic zone" assemblages were non-migrating (e.g. some female *P. elongatus*) and were probably exploiting the primary production, in which case localized phytoplankton concentrations may have been a constraint upon vertical migration. Advantages of such behaviour are obvious, especially for egg production after the long arctic winter. Surface concentrations of the predator *S. elegans* may have been associated with increased prey biomass.

Some crustaceans living during the day near or on the bottom rose towards the surface at night. Although mysids and epibenthic amphipods were found in the 01.01 and 07.26 hrs LHPR hauls, numbers were so low compared with those in the epibenthic sledge that it probably indicates that most underwent migrations below depths sampled by the LHPR.

Hyperbenthic fauna (here regarded as planktonic species and motile forms found swimming above the sediment) was abundant in the benthic sledge. Planktonic forms, such as *S. elegans*, have been noted near to the sediment before (7, 8). Temporal variations in density of hyperbenthos may be due to patchiness, vertical migration, changes in sampling efficiency etc. It is also difficult to separate hyperbenthos from benthic species never leaving the bottom with the Beyer's epibenthic sledge (9). However, even if few hauls were taken, diurnal vertical migration is suggested for chaetognaths, and calanoid copepods, with diminishing numbers near the bottom during the dark hours. Reverse vertical migration is indicated for the amphipod *R. macropus* which had the highest densities during the dark hours. The present study emphasises the influence of typically planktonic forms on the epibenthic community.

### ACKNOWLEDGEMENTS

We thank the Captain and men of R.V. *Johan Ruud* for their help, H.G. Hunt for advice in connection with LHPR data handling, U. Normann for computer expertise, and Mss M. Eriksen, S. Espelid, V. Frivoll and B. Vaaja for technical help. The work was financially supported by the Norwegian Fisheries Research Council (NFFR).

### REFERENCES

(1)  Hardy, A.C., 1953. Some problems of pelagic life. In Essays in marine biology, pp. 101-121. Edinburgh: Oliver & Boyd.
(2)  Anon, 1976. Norsk oseanografi, status og perspektiver. 246 pp. Oslo: Norsk Oseanografisk Komite og Norges Almenvitenskapelige Forskningsråd.

(3)  Longhurst, A.R., Reith, A.D., Bower, R.E., & Seibert, D.L.R., 1966.  A new
     system for the collection of multiple serial plankton samples.  Deep
     Sea Research, 13, 313-222.
(4)  Hesthagen, I.H., 1970.  On the near-bottom plankton and benthic inverte-
     brate fauna of the Josephine Seamount and the Great Meteor Seamount.
     Meteor Forschungsergebnisse.  Reihe D, 8, 61-70.
(5)  Cushing, D.H., 1951.  The vertical migration of planktonic Crustacea.
     Biological Revues, 26 (2), 158-192.
(6)  Russell, F.S., 1927.  The vertical distribution of plankton in the sea.
     Biological Revues, 2 (3), 158-192.
(7)  Beyer, F., 1958.  A new, bottom-living Trachymedusa from the Oslofjord.
     Description of the species, and a general discussion of the life
     conditions and fauna of the fjord deeps.  Nytt magasin for zoologi,
     6, 121-143.
(8)  Jakobsen, T., 1971.  On the biology of Sagitta elegans Verrill and
     Sagitta setosa J. Muller in Inner Oslofjord.  Norwegian Journal of
     zoology, 19, 201-225.
(9)  Anger, K. & Valentin, C., 1976.  In situ studies on the diurnal activity
     pattern of Diastylis rathkei (Cumacea, Crustacea) and its importance
     for the "hyperbenthos".  Helgolander wissenschaftliche Meeresunter-
     suchungen, 28, 138-144.

# FACTORS AFFECTING THE IMPINGEMENT OF FISHES ON POWER STATION COOLING-WATER INTAKE SCREENS

**T.E. Langford, N.J. Utting and R.H.A. Holmes**

*Central Electricity Research Laboratories, Marine Biological Laboratory, Fawley Power Station, Fawley, Southampton, Hampshire*

ABSTRACT

Large numbers of fishes may be trapped on cooling-water intake screens at power stations. Massive ingress can cause operational difficulties and even temporary closure of the power station. Also, the continuous removal of a fraction of a population could affect the survival of a species in a particular locality. This paper describes the initial research into the factors which influence the catches of fishes at different sites on the British coast and summarizes briefly the behavioural mechanisms involved in their interaction with power station structures and operations.

## INTRODUCTION

A large modern power station sited on the coast, abstracts some 50-60 million gallons (about $63m^3/sec^{-1}$) of cooling water each hour. Before reaching the intake pumps the water is passed through grids with vertical bars about 15 cm apart which remove coarse debris such as logs, oil drums or large masses of weed. Following this, the water passes through finer screens of metal mesh with 6 mm apertures, and these fine screens remove weed, invertebrates and fishes. These fine screens are usually of the drum or band-type, rotated mechanically and washed with water sprays to remove the debris.

At some sites very large numbers of fish may be caught on these fine screens. For example, Holmes (1975) reported weekly catches of up to 60,000 small fish on the intake screens at Fawley power station in January 1974. Sharma and Freeman (1977) reported that at one inland site in the United States over 19 million fishes were impinged on screens during the whole of 1975. Mortalities of fish caught on screens often approaches 100%. In North America, concern is being expressed about the effect of impingement mortalities on the populations of some small species and on recruitment. Already a fine of over $1.6M. has been levied on a power company for killing small fish and the United States Environmental Protection Agency (EPA) has proposed criteria for intake siting and design which, if actually adhered to would be extremely expensive. In Britain, a massive influx of sprats (*Sprattus sprattus*) blocked and damaged the cooling water intake screens at Dungeness nuclear power station and the resulting loss of generation and repairs cost the CEGB over £1M. sterling ($2M), (Langford 1977).

Concern over impingement of fishes is centred on two aspects:-

     1. The potential effects on local or migratory fish populations of commercial and non-commercial species.

     2. The loss of generating capacity and damage caused by sudden

screen blockages.

At present research is in its early stages but the main objectives of the programme are:-

a) to investigate the behavioural and physiological stimuli which cause various species to enter intake areas, (feeding, breeding and dispersal movements).

b) to establish the biological significance of the numbers and size of fish impinged, to the populations of various species in different localities.

c) to establish methods of predicting fish catch and particularly massive ingresses.

d) to investigate and devise where necessary or practicable, methods of deflecting fish or avoiding impingement mortalities.

This paper summarizes very briefly some of the observations made at three power stations during the winters of 1975/76 and 1976/77, together with data on seasonal factors affecting fish catches on screens.

## SITES AND METHODS

The three power station sites studied are listed in Table 1.

### TABLE 1

| Site | Capacity | Location | Fuel | Intake | Studies |
|------|----------|----------|------|--------|---------|
| Fawley | 2000 MW | Southampton Water (Sea inlet) | Oil | Onshore Channel | 24-hr. tidal seasonal, daily surveys |
| Kingsnorth | 2000 MW | Medway estuary | Oil (Coal) | Onshore (No channel) | 24-hr. tidal surveys |
| Sizewell | 1320 MW | Suffolk Coast | Nuclear (Magnox) | Offshore (Tunnel to intakes) | 24-hr. tidal, plus trawling off intakes. |

The major differences between the stations are their locations, (i.e. on a sea-water inlet, an estuary and an open coast) and the design and siting of the intakes.   Fawley has the screens set at the landward end of a 600 m. long, dredged intake channel.   Kingsnorth has screens sited almost at the shoreline, with a very short dredged intake channel, while the Sizewell intake orifices are sited some 200 m offshore, and the screens at the landward end of a long, undersea tunnel.

The initial studies were aimed at finding the seasonal, diurnal, tidal and climatic factors involved in fish impingement at the various sites, and to obtain some indication of the mechanisms involved.   To do this, hourly collections of impinged fish were carried out over 24-hour and later 13-hour periods, at different phases of the tide.   Earlier studies (Holmes 1975), had indicated the seasonal patterns at one site (Fawley) in detail, from daily collections over an 18-month period.   Some evidence of climatic effects had also come from this long-term study.

At Sizewell, simultaneous analyses of otter-trawl catches, taken off the
intake, and intake screen catches, have been made, in co-operation with the
MAFF Fisheries Laboratory at Lowestoft.   These are being used to assess
species and size selectivity of the screen catches as to attempt to quantify
the screen catch in relation to the local population.

### RESULTS

The data summarised in this short paper are only a small part of those
collected so far.

### Seasonal Fluctuations in Fish Catches

At Fawley there was a marked seasonal variation in total screen catch with
peaks in winter and spring, and generally low catches in summer (Fig. 1).
There was a similar, but less pronounced variation in the diversity of species
caught.   The lowest number of species recorded in one week was 4,   the highest
23, and again diversity was generally lower in summer than in winter.

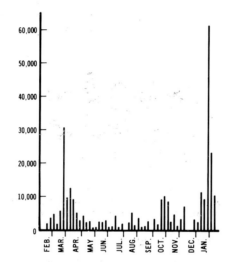

Fig.1. Fish on Fawley Generating Station Screens 1973-1974
Estimated Weekly Total Numbers

As might be expected, different species showed markedly different seasonal
patterns.  For example, herring (*Clupea harengus*) were caught mainly in
mid-winter and hardly at all in other seasons.   Sand smelt (*Atherina
presbyter*) were collected all year round but reached massive peaks in autumn
and winter, sometimes comprising most of the weekly catch, (Holmes 1975).
In contrast pout (*Trisopterus luscus*) were common all year round with
relatively smaller peaks in winter.   The eel (*Anguilla anguilla*) was one
of the few species as common in summer, as in winter, though numbers were
generally low.    The extreme variability of screen catches is illustrated
by the large peaks in total catch which occurred in March 1977 and January
1974.    The first was mainly sand smelts, while the second was mainly sprats
(*Sprattus sprattus*).

The data, however, show clearly one of the major active components influencing the 'impingement' problem, i.e. the seasonal migrations of species into inshore areas.    The migrations are probably part of feeding, breeding or dispersal cycles and these no doubt, vary with species though they have not been investigated for every species involved.

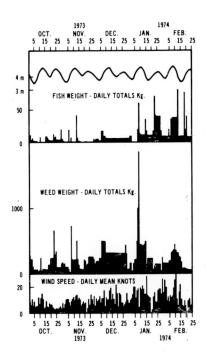

FIG. 2.    Daily Catches of Fish and Weed at Fawley Power Station in relation to tide height and wind speed.

## Daily Fluctuations and Climatic Factors

Within the general seasonal patterns there were considerable daily variations in catch at Fawley which may have been related to climatic conditions. (Fig.2), as well as fish presence in the intake area.    The peak daily catches did not seem to be related to the tidal phase, some occurring during neaps, some during spring tides.  Holmes (1975) analysed the fish and weed catches in relation to wind direction and velocity and suggested that catches were higher after heavy south-westerly winds, though this direction was actually away from the screens.

## Tidal and Diurnal Factors Affecting Catches

Detailed surveys showed differences in the influence of state of tide on catches at the different sites.    For example, at Fawley, there was a clear-cut double-peak in catches over 24-hours, with the largest proportion of the catch occurring in the 3-hour period over low water.    There was no evidence of a significant increase in catches during the hours of darkness.    Peak weed catches, i.e. of "passive" material, coincided with peak fish catch in one survey but not in others. (Fig.3).

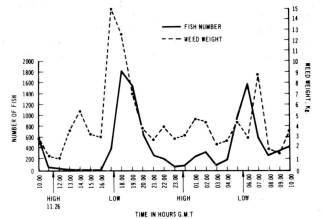

FIG. 3   Hourly Catches of Fish and Weed on Intake Screens at Fawley Power Station - November 20/21st 1975

At Kingsnorth, the patterns were generally similar to those at Fawley.

At Sizewell, which has an offshore intake, there was no clear pattern of catch which could be correlated with tide.   (Fig. 4), although there was some indication of a maximum during the mid-ebb period.

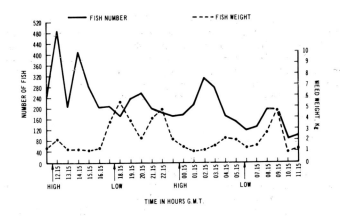

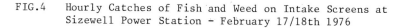

FIG.4   Hourly Catches of Fish and Weed on Intake Screens at Sizewell Power Station - February 17/18th 1976

## Effects of Power Station Operation on Catch

Low catches in summer were initially believed to be a result of lower

water usage arising from lower electrical generation at Fawley power station
during this period, although results do not indicate any direct relationship
(Holmes, 1975).      There was a higher weed-catch in summer and early winter,
though generation varied markedly from low to high during this period.
Higher fish catches occurred during the November-February period when
output increased, but catches fell again sharply after February, though
output did not fall until April.     Absence of fish in the area was obviously
affecting the catch more than pumping rates.

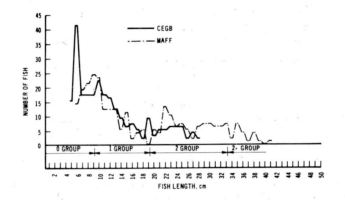

FIG. 5   Comparison of Length, Frequency Distribution of Whiting
          (*Merlangius merlangus*) Caught in Otter Trawls and on
          Intake Screens at Sizewell 1976/77.

At Sizewell otter-trawl catches in winter (Fig.5) showed large populations
around the intake and at that time abundance in trawls was similar to that
on screens.      However, in a summer survey, when the power station was
operating only half of its plant, the otter trawl catches were very large
in comparison to catches on the screens.      These data have yet to be
quantified and analysed in detail, though they suggest that at Sizewell
the amount of generation at the station influences catch strongly.

## Sizes of Fish Caught on Screens

The majority of fish caught on intake screens tend to be in the 0+ and 1+
groups, or specimens of various small species.      In the comparisons between
otter-trawl catches and screen catch at Sizewell the whiting catch off
the intake was of a similar structure to that in the screen catch on two
occasions.      However, on a third occasion the composition of screen catch
was quite different from the trawl catch, apparently suggesting a marked
selectivity for the few fish in the 0+ group.      Further work should
clarify this selectivity both for whiting and other species.

## DISCUSSION

There are indications that the impingement of fish on cooling-water screens

depends on both "active" and "passive" factors.   The more important
are probably the active factors, i.e. the physiological mechanisms which
cause the seasonal migration of fish into intake areas.   Once the fish
are in the intake area, for whatever reason, there is a danger of
impingement, either because of active selection or random migration into
the intakes and thence to the screen wells, (i.e. the chambers in which
the band or drum-screens rotate).   Once in the screen-wells the fish
are probably disorientated by turbulence and varying current velocities.
In the relatively simple system at Fawley and Kingsnorth, the screen-wells
are full of water at high tide.   Current velocities and turbulence are
at their minimum.   As the tide falls, turbulence increases and velocities
increase toward the screen surface.   At some point, i.e. just before
low tide, fishes trapped in the screen-wells are probably forced on to
the screen as water velocities exceed their critical swimming velocity.
The difference in the Sizewell pattern is not yet fully understood.

At non-tidal sites, such as those on the Great Lakes or on rivers, the
active component, i.e. migration, brings the fish into the intake channel
and although there is no tidal effect, impingement may result through
exhaustion as the fish attempts to keep station in the intake current,
or through random mass movements actively following the current.

In most situations, young, or small fishes are the main victims of
impingement and although these may each be regarded as a potential adult
by the layman, modelling studies and population dynamics studies demonstrate
that their real biological significance is considerably less since only
a small fraction of the juvenile population reach the mature adult stage.
(Englert et al 1976).   As far as deflection or rescue are concerned, the
installation of costly structures should depend very much on the actual,
rather than hypothetical adverse effects on the survival of species,
populations, or on commercial catches, and in no case has this been
determined as yet.   There can only be two basic methods however,
i.e. deflection away from the screen area or collection and removal from
screen-wells before impingement occurs.   A number of schemes for both have
been suggested, devised or are under construction in various North American
plants, though the economics of such work have not yet been quantified
(N.T.I.S. Report 1973).

The prediction of massive ingresses of fish for operational purposes
provides a greater challenge, but obviously, there are both biological
and climatic factors involved.   The sporadic nature of the problem makes
predictive studies more difficult.

In both fields, research is continuing and it is hoped that the significance
of fish impingement on ecological grounds will be evaluated before
unnecessary and costly constraints are imposed or proposed in Europe.
The investigation of fish migrations and movements and behaviour in any
area is obviously necessary, both for operational and ecological predictions,
before sites for intakes for new stations are decided.

REFERENCES

Englert, T.L; Lawler, J.P., Aydin F.N. and Vachstevanous G.
    A model study of striped bass population dynamics in the Hudson River.
    Estuarine Processes 1 (1976)  ed. Martin Wiley, Academic Press, London.

Holmes, R.H.A.   ;Fish and weed on Fawley generating station screens.
    February - 1973 - January 1974.  Central Electricity Research
    Laboratories Laboratory Note  RD/L/N 129/75 17pp.

Langford, T.E.   Biological Problems with the use of sea-water for cooling.
    Chemistry and Industry 16th July,1977. pp.612-616

N.T.I.S. Report 1973   " A review of thermal power plant intake structure
    design and related environmental considerations.  Nat. Tech.Inf.Service
    (U.S. Dept. of Commerce)   Report HEDL/TME/73/24   56pp.

Sharma R.K. and Freeman, R.F. 1977.   "Survey of fish impingement at power
    plants in the United States. 1, "The Great Lakes".  Report of the Argonne
    Nat. Lab. Argonne, Illinois.   Report No. ANL/ES/56   218pp.

ACKNOWLEDGEMENTS

The authors wish to thank the Managers' and staff of Sizewell, Kingsnorth
and Fawley power stations for all their co-operation.   Also, thanks
to all members of the staff at the Fawley Marine Biological Laboratory
who have been involved in the long surveys at the various sites.   The
staff of the MAFF Fisheries Laboratory at Lowestoft carried out the trawl
surveys and Mr. J.P. Riley has kindly allowed us to use some of the data
for which we are extremely grateful.


The paper is published by permission of the Central Electricity Generating
Board.

# HABITAT SELECTION AND GAMES THEORY

**P.S. Meadows and J.I. Campbell**

*Department of Zoology, University of Glasgow, Scotland*

## ABSTRACT

Games theory analyses the safest strategy to be adopted in
conflict situations. We have applied it to the habitat preferences of marine animals where a conflict between species is likely
to occur, and have concluded that the safest field strategy for a
species to adopt may often be predictable.

## INTRODUCTION

One of the major problems encountered when considering the
influence of behavioural and physiological factors on the
distribution of animals, is the lack of theoretical framework
within which to view observational and experimental data (Meadows
and Campbell, 1972a,b). This paper explores the theory of games,
or analysis of conflict situations (Anon, 1972; Neumann and
Morgenstern, 1953). We show that it may be possible to predict
species distribution where the requirements of separate species
conflict with each other in the search for a preferred habitat.
Such conflict may be due to territoriality, aggressiveness,
limiting population density, or predation, for example. We
consider firstly a simple hypothetical example of habitat preferences and predation (starfish/gastropod), and then apply games
theory in a more general ecological content.

## The starfish/gastropod game

Starfish are known to prey on gastropods, and the habitat preferences of a number of starfish and gastropods have been described
(c.f. Meadows and Campbell, 1972a). We may therefore construct a
hypothetical conflict as follows. Let two habitats A and B abut
under natural conditions, and let both be inhabited by a given
starfish and gastropod species. Under experimental conditions
(choice experiments) let the gastropod prefer A to B in the ratio
60:40, and the starfish prefer B:A in the ratio 60:40. Consider
three situations. Case 1: no predation by the starfish on the
gastropod in either habitat. Case 2: predation such that 50% of
any gastropods encountered by starfish are eaten in either habitat.
Case 3: predation such that 50% of any gastropods encountered in
habitat A, and 10% of any gastropods encountered in habitat B,
are eaten by the starfish. This data can be converted into games

theory notation, which will enable us to predict the safest strategy for each species under field conditions. The preference of 60% by the gastropod for habitat A is considered as a score (or reward) of 60/100 = 0.6 to the gastropod which it receives if it chooses A in the field. Similarly, the 40% preference by the starfish for habitat A becomes a score of 0.4 to the starfish if it chooses A in the field. The two scores (0.6 0.4) become the top left hand entries in Table 1, Case 1. Both the gastropod and the starfish have two alternatives : habitat (Row) A or B, and habitat (Column) A or B, respectively. The gastropod's safest field strategy, knowing its own and its opponents preferences, is in mathematical terms to assess the minimum score obtainable from each row (Row A, min (0.6, 0.6) = 0.6; Row B, min (0.4, 0.4) = 0.4) and to select the maximum of these, Row A (max. (0.6, 0.4) = 0.6). In field terms this means choose habitat A. The starfishes safest field strategy, knowing its own and its opponents preferences, is to assess the minimum score from each column, and to select the maximum of these, column B (max. (0.4, 0.6) = 0.6). In field terms this means choose habitat B. So far we have said no more than that the safest strategy for each species in the field is to choose the habitat preference in laboratory choice experiments. This must be so because at this stage no conflict of interests has occurred.

TABLE 1   Gastropod/Starfish pay-off tables

(Ga = gastropod, St. = starfish)

Case 1   No predation by starfish

| | | Starfish alternatives (Column A or B) | | | | Row min (Ga.) |
| | | A | | B | | |
| | | Ga. | St. | Ga. | St. | |
|---|---|---|---|---|---|---|
| Gastropod alternatives (Row A or B) | A | 0.6 | 0.4 | 0.6 | 0.6 | 0.6 max. |
| | B | 0.4 | 0.4 | 0.4 | 0.6 | 0.4 |
| Column minimum (st.) | | | 0.4 | | 0.6 max. | |

The situation becomes more interesting when cases 2 and 3 are analysed (Table 1). Here, a 50% predation has been taken as reducing the gastropod's score by 50%, and a 10% predation as reducing the gastropod's score by 10%. For example, in case 2, top left hand entry, 0.6 becomes 0.3. When the 50%/50% and 50%/10% predations in cases 2 and 3 are analysed (Table 1), there is no difference between case 1 and 2, but in case 3, the differential mortality in the two habitats has altered the gastropod's best field strategy to habitat (row) B, the less preferred habitat in the laboratory choice experiments. A conflict between habitat preferences and differential mortality has altered the gastropod's safest field strategy.

Case 2   Predation by starfish.   P = 0.5 for habitat A and B.

| Starfish alternatives (Column A or B) | | | | | | Row min (Ga.) |
|---|---|---|---|---|---|---|
| | | A | | B | | |
| | | Ga. | St. | Ga. | St. | |
| Gastropod alternatives (Row A or B) | A | 0.6 ↓ 0.3 | 0.4 | 0.6 | 0.6 | 0.3 max. |
| | B | 0.4 | 0.4 | 0.4 ↓ 0.2 | 0.6 | 0.2 |
| Column min (st.) | | | 0.4 | | 0.6 max. | |

Case 3   Predation by starfish.   P = 0.6 for habitat A,
                                   P = 0.1 for habitat B.

| Starfish alternatives (Column A and B) | | | | | | Row min* (Ga.) |
|---|---|---|---|---|---|---|
| | | A | | B | | |
| | | Ga. | St. | Ga. | St. | |
| Gastropod alternatives (Row A or B) | A | 0.6 ↓ 0.3 | 0.4 | 0.6 | 0.6 | 0.3 |
| | B | 0.4 | 0.4 | 0.4 ↓ 0.36 | 0.6 | 0.36 max. |
| Column min (st.) | | | 0.4 | | 0.6 max. | |

### A general application of games theory

Games theory quickly becomes complicated. In order to understand its general ecological implications we have therefore restricted ourselves to conflicts between two species in which each species has only two or three alternatives, and to conflicts where one species' gain is the other's loss, in a financial analogy if one species wins £5 by its choice, the other loses £5. These are called zero sum games since £5 - 5 = £0. Let two species, X and Y, each have three habitats from which to choose (X : $A_1$, $A_2$, $A_3$. Y : $B_1$, $B_2$, $B_3$). In general $A_i \neq B_j$, although conceptually it is simpler to specify $A_1 = B_1$, $A_2 = B_2$, $A_3 = B_3$, in which case the two species are competing for shared habitats. Let the pay-off metrix, equivalent in form to Table 1,

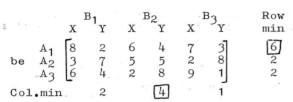

|  |  | $B_1$ | | $B_2$ | | $B_3$ | | Row min |
|---|---|---|---|---|---|---|---|---|
|  |  | X | Y | X | Y | X | Y |  |
|  | $A_1$ | 8 | 2 | 6 | 4 | 7 | 3 | [6] |
| be | $A_2$ | 3 | 7 | 5 | 5 | 2 | 8 | 2 |
|  | $A_3$ | 6 | 4 | 2 | 8 | 9 | 1 | 2 |
| Col.min |  | 2 | | [4] | | 1 | | |

where X chooses rows

and Y columns. We define the scores as being obtained from laboratory experiments (choice, predation etc.); since we are talking in general terms, we can regard the (8, 2) top left hand entry as an integer quantification of the suitability of habitat $A_1$ to X (score 8), when Y chooses $B_1$ (and scores 2), or conversely the suitability of habitat $B_1$ to Y (score 2) when X chooses $A_1$ (and scores 8). As before (Table 1) X's safest strategy, whatever Y chooses, is habitat $A_1$ (max. (min. (8, 6, 7), min. (3, 5, 2), min. (6, 2, 9)) = max. (6, 2, 2) = 6 = $A_1$), and X's score is then 6. By similar reasoning Y's safest strategy is habitat $B_2$, whatever X chooses. An arithmetical simplification is usually applied to data of this sort. Since the total gain for every pair of choices is constant ($A_1$ + $B_1$ = 8 + 2 = 10, . . .,$A_3$ + $B_3$ = 9 + 1 = 10) 0.5 x 10 is subtracted from each reading. For example ($A_1$, $B_1$) changes from (8, 2) to (+3, -3), and ($A_3$, $B_3$) from (9, 1) to (+4, -4). It is now obvious that Y's scores are the negatives of X's scores, and so one can ignore Y's scores with no loss of information, and obtain a simplified pay-off matrix showing only

$$\text{X's gains} \quad \begin{bmatrix} +3 & +1 & +2 \\ -2 & 0 & -3 \\ +1 & -3 & +4 \end{bmatrix} \quad \begin{matrix} \boxed{+1} \\ -3 \\ -3 \end{matrix}$$
$$\quad\quad\quad\quad\quad +3 \quad \boxed{+1} \quad +4$$

where the best strategies remain $A_1$ for X, (+1), and $B_2$ for Y, (+1). Careful thought shows that since Y's scores are the negative of X's, Y must now choose the minimum of the column maxima, X's best strategy for its highest score is therefore $x = \max_i (\min_j a_{ij})$ and Y's best strategy for its highest score is $y = \max_j (\min_i (-a_{ij})) = -\min_j (\max_j a_{ij})$, where i = i'th row, j = j'th column, and $a_{ij}$ = entry in row i and column j in the pay-off matrix ($a_{11}$ = +3, , $a_{33}$ = +4). The game we have considered is defined as having a stable solution, because if Y chooses $B_2$, then X can do no better than choose $A_1$ (in col. $B_2$, +1>0, +1>-3, and +1 is in row $A_1$). Conversely if X chooses $A_1$, Y can do no better than choose $B_2$, remembering that Y's scores are the negative of X's and hence that the inequality sign reverses (in row $A_1$, +1<+3, +1<+2, and +1 is in row $B_2$). In this game, neither species can improve its score unless the other changes its choice, and so there is a stable solution, $A_1$ $B_2$, where x + y = 0, i.e. (+1) + (-1) = 0. A zero sum two species game has a stable solution if and only if x = -y, where x = -y = V defined as the value of the game. The value of the above game is +1, the entry in $A_2$ $B_2$. In all zero sum games with a stable solution, the value of the game is the entry which is the smallest in its row and largest in its column. Clearly this sort of game can be extended to situations in which both species X and species Y have

many alternatives, and even to include more than two species.
However the pay-off matrices then become complex.

Unfortunately many conflict situations which occur naturally and
which can be modelled by games theory, do not have stable solutions.
In these, species X cannot find a habitat which is the safest choice
for itself as well as for its opponent Y;  there is no mutually
beneficial choice of habitats.  Consider species X and Y choosing
habitats $A_1$ and $A_2$, and $B_1$ and $B_2$, respectively.  Let the pay-off
matrix be

$$
\begin{array}{cc}
 & B_1 \qquad\quad B_2 \\
\begin{array}{c} A_1 \\ A_2 \end{array} &
\left[\begin{array}{cc} -2 & +4 \\ +3 & -1 \end{array}\right]
\begin{array}{c} -2 \\ -1 \end{array} \\
 & +3 \qquad\quad +4
\end{array}
\qquad \text{where as usual only X's scores are}
$$

entered, so that -2 means a loss of 2 to X but a gain of 2 to Y.
The game begins.  X chooses $A_2$ since its maximum possible loss is
only -1, rather than -2 if it chooses $A_1$.  Y now considers its
choice.  Since X has chosen $A_2$, Y gains 1 if it chooses $B_2$ but
loses 3 if it chooses $B_1$, so Y chooses $B_2$.  X considers its next
choice.  Since Y has chosen $B_2$, X gains 4 if it chooses $A_1$ but
loses 1 if it chooses $A_2$, and so chooses $A_1$.  By similar reasoning
Y's next choice is $B_1$, and then X's next choice $A_2$ again.  An
infinitely repeating sequence of all the choices emerges ($A_2$ $B_2$
$A_1$ $B_1$    $A_2$ $B_2$ $A_1$ $B_1$ ......... ).  There is thus no mutually beneficial choice of habitats.  No entry in the matrix is the smallest
in its column while being the largest in its row, x + y <0 (-1 +
(-3) <0), the game has no stable solution, and no obvious best
strategy exists for either species.  Surprisingly, it is possible
to suggest a best long term strategy for X and Y in these circumstances by using probability theory.  Consider the total gain to
X over a large number of choices, say 100, of habitats (i.e. rows)
$A_1$ and $A_2$, if X chooses $A_1$ m times out of 100 and $A_2$ 100 - m
times out of 100 ($0 \leqslant m \leqslant 100$).  This is equivalent to X having a
probability of p for choosing $A_1$ and 1-p for choosing $A_2$ ($0 \leqslant p \leqslant 1$).
If species Y now chooses habitat (column) $B_1$, X is restricted to
a loss of -2 or a gain of +3, and X's expected gain over many
choices is -2p +3 (1-p) = 3 -5p.  Similarly if Y chooses $B_2$, X's
expected gain is 4p + (-1) (1-p) = 5p -1.  (3 -5p) and (5p -1)
when plotted on the ordinate for different values of p on the
abscissa ($0 \leqslant p \leqslant 1$) give two intersecting straight lines (Fig. 1,
left hand graphs).  Now careful analysis indicates that X's best
strategy is defined by the point of intersection (0.4, +1), which
is calculated as 3-5p = 5p-1 hence p = 0.4, 3-5p + 3-(5 x 0.4) =
+1 and X's gain over a large number of choices.  In other words
X should choose habitat (row) $A_1$ with a probability of 0.4 (i.e.
40% of the time) and habitat (row) $A_2$ with a probability of
1-0.4 = 0.6 (i.e. 60% of the time).  We can undertake a similar
analysis for species Y.  Let Y choose $B_1$ with a probability of q,
and $B_2$ with a probability of 1-q.  If species X chooses habitat
$A_1$, Y's expected gain over many choices is -2q + 4 (1-q) = 4-6q,
while if X chooses $A_2$, Y's expected gain is 3q + (-1) (1-q) = -1
+ 4q.  These equations are plotted for different values of q on
the right hand graph of Fig. 1.  Y's best strategy is then defined
by the intersection of the two lines (0.5, +1), calculated from
4-6q = -1 + 4q hence q = 0.5, and 4-6q = 4 -(6 x 0.5) = + 1,

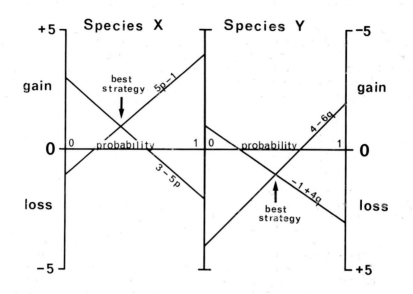

Fig. 1. Unstable game.  Probability model.

remembering that positive values, being X's gains are Y's losses;
the ordinates have been reversed on the right hand graph to allow
for this.  In fact even Y's best strategy will give it an overall
long term loss (+1), since the intersection is below the zero gain
time.  The intersection (0.5, +1) shows that Y should choose the
two habitats (columns) $B_1$ and $B_2$ equally often (q = 0.5, 1-q =
1-0.5 = 0.5).  It can be seen, therefore, that in this more difficult situation it is still possible for X and Y to adopt behavioural
strategies which in the long term will give them a maximum predictable gain (species X) or minimum predictable loss (species Y).

Our analysis started with a hypothetical example, the starfish/
gastropod game;  we then considered games theory in a more general
ecological context of competition for and choice of habitats.  We
were able to define in ecological terms games with a stable solution, and then to consider the more difficult unstable  games which
can only be analysed by probability theory.  The use of these ideas
in predicting species distribution from laboratory and field experiments clearly depends on assigning a meaning to scores entered in
the pay-off matrix.  If these scores are based on quantified
information such as preferences, physiological and lethal limits,
predation rates, and population density limits, we feel that games
theory will lead to a deeper understanding of the interplay of
factors governing animal distribution.  It may even be possible
to  predict  exactly  distribution in the field, and to state
which of these distributions are stable and which are unstable.

REFERENCES

Anon,  Theory of Games, Open University m201, 28, 1-44 (1972).

P.S. Meadows and J.I. Campbell,  Habitat selection by aquatic
     invertebrates,  Adv. Mar. Biol. 10, 271-382 (1972a).

P.S. Meadows and J.I. Campbell,  Habitat selection and animal
     distribution in the sea: the evolution of a concept,  Proc.
     R. Soc. Edin. B. 73, 145-157 (1972b).

Neumann, J. von and Morgenstern, O. (1953)  Theory of games and
     economic behaviour,  Wiley, New York.

# IN SITU OBSERVATIONS ON THE BEHAVIOUR AND BIOLOGY OF THE TROPICAL SPIDER CRAB *STENORHYNCHUS SETICORNIS* HERBST (CRUSTACEA, DECAPODA, BRACHYURA)

**Gerd Schriever**

*c/o Biologische Anstalt Helgoland, Meeresstation, 2192 Helgoland, F.R. of Germany*

## ABSTRACT

During saturation diving from the American underwater laboratory HydroLab at Freeport,Grand Bahama,it was possible to make observations on the arrow crab Stenorhynchus seticornis for more than five hours per day. 25 species of the arrow crabs were found on a coral head of about 51 $m^2$, the population density is about 1 crab per 2 $m^2$.

At daytime the crabs prefer well protected locations in crevices,holes or between the tentacles or arms of crinoids and sea anemones.At night they were found on exposed locations,on soft corals or gorgonians.At dawn they descend from the soft corals and return to their daytime location.This diurnal rhythm seems to be a sort of negative phototaxis. Two tests show that the crabs seek dark and protected places during daylight.

The extreme length and spininess of the appendages make the crabs difficult to eat.One fish tried to catch a crab,but it was eaten only after all or most of its legs were dropped.

Two different populations in 18 - 21 m and 45 - 65 m water depth showed significant differences in the development of sexes.The "deep water" population was greater in size and it is postulated that mature and older crabs live in deeper water than do juveniles.

## INTRODUCTION

There is very little information available about tropical spider crabs. The arrow crab Stenorhynchus seticornis is common in the Atlantic Ocean from North Carolina,USA to Rio de Janeiro and on the African coast from Madeira and the Canary Islands to Angola (Ref. 1.,5.).The crabs settle to 1500 m depth and prefer hard bottom,gravel,corals and sandy bottom. Barr (2) made the first investigations on the behaviour of arrow crabs from the American underwater laboratory Tektite II at Lameshure Bay, Virgin Islands.

In 1974 and 1976 it was possible to study the behaviour and biology of Stenorhynchus seticornis Herbst in the coral reefs of Freeport,Grand Bahama.By saturation diving from the American underwater laboratory HydroLab,it was possible to make observations on the crabs for more than 5 hours per day and to follow their diurnal rhythm.

## OBSERVATIONS AND RESULTS

### Population Density

The main observation area chosen was a coral head of about 51 $m^2$.  This
coral head was situated directly beside the HydroLab, in an area of high
diving activity and covered by the green algae Halimeda spec. and
Acetabularia spec., the porifera Agelis spec. and Haliclona rubens, the
the hydrozoa Milepora alcicornis, the gorgonians Gorgonia ventalina and
several species of soft corals.  During the observation time a maximum
number of 25 Stenorhynchus seticornis was found.  In daytime the crabs
sat on sheltered places, between crevices or the tentacles of the
actinians Bartholomea spec. and Lebrunea spec. and the arms of the
crinoids Nemaster rubiginosa and Nemaster discoidea.  Occasionally there
were more than 2 crabs at such sheltered places.  68 % of all crabs
were found o together with the actnians and crinoids.

The crabs obviously walk actively between the arms and tentacles of the
actinians and crinoids.  It was not possible to find out why the crabs
prefer these sheltered places and did not use all crevices and holes of
the coral head.

The population density on this coral head was about 1 crab per 2 $m^2$.
Barr (2) reported a population density of 1,5 - 2 crabs per $m^2$ at
Lameshure Bay, Virgin islands.  He counted all crabs along two transacts
from the underwater laboratory TEKTITE II and the high population density
seemed to depend on the water turbulence and turbidity resulting from
the diving activities along the transacts which provided suitable feeding
areas for the crabs.  The same conditions were found near the HydroLab
and it is assumed that the population density at Lameshure Bay is
higher than in the Bahamian coral reefs.

### Preferred Location and Diurnal Rhythm

During the day Stenorhynchus seticornis showed a characteristic change
of location.  Five times a day, at 05.30 h, 10.30 h, 15.30 h, 18.30 h
and 22.30 h all crabs in the observation area were counted and their
location checked, Table 1.  During the daytime at 10.30 h and 15.30 h,
all crabs were in sheltered places.  It was not possible to find all
crabs because they were hidden in crevices or holes of the coral head.
At evening twilight, 18.30 h, the arrow crabs started to climb up the
coral head, looking for exposed locations.  When they had reached such
a place, the crabs sat against the current and started to filter small
particles and plankton out of the water.  The animals spread out their
legs and sometimes removed the adhered particles from the legs and
carapace with their chelipeds.  In this position the arrow crabs could
be found the whole night.  Sometimes the crab left this exposed place
during the night and returned to its daytime location.  Once there,

it started immediately to eat the material from its legs and carapace.
At dawn, 05.30 h, all crabs descended from their exposed locations and
returned to their former daytime locations.    Contrary to statements by
Barr (2), feeding activities of most arrow crabs were visible only at
night and dawn, but not during daytime.    Only two <u>Stenorhynchus seti=</u>
<u>cornis</u>, sitting on sandy bottom under the coral head, sometimes fed
during the day.

TABLE 1    Tabular Listing of Animals Observed during
Investigations of Day-Night Rhythm

| Location/Time | 05.30 | 10.30 | 15.30 | 18.30 | 22.30 |
|---|---|---|---|---|---|
| hard coral | 7 | 3 | 3 | - | 2 |
| hc + crin. | 1 | 7 | 4 | - | 1 |
| hc + anth. | - | 1 | 2 | - | - |
| porifera | 3 | 5 | 4 | - | - |
| por. + anth. | 1 | 5 | 4 | 1 | 1 |
| soft coral | 3 | - | - | 8 | 6 |
| sc + crin. | - | - | 1 | - | 1 |
| hc exposed | 5 | - | - | - | 3 |
| por. exposed | - | - | - | 2 | 2 |
| sheltered % | 60 | 100 | 100 | 9,1 | 26,7 |
| exposed % | 40 | 0 | 0 | 90,9 | 73,3 |

| hc | = hard coral | | por. | = porifera |
|---|---|---|---|---|
| crin. | = crinoid | | sc | = soft coral |
| anth. | = anthozoa | | | |

## Negative Phototaxis

It seems that the diurnals rhythm is a sort of negative phototaxis.    To
show further light dependent reactions two tests were performed.

1.    During daytime 10 adult arrow crabs were taken out of their sheltered
places and brought on to the light sandy bottom at a distance of about
3 - 4 m from a large coral head.    At first the crabs looked around and
waited for a short time, then about 4 minutes later they started immedi=
ately toward the shadow of the coral head.

2.    Again, 10 adult arrow crabs were placed on to the light sandy
bottom and the diver stayed on the bottom at a distance of about 1 m.
The dark figure and the shadow of the diver were picked up by the crabs
at once.    They went to the darkest place, that is, the arms and knees
of the diver and always kept contact with the sheltering object.

Beside the diurnal rhythm these tests showed the nagytive phototaxis of
<u>Stenorhynchus seticornis</u>.    The time of reaction depends on the difference
in light intensity of the offered objects.    Nearly the same behaviour

is shown by the boreal majid spider crab <u>Hyas araneus</u>.   Quantitative
light measurements to test the threshold of irritation were not possible.
When the arrow crabs were illuminated by a searchlight at night, they
left their exposed places on the coral head and started to descend after
a maximum of 30 seconds.

## Defense Mechanism

During the whole observation period no <u>Stenorhynchus seticornis</u> was
caught by a predator.During daytime the arrow crabs were hidden in
sheltered places, at night they were sheltered by the dark.   At night
sometimes the crabs were illuminated up to 15 minutes but no one was
ever eaten by a fish.   Therefore one big adult specimen was placed on
the light sandy bottom during daytime.   Some minutes later different
fish species, angle fishes, yellow tail snappers and small groupers
surrounded the arrow crab.<u>Stenorhynchus seticornis</u> pressed its carapace
on the bottom and spread out its long spiny legs.   Only a hogfish
(<u>Lachnolainus rufus</u>) tried to eat the arrow crab but spit it out at once.
The extreme length and the spininess of the appendages make the crab
difficult to eat.   Only after most of the crab's legs were dropped was
it eaten.   Barr (2) described the same behaviour of a fish at Lameshure
Bay, Virgin Islands.   Obviously these attacks depend on injury; the
spreading of blood induces the fish to attack and eat the arrow crab.
The crab's anatomy provides a passive defense mechanism against fish.

## Population Structure

The investigation of the <u>Stenorhynchus seticornis</u> population around the
HydroLab, water depth 18 - 21 m, and at the coral reef edge, water depth
40 - 65 m, showed distinct differences.

At the end of the mission 47 arrow crabs were collected around the
HydroLab and fixed.   In the laboratory the sex and carapace length and
width were determined.   The single development stages of the sexes were
divided into pre- and post puberty stages (Ref. 4).   At 18 - 21 m depth
there was a significant majority of 61,7 % males to 38,3 % females.
A differentiation of pre- and post-puberty   stages showed in both sexes
a relationship of 73,4 % pre-puberty stages to 26,6 % post-puberty.
Only three post-puberty females and eight post-puberty males were found.
The average length of the pre-puberty males was 7,2 mm (s.d. 1,6 mm),
the post-puberty males were 10,5 mm long (s.d. 2,0 mm).

At 40 - 65 m depth the coral reef edge showed quite another population.
The reef fell vertically down from about 45 m to more than 100 m.
Overhangs, crevices and small and large holes were present and settled
by large crinoids, sea urchins, porifera and anthozoa.   The population
density of <u>Stenorhynchus seticornis</u> was much smaller than at the HydroLab
area.

Because of the great depth, observation and investigation time was
limited to one hour during daytime only.   59 arrow crabs were found,
74,6 % preferred crevices and the arms or tentacles of the crinoid
<u>Nemaster rubiginosa</u> and the anthozoa <u>Bartholomea spec.</u>.   Not all species
could be reached by the diver, because the arrow crabs fled into the
inner crevices.

Collected Stenorhynchus seticornis were much larger, average carapace
length 12,2 mm, than that species collected in the "shallow water",
average carapace length 8,0 mm.   The different sexes showed a more
pronounced variation.   The post-puberty males were 2,3 mm longer than
the species of the "shallow water", the four pre-puberty males were
1,8 mm longer.   The post-puberty females were 1,9 mm longer than the
species of the HydroLab area.   No pre-puberty females were found here.

A comparison of these two populations showed statistically significant
differences.   At the HydroLab area   the relationship of pre-to post-
puberty arrow crabs was 76,6 % to 23,4 % to the pre-puberty species.
At 40 - 65 m water depth this relationship was just the opposite.   It
is postulated that the crabs migrate into deeper water after or just
before the moult of puberty (Ref. 4).   Dons (3) described the migration
into deeper water of the adult boreal spider crab Hyas araneus.   It
was not possible to solve this problem due to limited time of investigation.
Contrary to the present findings Yang (6) described two different
Stenorhynchus species from shallow water and greater depth.   He found
anatomical differences at the first larval zoea stage and in the adults.
Such differences were not found in the present study.   Obviously the
differences are between crabs from shallow water and crabs from more
than about 150 m depth.

### CONCLUSIONS

The arrow crab Stenorhynchus seticornis Herbst showed a notable negative
phototaxis.   This negative phototaxis is correlated with a diurnal
rhythm, which involves a distinct changing of location during day and
nighttime.   The crabs showed an excellent homing ability when they
returned to their daytime location at dawn.   The crabs' anatomy provides
a passive defense mechanism against fish.   The extreme lengh and
spininess of the appendages make them difficult to eat.   Adult crabs
seem to migrate into deeper water,   There are no obvious predators on
Stenorhynchus seticornis.   The arrow crabs clean the reef of organic
matter and serve as scavengers of the coral heads (Ref. 2).

### ACKNOWLEDGMENT

The auther is indebted to the Deutsche Forschungsgemeinschaft for
financial support and wishes to thank the National Oceanic and Atmos=
pheric Administration and the MUS&T-Programm of the U.S. Department of
Commerce for the opportunity to take part in the project SCORE at
Freeport, Bahama.   Dr. J. Markham, Biologische Anstalt Helgoland,
many Thanks for reading the English manuscript.

REFERENCES

(1)    Alvarez, E.S., 1974.    Crustaceos Decapodos del Archipelageo
        Canario.  I.  Contribucion al conocimiento de las especies
        de Braquiuros (Crustacea, Decapoda, Brachyura).    Boletin del
        Instituto Espanol de Oceanografia, Madrid, 182, 3 - 31

(2)    Barr, L., 1971.    Observations on the biology and the behavior of
        the arrow crab Stenorhynchus seticornis Herbst, in Lameshure
        Bay, St. John, Virgin Islands.    In TEKTITE 2, Scientists in
        the Sea, (Ed. U.S. Department of Interior, Washington D.C.),
        VI - 213 - 220.

(3)    Dons, C., 1912/13.    Slegten Hyas.    Tromsø Museums Årshefter,
        Tromsø, 34, 115 - 178.

(4)    Hartnoll, R.G., 1965.    The biology of Manx spider crabs.    Pro=
        ceedings of the zoological Society London, 141, 423 - 496.

(5)    Williams, A.B., 1965.    Marine decapods Crustaceans of the Caro=
        linas.    Fishery Bulletin.    Fish and Wildlife Service.
        United States Department of Interior, Washington D.C.,65, 1-298.

(6)    Yang, W.T., 1976.    Studies on the western Atlantic arrow crab
        Stenorhynchus (Decapoda,Brachyura,Majidae).    I.  Larval
        characters of two species and comparison with other larvae of
        Inachinae.  Crustaceana 31 (2), 157 - 177.

# LEARNING IN THE STARFISH
# *MARTHASTERIAS GLACIALIS*

## Tine Valentincic

*Institute of Biology and Department of Biology, Askerceva 12, 61000
Ljubljana, Yugoslavia*

ABSTRACT

The starfish <u>Marthasterias glacialis</u> learns to avoid food models with implanted
electrodes if a mild electric shock is delivered at the beginning of the consummatory phase of the feeding response.   The number of negative reinforce-
ments necessary to produce avoidance response decreases during approximately
20 successive trials.   High frequency of learned responses stabilizes in
later presentations.   "Loss of learnt response" may occur after initial
success and after a few trials learnt avoidance responses reappear.   Two
possibilities for this phenomenon are discussed:   operation of two different
memory systems and a new ethological approach based on state of central filtering mechanisms.   Relatively good retention of avoidance response was demonstrated after an interval of 24 hours.

INTRODUCTION

Learning in echinoderms has been the subject of relatively few studies in the
past.   The reasons for this unusual delay in the research of learning abilities is such an ecologically important phylum originates from a basic misunder-
standing of echinoderm behaviour.   It originates from the work of Von Uexkull
(8) who described sea urchins as a "republic of reflexes".   It was long considered that this animal group possesses nothing corresponding to behaviour
patterns in which drive and internal coordination can be discovered.   Thorpe
however quotes in his book several authors who provided good examples
(7) of simple behaviour patterns.   Evidence for feeding drive dates as far
back as the work of Romanes (5) who showed that feeding in starfish cannot be
induced by external stimuli alone.   Earlier work by the author (9) has shown
a good example of how motivational states for feeding behaviour can be controlled by "controlled starvation" in <u>Marthasterias glacialis</u>.

Good reviews of research in echinoderm learning have appeared in last ten
years, notably Refs: 1,4,11.   Associative learning in echinoderms has been
the subject of work by Diebschlag (2), Sokolov (6), and Landenberger (3).

Avoidance responses based on tactile and light intensity discrimination were
conditioned in some cases by touching or shocking animals when they tried to
escape from the central part of the experimental chamber onto a periphery
different either in substratum structure or in illumination.   In my opinion
Diebschlag's experiments have a good ethological basis since animals exhibited
a single simple behavioural pattern - escape response, which was modified by
punishment.   Sokolov (6) also attempted to train asteroids (<u>Asterias rubens</u>)
on the basis of tactile discrimination of substrates.   His experiments were
run in two-choice apparatus with rough bottom in one and smooth bottom in the

other part of the tank.    Food reinforcement was used during the training with
the intention of changing the animal's preference for substrate.    His results
indicate that a learnt response develops in at least some animals.    It is
most probable that difficulties in such experiments originate from the fact
that the experimenter manipulates the animal when putting it into the two-
choice apparatus.    This action induces escape behaviour, which cannot be
reversed by feeding stimuli for a relatively long period (unpublished observations).    Landenberger worked with the Pacific starfish Pisater giganteus,
and trained the animals to move to the bottom of a dark tank when the light
was turned on.

Evidences for associative learning in Marthasterias glacialis are reported in
this paper.    Feeding drive in this animal can be induced in a controlled
manner and under this condition it is possible to train the starfish to avoid
"electric" food models.

### MATERIALS

The sea stars were collected on the rocky  bottom of the upper infralittoral
zone in the Gulf of Rijeka.    They were kept at suitable feeding motivation
level (see 9 and 10) in experimental aquarium at the Institute of Biology in
Ljubljana.    Different behavioural experiments on chemoreception and learning
were conducted with the same group of 60 animals during a period of two years.
Filtration and aeration facilities provided a good quality of sea water in this
closed system :  temperature $20^oC$, salinity $35^o/oo$, oxygen saturation 90 - 98%.
The content of microconstituents did not attain values higher than:  $NH_3$ (after
intense feeding) = 2,27 µg/l,  N - $NO_2$ = 0,21 µg/l,  P - $PO_4$ = 1,45 µg/l, P -
organic 0,62 µg/l,  $SiO_2$ = 1,1 µg/l.  Marked accumulation of nitrates (60 µg/l)
did not interfere with the behaviour of the animals.    Illumination was kept
constant.    The animals were fed mostly with mussels and gastropods.

Learning experiments were conducted with animals which were left undisturbed
in small experimental aquaria (20 x 20 x 20 cm) for a period of 20 days.

### EXPERIMENTAL METHOD

Cotton was moulded together with 1 cm long free copper or silver wires of an
ordinary PVC isolated cable to yield a food model 1 cm in diameter which was
soaked in 5 x $10^{-2}$ M solution of L-cysteine to provoke a feeding response (10).
The food model was connected through a switch to phase for AC electro-shocks
or to + pole for DC shocks.    The ground electrode (silver wire) or - electrode
were placed 1 cm deep in the center of the experimental aquarium.    The appetitive phase of the feeding response was then triggered by introducing 0.5 ml
of the stimulating liquid into the container and the experiment was started
5 minutes later when the animal was actively searching for food.    Concentration of the stimulating chemical (L-cysteine in all experiments) was rapidly
raised in the vicinity of the food model from $10^{-5}$ M initial concentration to
a higher one.    The animal "quicly" attacked the model.    The phases of feeding response 1 - 4 (see Refs. 9 and 10) are considered here to be appetitive
behaviour, phases 5 and 6 to be the consummatory phase of the feeding response.
Thus at the beginning of the consummatory phase the tube feet touch the model
as shown in Fig. 1.    Electric shocks of 6 to 9 V (duration 0.2 - 0.3 sec.)
were delivered through the model 6 seconds after the animal touched the cotton
and repeated until avoidance response occurred.    This consisted of a retraction of the affected tube feet, lifting or shortening of the affected arm, and
in most cases escape in the opposite direction ensued (Fig. 2).    The voltage

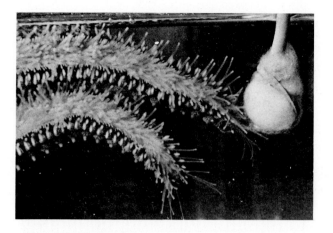

Fig. 1 Beginning of the consummatory phase of the feeding response in
Marthasterias glacialis

Fig. 2 Avoidance response to electric shock

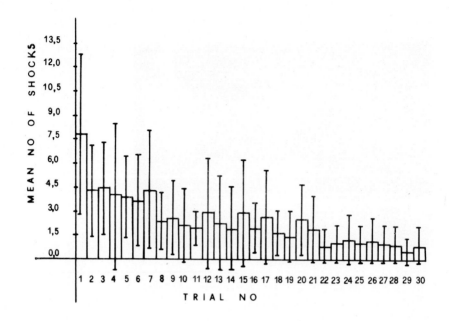

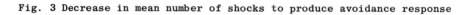

Fig. 3 Decrease in mean number of shocks to produce avoidance response

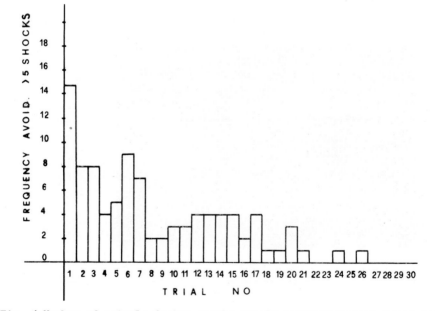

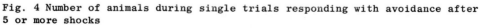

Fig. 4 Number of animals during single trials responding with avoidance after
5 or more shocks

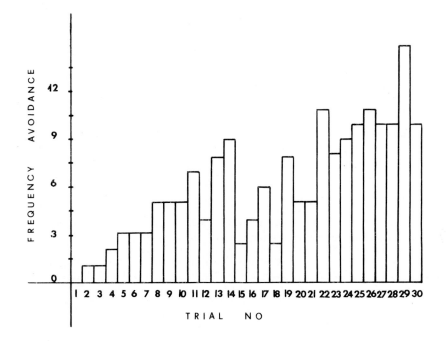

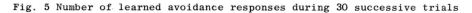

Fig. 5 Number of learned avoidance responses during 30 successive trials

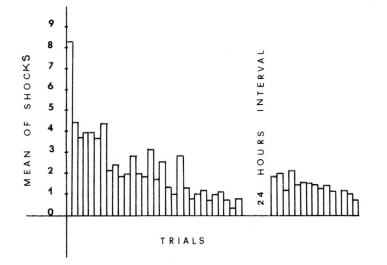

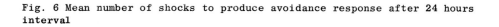

Fig. 6 Mean number of shocks to produce avoidance response after 24 hours interval

of shocks was selected during the first three punishments for each animal at
the level just sufficient to produce an observable response of the tube feet
touching the cotton.    If the animals attacked the food models several times in
succession, each attack was considered as a separate trial.    After the starfish
associated the surface structure of the cotton with "pain", avoidance response
occurred 2 to 6 seconds after the contact and no negative reinforcement was
delivered.    Twenty animals were used in these experiments which ranged in size
from 5 to 18 cm in diameter.

### RESULTS

As shown in Fig. 3 the number of shocks to produce an avoidance response decreased in an irregular manner from 1st to approximately 20th trial.    Data for
the individual animals indicate that learning is initially rapid, but after
that a second increase in the number of shocks for single avoidance appeared in
a few trials.    Some other animals behaved even more irregularly with two or
three losses of learnt response in the course of training.    High standard
deviation in trials 12 to 15 can be explained in this way.    Figure 4 illustrates the frequency is high in the first 7 trials when the animals can still
be considered as naive and increases again in sessions 12 to 15.    A rapid
drop in the mean number of shocks from the first to the second trial can be of
dual origin:   learning or arousal for avoidance response.    The first considerable step in learning seems to appear after 7 trials and a relatively unstable
situation persits for a further 14 sessions.    Later learned avoidance responses or avoidance after a single shock predominated.    Experiments with
individual starfishes lasted from 75 to 120 minutes.    Figure 5 illustrates
the frequency of learned avoidance responses showing something like bimodal
distribution with "loss of learnt response" in trials 15 to 21.    Further
training did not markedly improve performance and feeding response often ceased
after 40 trials.    Good retention of avoidance response was demonstrated after
a 24 hour interval (Fig. 6).

### DISCUSSION

The results clearly demonstrate the ability of the starfish Marthasterias
glacialis to associate contact of the tube feet with the surface structure of
the food model, with avoidance response.    Observations of predator-prey relationships confirmed that this kind of learning also occurs in nature.    Lima
inflata successfully defends itself with tentacles provoking a typical avoidance response in Marthasterias glacialis.    A successive sequence of attacks
of the predator resembles closely the experiment described.    Similar behaviour
was sometimes observed with the sea urchin Paracentrotus lividus whose pedi-
cellaria can be used in effective punishment of the starfish.

Two possible causes of the unexpected dual distribution of the avoidance responses shown in Fig. 5 are apparent.    The first possibility is a two-stage
memory system.    Short-term memory would build up in few successive trials and
decay once or several times in the course of learning.    The long-term memory
would be a slowly operating system reaching its peak after some 20 trials and
decaying only little in 24 hours.    This theory is attractive but to my opinion
incorrect.    Even if the time courses of this phenomenon agrees closely with
that described in some cephalopods, it seems unlikely that short-term memory
would be not re-established in each successive trial.    An alternative explanation can be based on more ethological grounds.    We can consider feeding behaviour and avoidance behaviour in Marthasterias glacialis as flexible behaviour patterns which may be triggered by convenient stimuli.    The state of

central filtering mechanisms may determine which kind of behaviour will predominate in successive trials.    Electric shocks were probably influencing
the intensity of feeding behaviour as well as releasing an avoidance response.
Association between food model surface and "pain" may be formed obeying a
single learning curve.    Learned avoidance response will in any particular
trial depend on the position on the learning curve attained by past experience
and on the state of central filtering mechanisms.    Animals may thus be more
in the feeding or in the avoidance mode.    Even if the avoidance response is
firmly established we can expect that the consumatory phase of the feeding
response will predominate at least on some occasions.

## REFERENCES

(1)     Binyon, J., 1972.    Physiology of Echinoderms.    Oxford: Pergamon
         Press.

(2)     Diebschlag, E., 1938.    Ganzheitliches Verhalten und Lernen bei
         Echinodermen.    Zeitschrift fur Vergleichende Physiologie, 25,
         625-654.

(3)     Landenberger, D. E., 1966.    Learning in the Pacific starfish Pisaster
         giganteus.    Animal Behavior, 15, 414-418.

(4)     Reese, E. S., 1966.    The complex behavior of echinoderms.    In Phy-
         siology of Echinodermata. (Ed. R. A. Boolootian).    New York:
         Interscience Publishers, John Wiley & Sons.

(5)     Romanes, G. J., 1885.    Jellyfish, Starfish, and Sea Urchins.    London.

(6)     Sokolov, V. A., 1961.    Tactile conditioning of the starfish Asterias
         rubens.    Murmanskii morskoi Biologicheskii Institut.    Trudy, 3,
         49-54.

(7)     Thorpe, W. H., 1956.    Learning and Instinct in Animals.    London, W.
         C. 2:    Methuen and Co. Ltd.

(8)     Uexkull, J. von, 1897.    Uber Reflexe bei den Seeigeln.    Zeitschrift
         fur Biologie, 34, 289-318.

(9)     Valentincic, T., 1973.    Food finding and stimuli to feeding in the
         sea star Marthasterias glacialis.    Netherlands Journal of Sea
         Research, 7, 191-199.

(10)    Valentincic, T., 1975.    Amino - acid chemoreception and other releas-
         ing factors in the feeding response of the sea star Marthasterias
         glacialis (L.).    Proceedings of the 9th Symposium on Marine
         Biology, 693-705.    Aberdeen: Aberdeen University Press.

(11)    Willows, A. O. D. & Corning, W. C., 1975.    The Echinoderms.    In
         Invertebrate Learning, Vol. 3, (Ed. W. C. Corning, J. A. Dyal,
         and A. A. D. Willows).    New York and London: Plenum Press.

# REPRODUCTION AND
# DEVELOPMENT

# ENVIRONMENTAL INFLUENCES ON GROWTH AND SEX RATIO IN DIFFERENT EELS POPULATIONS (*ANGUILLA ANGUILLA* L.) OF ADRIATIC COASTS

**Giuseppe Colombo and Remigio Rossi**

*Institute of Zoology, University of Ferrara, Italy*

## ABSTRACT

The AA. examined 260 yellow eels and 2939 silver eels from lagoons of Northern Adriatic coasts for sex, age and growth. The sex ratio of migrating silver eels is seen as a response to sex determination to environmental conditions. It is suggested that the distance of the actual biomass from the carrying capacity of the ecosystem is one of the main factors that regulates the rate of growth and sex differentiation of females from intersexual yellow eels.

## INTRODUCTION

Eels represent an important source of food in Europe and Japan. Their biology has been recently discussed in some books and reviews (Ref. 1,2,3,4,5).
The life cycle of the European eel (Anguilla anguilla L.) in continental waters goes through three stages (elvers–yellow eels–silver eels), called with different names according to their morphological appearance, and are fished by different methods, in relation to their behaviour.

## SEX RATIO

We determined the sex ratios by gonad inspection of populations samples of silver eels catched during the whole fishing season in lagoons of Western Adriatic coasts. The results are shown in Table 1.
The observed average lengths of silver eels are similar to those found by Frost (6, 7) in England and North Ireland, by Rasmussen (8) in Denmark and by Deelder (9) in Holland, but North Europe silver eels are older, ranging from 7 to 9 years for males and about 11 to 13 for females. Eels of South Europe grow faster since in Southern regions they have a longer feeding period. The average attained size is about the same.
In silver eels there is a net sexual dimorphism since males become silver at a younger age than females and these attaine a much larger size than males. Sex of the silver eels can be easily distinguished by the size of the animals and thus one might determine the sex ratio with little error.
Sex ratio of silver eel populations vary widely in different environments even from year to year (Ref. 10, 11, 5, 12).
The exact mechanism of genetic sex determination in eels has not yet been demonstrated and it will remain so, as breeding is impracticable. A heteromorphic pair of chromosomes was described in European, American and Japanese eels (Ref. 13). However some doubt still remains, because the number of animals stu-

313

G. Colombo and R. Rossi

TABLE 1  Statistics of Silver eels of Northern Adriatic Coasts

| | Water surface (ha) | Salinity (mean) ‰ | Yield Kg/ha | Males % | Length (cm) ♀ | Length (cm) ♂ | AGE (y) ♀ | AGE (y) ♂ |
|---|---|---|---|---|---|---|---|---|
| 5 lagoons of PO DELTA and VENICE (Northern Adriatic) | from 310 to 1500 | 24-28 | 6-25 | 5-10 | 1049<br>59.4 ± 4.8<br>47-80 | 82<br>42.4 ± 4.7<br>36-48 | 136<br>6.9 ± 1.9<br>4.5-14.5 | 82<br>4.8 ± 2.6<br>1.5-10.5 |
| VALLE NUOVA (Near Comacchio) | 1800 | 15 | 7 | 7 | 276<br>65.5 ± .2<br>56-78 | 22<br>46.6 ± .6<br>42-54.6 | 127<br>4.6 ± .1<br>3.5-9.5 | 22<br>4.2 ± .2<br>3.5-7.5 |
| COMACCHIO lagoons | 10000 | 25 | 16 | 24 | 421<br>56.1 ± .4<br>39-100 | 131<br>43.1 ± .2<br>37-52 | 421<br>7.1 ± .1<br>3.5-14.5 | 131<br>4.7 ± .1<br>3.5-9.5 |
| Culture in ponds with artificial feed (Comacchio) | pond of 1600 m² | 25 | 7500 | 89 | 32<br>50.5 ± 2.7<br>46-68 | 250<br>40.6 ± 3.8<br>31-51 | 24<br>3.4 ± .2<br>2.5-4.5 | 48<br>2.6 ± .1<br>2.5-3.5 |
| LESINA lagoon (Southern Adriatic) | 5100 | 15 | 5 | 82 | 62<br>60.7 ± .7<br>51-74 | 289<br>42.6 ± .2<br>33-51 | 62<br>3.4 ± .1<br>2.5-6.5 | 289<br>2.5 ± .03<br>1.5-6.5 |
| VARANO lagoon (Southern Adriatic) | 7000 | 17 | 2 | 93 | 22<br>57.6 ± 1.2<br>51-72 | 303<br>40.5 ± .1<br>31-48 | 22<br>3.8 ± .1<br>3.5-5.5 | 303<br>2.6 ± .02<br>1.5-7.5 |

died is low, the sex of the animals has not always been determined and mainly
because the morphology of the heterochromosomes described is different.
Sex ratio of population samples of <u>silver eels</u> can   vary for many reasons.

### Difference of Behaviour between Sexes.

Distributional variations in sex ratio could be explained by different migratory tendencies between sexes (Ref. 2) or by different food seeking behaviour of
the larger and faster growing females (Ref. 5). Male silver eels migrate earlier in autumn than females (Ref. 3) and thus it is necessary to have samples
of the whole period of migration.

### Differential Mortality.

It is difficult to measure it in eel  populations and there are no reported data. A particular type of differential mortality caused by fishing effort is
that of Lesina and Varano lagoons, where eels are fished by eel-pots: in this
way all eels of market size are catched, including a large proportion of faster
grown yellow females, whilst the small males may escape. However in collecting
only silver eels, as in the other samples reported in Table 1, different sex
ratios are observed also in similar and proximate lagoons, and differential
mortality is out of the question.

### Effects of the Environment on Sex Differentiation (metagamic determination)

Many Authors  infer  that metagamic determination is the most important factor
and we also subscribe to this view.

### SEX DIFFERENTIATION

Histological changes of the gonads during the sexual differentiation were extensively reported by Grassi (14), Rodolico (15), D'Ancona (16, 17).
We examined the gonads of 260 yellow eels in two samples fished during a year
in Comacchio lagoons. Out of these 95 were histologically examined since we
found useless to examine with the microscope the large ovaries of the bigger
yellow eels above 50 cm of length

TABLE 2  Sex Distribution of yellow eels against length $(N, \bar{x} \pm s.e.)$

| LENGTH cm | Undifferentiated | | Males | | Undiff. + Males | | Females | |
|---|---|---|---|---|---|---|---|---|
| 20–24 | 12 | 1.12 ± .17 | | | 12 | 1.12 ± .17 | | |
| 25–29 | 36 | 1.51 ± .06 | 2 | 2.00 ± .50 | 38 | 1.63 ± .07 | 11 | 1.68 ± .40 |
| 30–34 | 6 | 1.67 ± .17 | 8 | 1.75 ± .16 | 14 | 1.71 ± .11 | 19 | 2.13 ± .49 |
| 35–39 | 1 | 2.50 | 1 | 2.50 | 2 | 2.50 | 28 | 2.64 ± .75 |
| 40–44 | | | 2 | 5.00 ± .50 | 2 | 5.00 ± .50 | 18 | 3.39 ± .83 |
| Over 45 | | | | | | | 116 | from 3.5 to 14.5 |

Males of Table 2 include all the animals with Syrski organ, i.e. a small thread
more or less lobulated. This is the gonad which develops from the undifferentiated one of the smallest eels, without changing its overall organisation

G. Colombo and R. Rossi

TABLE 3  Sex distribution of yellow eels against age $(N, \bar{x} \pm s.e.)$

| AGE | Undifferentiated | | Males | | Undiff. + Males | | Females | |
|---|---|---|---|---|---|---|---|---|
| 0-1 | 6 | 24.4 ± .6 | | | 6 | 24.4 ± .6 | | |
| 1-2 | 41 | 26.8 ± .4 | 7 | 30.9 ± .6 | 48 | 27.4 ± .4 | 20 | 30.8 ± .6 |
| 2-3 | 8 | 28.6 ± 1.3 | 4 | 32.9 ± 1.6 | 12 | 30.0 ± 1.1 | 38 | 36.8 ± .7 |
| 3-4 | | | | | | | 23 | 42.8 ± .7 |
| 4-5 | | | 1 | 41.2 | 1 | 41.2 | 28 | 49.0 ± .8 |
| 5-6 | | | 1 | 43.3 | 1 | 43.3 | 39 | 51.4 ± .8 |
| Over 6 | | | | | | | 44 | from 46.6 to 79.9 |
| TOTAL | 55 | | 13 | | 68 (26 %) | | 192 (74 %) | |

(Fig. 1). The germ band, from the undifferentiated stages, lengthens and enlarges mainly by the increase of the somatic tissue. In testis the somatic tissue separates the germ cells in tubules, and here spermatogonia are grouped and later will form spermatocytes nests (Fig. 2 and Fig. 4). You can see all the steps among the above outlined structures. Only in the longest males a tubular organisation of the germ cells predominates. But all yellow eels from 25 cm, classified as undifferentiated, or as males with Syrski organ, at microscopical examination show few or many oocytes inside the tubules and these are adjacent to spermatogonia or spermatocytes, irrespective of animal length and age (Fig.3). Grassi (14) stated that it is very rare to find males (yellow) without oocytes. The differentiation of the ovary is characterized by the formation of threads of oocytes in 2nd period of growth, with basophilic cytoplasm. Then threads fold and a characteristic ribbon-like organ appears (Fig. 5 and Fig. 6).
We saw well differentiated ovaries with a clear macro- and microscopic structure in small yellow eels of 26 cm of length. No ovaries with threads of oocytes were found to have nests of spermatocytes, whereas 3 yellow eels, 35 to 43 cm long, with a Syrski organ showed ovaries with oocyte threads still well compact.
We are inclined to conclude that European eels develop first as intersexes, that means yellow eels with gonads having a testicular structure (intersexual males) containing spermatogonia and early spermatocytes, plus oocytes. This kind of gonad in yellow eels, from a wide range of length and age, differentiates into ovary.
We also examined the histological sections of the testes of silver eels of different lengths and ages taken from samples of lagoons. Almost all testes contain few nests of spermatids and bundles of spermatozoa in a gonad largely immature, but we did not succeed in finding oocytes when silver characteristics were well apparent.
Histological examination of 34 male silver eels from the yield of ponds where eels are kept    crowded    (7500 Kg/ha) and artificially fed shows that some of the longest ones have oocytes in a testicular structure. (The probability

calculated by Fisher's exact method is P < .001)

TABLE 4  Frequencies of Testes with oocytes
in artificially reared silver males

| LENGTH cm | 30-34 | 35-39 | 40-44 | 45-49 | 50-54 | Total |
|---|---|---|---|---|---|---|
| With oocytes | - | - | 1 | 8 | 4 | 13 |
| Without oocytes | - | 2 | 9 | 8 | 2 | 21 |
| Total | | 2 | 10 | 16 | 6 | 34 |

In eels from these crowded ponds many testes contain nests of spermatids and
bundles of sperms together with oocytes. There is no relation between presper-
matogenesis and presence of oocytes (the probability calculated by Fisher's
exact method is not significant). Therefore it seems that completion of sperma-
togenesis is not inhibited by the presence of oocytes in the gonad. It must be
noticed that in these crowded ponds silver eels attain  the same total length
in less time than in the nearer Comacchio lagoons, in similar abiotic conditions,
temperature and salinity. The main differences are crowding     by artificial
food and the  changed  sex ratio. The same results are found in Japanese eel-
farms for Japanese as well as European eels (Ref. 18).
Table 3 shows that in natural conditions there are statistically significant
differences in length between males and females of the same age group, and the
slower growing eels remain undifferentiated or become males (intersexual).
Yellow female eels are bigger than males, but there is no evidence if the eels
which have become female grow faster, or if the faster growing eels become females.
In artificial conditions and on the Southern Adriatic coast as in Lesina and
Varano lagoons, eels grow very fast and there is a large proportion of males.
Sex determination therefore is not a simple trophic question, but other factors
(temperature, density) also regulate the final sex ratio.


SEX RATIO as a MEAN for ECOLOGICAL HOMEOSTASIS

The results of the reported investigations gives evidence that in eel  populations the sex ratio is regulated by environmental factors.
The eels are juvenile intersexes with a male structure gonad and this suggests
in favour of a polygenic system of sex determination.

Apart  from those early differentiating by the presence of most of the genes
of their sex, male eels differentiate definitively only when they reach the
silver stage. Whereas females differentiate from the intersexes during the yellow phase. We suggest that many females differentiate, as much as the area of
growth can carry, and the abiotic conditions, mainly temperature, allow.

In crowded conditions, in artificial ponds, or in wild ecosystems when natural
recruitment is increased artificially with small yellow eels (Ref. 12), or in
warmer waters as in Southern regions, the ultimate result is the large proportion of silver males in the production.

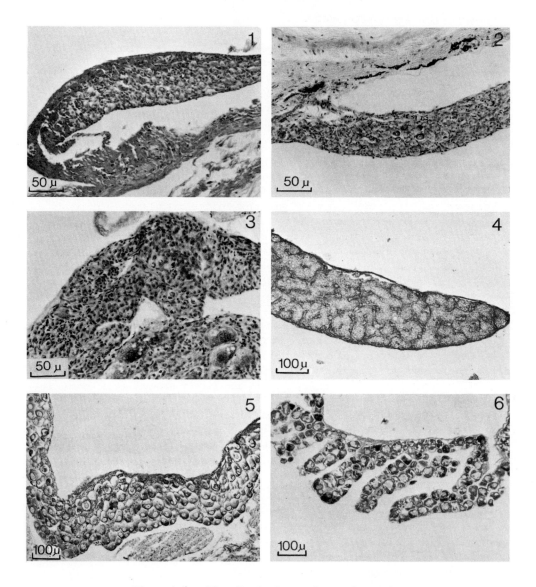

Figg. 1–6.  Histological sections of gonads

(1) Undifferentiated gonad of a 30 cm yellow eel; (2) testis of yellow eel
of 28.5 cm; (3) testis of yellow eel of 36.9 cm;  (4) testis of silver eel
from crowded ponds containing oocytes; (5) ovary of yellow eel of 37 cm;
(6) ovary of yellow eel of 32 cm.

Crowding    may have two effects. (1) In favourable conditions eels of both
sexes reach in advance the silver stage and then migrate out. (2) The proportion of intersexes which differentiate into females is reduced, most become
silver males, which consume less and migrate out earlier. Both these mechanisms
result in a subtraction of biomass from the ecosystem and therefore the distance of the actual biomass from the carrying capacity of the ecosystem can be
considered mainly    responsible for the final sex ratio (Fig. 7).

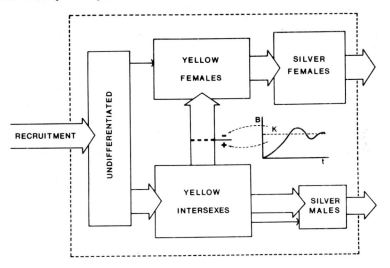

Fig. 7   Compartment model of biomass change of an eel   population
in a closed ecosystem controlled by carrying capacity (K)

The values of the carrying capacity (K) differ in any ecosystem since it depends
not only on crowding    and intra and interspecific competition,   but on all
the environmental conditions, biotic and abiotic of the system. The abiotic conditions (stressing factors, temperature) seem to be the most important in the
Lesina and Varano lagoons.

### REFERENCES

(1)    Bertin, L., 1956.    Eels, a biological study. 192 pp. Cleaver-Hume Press,
London.

(2)    D'Ancona, U., 1960.    The life cycle of the Atlantic eel. Symposium of the
Zoological Society of London, 1, 61-75.

(3)    Deelder, C.L., 1970.    Synopsis of biological data on the eel, Anguilla
anguilla. Fisheries Synopsis n. 80. F.A.O. Rome.

(4)    Tesch, F.W., 1973.    Der Aal. 306 pp. Paul Parey, Hamburg.

(5)    Sinha, V.R.P. & Jones, J.W., 1975.    The European freshwater eel. 146 pp.
Liverpool University Press, Liverpool.

(6)    Frost, W.E., 1945.    The age and growth of eels (Anguilla anguilla) from

the Windermere catchment area. Journal of Animal Ecology, 14, 26-36, 106-124.

(7)    Frost, W.E., 1950.    The eel fisheries of the River Bann, Northern Ireland and observations on the age of the silver eels. Journal du Conseil permanent international pour l'exploration de la mer, 16, 358-383.

(8)    Rasmussen, C.J., 1952.    Size and age of the silver eel (Anguilla anguilla L.) in Esrum Lake. Reports of the Danish Biological station, 54,3-36.

(9)    Deelder, C.L., 1957.    On the growth of eels in the IJsselmeer. Journal du Conseil permanent international pour l'exploration de la mer, 23, 83-88.

(10)   D'Ancona, U., 1946.    Observations sur la proportion des sexes chèz les anguilles des lagunes littorales de l'Adriatique. 13e Biologisch Jaarboek, Dodonea, 261-269.

(11)   Penàz, M. & Tesch, F.W., 1970.    Geschlechtsverhaltnis und wachstum beim Aal (Anguilla anguilla) and verschiedenen lokalitaten von Nordsee und Elbe. Berichte der Deutschen Wissenschaftlichen Kommission fur Meeresforschung, 21, 290-310.

(12)   Parson, J., Vickers, K.U. & Warden, Y., 1977.    Relationship between elver recruitment and changes in the sex ratio of silver eels (Anguilla anguilla L.) migrating from Lough Neagh, Northern Ireland. Journal of Fish Biology, 10, 211-229.

(13)   Park, E.H. & Kang, Y.S., 1976.    Karyotype conservation and difference in DNA amount in Anguilloid Fishes. Science, 193, 64-66.

(14)   Grassi, B., 1919.    Nuove ricerche sulla storia naturale dell'anguilla. Memorie del Regio Comitato Talassografico Italiano, 67, 1-141.

(15)   Rodolico, A., 1933.    Differenziamento dei sessi ed ovo- spermatogenesi nell'anguilla. Pubblicazioni della Stazione Zoologica di Napoli, 13, 180-278.

(16)   D'Ancona, U., 1943.    Nuove ricerche sulla determinazione sessuale della Anguilla. Archivio di Oceanografia e Limnologia, 3, 159-265.

(17)   D'Ancona, U., 1957.    Nuove ricerche sulla determinazione sessuale della Anguilla. Le influenze ambientali sul differenziamento della gonade. Archivio di Oceanografia e Limnologia, 11, 69-111.

(18)   Egusa, S., 1970.    Notes on Sex and Growth of European eels, in Freshwater Eel-rearing Ponds. Bulletin of the Japanese Society of Scientific Fisheries, 36, 1024-1025.

# SOME ASPECTS OF FISSION IN
# *ALLOSTICHASTER POLYPLAX*

**R.H. Emson**

*Zoology Department, King's College, London*

ABSTRACT

The process of fission in A. polyplax is described.   Evidence as to the
causes of fission is presented as well as data on the incidence of the phenomenon in natural populations.   The value of  the phenomenon as a means of
asexual reproduction is discussed.

INTRODUCTION

The phenomenon of fission in starfish is one which has interested a number of
workers and a variety of theories as to the causes have been put forward (see
Clark (2) for review).   There is nevertheless a lack of observations on
living animals.   There have been few attempts to induce fission experimentally and the process of fission in naturally splitting animals appears not to
have been described.

MATERIAL

The present observations were made on A. polyplax, a small forcipulate starfish of the family asteriidae, found in New Zealand and South Australia.   In
New Zealand it is found in small numbers in pools at the low water mark and
under rocks on a variety of sheltered and semi-exposed rocky shores.   A
single large population was found on a West Coast boulder shore (Raglan),
exposed to continuous water movement due to swell but protected from the
severe wave action general on this coast.   Figures for incidence of fission
and other population parameters are based on material collected at this site.

A. polyplax is a small starfish, the largest individuals in the present study
having an arm length of 29 mm.   The arm number is most often eight and the
majority of animals are composed of two "halves" unequal in size, each with four
arms (usually markedly different in length), two madreporites and an anus.
It is carnivorous, and strongly photonegative, moving to shaded positions in
the laboratory tanks and, in the field, being found only on the undersides of
stones and boulders or in deep shade.

OBSERVATIONS

Characteristics of the Field Population.

Two collections of animals were made at Raglan in June and August and the
following data obtained.

(a) Frequency of specimens showing evidence of fission within the population.
The proportion of obviously split specimens was 91% in June and 89% in August.
Of the remaining 10% in which fission was not detectable, some may have re-

generated to a point where no distinction between parts was visible but the majority were individuals with an unusual arm number which may have been non-fissiparous.

(b) <u>Arm number</u>
The analysis of arm number is shown in Table 1a and the relative numbers of large and small arms in Table 1b.   It is clear that 8 is the usual number and that of the 39% which do not have 8 arms 73% have 7 or 9 arms.   Table 1b also shows that the majority of animals with four large arms regenerate four new ones.   The tendency of animals with 5 or 3 arms to regenerate the number necessary to return the total to eight is, however, not pronounced, most of these animals also regenerating four arms.

### TABLE 1    Arm Number in Allostichaster polyplax

a.   Total arm numbers

| Arm number | Number of individuals |
|---|---|
| 3 | 1 |
| 4 | 22 |
| 5 | 8 |
| 6 | 19 |
| 7 | 70 |
| 8 | 300 |
| 9 | 73 |
| 10 | 2 |

b.   Relative numbers of large and small arms

| Small arm number | Large arm number | | | | | | | |
|---|---|---|---|---|---|---|---|---|
|  | 2 | 3 | 4 | 5 | 6 | 7 | 8 | 9 |
| 0 | 0 | 1 | 22 | 7 | 4 | 11 | 28 | 3 |
| 1 | 0 | 0 | 1 | 11 | 2 | 3 | | |
| 2 | 0 | 0 | 3 | 2 | 3 | | | |
| 3 | 0 | 2 | 27 | 9 | 0 | | | |
| 4 | 1 | 28 | 241 | 37 | 2 | | | |
| 5 | 2 | 19 | 31 | | | | | |
| 6 | 1 | 2 | | | | | | |
| 7 | 1 | | | | | | | |

(c) <u>Large arm size</u>
The length of the largest arms of all specimens (R) from both populations were measured.   In neither set of data is any animal smaller than R=7mm found and the greatest arm length is R=29mm.   The absence of smaller specimens indicates either that all of the previous year's recruits have achieved this size, or that recruitment is irregular.   Comparison of the data for June and August reveals relatively little difference, indicating that growth is slow at this time.

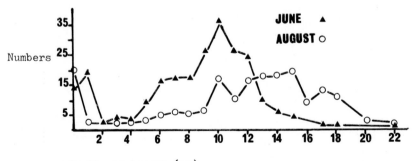

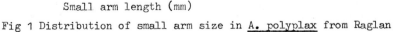

Small arm length (mm)

Fig 1 Distribution of small arm size in <u>A. polyplax</u> from Raglan

(d) <u>Small arm size</u>

The data derived from measurement of small arm size (r) is shown in Fig. 1.
It can be seen that there is a distinct peak in both sets of data and that the
peak of arm size has shifted between June and August from a mean value of 8.8
to 11.3.    This clearly represents the average growth of the regenerating arms
during this period.    Thus the average growth per month over the period is 1.25
mm.    This growth has occurred during the winter and, since growth in starfish
is both temperature and food dependent, it is reasonable to suppose that growth
in summer would be considerably greater.    The presence of the distinct peak in
arm size indicates that there is a period of higher incidence of fission.
Given a higher growth rate in summer, it seems very likely that the peak period
of fission occurs in the mid-late summer.    While there is clearly higher incidence of fission at one time of year, fission does occur at all seasons.
Small samples examined in April and November had a proportion which had recently split among them and the June and August samples contained 6% and 7% of
recently split individuals

Fig 2 a. Characteristic posture of splitting animal. b. Intermediate phase of
fission. c. Close-up of splitting animal showing tube foot posture. d. Final
stages of fission.

The Process of Fission

By the time that external evidence of fission is obvious, the process is
already advanced.    The most obvious evidence is usually that the two sets of
arms are arranged to oppose each other (Fig 2a).    Close inspection reveals
that at the point where the opposing arms leave the disc, a small split can
be seen.    At this point in the time sequence, if such an animal is inverted,
it will right itself rapidly and in a co-ordinated fashion and after some
normal movement may resume the original posture, indicating that early in the
sequence, the nerve ring remains intact.

Subsequently, the split between the plates can be seen to have deepened and a
stage is reached at which, if it is inverted, the animal cannot turn itself

back as a functional unit.   It seems apparent that the nerve ring has now
been severed and that the animal has separated into two parts.   The two
"halves" do usually right themselves but may take some time.   They may do so
having introduced a twist in the aboral tissue.   At this stage (separation
into two parts), a pronounced groove may be present on the aboral surface
along the line of junction between the two "halves" of the animal.   Inspection
of the animal reveals that the two sets of tube feet are either stepping
towards the tips or are attached to the substratum with the disc further away
from the mouth of the animal than the tube foot base (Fig 2 c).   This arrangement of the tube feet in opposing sets which are tending to pull outwards from
the centre of the animal in such a way as to pull the two "halves" apart is
clearly the reason why splitting occurs.

The part of fission from first separation of the animal into two functional
units to complete separation of the lower "halves" so that the "halves" are
linked only by the aboral (dorsal) tissues, is relatively rapid.   As the
separation of the oral part of the animals, once the plates are separated,
requires only the tearing of the walls of the gut, this is not surprising.
Since most animals split along the line of previous fission, there is a line
of weakness along which separation may occur.   However, although the ventral
tissues part easily, this is not the case with the aboral integument.   The two
sets of tube feet now exert a strong pull away from the area of split, forcibly
stretching these tissues (Fig 2 b, d).   The tissues in this region are strong
and some time may elapse before the connective tissue between the plates
breaks down completely.   The time taken for complete fission is from 8-24
hours.   Subsequent to the breakdown of tissues, the two new animals usually
remain motionless for some time.

## The Cause of Fission

Characteristics of splitting animals.   Size.   Examination of the animals
found splitting in the laboratory reveals that most animals which split have
the two "halves" of the body equivalent or near equivalent in size.   A typical
example is that shown splitting in Fig 2 where the difference in size of the
two parts is negligible.   Only when tank conditions became extreme did animals with large differences in arm size ratio show any tendency to split. The
growth pattern already observed would produce animals with arms with high r/R
ratio at the period of maximum incidence of fission.

Behaviour.   A. polyplax moves very little under laboratory conditions and is
strongly photo-negative.   It was clear, however, that movement is normally in
the direction of the largest arms, as one would expect, although sideways
movement, i.e. parallel to the line of previous fission, did also occur.
Animals whose arms were reaching equivalence in size did not show a noticeably
lesser tendency to move in the direction of the larger arms.   A. polyplax
maintains, or can exert, a very strong hold on the substrate, to the extent
that forcible removal causes a large number of tube feet to break off, leaving
the sucker disc attached to the substratum.   On uneven or rounded surfaces,
such a movement could result in outward pulls from the centre, particularly,
as is often the case, the eight arms align themselves in a 4 + 4 arrangement.
This clamping down action occurs in the laboratory in response to touch,
sudden strong water movements and similar mechanical stimuli and inevitably
follows removal for examination whether or not the individual was previously
gripping the rock.

Circumstances in which fission was induced. (a) <u>In transit from New Zealand to</u> <u>U.K.</u> Of 31 individuals, 2 split en route, another individual died and two autotomised single arms.   These animals were subjected to very low temperatures in transit as well as mechanical shock.   Several others had r/R ratios greater than 0.75 but did not divide.

(b) <u>In the laboratory.</u>   On several occasions fission occurred in a few animals after relatively large temperature changes in the holding tanks.   This was more often when the temperature was raised and also occurred when tank conditions became poor as a result of failure of circulation.   On two occasions, animals were found splitting while feeding on or after having fed on <u>Mytilus</u> <u>edulis</u> (L).   In one case, the mussel and starfish were clearly juxtaposed in such a way that the edges of the mussel shells could have cut the starfish tissue.   In both instances, the "halves" of the animal splitting were very similar in size.   Such was also the case when fission appeared to have been induced by temperature change.   Anoxia due to death of other animals in the tank and/or circulation failure also caused some instances of fission.   When however, tank conditions became so poor that some animals were in a moribund state, a higher proportion of the population split, including animals with a greater difference in relative arm size.

(c) <u>Experimental induction.</u> Stimuli which might occur in nature were applied in attempts to induce fission.   All animals used in experiments had a high r/R ratio.   1. Entrapment.   4 specimens had 3 arms trapped but not crushed. Of these 2 escaped but, in pulling free, left one arm behind;   the others freed themselves without damage.   There was no attempt to split.   2.   Three specimens were damaged by crushing the arms on one side.   Neither autotomy of the damaged arms nor fission occurred.   3.   Dilution.   Experimental reduction of the seawater concentration to 50% of original resulted in rapid mortality but no evidence of fission.   10% reduction of salinity resulted in loss of mobility but no splitting.

(d) <u>Artificial induction through cutting the nerve ring.</u>   From observation of fission, it seems that breakdown of the nerve ring is required before fission will occur.   If this is so, artificial section of the nerve ring at one or two places should result in fission.   It is possible, however, that division of the plates automatically results in breakdown of the nerve ring and subsequent fission.   The following experiments have been undertaken on animals with a high r/R ratio.   1.   Section of the nerve ring at two places.   2.   Section of the nerve ring at a single side of the junction of the two "halves" of the animal.   3.   Cutting the epidermis and partially separating the plates at the junction between the two "halves" of the animal.   4.   Cutting the aboral (dorsal) tissues above the junction.

Of these experiments those involving double section of the nerve ring resulted in the experimental animals splitting in the same way as those dividing spontaneously.   None of the other experimental situations resulted in an attempt to split.   The low number of experiments undertaken is attributable to the fact that animals with high r/R ratios were few in number.

## Further Aspects of Fission

<u>Plane of fission.</u>   It is clear that for the majority of animals, the plane of fission is along that of the previous split, because there is here an obvious line of weakness.   Division can, however, occur at right angles to the previous line of fission.   Such instances were, nevertheless, rare.

<u>Survival of split animals.</u> The survival of split animals in the field is unknown but, if laboratory experience is relevant, should be of a high order.

Both "halves" of spontaneously dividing animals clearly survive without
difficulty and become functional animals rapidly.    This even applies to animals which have split as a result of poor water conditions and in which one
"half" is relatively small.    The smallest animals to have successfully regenerated (r/R=0.33+) had R=5mm.    There seems little doubt that each normal
split is capable of producing two new animals.    Even artificially cut animals,
which took much longer to heal the cut surface, survived in the laboratory for
50 days, by which time all had obvious regenerating arms.    The potential
longevity of <u>A. polyplax</u> in the field is unknown but the survival of animals
in the laboratory for up to 4 years, albeit at lower temperatures than those
of the natural environment, suggests a long lifespan, as does the fact that the
species produces small eggs and hence, planktotrophic larvae.    Fission on an
annual basis, therefore, would potentially result in a possible 32 animals at
the end of five years.    It is clear that a considerable potential for asexual
reproduction exists.

<u>Recovery and regeneration</u>.    The return of split animals to a normally func-
tioning state is rapid.    Within 2 weeks, animals can be found feeding with
the remaining portion of the cardiac stomach extended.    Examination of sections through split animals reveals that after 1 day, the broken ends of
aboral tissue have fused with the torn gut tissues.    Re-organisation follows
and sections taken of animals 1 week post-fission revealed clearly visible
primordia.    After 2 weeks all four arm buds were clearly visible on living
animals and average small arm length was 5mm after 16 weeks.    Other details
of the regeneration process seem similar to those reported by Yamazi (8) and
Tartarin (7) and will not be further considered here.

Fig 3 a. Diagram showing position of experimental cuts.
       b. Result of experimental cut.

<u>Control of the number of regenerating arms</u>.    From the field data it was seen
that the tendency to regenerate a number of arms very similar to those lost is
considerable.    It seems that the number of arms regenerated is controlled by
the amount of disc available for new arms.    Thus the normal situation is that
two arms develop on the exposed disc adjacent to the existing arms and a further pair develops between them.    As the amount of disc left when a 7 or 9
armed animal splits is extremely similar to that of an 8 armed animal, the
development of 4 arms here also is to be expected.    If the disc area exposed
is the controlling factor, one would expect to be able to produce animals with
10 arms by judicious surgery.    To ascertain whether this was the case, animals
were cut as shown in Fig 2a and left to regenerate.    Figure 2b shows an
example of a 10 armed animal so produced.    It is clear that disc area exposed
is fundamental to the determination of the number of arms regenerating.

## DISCUSSION

The observations and experiments reported here strongly suggest that the normal cause of fission in A. polyplax is the appearance of co-dominance in opposing arm groups of the animal, which, when a stimulus causes the tube feet to attach strongly or alternatively to step in opposite directions, results in the tearing of the aboral tissues and the fracture of the nerve ring usually along the line of weakness of the previous division.    An important consideration is that the effector organs involved in the fission are the tube feet, which are under the control of the nervous system.    Since both are in close contact with the external medium they are likely to be immediately affected by changes in it as the tissues of echinoderms are highly permeable.    It will be noted that the peak of fission appears to be in summer, when temperature change likely on exposure to the air will be considerable and when the r/R ratio will be close to unity.    Temperature fluctuation and a tendency to periodic anoxia are also characteristic of rock pools in summer.    The failure of the experiments involving mechanical damage does not detract from the hypothesis since damage to an arm is unlikely to cause that arm to grip strongly, in fact retraction of the tube feet usually occurs.

Earlier workers have observed that fission often follows on a period of stress and it has been previously suggested that equivalence of the two "halves" may be important.    It has, however, been suggested that an internal change, presumably of a chemical nature is necessary and one author (Tartarin 7) attributes fission in Coscinasterias tenuispina to sharp edged food.    In this and another species of this genus (C. acutispina Stimpson) (Yamazi 8) it has been remarked that equivalence of size is not a feature of splitting animals.

On present evidence, chemical involvement in the process seems unlikely and the experiences of Tartarin, who kept C. tenuispina for 2 years in floating cages in the sea without a single occurrence of fission, supports this view.    If fission were dependent upon a chemical build up, some of these animals should have split, since specimens on the sea bottom close by split during the same period.    The absence of fission in these specimens led Tartarin to postulate that eating sharp edged food was the cause of fission since this was the only difference he could discern between his captive animals and those in the adjacent wild populations.    While such an explanation may be adequate for C. tenuispina and, from evidence presented earlier, could possibly be the cause of fission in some instances in A. polyplax, it is clearly not the only cause in the latter species.

Whether the explanation of fission made for A. polyplax can be applied to all other fissiparous species is debatable.    Some species show considerable similarities with A. polyplax, others, members of the genus Coscinasterias, considerable differences.
Nepanthia belcheri Perrier (Kenny 5), C. tenuispina at Bermuda (Crozier 3), Sclerasterias richardi Perrier (Falconetti 4) and the Sclerasterias species examined by Fisher (5) all show a high r/R ratio at fission and all of these except S. richardi are from the intertidal and, moreover, show the highest incidence of fission in summer.    Asterina wega Perrier (Achituv 1) also is intertidal but no data is available on the conditions under which fission occurs in this species.    For all these species the mode of fission attributed to A. polyplax seems possible.    C. acutispina and C. tenuispina in the Mediterranean, however, both split when the arm groups are very different in size and, in C. tenuispina at least, often at right angles to the line of previous fission.    For these, an alternative explanation is apparently

required, possibly damage, as Tartarin suggests.    Certainly the genus
Coscinasterias, when alive, has a very flexible, elastic and loosely constructed body (fission when cut artificially takes only a few minutes compared with
hours for A. polyplax).    The fact that it is small intertidal specimens of
C. acutispina which split would support the view that mechanical damage is
important but Yamazi (8) does not believe mechanical damage to be the cause
of fission.    My own observations on Coscinasterias calamaria confirm this
view since an extensive series of experiments involving this kind of stimulus
gave negative results.    This genus requires further study.

The A. polyplax population examined contained few animals not showing evidence
of fission.    Of these, some had 5 or 7 arms and may have a lesser tendency to
form functional "halves", the others were predominantly larger specimens.    It
may be, therefore, that as with several other fissiparous species, the tendency
to split is less in large specimens, as a result perhaps of increased strength
of the tissues linking the plates and thus the arms.

It would seem that such a situation is not often achieved by A. polyplax
although there may be sub-littoral populations in which it is the case.    It
is, however, a common feature of fissiparous species.    The abundance of food
may be important in determining if and when a fissiparous species splits.
Allostichaster insignis Farquhar for example, living in shallow water on a
mussel bed in Wellington harbour (N.Z.), shows a low incidence of fission and
the population contains a high proportion of large animals in which fission is
not apparent.    These animals have conditions of high food availability and
are subject to few of the stresses undergone by intertidal forms.    There
seems little doubt that there is a connection between these facts and that,
in this species at least, the combination of plentiful food and quiet conditions results in less fission.

Fission is clearly a fundamental feature of the life history of A. polyplax.
The animal is small and relatively rare except in a few widely separated
areas.    The size frequency data from Raglan revealed an absence of very small
animals which can be interpreted as an indication that successful recruitment
from sexual reproduction at this site is erratic.    This is not surprising
since, despite the small size, A. polyplax does not have large eggs and
direct development and it is clear both that the reproductive output must be
small and that the chances of survival of the resulting larvae are low.    My
experience indicates that full maturity is uncommon.    Some animals were
available in the period at which gonad development should be at or nearing
the peak (December) and of these,only those with a high r/R ratio had
significant gonads and even in these animals the gonads were not large.    It
is apparent that, in any terms, asexual reproduction by fission must be
extremely important for the survival of the species.    At the very least, if
sexual reproduction is periodically successful, fission will allow the population numbers to build up so that when gamete release occurs, the output is
greatly increased and therefore more likely to be successful.    If sexual
reproduction very rarely succeeds, then the fission process would be essential
to the continuation of the species in the short term.    In the unlikely event
that sexual reproduction is never successful, the process would provide the
only reproductive method of the species.

## ACKNOWLEDGEMENTS

I thank Professor J.E. Morton for the original opportunity to study
A. polyplax, and T. Beckett for sending live material to me in London.

## REFERENCES

(1)    Achituv, Y., 1969.    Studies on the reproduction and distribution of
       Asterina burtoni Grey and Asterina wega Perrier (Asteroidea) in the
       Red Sea and Eastern Mediterranean.    Israel Journal of Zoology, 18,
       329-342.

(2)    Clark, A.M., 1967.    Variable symmetry in fissiparous Asterozoa.
       Symposia of the Zoological Society of London, 20, 143-157.

(3)    Crozier, W.J., 1920.    Notes on some problems of adaptation.   2. On the
       temporal relations of asexual propagation and gametic reproduction
       in Coscinasterias tenuispina;   with a note on the direction of
       progression and the significance of the madrepores.    Biological
       Bulletin of the Marine Biological Laboratory, Woods Hole, 39,122-128.

(4)    Falconetti, C., Fredj-Reygrobellet, D. et Fredj, G., 1976. Sexualite
       et fissiparite concomitantes chez l'asterie Sclerasterias richardi;
       premieres donnees.   Marine Biology, 34, 247-257.

(5)    Fisher, W.K., 1925.    Asexual reproduction of the starfish Sclerasterias.
       Biological Bulletin of the Marine Biological Laboratory, Woods Hole.

(6)    Kenny, R. 1969.    Growth and asexual reproduction of the starfish
       Nepanthia belcheri (Perrier).    Pacific Science, 23, 51-55.

(7)    Tartarin, A., 1953.    Observations sur les mutilations, le regeneration,
       les neoformations et l'anatomie de Coscinasterias tenuispina.
       Recueil des Travaux de la Station Marine d'Endoume, Faculte des
       Sciences de Marseille, 10, 1-107.

(8)    Yamazi, I. 1950.    Autotomy and regeneration in Japanese sea-stars and
       ophiurans.    1. Observations on a sea-star Coscinasterias acutispina
       Stimpson and four species of ophiurans.    Annotationes zoologicae
       japonenses, 23, 175-186.

# ENVIRONMENTAL CONTROL OF REPRODUCTION IN THE POLYCHAETES *EULALIA VIRIDIS* AND *HARMOTHOE IMBRICATA*

## P.R. Garwood and P.J.W. Olive

*Zoology Department, University of Newcastle upon Tyne,*
*Newcastle upon Tyne NE1 7RU, England*

### ABSTRACT

The effects of environmental daylength and temperature on the progress of vitellogenesis in two species of polychaete, Harmothoe imbricata and Eulalia viridis, have been investigated using controlled environment cabinets. H. imbricata grows two cohorts of oocytes, the second only entering vitellogenesis after the spawning of the first. Low temperature accelerates the growth rate of the first cohort, but slows down growth of the second. Moderately long daylength produces the fastest growth in both cohorts, but the influence of daylength on the second is much less marked. E. viridis grows a single batch of oocytes, later in the year, and initiation of vitellogenesis is dependent upon the temperature rising above a critical level (between $5^{\circ}$ and $10^{\circ}C$). The rate of vitellogenesis is then controlled directly by temperature, whilst daylength is of little or no importance. The roles of daylength and temperature in the control of the two waves of vitellogenesis in H. imbricata and the single wave in E. viridis have been interpreted in terms of the evolution of an appropriate reproductive strategy.

### INTRODUCTION

There seems to be general agreement that "environmental" factors are responsible for determining the timing of the breeding season in animals with "discrete iteroparous" reproduction (Olive and Clark, in press), but with only a few exceptions (e.g., Barnes 1975), it has not been demonstrated what these environmental factors are, nor what processes they control. Part of the problem is that spawning occurs after a protracted period of gametogenesis, and as Clark (1965) pointed out more than ten years ago, synchronising environmental inputs may occur both early and late in the process of gametogenesis.

We have attempted to simplify the problem by concentrating on two species of common littoral polychaetes, Harmothoe imbricata and Eulalia viridis, in which vitellogenesis takes place synchronously shortly before the breeding season. The basic life histories of the two animals have already been described (Daly 1972 and Olive 1975a) and in this report, we shall concentrate on the effects of temperature and daylength on the vitellogenic phases of the two species, using controlled artificial environments.

331

Harmothoe imbricata

Specimens were collected from underneath rocks in the intertidal zone to the
north of Cullercoats Bay, Tyne and Wear, and brought back to the laboratory
in a vacuum flask.    Animals were maintained individually in plastic beakers
containing 80-100 ml sea water, placed in water baths, the temperature of
which was controlled by Churchill Thermochiller Units.    Artificial light,
where employed, was provided by   single 15 watt bulbs, housed in light proof
boxes containing the water baths.    Chopped Malacoceros fuliginosa was provided once or twice per week as food, and the sea water in the beakers was
renewed regularly.    Oocyte sampling and estimation of modal oocyte diameters
was based on the methods of Daly (1972), and the midpoint of the modal oocyte
size class used in the calculation of the modal oocyte volume.    As oocytes
approached full size, heterosexual pairs were set up and checked each morning
to determine the spawning date.    Eggs are always spawned between 10 p.m. and
8 a.m., and are retained under the elytra of the female until the trochophore
stage.

Eulalia viridis

Animals were collected from crevices in the upper intertidal zone in Cullercoats Bay, and were maintained individually in the laboratory in plastic pots
containing 100 ml of filtered sea water and several small stones.    The pots
stood in Gallenkamp cooled incubators, giving a variety of light and temperature regimes.    None of the animals were fed during experiments.    From time
to time, samples of native shore animals were collected, and their maturity
assessed.    The sexual maturity of Eulalia viridis was assessed from oocyte
frequency histograms and staging sequence after Olive (1975a, b) as follows:
Stage 1. Maximum oocyte diameter less than 40 μm.    Stage 2. Maximum oocyte
diameter between 40 and 80 μm.    Stage 3. Maximum oocyte diameter greater
than 80 μm.    Stage 4. Maximum oocyte diameter greater than 80 μm, and the
majority of oocytes larger than 80 μm.

RESULTS

Vitellogenesis and environmental conditions

Environmental temperature in the littoral zone at Cullercoats, as determined
from records of circulating sea water at the Dove Marine Laboratory (heavier
line), supplemented by recordings of surface water temperature in Cullercoats
Bay (lighter line), and effective daylength as the period between sunrise and
sunset (stippled area) are shown in Fig. 1.    H. imbricata undergoes vitellogenesis in two successive waves, the second following immediately after the
oocytes grown in the first have been spawned (Daly 1972).    The first wave of
vitellogenesis coincides with both the coldest conditions, and the shortest
daylengths, whereas the second wave occurs during a period of increasing
environmental daylength and temperature.    Vitellogenesis in E. viridis occurs
later, not starting in most individuals until May, and this species spawns in
midsummer in this locality.    The two species show conveniently contrasting
relationships between the timing of the major period of oocyte growth and
natural environmental conditions, and the effects of temperature and daylength
on this growth phase have been examined experimentally independently in the
two species.

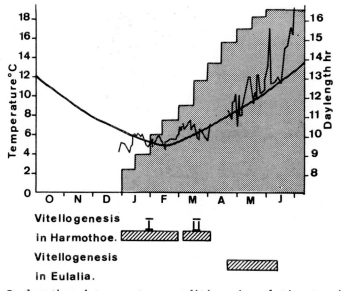

Vitellogenesis
in Harmothoe.

Vitellogenesis
in Eulalia.

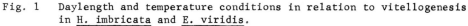

Fig. 1    Daylength and temperature conditions in relation to vitellogenesis
in H. imbricata and E. viridis.

Experimental Results - Harmothoe imbricata

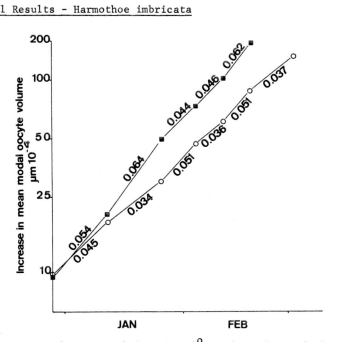

Fig. 2    Oocyte growth in H. imbricata at $4^{\circ}$C under ambient lighting (O)
and a constant 13L:11D regime (■).

The first wave of vitellogenesis from mid-December to March.     The correlation between the onset of this phase and the annual minimum daylength (see Fig. 1) suggested that daylength might be an important influence.     The first experiment, designed to test this hypothesis, involved sampling of oocytes from two groups of eight females, kept under ambient light conditions, or in a constant 13L:11D regime, both at a constant $4^{\circ}C$.     Figure 2 shows oocyte growth in the two groups as the increase in mean modal oocyte volume.     Growth at 13L:11D is considerably faster than under ambient conditions.     The figures alongside the two curves are the instantaneous relative growth rates (K) as calculated from the formula:

$$K = \frac{l_n V_2 - l_n V_1}{t_2 - t} \qquad \text{(Brody, 1945)}$$

Where $V_1$ and $V_2$ = mean modal oocyte volumes at times $t_1$ and $t_2$.

If overall values of K are calculated for individual animals, the mean value is significantly greater at 13L:11D than at ambient (0.0558 ± 0.0069 compared with 0.0439 ± 0.0097, t = 2.836, P = <0.02).

The results of a more extensive experiment, involving the manipulation of both daylength and temperature conditions, is shown in Fig. 3.     Groups of females were kept at three constant temperatures, $15^{\circ}$, $10^{\circ}$ and $5^{\circ}C$, with two light regimes, simulated ambient and constant 12L:12D, at each temperature.     In addition, a 16L:8D regime was employed at $5^{\circ}C$ only.

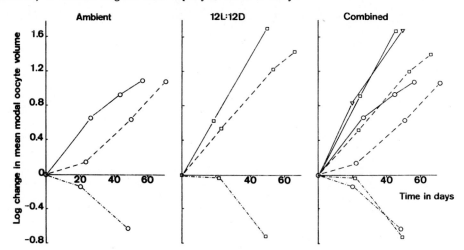

Fig. 3.   Oocyte growth in H. imbricata under various daylength and temperature conditions.   O Ambient lighting   □ Constant 12L:12D   ▽ Constant 16L:8D   ———  $5^{\circ}C$   --- $10^{\circ}C$   ----- $15^{\circ}C$.

Overall instantaneous relative growth rates under the various conditions were compared using an S.N.K. ranked analysis of variance (Sokal and Rolf, 1969). Oocytes grew fastest at $5^{\circ}C$, slower at $10^{\circ}C$ and at $15^{\circ}C$ growth was negative due to degeneration of the larger oocytes, and in both light regimes the differences in growth rates between the three temperatures were significant. At $5^{\circ}$ and $10^{\circ}C$, the rate of growth was significantly faster under the 12L:12D regime compared with ambient conditions, reflecting the greater rate of accumulation of "daylight hour days" at 12L:12D, whereas at 15°C, degeneration of the larger oocytes occurred under both light regimes.    Animals kept at long (16L:8D) daylength at 5° C showed faster growth than those under ambient conditions, but there was no significant difference when compared with growth at 12L:12D.

The first wave of vitellogenesis is, then, influenced considerably by both light and temperature, being fastest at low temperature and moderately long daylength, whilst increasing daylength beyond a value of 12L:12D has little further accelerating effect.    High temperature (15°C) completely suppresses oocyte growth.

The second wave of vitellogenesis from March to April.    The second cohort of oocytes, which enter vitellogenesis only after the spawning of the first, grow rapidly under conditions of increasing daylength and temperature (see Fig. 1).    Because of the brevity of this phase, modal oocyte diameter measurements are not a feasible method for monitoring growth, but the time interval (T) between successive spawnings in individual animals can conveniently be used as a measure of the rate of oocyte growth.    The mean spawning interval for animals kept under a variety of conditions (Table 1), shows that in contrast to the first cohort of oocytes, the rate of growth of the second is largely unaffected by daylength, although it is slower at 8L:16D, and significantly so, with all but one of the other 5° C groups.    Growth can occur at 15°C, and indeed growth at this temperature is faster than at any of the others.    Daylength and temperature both affect this second wave of vitellogenesis, which is slowest at low temperature and short daylength, but their influence is greatly reduced, with only extreme values producing significant changes in growth rate.

TABLE 1.    The effects of various daylength/temperature combinations

on the duration (T) of the second wave of vitellogenesis

in H. imbricata

| Temperature | 15 | 10 | Ambient | 5 | 5 | 5 | 5 | 5 | 5 |
|---|---|---|---|---|---|---|---|---|---|
| Daylength | Ambient | Ambient | Ambient | Ambient | 16L:8D | 13L:11D | 12L:12D | Ambient | 8L:16D |
| Mean T | 24.36 | 28.2 | 31.55 | 32.5 | 32.9 | 33.29 | 33.26 | 35.92 | 37.2 |
| $s^2$ | 5.62 | 6.71 | 1.54 | 7.3 | 12.25 | 4.58 | 17.64 | 13.1 | 30.4 |
| ^ | 11 | 5 | 9 | 24 | 16 | 7 | 11 | 8 | 17 |

S.N.K.

Eulalia viridis

There is a strong correlation between the proportion of females with oocytes >50 and 80 μm in diameter and sea temperature (r = 0.89, 0.88, P <.001) and since this period is also one of increasing daylength, there is an equally good correlation with daylength (r = 0.89, 0.88, P = <0.01).

An experiment was performed in March, prior to the natural onset of vitellogenesis, to determine whether it was increasing daylength or the rising temperature conditions that was responsible for the initiation of oocyte growth.    Animals in Stage 1 of vitellogenesis or Stage 2 (with only a few

oocytes 40-80 μm in diameter) were maintained at 5°C with short (8L:16D) and
long (16L:8D) daylength, or at 10°C with short, long or split long (8L:4D,
8L:4D) daylength.    The pooled oocyte frequency histograms for days 0, 28 and
56 (Fig. 4) show that at 5° C no oocyte growth occurred, whereas at 10° C a
population of vitellogenic oocytes developed.

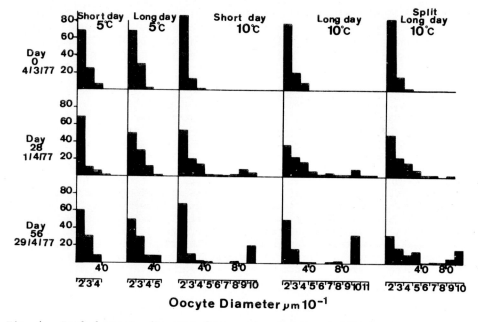

Fig. 4    Pooled oocyte diameter frequencies for E. viridis kept
          under 5 different light/temperature regimes.

The individual animals maintained at 5° C remained, with one exception, in
Stages 1 and 2 but, in contrast, many of the 10° C maintained animals developed to Stages 3 and 4 (Table 2).    After 56 days, the originally homogeneous
experimental sets have separated into two homogeneous subsets.    The animals
maintained at 10° C under split long daylength were slower to respond than
the other ones at 10° C;   after 28 days they did not differ significantly
from those kept at 5°C.    Constant short daylength does not inhibit vitellogenesis under appropriate temperature conditions, and exposure to long daylength does not alone initiate more rapid vitellogenesis.    At the beginning
of May, the shore population contains a small proportion of Stage 3 animals
and the majority of the females have at least some oocytes greater than 50 μm
in diameter.    At this time, a second experiment was performed in which
animals were maintained at 5°, 10°, 15° and 20° C, for 21 days under a long
daylength regime.    The results show very clearly a progressive influence of
environmental temperature on the rate of vitellogenesis.    In Fig. 5, oocyte
frequency histograms confirm that little or no oocyte growth occurs at the
lowest temperature;   the proportion of larger oocytes, however, increases
progressively in animals maintained at 10°, 15° and 20° C.    There is a
significantly higher proportion of the more mature females at each success-
ively higher temperature (Table 3);   a posteriori tests confirm that after
21 days at these temperatures the sets have become heterogeneous.

TABLE 2.    Sexual maturity of _Eulalia viridis_ in different
environmental conditions

| Set | Environmental conditions | Day 0 Stage | | | | Day 28 Stage | | | | Day 56 Stage | | | |
|---|---|---|---|---|---|---|---|---|---|---|---|---|---|
| | | 1 | 2 | 3 | 4 | 1 | 2 | 3 | 4 | 1 | 2 | 3 | 4 |
| A | 5°C  8L  16D | 15 | 9 | 0 | 0 | 15 | 9 | 0 | 0 | 9 | 7 | 0 | 0 |
| B | 5°C  16L  8D | 15 | 7 | 0 | 0 | 9 | 13 | 0 | 0 | 8 | 10 | 1 | 0 |
| C | 10°C  8L  16D | 18 | 4 | 0 | 0 | 2 | 12 | 5 | 2 | 9 | 2 | 2 | 3 |
| D | 10°C  16L  8D | 11 | 12 | 0 | 0 | 5 | 5 | 11 | 1 | 5 | 0 | 7 | 7 |
| E | 10°C 8L 4D 8L 4D | 18 | 5 | 0 | 0 | 6 | 15 | 0 | 1 | 1 | 6 | 0 | 5 |
| A posteriori test | | A B C D E | | | | A B E | | C D | | A B | | C D E | |
| $G_H$ | | 7.46 n.s. | | | | 68 | | p< .001 | | 34.8 | | p< .001 | |

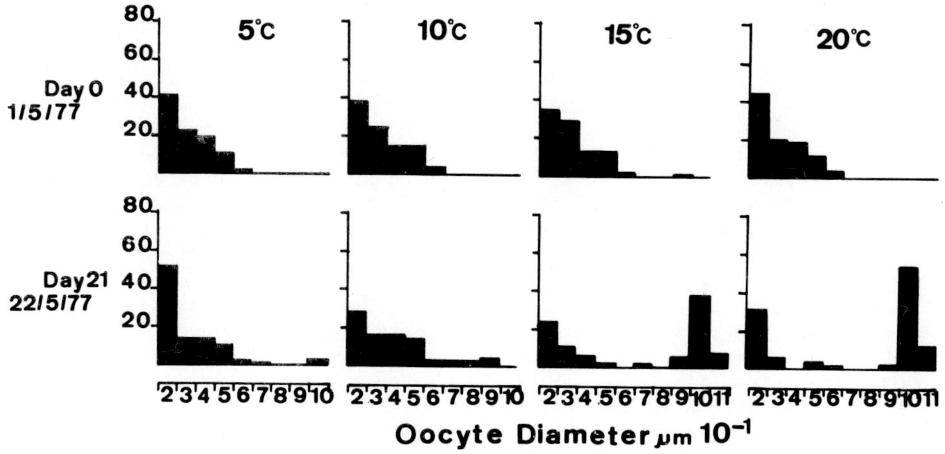

Fig. 5    Pooled oocyte diameter frequencies for _E. viridis_ kept at
4 different temperatures.

TABLE 3.    Sexual maturity of _Eulalia viridis_ in 4 different
temperature regimes

| Set | Constant Temperature Conditions | Day 0 Stage | | | | Day 21 Stage | | | |
|---|---|---|---|---|---|---|---|---|---|
| | | 1 | 2 | 3 | 4 | 1 | 2 | 3 | 4 |
| A | 5°C | 3 | 14 | 2 | 0 | 2 | 12 | 5 | 0 |
| B | 10°C | 4 | 17 | 1 | 0 | 3 | 11 | 7 | 1 |
| C | 15°C | 3 | 16 | 2 | 0 | 2 | 1 | 12 | 6 |
| D | 20°C | 3 | 18 | 2 | 0 | 0 | 0 | 10 | 13 |
| A posteriori test | | A B C D | | | | A B C D | | | |
| $G_H$ | | 0.8 n.s. | | | | 412 P< .001 | | | |

DISCUSSION

In both H. imbricata and E. viridis, it has been possible to identify environmental conditions which govern the rate of vitellogenesis, and in both species
these conditions result in synchronous development of germ cells within the
population.

The oocytes of the first wave of vitellogenesis in H. imbricata develop
earliest, under conditions of cold (around the minimum) temperature, and daylength increasing from its minimum value.    The rate of growth during this
phase has been shown to be influenced by both these factors being fastest at
low temperature and moderately long daylength.    High temperature inhibits
vitellogenesis, resulting in the degeneration of large oocytes, leaving a
pool of small previtellogenic ones.    These remain viable, and are capable of
growing once the animals are returned to suitably low temperatures.    Daylength increases also accelerate the rate of growth, up to a maximum at about
12L:12D, beyond which further increase has little effect.

In contrast, the second cohort of oocytes, growing under conditions of
increasing temperature and daylength, is relatively unaffected by the environment.    Its rate is reduced by decreased temperature, getting progressively
slower from $15^{o}$ C down to $5^{o}$ C, a complete reversal of the situation for the
first cohort of oocytes, and in addition, the effect of temperature is much
less marked.    This reversal in effect of temperature reflects the differences
in the natural temperature conditions to which animals would be exposed on the
shore during these two phases.    Similarly, daylength is of greatly reduced
importance in its effect on the second cohort, although the direction of this
effect remains apparently unchanged.    The reduction in sensitivity of the
second cohort to both temperature and daylength conditions is a reflection
of the much faster growth of this cohort (some $2\frac{1}{2}$ times as fast as the first).
The reasons for the faster growth of the second cohort of oocytes compared
with the first, is not fully understood, but the work presented here shows it
cannot be explained simply in terms of differences in environmental conditions,
and must, therefore, have its foundations in some endogenous factor.

The oocytes of E. viridis develop later than those of H. imbricata.    They
have been accumulating in the coelom since the previous September, but
throughout this period they have remained small.    Once vitellogenesis is
initiated, the growth of the more advanced oocytes in each female is rapid,
and full sized oocytes approximately 100 - 120 µm in diameter, soon develop.
The rather sudden onset of oocyte development has suggested that there may
be some switch-like mechanism controlling the onset of vitellogenesis (Olive
1977) and it has been shown that the supra-oesophageal ganglion of E. viridis
releases a hormone which is essential for vitellogenesis (Olive 1975, 1976).
More recent experiments have confirmed the importance of this hormone but
they do not support the idea that the progress of vitellogenesis is controlled
by an "on-off" hormonally mediated switch.    Instead, as we have shown, sexual
development appears to be controlled progressively by increasing environmental
temperature.    The experiments suggest that low environmental temperature has
a direct limiting effect on the progress of gametogenesis in the early Spring,
and that daylength has no role in controlling vitellogenesis.

Our studies on these two species show clearly that there is no simple
relationship between temperature, light and reproduction.    Each has evolved
a particular relationship between the environmental conditions it experiences

and the physiological processes involved in sexual maturation, such that they
mature at the "appropriate" time of year.   The timing of the breeding season
is, we presume, controlled by a set of as yet unknown factors influencing
larval development and effective recruitment.   Of particular interest is
the observation that even within a species, the precise relationship between
the gametogenic processes and environmental conditions is not necessarily
fixed.   We conclude that this relationship is one of the variables upon
which natural selection can act during the evolution of an appropriate
reproductive strategy, and that in each species it is an effect of selection
for a particular breeding season, but not the ultimate cause of the timing of
the breeding season.   It would be of great interest to examine the relationship between vitellogenesis and environmental conditions in other parts of
the geographic range of these two species.

## REFERENCES

Barnes, H., 1975.  Reproductive rhythms and some marine invertebrates;  an
    introduction.   Publicazione dell Stazione Zoologica, Napoli, 39
    (supplement):  8-25.

Brody, S., 1945.  Bioenergetics and growth.   1023 pp.  New York:  Reinholdt
    Publishing Co.

Clark, R.B., 1965.  Endocrinology and the reproductive biology of polychaetes.
    Oceanography and Marine Biology, Annual Review, 3:  211-255.

Daly, J.M., 1962.  The maturation and breeding biology of Harmothoe imbricata
    (Polychaeta:  Polynoidae).   Marine Biology, 12:  53-66.

Olive, P.J.W., 1975a.  The reproductive biology of Eulalia viridis (Muller)
    in the North Eastern U.K.  Journal of the Marine Biological Association of
    the United Kingdom, 55·  313-326.

Olive, P.J.W., 1975b.  A vitellogenesis promoting influence of the prostomium
    in the polychaete Eulalia viridis (Muller) (Phyllodocidae), General and
    Comparative Endocrinology, 26:  266-273.

Olive, P.J.W., 1976.  Further evidence of a vitellogenesis-promoting hormone
    and its activity in Eulalia viridis (L.) Polychaeta:  Phyllodocidae.
    General and Comparative Endocrinology, 30:  397-403.

Olive, P.J.W., 1977.  Observations on the reproductive cycles, gametogenesis
    and endocrinology of the polychaete Eulalia viridis (Phyllodocidae) and
    Nephtys hombergi (Nephtydae).  In Advances in Invertebrate Reproduction,
    1:  389-403.  (Ed. K.G. and R.G. Adiyodi).  Proceedings of the First
    International Symposium on Reproductive Physiology of Invertebrates.

Olive, P.J.W. and Clark, R.B. (in press).  Reproduction.  In Annelid
    Physiology.  (Ed. P. Mill) New York:  Academic Press.

We wish to acknowledge the award of an S.R.C. studentship to P.R. Garwood
and a N.E.R.C. grant award to P.J.W. Olive, and the able technical assistance
of Miss P. Newman in some of the work.

# INFLUENCE D'UNE TEMPERATURE ELEVEE SUR LE RYTHME DE PONTE ET LA FECONDITE DES POPULATIONS MEDITERRANEENNES DE *SCOLELEPIS FULIGINOSA* (ANNELIDE: POLYCHETE) EN ELEVAGE AU LABORATOIRE

## Jean-Pierre Guérin et Jean-Pierre Reys

*Laboratoire d'Hydrobiologie Marine et Station Marine d'Endoume, Centre Universitaire de Luminy, 13288 Marseille Cedex 2, France*

ABSTRACT

The effect of elevated temperature ($27^\circ$C - never reached in natural conditions in the Gulf of Marseilles) was tested with regard to longevity and fecundity of Scolelepis fuliginosa reared in the laboratory.    32 pairs were studied, some being maintained at the constant temperature of $27^\circ$C, others were reared at $27^\circ$C for several weeks and then brought down to $19^\circ$C. Overall, 954 broods were reared which gave $2,5 \cdot 10^6$ eggs, average egg-laying rhythm being 3,52 days.   Egg-laying rhythm and fecundity did not show any significant differences between $19^\circ$ and $27^\circ$C.   We can conclude that elevated temperature has no inhibitory effect on reproduction at least for Mediterranean Sea populations of Scolelepis fuliginosa.    This suggests that, in the natural populations, trophic conditions make egg-laying possible only in winter and spring.

### INTRODUCTION

L'étude du méroplancton révèle qu'un bon nombre d'espèces de Polychètes se reproduisent à une époque relativement précise de l'année, que ce soit en hiver ou en été.   Inversement, un contingent assez restreint d'espèces paraît apte à se reproduire pratiquement à longueur d'année, sauf parfois pendant les époques les plus chaudes : c'est le cas, notamment, des populations méditerranéennes de *Scolelepis fuliginosa* Claparède.   Précédemment (Guérin, 1973) nous avions indiqué que l'arrêt des émissions de cette espèce dans le milieu naturel en période estivale, ne semblait pas lié à un effet direct de l'augmentation de la température, mais plutôt à un effet indirect, les animaux ne trouvant plus de nourriture en quantité suffisante pour assurer leurs besoins métaboliques pendant cette période.   D'après cette hypothèse, la température ne serait plus le seul facteur à considérer pour rendre compte de la séquence de phénomènes à l'origine de la reproduction des Polychètes, comme Bhaud (1972) l'avait déjà souligné.

La réalisation au laboratoire, d'élevage en cycle complet des populations méditeranéennes de *Scolelepis fuliginosa*, était une occasion de tester expérimentalement l'effet réel de la température sur le rythme de ponte et la fécondité de cette espèce dans des conditions thermiques et trophiques bien contrôlées.

### MATERIEL ET METHODES

#### Conditions d'élevage

Les animaux adultes sont maintenus, comme précédemment (Guérin, 1973), dans des

récipients d'une contenance de 200 cm$^3$, à raison d'un couple par récipient. La
nourriture est exclusivement constituée par du "Tetramin" que nous avons utilisé
tel qu'on le trouve dans le commerce. Les animaux sont nourris en principe quotidiennement. Les renouvellements d'eau dans les bacs ont lieu tous les 15
jours environ, d'une manière synchrone dans tous les récipients.

Les expériences ont été menées à deux températures différentes : 19° et 27°C.
Signalons que les animaux maintenus à température élevée ont subi des conditions d'éclairement plus intense que les animaux maintenus à 19°, les fenêtres
du local où se déroulaient les expériences à forte température n'étant pas
pourvues d'un écran de polystyrène, situé derrière les vitres, comme c'est le
cas pour le local réfrigéré.

## Origine des animaux et déroulement des expériences

Nous avons étudié le rythme de ponte et la fécondité de quatre groupes d'animaux issus de la souche vivant au laboratoire à la température de 19± 0,5°C
depuis de nombreuses générations, et d'un groupe constitué d'individus provenant
de larves récoltées dans le méroplancton.

Le groupe A est issu de larves écloses avant le 20/8/1972 au laboratoire et qui
a été transféré à 27°C à compter du 25/11/1972 : il est composé de 5 couples.
Le groupe B, issu d'une ponte du 1/9/1972 est constitué par les individus qui
se sont développés le plus rapidement, les adultes ayant été élevés jusqu'à la
maturité sexuelle à 19°C ; le transfert à 27° a eu lieu le 3/11/1972 ; ce groupe a un effectif de 10 couples. Le groupe C est constitué par des individus
issus de la même ponte que B, mais qui se sont développés plus lentement que
ceux constituant le groupe précédant ; dans ce cas également la maturité sexuelle a été acquise à 19° et le transfert à 27° a eu lieu le 3/12/1972, pour les
10 couples de ce groupe. Enfin, le Groupe D est formé par des adultes issus de
larves méroplanctoniques récoltées le 15/12/1972, élevées à 19° ; sept couples
ont été placés à 27° le 25/1/1973.

Les animaux du groupe A sont restés à 27° jusqu'à la fin de l'expérience, fixée
arbitrairement au 1/4/1973. Par tirage au sort, les couples du groupe B portant un indice impair (désigné par $B_i$ ) et les couples du groupe C portant un
indice pair ($C_p$) ont été transférés de 27 à 19° le 16/1/1973. Les deux autres
séries ($B_p$) et ($C_i$) ainsi que le groupe D sont restés en permanence à 27°C.

Pour comparer le rythme de ponte et la fécondité des divers groupes nous avons
utilisé des tests non paramètriques en raison de l'hétérogénéité des variances.
Il s'agit du test H de Kruskal-Wallis, éventuellement suivi d'une comparaison
multiple (STP in Sokal et Rohlf, 1969) et du test T de Wilcoxon pour séries ap-
pareillées.

## Récolte des pontes et détermination du nombre d'oeufs

La récolte des pontes (déposées la nuit) doit se faire quotidiennement, si l'on
veut fixer les embryons avant leur éclosion, c'est à dire avant leur dispersion
dans le bac d'élevage. Ces pontes sont agglomérées dans du mucus (Guérin,
1974). Elles ont été fixées au formol non neutralisé, ce qui a provoqué la dis-
parition du mucus après plusieurs mois, d'où libération des oeufs. Ceux-ci ont
alors été déposés dans une cuve de Dollfus, le dénombrement portant sur 30 cases disposées selon deux rangées orthogonales, 10 dans un sens, 20 dans l'autre.

RESULTATS

## Mortalité et durée de vie sexuelle

Nous avons déjà signalé que les expériences avaient été volontairement inter-
rompues le 1/4/1973. En fonction du calendrier du début des expériences on
constate donc que celles-ci avaient une durée maximum prévisible. Lorsque les
expériences ont pris fin, de nombreux couples étaient encore en vie et conti-
nuaient à se reproduire : nous ne ferons donc que le bilan des individus qui
sont morts avant la fin de l'expérience.

Groupe A. Les premières pontes intervenant entre le 26 et le 29/10/1972, la
durée de l'expérience était fixée arbitrairement à 154 jours. Sur 5 couples,
2 sont morts avant la fin de l'expérience, respectivement au 130e et 135e jour,
après avoir déposé 32 pontes.

Groupe B. Les reproductions ayant commencé plus tard, la durée maximum est réduite à 147 j. Un seul couple est mort avant la fin de l'expérience, à 112 j,
après avoir déposé 32 pontes.

Groupe C. Rappelons que les individus qui composent ce groupe sont issus de la
même ponte que ceux du groupe B, mais que leur vitesse de croissance a été moins
rapide. La durée maximum de l'expérience est de 116 j. Dans ce groupe la mortalité a été assez importante, puisqu'elle intéresse, d'une part, deux couples
maintenus à 27°, qui sont morts respectivement après 59 et 83 j d'expérience
en ayant déposé 15 et 24 pontes, et, d'autre part, 3 couples transférés à 19°,
morts respectivement après 84, 88 et 94 j d'expérience, en ayant produit 21,
25 et 29 pontes.

Il est intéressant de souligner cette disparité entre les séries B et C où les
animaux qui ont eu une croissance laborieuse (groupe C) semblent moins résis-
tants et ont une durée de vie notablement réduite par rapport à ceux dont la
vie larvaire s'est déroulée plus rapidement (groupe B). Notons également que
le maintien des élevages à forte température n'influe pas sur la mortalité.

Groupe D. Le groupe D est composé de 7 couples constitués à partir de larves récoltées dans le méroplancton. Trois de ces couples sont morts après des durées
de vie sexuée (à partir de la première ponte) assez faibles de 32, 47 et 50 j,
en ayant déposé respectivement 8, 14, et 7 pontes. Il semble, comme cela a été
confirmé par des données récentes sur la composition chimique élémentaire (Guérin et Kérambrun, 1976), que les animaux issus du milieu naturel, que ce soit à
l'état de larves ou d'adultes, s'adaptent mal aux conditions de vie du laboratoire.

## Présentation globale des résultats

La présentation globale des résultats concernant la fécondité figure au tableau
1.

On voit qu'en fonction de la durée de vie sexuelle (intervalle de temps compris
entre la date de la première ponte et la date de la dernière ponte - ou la fin
de l'expérience) le nombre de pontes déposées est important. Ceci représente
une amélioration par rapport aux premiers résultats (Guérin, 1973). Cette cons-
tatation est intéressante si l'on considère que les élevages se sont déroulés à
des températures nettement plus élevées que précédemment, c'est à dire dans des
conditions plus délicates.

Nous constatons également que la fréquence moyenne de ponte varie assez peu
d'une série à l'autre, les valeurs extrêmes de l'intervalle moyen qui sépare
deux pontes successives étant respectivement de 3,35 et 3,87 j.  Par contre il
y a des différences notables dans la production journalière d'oeufs, qui apparaît particulièrement faible dans le groupe A mais importante dans le groupe
C, malgré la mortalité qui a affecté les animaux de ce dernier groupe.

TABLEAU 1. Comparaison du nombre de pontes, du rythme de ponte et de la fécon-
           dité des différents couples pendant toute la durée de l'expérience.

| Groupe | Nb de couples | Durée de vie sexuée cumulée | Nb de pontes | Nombre d'oeufs | Fréquence de ponte | Production oeufs/jours |
|--------|--------|--------|--------|--------|--------|--------|
| A | 5 | 675 (135) | 174 (33,8) | 364 140 (72 828) | 3,87 | 539 |
| B | 10 | 1 296 (129) | 386 (38,6) | 1 037 480 (103 748) | 3,35 | 801 |
| C | 10 | 987 (98) | 293 (29,3) | 828 650 (82 865) | 3,36 | 840 |
| D | 7 | 368 (52) | 101 (14,4) | 276 010 (39 430) | 3,64 | 750 |
| Totaux | 32 | 3 326 | 854 | 2 506 280 | | |

## Effet de la température sur la fréquence de ponte

Il apparaît que le nombre moyen de pontes par semaine (choisi comme unité de
travail) ne diffère pas significativement entre les trois groupes A, B et C au
cours des 6 premières semaines d'expérience, pendant lesquelles les conditions
étaient identiques pour tous les couples (H = 4,01 ; 0,05 < P < 0,10) Le nombre moyen général de pontes par semaines est de 1,9 et varie de 1,6 pour le groupe A à 2,9 pour le groupe B et 1,8 pour le groupe C.

Pour tester l'influence de la température nous avons considéré, dans les 2 séries
du groupe B et les 2 séries du groupe C, le nombre de pontes de chaque couple
6 semaines avant et 6 semaines après le changement de température.  Ces données
sont regroupées·dans le tableau 2.

TABLEAU 2. Evolution du nombre de pontes et de la fécondité des différents grou-
           pes d'individus 6 semaines avant ou après l'éventuel changement de
           température.

| Groupes | 6 semaines avant le 16/1/1973 | | 6 semaines après le 16/1/1973 | |
|--------|--------|--------|--------|--------|
| | Nb de pontes | Nb d'oeufs | Nb de pontes | Nb d'oeufs |
| Bp ($\theta$ cte) | 59 | 113 560 | 79 | 244 130 |
| Bi ($\theta$ var) | 51 | 140 510 | 60 | 181 240 |
| Ci ($\theta$ cte) | 56 | 109 740 | 51 | 146 660 |
| Cp ($\theta$ var) | 54 | 68 950 | 68 | 233 320 |

On constate que la différence n'est significative (test de Wilcoxon) ni pour
les 5 couples de la série Bi (T = 3,5 avec P > 0,05), ni pour les 5 couples de
la série Cp (T = 3 avec P > 0,05), qui ont toutes deux subies le changement de

température le 16/1/1973.

De même, les témoins du groupe Bp et Ci ne montrent pas de différences.

Compte tenu de ces résultats nous avons étudié l'évolution de la fréquence de ponte en fonction de l'âge des animaux.  La Fig. 1 représente le nombre moyen cumulé de pontes par semaine pour chaque groupe (pour les groupes B et C nous avons différencié les couples ayant subi le changement de température de ceux qui sont restés en permanence à 27°C).  On remarque que les points sont assez bien alignés, ce qui permet de conclure que l'âge des animaux n'influe pas sur la fréquence de ponte pendant la période considérée (maximum de 19 semaines).

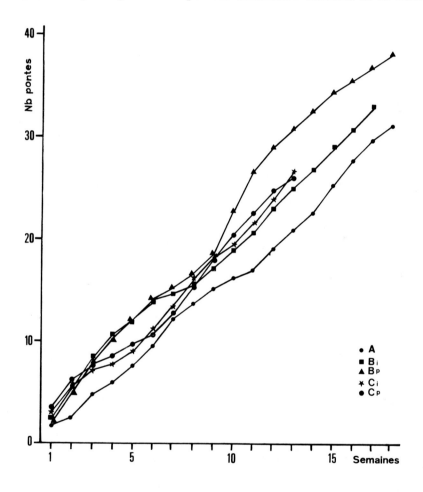

Fig. 1. Nombre moyen cumulé de pontes par semaine des différentes séries.

De même pour le rythme de ponte, nous considérerons le nombre moyen d'oeufs pondus par semaine par les trois groupes (tableau 2). En comparant le nombre d'oeufs produits pendant les 6 premières semaines à l'aide du test de Kruskal-Wallis, la différence est hautement significative (H = 10,89 avec P> 0,01). En effectuant une comparaison multiple des groupe 2 à 2 on constate, au seuil de $\alpha$ = 0,05, que le groupe A diffère du groupe B, mais que le groupe C ne diffère pas des 2 autres ($U_{th}$ = 32,6, $U_{A/B}$ = 36, $U_{A/C}$ = 31, $U_{B/C}$ = 30).

Pendant cette période, le nombre moyen général d'oeufs pondus par semaine est le plus élevé pour le groupe B : 29 765 oeufs/semaine, et le plus faible pour le groupe A : 10 856, alors que le groupe C a une fécondité intermédiaire : 17 876.

## Effet de la température sur la fécondité

L'effet de la température sur la fécondité a été testé de la même manière que pour les pontes. Le nombre d'oeufs pondus par chaque couple, pendant une durée de 6 semaines avant et 6 semaines après le changement de température, est significativement différent pour le groupe Cp (T = O avec P <0,03). Pour le groupe Bi la différence est significative avec une probabilité très faiblement supérieure à 0,05 ( T = O pour P < 0,06). Mais, contrairement au nombre de pontes, les témoins des groupes Bp et Ci montrent ici également une différence significative entre les deux mêmes périodes (T = O pour P< 0,03).

Si nous considérons la figure 2, qui représente le nombre moyen cumulé d'oeufs pondus par semaine par les 5 groupes, on s'aperçoit qu'il y a une modification de la pente à un moment donné, qu'il y ait eu ou non changement de température. Cette rupture de pente est nette pour le groupe A et les 2 séries Ci et Cp, un peu moins marquée dans le cas des séries Bi et Bp. En outre, il faut remarquer que le changement de fécondité correspond à des durées de vie sexuée différentes (13$^e$ semaine pour le groupe A, 5$^e$ semaine pour la série Ci).

## DISCUSSION

Ces résultats montrent, d'un point de vue pratique, que les élevages de cette espèce sont bien au point et sont réalisables dans des conditions de production satisfaisantes dans des bacs de faible volume.

D'un point de vue écophysiologique, il convient d'insister sur les capacités d'adaptation de cette espèce à des conditions de vie artificielles : eau stagnante renouvelée peu fréquemment, et surtout, pour les animaux maintenus à 27°, température élevée qui ne s'observe jamais dans le Golfe de Marseille, même en surface.

Le point le plus intéressant réside dans le fait que ces températures élevées n'affectent ni le rythme de ponte ni la fécondité des animaux, et ceci est probablement dû au fait que les animaux disposent de nourriture en quantité suffisante. Cette affirmation est étayée par les observations de quelques auteurs sur des populations naturelles : Ainsi Southward et Southward (1958) ont montré que des populations d'*Arenicola ecaudata* établies dans une station où ils trouvaient une nourriture abondante, se reproduisaient plus fréquemment que d'autres populations qui ne bénéficiaient pas de conditions semblables ; Olive (1970) a fait des constatations de même nature à propos de *Cirratulus cirratus*, ce qui est confirmé par Gibbs (1971).

Il semble donc qu'il y ait une liaison directe entre la quantité de nourriture disponible et les possibilités d'élaboration des gamètes. Cependant le fait de posséder des gamètes ne signifie nullement que les animaux ont la possibilité de les émettre. C'est ainsi que nous avons pu montrer expérimentalement (Guérin, 1977) que les *Scolelepis ciliata* et les populations atlantiques de *S. fuliginosa* ne sont susceptibles d'émettre leurs gamètes que dans une eau suffisamment riche en oxygène dissous. Cette limitation n'existe pas pour les populations méditerranéennes, qui, bien que caractéristiques de milieux pollués,

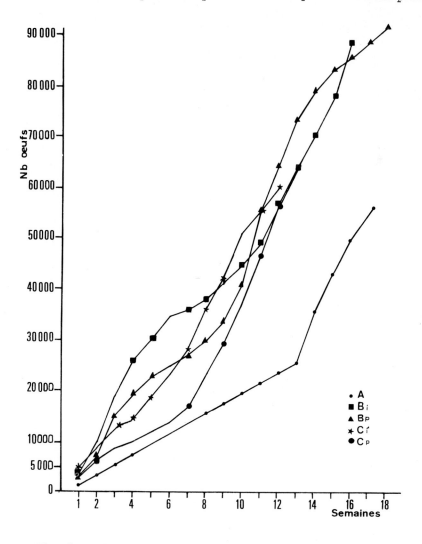

Fig. 2. Nombre moyen cumulé d'oeufs pondus par semaine.

peuvent pondre dans des eaux très pauvres en oxygène dissous grâce à la sécré-
tion de mucus qui entraîne les oeufs dans les couches superficielles, plus riches
en oxygène, et où se déroulera le développement larvaire.  En élevage, les pontes sont déposées dans le ménisque superficiel où, même à 27°C, les embryons
trouvent une quantité d'oxygène suffisante  pour effectuer leur développement
dans de bonnes conditions.

Enfin un dernier point à souligner réside dans l'existence d'une rupture de
pente sur les graphiques représentant la production d'oeufs en fonction du
temps.  Il faut noter que cette accélération n'est pas synchrone pour tous les
couples : elle n'est pas due  à des facteurs externes.  En fait, la reproduction commence très tôt chez ces Polychètes, avant même que la croissance soma-
tique ne soit terminée.  On peut donc estimer que, dans une première phase,
les animaux pondent tout en continuant leur croissance : la production d'oeufs
est alors assez faible ; dans une seconde phase la croissance est terminée ou
très ralentie :  la totalité de l'énergie disponible est alors utilisée pour
la production de gamètes, qui devient très importante.

## REFERENCES

Bhaud, M., 1972.  Quelques données sur le déterminisme écologique de la repro-
    duction des  Annélides Polychètes. *Marine Biology*, 17, 115-136.

Gibbs, P.E., 1971.  A comparative study of reproductive cycles in four polychae-
    tes species belonging to the family Cirratulidae. *Journal of the Marine Bio-
    logical Association of the United Kingdom*, 51, 745-771.

Guérin, J.-P., 1973.  Premières données sur la longévité, le rythme de ponte et
    la fécondité de *Scolelepis* cf. *fuliginosa* (Polychète, Spionidé) en élevage.
    *Marine Biology*, 19, 27-40.

Guérin, J.-P., 1974.  Rôle du mucus entourant la ponte dans la survie des em-
    bryons et la vitesse de croissance des larves de *Scolelepis fuliginosa* Cla-
    parède (Annélides Polychètes).  *Comptes rendus des Séances de l'Académie des
    Sciences Paris*, 279, D, 363-366.

Guérin, J.-P., 1977.  La vie larvaire chez les Annélides Polychètes et les Mol-
    lusques (Bivalves et Gastéropodes).  Etude écophysiologique et expérimentale.
    *Thèse de Doctorat d'Etat*, 240 pp., Université d'Aix-Marseille.

Guérin, J.-P. & Kerambrun, P., 1976.  Première données sur la composition chi-
    mique élémentaire de  *Scolelepis fuliginosa*  (Annélide Polychète).  Influence
    des conditions d'élevage. *Comptes rendus des Séances de l'Académie des Scien-
    ces, Paris*, 283, D, 659-661.

Olive, P.J.W., 1970.  Reproduction of a Northumberland population of the poly-
    chaete  *Cirratulus cirratus*.  *Marine Biology*, 5, 259-273.

Sokal, R.R. & Rohlf, F.J., 1969. *Biometry*, 776 pp., San Francisco:W.H. Freeman
    & C°.

Southward, E.C. & Southward, A.J., 1958.  The breeding of  *Arenicola ecaudata*
    Johnston and *A. branchialis* Aud. and Edw. at Plymouth. *Journal of the Marine
    Biological Association of the United Kingdom*, 37, 367-386.

# THE EFFECT OF SALINITY AND TEMPERATURE ON THE POST-LARVAL GROWTH OF THE CRAB *RHITHROPANOPEUS HARRISII*

**Richard G. Hartnoll**

*Duke University Marine Laboratory, Beaufort, N.C., U.S.A. and Department of Marine Biology, Liverpool University, Port Erin, Isle of Man\**

## ABSTRACT

Growth from the first to the sixth post-larval instars was followed in nine salinity-temperature combinations. About 40 isolated crabs were maintained in each regime and survival, moult increment and intermoult duration monitored. Significant mortality was limited to the lowest ($20^{\circ}C$) temperature series, where it increased from 2% at 7.5‰ to 55% at 32.5‰. Intermoult duration was little affected by salinity, but increased at lower temperatures. Moult increment decreased with size, increased with temperature, and varied with salinity in the order 20 > 32.5 > 7.5‰. The mean size of the sixth instar ranged from 3.5 mm ($20^{\circ}C$, 7.5‰) to 5.0 mm ($30^{\circ}C$, 20‰). Relationships are derived between carapace width on one hand, and intermoult period, moult increment and coefficient of variation of instar size on the other. These are used to generate growth curves and population models.

## INTRODUCTION

Few investigations of intermoult duration and moult increment in crabs have used specimens of known post-larval instar number, except for some studies on Carcinus maenas (Refs. 4 & 10) and Cancer anthonyi (Ref. 1). Only Klein Breteler (4) has looked into the effects of environment in any detail. The present study set out to rear the early post-larval instars of the small euryhaline xanthid crab Rhithropanopeus harrisii (Gould) in a matrix of nine salinity-temperature combinations. Individuals were isolated so that each ecdysis could be monitored, and survival, moult increment and intermoult period accurately related to instar number.

## METHODS

Berried females of R. harrisii were collected in the Cape Kennedy area of Florida and maintained in the Beaufort Laboratory at 20‰ and 20 or $25^{\circ}C$ until the larvae hatched. The larvae were reared by Dr Costlow's team in nine salinity-temperature combinations (20, 25 & $30^{\circ}C$; 7.5, 20 & 32.5‰) as the control series of a larval growth experiment which terminated when the megalopae moulted to the first crab instar. I then took over the specimens and reared them through to the sixth crab instar. The number of individuals per regime ranged from 35 to 77, and altogether 405 crabs were reared.

\*Present address.

TABLE 1   Results of the Laboratory Rearing of Post-larval R. harrisii

| | Instar/moult no. | 20°C 7.5‰ | 20°C 20‰ | 20°C 32.5‰ | 25°C 7.5‰ | 25°C 20‰ | 25°C 32.5‰ | 30°C 7.5‰ | 30°C 20‰ | 30°C 32.5‰ |
|---|---|---|---|---|---|---|---|---|---|---|
| Carapace width (mm) of instar no. | 1 | 1.44 ± 0.02 | 1.55 ± 0.02 | 1.48 ± 0.02 | 1.43 ± 0.02 | 1.49 ± 0.02 | 1.48 ± 0.02 | 1.43 ± 0.02 | 1.55 ± 0.02 | 1.54 ± 0.03 |
| | 2 | 1.87 ± 0.03 | 2.02 ± 0.02 | 1.86 ± 0.04 | 1.85 ± 0.03 | 1.94 ± 0.03 | 1.86 ± 0.02 | 1.89 ± 0.04 | 2.03 ± 0.03 | 1.97 ± 0.05 |
| | 3 | 2.26 ± 0.04 | 2.50 ± 0.04 | 2.26 ± 0.05 | 2.25 ± 0.04 | 2.43 ± 0.05 | 2.27 ± 0.04 | 2.39 ± 0.05 | 2.63 ± 0.04 | 2.47 ± 0.08 |
| | 4 | 2.63 ± 0.05 | 2.96 ± 0.05 | 2.64 ± 0.07 | 2.71 ± 0.07 | 2.97 ± 0.08 | 2.73 ± 0.06 | 2.97 ± 0.07 | 3.33 ± 0.06 | 3.11 ± 0.11 |
| | 5 | 3.02 ± 0.06 | 3.48 ± 0.08 | 3.07 ± 0.12 | 3.18 ± 0.09 | 3.55 ± 0.11 | 3.22 ± 0.07 | 3.57 ± 0.10 | 4.05 ± 0.09 | 3.76 ± 0.12 |
| | 6 | 3.48 ± 0.09 | 3.93 ± 0.11 | 3.57 ± 0.18 | 3.66 ± 0.12 | 4.38 ± 0.15 | 3.95 ± 0.12 | 4.28 ± 0.13 | 4.97 ± 0.10 | 4.57 ± 0.15 |
| Duration (days) of instar no. | 1 | 6.8 ± 0.6 | 6.1 ± 0.3 | 9.6 ± 0.4 | 5.3 ± 0.3 | 5.6 ± 0.2 | 6.6 ± 0.8 | 4.4 ± 0.2 | 3.9 ± 0.4 | 4.5 ± 0.2 |
| | 2 | 11.6 ± 1.0 | 9.7 ± 0.4 | 12.1 ± 1.0 | 7.2 ± 0.9 | 7.0 ± 0.8 | 7.8 ± 1.0 | 4.1 ± 0.3 | 4.6 ± 0.3 | 4.3 ± 0.3 |
| | 3 | 15.2 ± 1.0 | 15.9 ± 1.7 | 13.8 ± 1.2 | 9.5 ± 1.1 | 9.0 ± 1.2 | 9.3 ± 1.4 | 5.9 ± 0.8 | 5.5 ± 0.7 | 5.2 ± 0.4 |
| | 4 | 18.2 ± 1.3 | 21.6 ± 2.2 | 12.7 ± 0.9 | 16.5 ± 2.9 | 13.1 ± 2.0 | 13.4 ± 1.4 | 9.2 ± 1.5 | 9.8 ± 1.2 | 9.1 ± 1.6 |
| | 5 | 19.8 ± 1.7 | 18.3 ± 1.9 | 14.3 ± 2.2 | 25.7 ± 3.0 | 22.0 ± 2.3 | 16.7 ± 2.2 | 17.9 ± 2.1 | 15.6 ± 1.3 | 16.0 ± 1.9 |
| % moult increment at post-larval moult No. | 1 | 29.6 ± 1.2 | 30.3 ± 0.9 | 25.0 ± 1.4 | 29.1 ± 1.1 | 29.3 ± 1.3 | 26.0 ± 1.8 | 31.8 ± 1.4 | 31.0 ± 1.4 | 29.6 ± 1.2 |
| | 2 | 20.7 ± 0.9 | 23.9 ± 1.1 | 21.0 ± 1.1 | 21.9 ± 1.3 | 25.2 ± 1.5 | 21.7 ± 1.1 | 26.5 ± 1.2 | 29.6 ± 1.2 | 25.0 ± 1.5 |
| | 3 | 16.4 ± 0.7 | 18.3 ± 1.0 | 17.8 ± 1.4 | 20.1 ± 1.2 | 22.2 ± 1.2 | 20.4 ± 1.1 | 24.1 ± 1.2 | 26.5 ± 1.7 | 25.8 ± 1.0 |
| | 4 | 14.8 ± 0.6 | 18.2 ± 1.0 | 15.5 ± 2.4 | 17.3 ± 1.0 | 19.7 ± 1.2 | 18.1 ± 1.1 | 20.1 ± 1.1 | 21.7 ± 1.1 | 25.1 ± 1.3 |
| | 5 | 14.3 ± 0.8 | 15.9 ± 1.0 | 15.8 ± 1.1 | 14.8 ± 0.8 | 23.2 ± 1.2 | 22.2 ± 1.5 | 19.7 ± 1.2 | 22.6 ± 0.9 | 21.1 ± 1.1 |
| % survival to end of instar no. | 1 | 100 | 100 | 87 | 100 | 100 | 97 | 100 | 98 | 100 |
| | 2 | 98 | 100 | 82 | 100 | 100 | 97 | 100 | 98 | 100 |
| | 3 | 98 | 99 | 79 | 100 | 100 | 97 | 100 | 98 | 100 |
| | 4 | 98 | 81 | 62 | 100 | 100 | 97 | 100 | 98 | 100 |
| | 5 | 98 | 65 | 45 | | | 97 | 100 | 98 | 97 |
| No. in series at commencement | | 59 | 77 | 37 | 39 | 40 | 36 | 35 | 44 | 38 |

One crab was kept in each compartment of a transparent polystyrene box with a hinged lid.  The first to third instars were kept in boxes with compartments measuring 34 x 34 x 30 mm deep, the fourth to sixth instars in larger compart-ments of 52 x 52 x 52 mm deep.  These compartments were filled to about 15 mm depth with some 20 and 40 ml of water respectively.  The crabs were kept under a 12/12 light/dark cycle in three environmental cabinets maintained at 20, 25 and 30°C, and within each cabinet series were kept at 7.5, 20 and 32.5‰.  Sea water was collected offshore from Beaufort at 33-35‰, filtered, diluted appropriately with demineralised water and brought to the correct temperature before use.  This filtered water was by no means sterile, but there were no bacterial growth problems.  In the two higher salinities some algae grew on the boxes and the crabs, but without obvious ill effect.  The water was changed every third day.  The crabs were fed daily on an excess of newly-hatched Artemia nauplii, and checked to see whether they had moulted. Dead crabs and cast integuments were preserved in 70‰ alcohol : although some crabs had started to eat their casts it was only rarely that they could not be accurately measured.  The standard dimension used was the maximum width of the carapace, which was determined with an eyepiece graticule in a stereo-microscope.

RESULTS

The results for the nine series of crabs are summarised in Table 1.  Where appropriate mean values and 95% confidence limits are given.

Survival

The range of environments used in this programme was clearly too limited to determine the tolerance of post-larval R. harrisii.  There was no significant mortality at 25 or 30°C.  At 20°C the mortality between the first and sixth post-larval instars increased with salinity, from 2% at 7.5‰ to 55% at 32.5‰. This was not because development took longer at the higher salinities, for the series at 32.5‰ reached the sixth instar faster than the 7.5‰ one (see below).  Clearly environment has different effects on survival and on inter-moult period.  Larval mortality has been investigated under the same environ-mental conditions (Ref. 2).  The combined zoeal stages had over 25% mortality in several regimes, and over 50% at 20°/7.5‰, but low mortality in those two series where the young crabs showed highest mortality.  The megalopae had maximum mortality at 25°C/32.5‰ and 30°C/32.5‰.  So different environ-ments are optimal for the survival of the zoeas, the megalopa and the young crab instars : this may be partly because the material used in the larval studies came from near Beaufort, and that in this post-larval work from Florida.  Adult R. harrisii usually occur in salinities of less than 20‰ (Ref. 2), so some intolerance of higher salinities by the post-larvae is not unexpected.

Intermoult Period

Post-larval moults are plotted against age in Fig. 1 for the three series at 25°C and the three at 20‰.  The only effect of the range of salinity employed here was a slight acceleration of moulting at higher values.  This range also has little effect on larval duration (Ref. 3).  Increased temperature produces a much more obvious reduction in intermoult period, which is prominent in the first three instars but not maintained subsequently. This is because average instar size increases with temperature (see below), and intermoult period increases with size.  This size-effect masks the accelerating action of increased temperature.

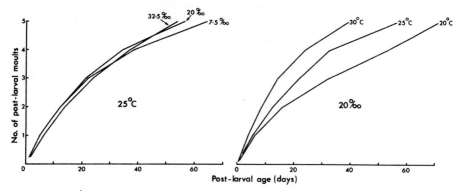

Fig. 1.  R. harrisii : post-larval moults plotted against age.

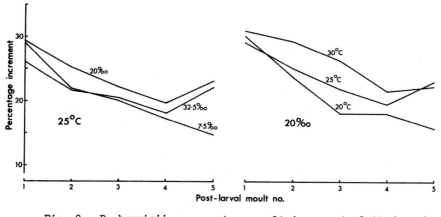

Fig. 2.  R. harrisii : percentage moult increment plotted against
post-larval moults.

## Moult Increment and Growth Rate

When the percentage increase in size is plotted against the sequence of post-
larval moults (Fig. 2) there are some irregularities, notably in the 25°C
series, but also several clear trends.  The increment decreases with size.
It increases with temperature over the range 20-30°C.  It varies with salinity
in the sequence 20 > 32.5 > 7.5‰.  Since the environment affects moult
increment it must also affect instar size, and Fig. 3 shows the effect of
temperature - the more significant variable - on instar size.  As the temperature rises the mean size of each instar increases.  There is little difference
in the first instar, but by the sixth the mean carapace width ranges from
3.48 mm (20°C, 7.5‰) to 4.97 mm (30°C, 20‰).

The relationship between instar size and post-larval age is influenced by
environment in a more complex fashion, since the effects on both moult
increment and intermoult duration are involved.  Different salinities are
optimal for short intermoult period (32.5‰) and large moult increment (20‰),
but the latter effect is dominant and the growth rate increases in the

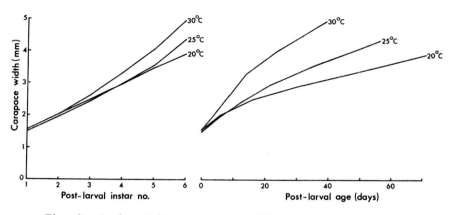

Fig. 3. <u>R. harrisii</u> : carapace width plotted against post-
larval instars and post-larval age.

sequence 7.5 < 32.5 < 20‰.  On the other hand increased temperature favours
both short intermoults and large increments, so the growth rate is much
faster at higher temperatures (Fig. 3).  The shortened intermoult period at
higher temperatures is a general phenomenon of Crustacean growth, but the
increase of moult increment with temperature is quite unexpected.  In <u>Carcinus</u>
<u>maenas</u> the increment was similar at 15 and 20°C (Ref. 4).  In <u>Palaemonetes</u>
<u>varians</u> the increment declined from 20 to 30°C (Ref. 5), in <u>Cancer anthonyi</u>
from 16 to 22°C (Ref. 1), and in <u>Callinectes sapidus</u> from 20 to 34°C (Ref. 6).
Perhaps the converse relationship in <u>R. harrisii</u> is related to the high
ambient temperatures to which the Florida population is accustomed.

## Size Variation within Instars

<u>Carcinus maenas</u> is the only other crab for which there appears to be informa-
tion on the size variation within the post-larval instars (Ref. 3).  The most
convenient expression of this variation is as the coefficient of variation,
'v'.

v = standard deviation of mean X 100 / mean

It can be appreciated from Table 1 that in each of the nine series the value
of v increases from one instar to the next, an inevitable consequence of the
considerable variation in moult increment.  To be useful this increase of v
needs to be quantitatively related to carapace size, and the best correlation,
as well as perhaps the theoretically most appropriate relationship, is given
by the regression of v on log carapace width.  The parameters of this
regression for the two species are :

|  | Correlation Coeff. | Slope | Intercept |
|---|---|---|---|
| <u>R. harrisii</u> (all series combined) | 0.80 | 4.42 | 2.56 |
| <u>C. maenas</u> (after Ref. 3) | 0.97 | 2.96 | 2.55 |

The results are fairly similar.  It will be interesting to see, when data
becomes available, if other species show the same relationship.

### DISCUSSION

The immediate effects of environmental variation on early post-larval growth
have already been considered, but there is plenty of scope for further analysis.

This data on early growth can be used to generate growth curves and population models.

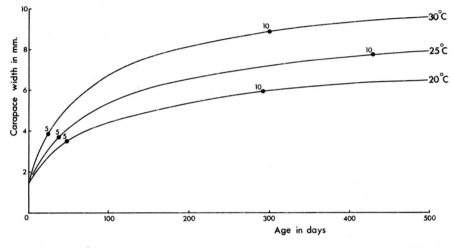

Fig. 4.  R. harrisii : predicted growth curves at a salinity of 20‰.

## Growth Prediction

Mauchline (7 & 8) has noted that in many decapods there is a good linear relation between log moult increment and pre-moult carapace size, and similarly between log intermoult period and carapace size.  These regressions have been determined for the three series of R. harrisii reared at 20‰, and used to produce growth curves (Fig. 4).  A maximum size is effectively reached within a year, ranging from 6.0 to 6.5 mm at 20°C up to 9.0 to 9.5 mm at 30°C. These predictions may be compared with the long term rearing results of Schneider (9) who kept R. harrisii from Florida at 25°C and 25‰.  His crabs measured 7.0 mm after 260 days, which is very close to the prediction of the 25°C trace in Fig. 4.  This agreement suggested that it might be interesting to look at some other species in the same way, and three larger species were chosen for which the necessary data on growth were available - Carcinus maenas (4), Cancer anthonyi (1) and Homarus americanus (8).  The regressions of log increment and log intermoult duration for R. harrisii and the other three species are presented in Fig. 5, and it is clear that as the size of the species increases the slope of both regressions is considerably reduced.  These regressions are used to generate the growth curves in Fig. 6, which predict very different maximum sizes for the species.  These maxima are quite close to those which occur, and so it appears that the parameters of early growth can be used to predict the final size reached by the species.

## Population models

The mean size of each instar has been calculated in the course of growth prediction, and the standard deviation of this mean can be derived using the regression of v on log carapace width (see above).  The mortality of  each instar must be estimated, and in the absence of any information on natural mortality major assumptions had to be made.  A constant 15% mortality at each ecdysis was assumed, together with an intermoult  mortality inversely proport- ional to carapace width and proportional to intermoult period, of a value of 15% for the first instar.  This permits the calculation of the proportional

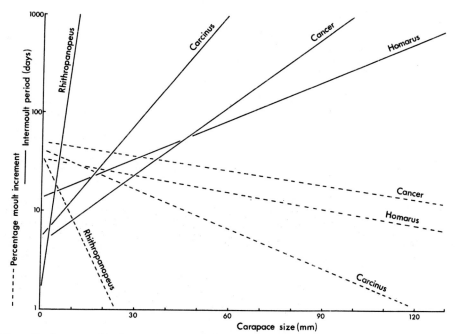

Fig. 5. Log moult increment and log intermoult period plotted against carapace size.

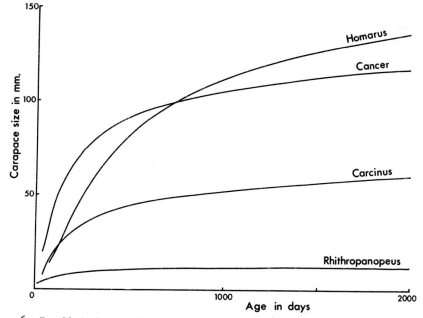

Fig. 6. Predicted growth curves based on the regressions in Fig. 5.

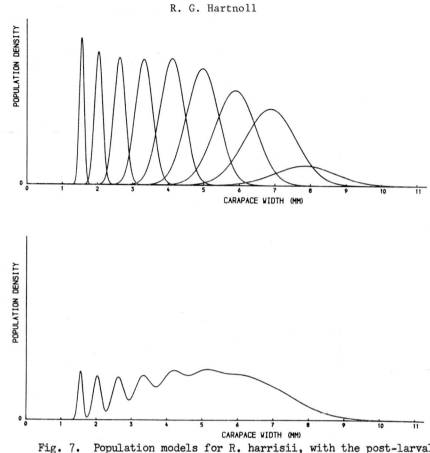

Fig. 7.  Population models for R. harrisii, with the post-larval
instars separated above and integrated below.

survival of a recruitment of first instars to each subsequent instar.  If
constant regular recruitment is now assumed, the proportion of each instar in
a steady state population is represented by its survival multiplied by its
duration.  A computer programme was prepared to use the above information to
plot size frequency distributions for each instar, and for the population as a
whole, and plots were prepared for R. harrisii (30°C, 20‰), Carcinus maenas
and Cancer anthonyi.  The regression of v on log carapace width for both
Rhithropanopeus and Carcinus were tried, and as the results were very similar
only the plots using the former are presented here (Figs. 7 & 8).  There are
interesting differences in the size distribution within the populations.  In
Rhithropanopeus there is a fairly even distribution over the whole range, but
in the other species this is not so, and the small specimens comprise only a
small part of the population.  This is rather unexpected, but it is a feature
which has been noted in natural populations of several large decapods.  The
other point of interest is that in all species only the first six instars
stand out from the cumulative curve.  The number of instars making up the
steady-state population are 9 in Rhithropanopeus, 18 in Carcinus and 14 in
Cancer, so that in the larger species size-frequency analysis will not permit
the discrimination of most of the instars.

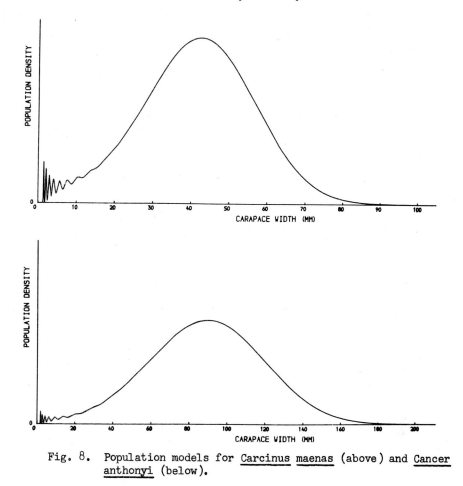

Fig. 8.  Population models for <u>Carcinus</u> <u>maenas</u> (above) and <u>Cancer</u>
<u>anthonyi</u> (below).

### ACKNOWLEDGEMENTS

I am very grateful to Dr John Costlow and his staff for help, facilities and
the provision of material at the Beaufort Laboratory.  Dot Coles and John
Bishop deserve my thanks for keeping the programme going whilst I was away
from Beaufort.  Brendan Cox at the Liverpool University Computer Laboratory
very kindly wrote and ran the population curve programme.

### REFERENCES

(1)  Anderson, W.R. & Ford, R.F., 1976.  Early development, growth and survival
        of the yellow crab <u>Cancer</u> <u>anthonyi</u> Rathbun (Decapoda, Brachyura) in
        the laboratory.  <u>Aquaculture</u>, 7, 267-279.

(2)  Costlow, J.D., Bookhout, C.G. & Monroe, R.J., 1966.  Studies on the larval
        development of the crab <u>Rhithropanopeus</u> <u>harrisii</u> (Gould).  1. The

effect of salinity and temperature on larval development.  Physiological Zoology, 39, 81-100.

(3)  Klein Breteler, W.C.M., 1975.  Growth and moulting of juvenile shore
      crabs, Carcinus maenas, in a natural population.  Netherlands Journal
      of Sea Research, 9, 86-99.

(4)  Klein Breteler, W.C.M., 1975.  Laboratory experiments on the influence
      of environmental factors on the frequency of moulting and the
      increase in size at moulting of juvenile shore crabs, Carcinus maenas.
      Netherlands Journal of Sea Research, 9, 100-120.

(5)  Knowlton, R.E., 1974.  Larval developmental processes and controlling
      factors in decapod Crustacea, with emphasis on Caridea.  Thalassia
      Jugoslavica, 10, 138-158.

(6)  Leffler, C.W., 1972.  Some effects of temperature on the growth and
      metabolic rate of juvenile blue crabs, Callinectes sapidus, in the
      laboratory.  Marine Biology, 14, 104-111.

(7)  Mauchline, J., 1976.  The Hiatt growth diagram for Crustacea.  Marine
      Biology, 35, 79-84.

(8)  Mauchline, J., 1977.  Growth of shrimps, crabs and lobsters - an
      assessment.  Journal du Conseil, 37, 162-169.

(9)  Schneider, D.E., 1967.  An evaluation of temperature adaptations in
      latitudinally separated populations of the xanthid crab Rhithropanoeus
      harrisii (Gould), by laboratory rearing experiments.  Ph.D. Thesis,
      Duke University.

(10)  Shen, C.J.,  1935.  An investigation of the post-larval development of
       the shore crab Carcinus maenas, with special reference to the
       external secondary sexual characters.  Proceedings of the Zoological
       Society of London, 1935, 1-33.

# THE RELATIONSHIP OF TEMPERATURE AND SALINITY TO LARVAL DEVELOPMENT IN MUSSELS (*Mytilus galloprovincialis* LAMARCK)

**Mirjana Hrs-Brenko**

*Center for Marine Research, "Rudjer Boskovic" Institute,
Rovinj - Yugoslavia*

## INTRODUCTION

A long reproductive season lasting from early autumn to late spring with
several spawnings has been established for the Mediterranean mussel (<u>Mytilus
galloprovincialis</u>) in the Adriatic Sea (1). During their reproductive season
the number of larvae in the plankton fluctuated, with an abundance of larvae
and heavy settlement in April and May (2, 3). Recently, optimal temperature
and salinity conditions were established by laboratory experiments for embryonic development (4). In the present paper larval development is described.
The results of the experiments are compared with field observations in an
effort to complete the knowledge on mussel larval development in natural conditions with regard to the most important ecological factors: temperature
and salinity.

## METHODS

The method for rearing mussel larvae in the laboratory has been described by
Hrs-Brenko and Calabrese (5) and Hrs-Brenko (6). In the present study four
experiments were conducted at 8 constant temperatures (from $10^{o}C$ to $27.5^{o}C \pm$
$0.5^{o}C$, at $2.5^{o}C$ intervals) and at 7 constant salinities (from $10^{o}/oo$ to $35^{o}/oo$
$\pm 1 ^{o}/oo$ at $5^{o}/oo$ intervals). Environmental sea water (from 36 to $37.5^{o}/oo$)
was used as a control. Filtered fresh well-water (not chlorinated) was used
for the preparation of salinities lower than the environmental salinity. A
mixture of the following algae: <u>Carteria</u> sp., <u>Chlamydomonas</u> sp., <u>Isochrysis
galbana</u>, <u>Monochrysis</u> <u>lutheri</u> and <u>Nanochloris</u> sp. was used daily as food for
the larvae.

## RESULTS AND DISCUSSION

<u>Effect of salinity and temperature on growth, survival and metamorphosis.</u>

As shown in Figure 1 the optimal temperature range for larval growth was found
to be from 20 to $25^{o}C$. Below $20^{o}C$ the growth rates were gradually retarded
by decreases in temperatures towards $12.5^{o}C$. The retardation of growth appears
to be the result of difficulties in the normal feeding of larvae at low temperatures (7). Above $25^{o}C$ growth of larvae was probably inhibited by temperatures
close to the upper tolerance limit and by an increased number of bacteria in
the medium. It is probable that the retarded growth of larvae was an effect
of high temperature ($27.5^{o}C$) because the observed interruption of sexual activity in summer months could indicate that mussels do not tolerate high sea
water temperatures during larval life. On the other hand, the oyster larvae
of warm water species, such as <u>Ostrea</u> <u>edulis</u>, showed undisturbed growth at
such high temperatures (8).

The optimal salinity range for growth was from 30 to 35°/oo.    Sometimes an
excellent increase in length occurred in salinities lower than 30°/oo and in
environmental salinities, but only at a temperature range optimal for growth.
It is evident, that the effects of temperature and salinity on growth of larvae
are significant when a low salinity (below 15°/oo) or a high temperature level
(27.5°C) is approached.    As shown in Figure 1, the largest increase in length
(100%) was always recorded at 20°C and at 30°/oo.

The survival of larvae was excellent at temperatures lower than 22.5°C and
over a wide range of salinities.    The optimal survival was drastically reduced in the low salinity of 10°/oo which could be close to the lower salinity
limit for survival of larvae (Fig. 2).    The increased mortality of larvae
above 22.5°C was probably the result of the synergistic effects of high temperatures and also partly by the increased number of bacteria.    The erratic
survival of larvae at 27.5°C could indicate a close approach to the upper
temperature limit for survival.    From the 7th to the 23rd day total mortality
of larvae advanced from the extremely low (10°/oo) towards higher salinities
(Fig. 1).

The beginning of larval metamorphosis was indicated by the appearance of the
"eyed" larvae when the larvae reach approximately 200 μm in length.    To reach
metamorphosis larvae required a time which varied from 12 to 68 or more days
at different temperature and salinity combinations (Fig. 2).    High temperatures
accelerate larval development, so that the first "eyed" larvae at high temperature appeared on the 12th day after fertilization.    Nevertheless, larval
development is considered to be successful at moderate temperatures (i.e. from
17.5 to 20°C), because development of larvae at such temperatures takes place
over a wide range of salinities.    A delay in appearance of "eyed" larvae is
a result of the retarded growth caused by the gradual decrease of experimental
temperatures.    Thus at 10°C the first "eyed" larvae did not appear before the
33rd day, but only in a narrow range of salinities (Fig. 2).    It is obvious
that temperatures lower than 17.5°C and higher than 20°C narrow the salinity
range favourable for larval development and metamorphosis.

The results evidently show that larval development to the stage of metamorphosis
is much more affected by low than by high salinities.    In 15°/oo and at temperature ranges from 10 to 15°C the majority of larvae survived for a considerable time (1 to 2 months), but only grew slightly and died before reaching the
settling size.    It seems that the low salinity limit below which there is no
development to metamorphosis, is between 10 and 15°/oo.

Summary of field and laboratory observations on larval life

Hrs-Brenko (1,2,3,4) has reviewed the results of recent field studies on reproduction, larvae and spat in the northern Adriatic Sea, together with laboratory evidence on the temperature and salinity requirements for embryonic and
larval development.

Study on the reproductive cycle indicates that the onset of the gametogenesis
is at the time of the summer when sea water temperature decreases.    During
autumn months mussels gradually reach sexual maturity and begin to spawn.
According to laboratory experiments the autumn released eggs can develop into
straight-hinge larvae in two days, owing to the moderate sea water temperatures
during this period.    Further development of larvae to settling size may be
successfully completed in approximately 30 or 40 days over a wide range of
salinities.    Field observations showed that there were a high number of young

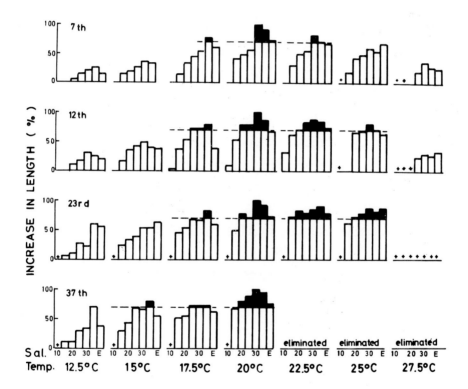

Figure 1.   Larval percent increase in length at different temperature and salinity combinations (+ dead larvae, E environmental salinity, optimal range in black).

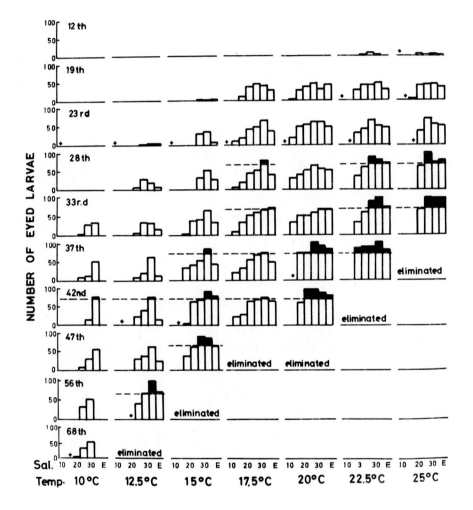

Figure 2.    "Eyed" mussel larvae percent at different temperature and salinity combinations from 12th to 68th day after fertilization (- no observation, + dead larvae, E environmental salinity, optimal range in black).

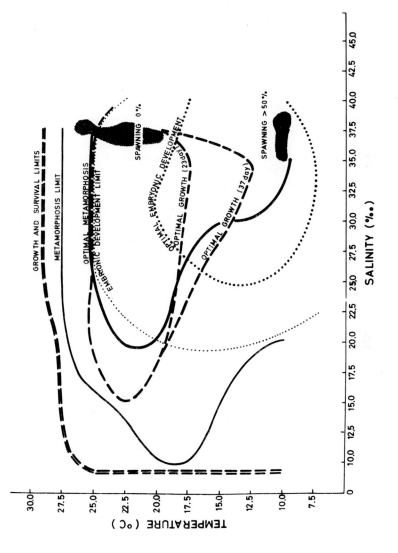

Figure 3.    The range of temperature and salinity requirements for mussel developmental stages.

mussels on seaweeds along the rocky shores (D. Zavodnik, private communication)
but hardly any on experimental plates exposed close to the coast in the late
autumn and winter.

In spite of intensive spawnings in early winter, only a few advanced larvae
together with many small sized larvae were found in plankton samples through
the cold season.    On the basis of laboratory results, the embryonic development of eggs released in winter is expected to be retarded from 3 to 5, or
even 8, days and larvae require about two months to reach metamorphosis.
Consequently, the appearance of spat in the field cannot be expected before
the end of February or the beginning of March.    Just about that time of a
year, a slight peak of advanced larvae and spat were regularly noticed, but it
varied with localities and years.    Low winter temperatures allow normal but
prolonged larval development with an excellent survival of larvae, but only in
the high salinity zones.    On the other hand, in the low salinity zones larvae
will never reach metamorphosis.    Therefore, in spite of a huge number of released eggs and an excellent survival of larvae in the laboratory it is believed
that a large number of larvae in the plankton will be lost in low salinity
zones owing to low temperatures and to other environmental stresses, predation
and dispersion during the long larval life.

In the field, repeated intensive spawnings, abundance of larvae, and heavy
settlement occur in the spring months when there is optimal temperature and
salinity in the coastal zones.    Towards the end of spring, mussels complete
their spawning season by producing less and less gametes, larvae and spat.
In optimal temperatures (17.5 - 20$^{o}$C) embryonic development will be completed
in two days.    At temperatures higher than 20$^{o}$C, the majority of released eggs
develop abnormally.    A few which develop normally into straight-hinge larvae
will grow well, but rarely survive, especially in the low salinity zones.

Temperature and salinity requirements for developmental stages of mussels in
the northern Adriatic Sea are given in Figure 3.    Temperature and salinity
limits are drawn free-hand, and, therefore are not shown precisely.    Moreover,
little variation in larval responses to the effects of constant temperature
and salinity can be expected especially at extreme levels, since in nature
both factors are cyclic rather than constant.

### ACKNOWLEDGEMENTS

I am very thankful to Professor C G Bookhout of Duke University Marine Laboratory, Beaufort, North Carolina, U.S.A. for language review of the manuscript,
and Mr Z Kalac and Mr G Sosic for technical help.    The support of the Self-
management Community of Interest for Scientific Research of SR Croatia is
acknowledged.

### REFERENCES

(1)      Hrs-Brenko, M., 1971.    The reproductive cycle of the Mytilus gallo-
            provincialis Lamk. in the northern Adriatic Sea and Mytilus edulis
            L. at Long Island Sound.    Thalassia Jugoslavica, 7, 533-542.

(2)      Hrs-Brenko, M., 1973.    The study of mussel larvae and their settlement
            in Vela Draga Bay (Pula, the northern Adriatic Sea).    Acqua-
            culture, 2, 173-182.

(3)     Hrs-Brenko, M., 1974.    The seasonal fluctuation of the mussel larvae
        in the northern Adriatic Sea.    Aquaculture, 3, 45-50.

(4)     Hrs-Brenko, M., 1974.    Temperature and salinity requirements for
        embryonic development of Mytilus galloprovincialis Imk.
        Thalassia Jugoslavica, 10, 131-138.

(5)     Hrs-Brenko, M., & Calabrese, A., 1969.    The combined effects of
        salinity and temperature on larvae of the mussel Mytilus edulis.
        Marine Biology, 4, 224-226.

(6)     Hrs-Brenko, M., 1973.    Gonad development, spawning and rearing of
        Mytilus sp. larvae in the laboratory.    Studies and Reviews,
        GFCM, 52 53-65.

(7)     Davis, H. C., & Calabrese, A., 1964.    Combined effects of temperature
        and salinity on development of eggs and growth of larvae of M.
        mercenaria and C. virginica.    Fishery Bulletin, 63, 643-655.

(8)     Davis, H. C., & Calabrese, A., 1969.    Survival and growth of larvae
        of the European oyster (Ostrea edulis L.) at different tempera-
        tures.    Biological Bulletin, Woods Hole, 136, 193-199.

# INFLUENCE DE LA TEMPERATURE SUR LA REPRODUCTION ET LA SURVIE DE QUELQUES NASSARIIDAE (MOLLUSCA, GASTEROPODA)

**Henri Massé, Claude Nodot et Anne-Marie Macé**

*Station Marine d'Endoume, 13007 Marseille, France*

ABSTRACT

Five species of Nassariidae living in shallow waters in Mediterranean Sea have been kept in laboratory tanks under controlled temperature conditions at 10, 15, 20, and 25°C. Cyclonassa donovani and Cyclonassa neritea spawned between 10 and 25°, Nassarius pygmaeus, Nassarius reticulatus, and Nassa mutabilis between 10 and 20°. The rate of development of the eggs increases rapidly with increased temperature. It is slower for the Cyclonassa which have a non-pelagic development than for the Nassarius which have a long pelagic planktotrophic life. Within each kind of development (pelagic or not), the smaller are the eggs, the faster the development rate is.
The lethal temperatures (L.T.50) of adults and larvae were not significantly different. No acclimation effect seems to occur on L.T.50 values for larvae reared at 10, 15, 20, or 25°. Spawning and young cleavage stages are the most critical period for the survival of these species as both adults and larvae can withstand high temperatures. These results are discussed in the context of thermal pollution problems.

## INTRODUCTION

La phase de reproduction est toujours un moment délicat dans le cycle vital d'une espèce. Aussi, étant donné l'accroissement de la pollution thermique en milieu côtier, il paraît intéressant d'étudier les effets de la température sur la reproduction de quelques représentants de la famille des Nassariidae, en particulier des espèces littorales susceptibles d'être soumises à des chocs thermiques plus ou moins prolongés.

## MATERIEL ET METHODES

### Animaux

Les Nassariidae étudiés vivent dans les sables fins infralittoraux, toutefois, l'espèce Nassarius reticulatus (Linné) se rencontre dans des fonds hétérogènes de sables vaseux parsemés de blocs rocheux ou de rhizomes de Phanérogammes mortes. Cyclonassa donovani (Risso) et Cyclonassa neritea (Linné) vivent dans l'horizon superficiel des sables fins infralittoraux, de la surface à 3 ou 4 m de profondeur. C. neritea affectionne les zones d'estuaire légèrement dessalées, tandis que C. donovani ne se rencontre qu'en mer ouverte (Picard, 1965). N. mutabilis (Lamarck) est une espèce caractéristique des sables fins bien calibrés infralittoraux en Mer Méditerranée, entre 4 et 10 m de profondeur. Nassarius pygmaeus (Lamarck) et N. reticulatus ont une répartition écologique plus large et supportent des sables vaseux. Les individus utilisés ont été récoltés entre 4 et 6 m de profondeur.

Elevages

Les animaux récoltés sont élevés dans des bacs thermostatés au degré près à 10,
15, 20, et 25°C. Le fond de chaque bac d'élevage est équipé d'un filtre biologique à sable, au travers duquel l'eau percole en permanence grâce à un exhaus-
teur à air comprimé.
Les Nasses sont enfermées par groupe de 10 individus dans des cages cylindriques
formées d'un tronçon de tuyau en P.V.C. de 15 à 22 cm de diamètre obturé à ses
deux extrémités par une toile de moustiquaire. Ces cages sont enfoncées dans le
sable du bac d'élevage ; les Nasses peuvent ainsi s'enfouir pendant leur période de repos. Elles sont alimentées deux fois par semaine avec des Bivalves
préalablement ouverts. Dès le début de la période de ponte, une inspection
quotidienne permet de prélever les oothèques déposées soit sur le pourtour de
la cage, soit sur les toiles de moustiquaire. Les oothèques sont transférées
dans de petites cages flottantes. Ces cages sont des segments de tuyau en P.V.C.
rigide de 4 à 10 cm de diamètre dont le fond est obturé par de la toile de fi-
let à plancton à maille de 90 μ . Cette toile retient les larves à leur éclosion et permet une bonne circulation de l'eau dans les cages. Leur flottabilité
est assurée par un anneau de polystyrène expansé encerclant l'extrémité supérieure. Elles peuvent être transférées à différentes températures dans les bacs
d'élevage, leur observation régulière permet de suivre le développement embryonnaire et de déterminer sa durée. De cette manière, il est possible d'obtenir de
nombreuses larves pouvant être utilisées dans les tests de température létale.

Tests de Résistance à la Température

Les tests de résistance consistent à exposer brutalement les animaux à des
températures élevées et constantes, s'échelonnant de 2 en 2 degrés entre 26 et
40°C. La méthode, inspirée de Kennedy et Mihursky (1971), a été décrite en dé-
tail par Bodoy et Massé (1977a). Selon le cas, des lots de 10 larves ou de 20
adultes sont plongés dans des bacs d'expérimentation. Les adultes sont immergés
directement dans les bacs. Ils peuvent s'enfouir dans le sédiment du filtre qui
recouvre le fond. Les contrôles sont effectués après 3, 6, 12, 24, 48, 72, et
96 heures. Les larves véligères sont préalablement introduites dans des tubes
flottants à l'aide d'une micro-pompe. Ces tubes, imaginés par B.L.S. Hardy
(communication personnelle) pour des élevages de Copépodes, sont des cylindres
en matière plastique de 15 mm de diamètre et de 25 mm de hauteur. Le fond des
tubes et leur bouchon sont respectivement garnis d'une toile à plancton à maille de 40 et 100 μ . Ils flottent verticalement en affleurant la surface de l'
eau. Les contrôles, effectués dans ce cas après 1, 2, 3, 6, 12, 24, et 48 heures
consistent à dénombrer les individus vivants et morts dans chaque bac de la
gamme. En ce qui concerne les Nassarius, les tests sont effectués sur les véligères libres d'une même cage flottante, aussitôt après l'éclosion. Les larves
ne sont pas réutilisées après leur contrôle. En ce qui concerne les Cyclonassa,
les tests sont effectués sur les larves avant l'éclosion. En effet, ces espèces
possèdent un développement direct, sans phase pélagique, et les oothèques con-
tiennent 1, rarement 2, exceptionnellement 3 embryons. Les manipulations n'étant
pas traumatisantes pour ces larves, elles sont remises à la température d'expérience après chaque contrôle. Les critères retenus pour déterminer la mort des
larves sont les suivants : absence de battements cardiaques, absence de mouve-
ments ciliaires, absence de réaction du pied à toute excitation.
Dans tous les cas, la courbe de mortalité obtenue en cumulant les pourcentages
d'individus morts, en fonction de l'augmentation de la température, permet de
déterminer la température létale pour 50% des individus (T.L.50).

RESULTATS

La Ponte

Sur les 5 espèces de Nasses mises en élevage à 10, 15, 20, et 25°, seules C. neritea et C. donovani ont pondu régulièrement à toutes les températures. N. pygmaeus, N. reticulatus, et N. mutabilis n'ont pas pondu à 25°. Chez N. reticulatus, les oothèques déposées à 25° étaient vides et non fertiles. Les pontes à 10° sont d'abord rares et irrégulières, elles sont produites après une longue période de maturation, un mois ou plus après celles obtenues à 15 et 20°. Chez C. neritea et C. donovani, le déclenchement de la ponte nécessite souvent un choc thermique de 5° ou plus, pendant un temps limité. Une fois déclenchée, la ponte se poursuit régulièrement à 10°. Ainsi, en Méditerranée, la température de 10° semble être une limite au-dessous de laquelle la reproduction de ces espèces n'est plus assurée. En mer ouverte, cette température est rarement atteinte, par contre, en hiver, elle est communément inférieure dans les estuaires et les lagunes marines. Au-dessus de 25°, chez C. neritea et C. donovani le nombre des pontes stériles croît très rapidement en fonction de la température au point de rendre la reproduction très aléatoire.

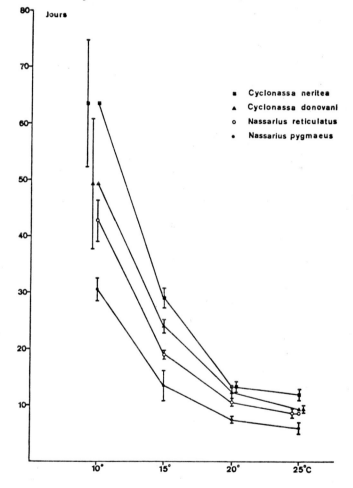

Fig. 1.   Durées du développement en fonction de la température.

Durée du Développement

La durée du développement correspond au temps qui s'écoule entre la ponte et
l'éclosion. D'après notre processus expérimental, deux facteurs peuvent être
pris en considération dans la détermination de cette durée : d'une part, la
température d'élevage des géniteurs, et, d'autre part, la température à laquelle
s'effectue l'embryogénèse, dans la cage flottante. La comparaison des observations montre que la température d'élevage des géniteurs n'a pas d'influence
significative sur la durée du développement, seule la température d'incubation
des oeufs influe. La figure 1 montre les résultats obtenus en regroupant les
données pour chaque température d'incubation, quelle que soit la température
d'élevage des géniteurs. Les intervalles de confiance des durées moyennes sont
calculés pour une probabilité de 95%.
Pour toutes les espèces, la durée du développement diminue rapidement avec
l'augmentation de la température. Les espèces sans phase pélagique ont une durée
de développement plus longue que celles à phase pélagique, toutefois, cet écart
tend à diminuer à 20 et 25°. La variabilité des résultats obtenus à 10°, chez
les Cyclonassa, semble en rapport avec l'éclosion. A la fin du développement
embryonnaire, tout se passe comme si les jeunes, en état de vie ralentie à 10°,
attendaient une augmentation de la température pour éclore. Ceci a été vérifié
expérimentalement, en réchauffant des oothèques maintenues à 10° pendant une
période égale à la durée moyenne de développement, on obtient souvent une éclosion dans les 24 heures qui suivent. Il faut noter également, que pour chaque
type de développement, direct ou indirect, l'espèce ayant les plus petits oeufs
(respectivement C. donovani et N. pygmaeus) possède la plus courte durée de
développement embryonnaire.

Résistance des Larves à la Température

La figure 2 montre les résultats des tests de température létale (T.L.50) effectués sur des véligères de N. reticulatus et des larves de C. neritea, obtenues à 4 températures de développement différentes. Pour chaque espèce, la
similitude des 4 tests indique que la température de développement a peu d'influence sur la résistance des larves. Des résultats identiques ayant été obtenus
pour les 4 espèces étudiées, il semble qu'il n'y ait pas d'effet d'acclimatation
sur la résistance des larves et ceci malgré la différence d'amplitude des chocs
thermiques entre les larves élevées respectivement à 10 et 25°.
Pour l'ensemble des tests effectués, les résultats obtenus en 24 heures d'exposition à un choc thermique sont cohérents, par contre, les valeurs de la T.L.50
obtenues à 48 heures peuvent être variables. Il est possible que ce phénomène
soit lié à l'état de jeûne des larves.
La figure 3 regroupe les courbes d'évolution des T.L.50 des larves et celles
des adultes de 4 espèces différentes acclimatées à 15°. Les T.L.50 des larves
sont relativement élevées, d'autant plus que la durée des tests est longue pour
des larves survivant sur leur réserve en vitellus. Le plus souvent, la résistance des larves est supérieure ou extrêmement proche de celle des adultes.

DISCUSSION

La distinction des sexes étant impossible sans une dissection des Nasses, le
nombre des femelles présentes dans chaque cage n'était pas connu, aussi aucune
étude quantitative n'a été faite sur le nombre d'oeufs pondus. Il semble d'ailleurs, selon Mattice (1975), que le nombre d'oeufs pondus varie de manière
significativement différente selon que les géniteurs sont soumis à une température constante, à une température variant en fonction des saisons, ou à une
température variant à la fois saisonnièrement et selon un rythme nycthéméral.

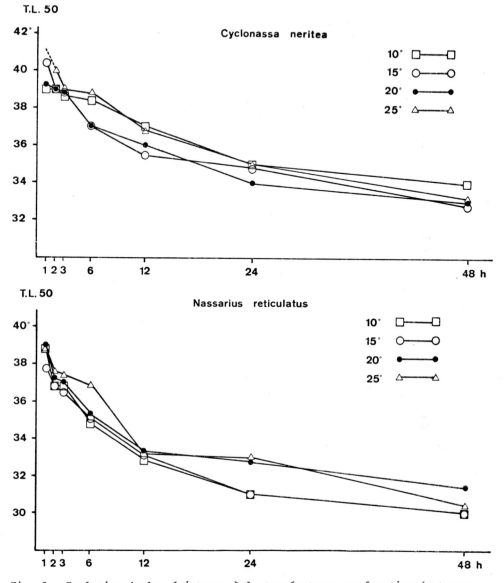

Fig. 2.  Evolution de la résistance à la température, en fonction du temps,
         Chez des larves obtenues à 4 températures de développement différentes

Cette dernière condition correspond à l'obtention du plus grand nombre d'oeufs.
En fait, notre but principal a été de fixer les limites thermiques compatibles
avec la ponte d'oothèques fertiles. En ce qui concerne les limites inférieures,
il est clair que les températures hivernales observées en mer ouverte en Méditerranée ne sont pas un facteur limitant de la ponte. Par contre, en ce qui
concerne les limites supérieures, il semble que les températures des eaux superficielles soient un facteur limitant pour ces espèces infralittorales toujours
immergées. Ces limites se situent autour  de 25° pour N. pygmaeus, N.reticulatus

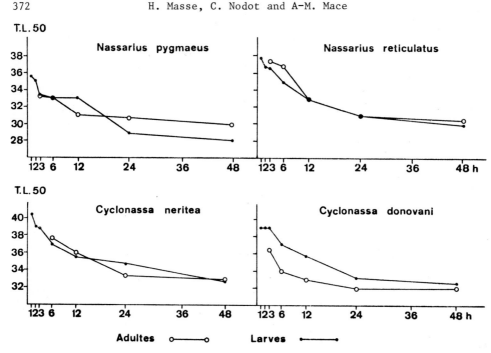

Fig. 3.   Comparaison des T.L.50 des larves et des adultes.

et N. mutabilis, entre 25 et 30° pour les Cyclonassa. Seules les espèces inter-
tidales très eurythermes peuvent pondre à des températures élevées, jusqu'à
35° pour Hydrobia ulvae selon Fish and Fish (1977). De plus, le pourcentage des
capsules ovigères qui avortent est beaucoup plus élevé à 25° qu'à 15 et 20°.
Il semble donc que l'embryogénèse soit très sensible aux températures élevées
comme cela a été montré pour N. pygmaeus par Bodoy et Massé (1977b). Toutefois,
le développement embryonnaire peut s'effectuer à des températures supérieures
au seuil qui bloque la ponte chez N. pygmaeus, N. reticulatus et N. mutabilis
puisque le développement embryonnaire a été observé à 25° pour ces espèces.
En ce qui concerne la durée du développement, les données que l'on trouve dans
la littérature sont très variables, e.g. Fioroni (1967), Castilla et Concina
(1976). Fretter et Graham (1962) donnent pour N. reticulatus une durée de
développement de 30 jours pour obtenir la libération des véligères, ce qui
correspond à des conditions thermiques assez basses, selon nos résultats. La
variabilité de ces données est due à l'influence importante de la température
sur la durée de développement. On peut considérer que l'accélération du développement est, entre 15 et 20°, un facteur très favorable au succès de la reproduction, en diminuant la durée d'exposition des oothèques aux conditions
hostiles du milieu, à un moment où elles sont particulièrement fragiles.
Une fois écloses, dans le cas des véligères, ou une fois le stade de larve
rampante atteint, dans le cas des Cyclonassa, les larves semblent beaucoup
plus résistantes à la température que pendant la phase précédente. Thorson
(1950) signale d'ailleurs, d'une manière plus générale, que les larves âgées
sont plus résistantes que les oeufs pendant les premières phases de l'embryogénèse.
Pour chaque espèce, la résistance aux températures élevées a été évaluée sur
les différentes phases du cycle vital. La synthèse des résultats obtenus permet
de mieux cerner les effets du facteur thermique.

Les adultes vivant à de faibles profondeurs, en particulier les Cyclonassa,
sont eurythermes, leurs T.L.50 sont donc élevées. Les larves, aussi bien les
véligères planctoniques que celles qui effectuent leur développement complet
dans une capsule ovigère, sont sensiblement aussi résistantes que les adultes.
Il semble donc que les phases critiques de la reproduction, du point de vue des
températures supérieures, soient, dans l'ordre, la ponte et l'embryogénèse.
Nous avons vu que la résistance des larves est peu dépendante de la température
de développement. Ce résultat s'oppose à ceux obtenus chez plusieurs espèces de
Mollusques adultes par différents auteurs et discutés par Bodoy et Massé (1977a).
Ceux-ci ont montré que les T.L.50 étaient d'autant plus élevées que les températures d'acclimatation saisonnières l'étaient. Par contre, cet effet d'acclimatation n'a pas été retrouvé chez différenres espèces de Copépodes Harpacticoïdes testées par Barnett, Dinet, Hardy et Nodot (communication personnelle).
Il semble donc que l'effet d'acclimatation soit très minime chez les petites
espèces, ou les formes larvaires, à métabolisme élevé.
Si l'on se place dans le contexte actuel de la pollution thermique marine, deux
effets majeurs doivent être considérés. D'une part, pour les véligères de
N. pygmaeus et N. reticulatus, qui appartiennent au méroplancton superficiel,
il existe un risque de transit dans les circuits de refroidissement des usines
utilisant l'eau de mer à cet effet. Dans ce cas, les larves sont brutalement
exposées à une forte élévation de température, puis à un refroidissement progressif entraînant une augmentation du temps d'exposition au choc thermique.
Si l'on se réfère aux courbes de la figure 2, on constate que les larves de ces
deux espèces sont extrêmement résistantes pour de courtes périodes, inférieures
à 3 heures. Ainsi, en tenant compte de la rapidité du transit dans les circuits
et malgré la phase de refroidissement, la durée des tests effectués dépasse
largement celle du choc thermique que peuvent subir les animaux vivant au voi-
sinage de ce type d'usine. D'un point de vue strictement thermique, en écar-
tant les incidences des chocs mécaniques et des synergies possibles avec d'autres polluants, tel que le chlore, nous pouvons dire que ces larves ont toutes
les chances de survivre à une forte élévation de la température n'excédant pas
toutefois 10° en été. En effet, à cette saison, la température des eaux superficielles en Méditerranée nord-occidentale peut dépasser 25°C.
Ceci confirme les observations de Barnett (1972) sur les véligères de Tellina
tenuis.
D'autre part, pour les adultes, il existe un risque de réchauffement dû à l'ar-
rivée d'une nappe d'eau chaude sortant des circuits de refroidissement et pous-
sée par les vents et les courants. En période hivernale, cette élévation de la
température peut induire la ponte des Nassariidae à un moment défavorable pour
les véligères, aussi bien au niveau de la nourriture disponible, qu'au niveau
de leur dispersion hors du plateau continental, les vents de Nord-Nord Ouest
étant dominants à cette saison en Méditerranée nord-occidentale (Massé, 1972).
De plus, la présence de la nappe d'eau chaude étant intermittente, au niveau
du fond, une fois la ponte déclenchée, le développement devra se faire à basse
température diminuant ainsi les chances de réussite en raison de l'allongement
considérable de la durée du développement, comme nous l'avons vu sur la figure
1. De plus, il faut considérer, dans le cas des véligères planctoniques, que la
durée de la phase pélagique est certainement, elle aussi, très liée à la température. En effet, d'après nos observations sur les Cyclonassa, chez qui l'embryogénèse et la vie larvaire se font à l'intérieur de l'oothèque, on peut dire
que la durée de la vie larvaire décroît, elle aussi, très rapidement avec l'élévation de la température (Fig. 1.). Dans le cas des véligères planctoniques,
même en supposant des conditions alimentaires satisfaisantes, l'éclosion dans
des eaux hivernales aura pour conséquence un allongement de la phase pélagique
correspondant à la durée de la vie larvaire, or cette phase est caractérisée
par une forte mortalité (prédation, dispersion) ce qui constitue un handicap

374 H. Masse, C. Nodot and A-M. Mace

supplémentaire dans le succès de la reproduction.

*Ce travail a été réalisé grâce au contrat de recherche n° 221.77.1.Env.F. passé entre l'Université d'Aix-Marseille II et la C.E.E., dans le cadre de son programme de recherche sur l'environnement.*

## REFERENCES

BARNETT, P.R.O., 1962. Effects of warm water effluents from power stations on marine life. Proceeding of the Royal Society of London, B, 180, 497-509.

BODOY, A. & MASSE, H., 1977a. Etude sur la résistance à la température de quelques Mollusques marins des côtes de Provence. Bulletin d'Ecologie, 8, (in the press).

BODOY, A. & MASSE, H., 1977b. Influence de la température sur la ponte et le développement embryonnaire de deux Mollusques Gastéropodes Prosobranches Polinices alderi (Forbes) et Nassarius pygmaeus (Lamarck). Haliotis, 7, (In the press).

CASTILLA, J.C. & CANCINO, J., 1976. Spawning behaviour and egg capsules of Concholepas concholepas (Mollusca : Gastropoda Muricidae). Journal of Marine Biology, 37, 255-263.

FIORONI, P., 1967. Quelques aspects de l'embryogénèse des Prosobranches (Mollusques, Gastéropodes). Vie et Milieu, 18 (1-A), 153-174.

FISH, J.D.,& FISH, S., 1977. The effects of temperature and salinity on the embryonic development of Hydrobia ulvae (Pennant). Journal of the Marine Biological Association of the United Kingdom, 57, 213-218.

FRETTER, V. & GRAHAM, A., 1962. British Prosobranch Molluscs. 755pp. London : Ray Society.

KENNEDY, V. & MIHURSKY, J.A., 1971. Upper temperature tolerances of some estuarine bivalves. Chesapeake Science, 12, 193-204.

MASSE, H., 1972. Contribution à l'étude de la macrofaune de peuplements des sables fins infralittoraux des côtes de Provence. VII Discussion, comparaison et interprétations des données quantitatives. Tethys, 4, 397-422.

MATTICE, J.S., 1975. Effect of constant and varying temperature on egg production of Lymnaea obrussa Say (Mollusca : Gastropoda).Verhandlungen Internationale Verein. Limnologie, 19, 3174-3178.

PICARD, J., 1965. Recherches qualitatives sur les biocoenoses marines des substrats meubles dragables de la région marseillaise. Recueil des Travaux de la Station Marine d'Endoume, 36, 1-160.

THORSON, G., 1950. Reproductive and larval ecology of marine bottom invertebrates. Biological Review, 25, 1-45.

# LABORATORY EXPERIMENTS ON THE SPAWNING OF *MACOMA BALTHICA;* ITS IMPLICATION FOR PRODUCTION RESEARCH

**P.A.W.J. de Wilde and E.M. Berghuis**

*Netherlands Institute for Sea Research, Texel, The Netherlands*

ABSTRACT

From 1974 the gonad development, the maturation of the gametes and the spawning in the common tellinid clam *Macoma balthica* was studied in the western Wadden Sea during 3 successive years. Spawning at will in the laboratory was induced by administration of a "standard" shock, consisting of a rise in temperature from 5 - 12.5° C in 5 min. In this way information on the spawning mechanism, the patterns of spawning and the amount of spawned gametes was obtained. Due to spawning *Macoma* loses about 25% of the weight of its soft parts. The calorific value of the sperm was 4.5; that of the eggs 5.9.
Spawning of the *Macoma* populations living on the tidal flats of the Wadden Sea takes place in the months of April and May during a number of separate spawning peaks, which are probably correlated with the particular temperature fluctuations described for tidal flat areas.

## INTRODUCTION

To obtain insight into the structure and functioning of the tidal mud-flats of the Wadden Sea, one of the research programs of the Netherlands Institute for Sea Research aims to study its ecological energetics. The problem is mainly tackled by the construction of energy budgets for the dominating fauna components (Ref. 1, 2, 3).

In the generally accepted energy equation for animals (C = P + R + F + U) the total energy input by food ingestion (C) always equals the sum of the energy fixed in tissues and gametes (P) and the energy lost by their own metabolism (R), and with the faeces (F) and urine (U). Instead of an independent determination of the separate terms of the equation, a number is in practice often derived from data for related species or is simply taken for granted. Hard to estimate and sometimes neglected is the energy lost during the liberation of the gametes in bivalves. Dissection of the ripe gonads is impossible in *Macoma* because of the complete intertwining of the ripe gonads with the alimentary canal and the digestive gland. Measuring of the weight loss of the animals due to spawning is not feasible because of the coincidence of the prolonged spawning season and the relatively short growing season (Ref. 4, 5).

The present study aims to assess this mode of energy release in *Macoma* by direct collection of the spawning products. This required a method by which spawning could be initiated at will in the laboratory. The background of this study is an ecological one.

Notwithstanding previous work on gonad development and spawning of *Macoma* by
Battle (6), Lammens (7) and Caddy (8), there was a need for further knowledge
of the gonad development, the maturation of the gametes and the exact spawning
season of the *Macoma* populations of the tidal mud-flats of the Wadden Sea. The
first part of the present study is devoted to the results of field observations.
The next section describes laboratory experiments in which spawning at will was
initiated, as well as investigations on the release mechanism. We were
successful in collecting sperm and eggs quantitatively; their calorific values
could be measured and the importance of spawning compared to production is
discussed. A final section discusses the significance of the observed spawning
mechanism in nature.

### ACKNOWLEDGEMENTS

Thank is due to Dr. H. Postma for his valuable comments.

### MATERIAL AND METHODS

Over one year old *Macomas* were sampled from an intertidal flat at Balgzand,
Station B (Ref. 9). The animals were washed out on the spot and transferred in
thermos containers. In the laboratory they were kept in running sea water at
5° C. The ages of the animals were determined by reading the year marks on the
shell (Ref. 7).
Ten specimens of each age group were killed in boiling water and the visceral
mass was externally examined with a stereo microscope. Observations were made
on the sex (♂, ♀, undifferentiated), the cycle of development of the gonads,
the maturation of the gametes, the first signs of spawning, the stage of
emptying and finally on the presence of parasites. *Macoma* was considered mature
if oocytes has tied off in the lumen of the follicles and the spherical eggs
averaged about 75 µ in diameter; further if testes were swollen, opaque white
in color and from tissue smears in sea water moving sperms could be obtained.
Caddy's arbitrary criterion, based on the line of extension of the gonads,
proved to be a useful help. The remaining animals were placed in shallow glass
boxes or were allowed to burrow in boxes filled with sediment, all provided
with running sea water of 5° C.

Positive thermal shocks were administered by transfer of the complete boxes
with *Macoma* into a container with running sea water of which the temperature
was adjusted at 12.5° C. Occurring spawnings were scored by visual observation.
Males and females are easy to recognize from the expelled gametes. For a
quantitative collection of gametes in separate animals *Macomas* from the 5° tank
were isolated during one night in 50 ml sea water at 12° C. Liberated sperm and
eggs were collected by filtration on 0.15 µ millipore filters. Salt was removed
by washing the filtrate with distilled water. The filters were dried in an
exsiccator. The amount of gametes was determined by weighing. As the gonads
generally are not emptied in one time, the individually marked animals were
allowed to burrow again in boxes at 5° for several days. Then it was tried to
induce spawning again, and so on.

Dr. Kees Kersting measured the calorific values of the gametes with a Parr 1411
calorimeter at the Limnological Institute of Amsterdam University.

### RESULTS AND INTERPRETATION

Seasonal Gonad Development and Spawning in the Field

Figure 1 presents a part of the results obtained in the successive years 1974 - 1977. The different age groups are taken together.

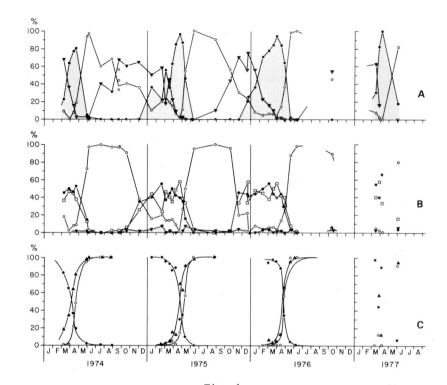

Fig. 1

A. Seasonal changes in the percentages of *Macoma* with non-developed (O) and developed (▼) gonads and with ripe gametes (●).

B. Percentages of undifferentiated specimens (O), males (●) and females (□) throughout the year. The black triangles (▼) represent trematode-infected animals.

C. Specimens loaded with ripe gametes but not yet spawned (●) and in which the first signs of spawning occurred (▲). The open circles (O) represent animals which have completely emptied gonads.

Figure 1.A. shows that after the gonads have emptied in late May, the reproductive organs almost disappear in both sexes. Large percentages of animals show non-developed gonads. The development starts already in July and August and in autumn and winter over 50% is well developed. The first specimens with ripe sperm and eggs are noticed in December. Their maximum numbers are reached in April. The animals spawn and the cycle is repeated. In general the year to year fluctuations are small, but the final maturation of the gametes may be delayed, probably in relation to weather conditions: compare spring '74 and '77 to '75 and '76, where in January already over 30% had ripe gametes.

In the period from June till November *Macoma* was called undifferentiated. Males and females were only recognizable from December up to May (see Fig. 1.B.). The calculated sex ratio was very close to 1 (1.065, n = 696). A sex ratio of 1

also held for the separate age groups over one year old, with the exception of
the group over 5 years old, showing a slight excess of males.

The black triangles (hatched area) in Fig. 1.B. show the fairly constant
percentage of about 3% of the animals infected by the trematode *Parvatrema
affinis*, which is known to cause sexual castration in *Macoma* (Ref. 10).

Figure 1.C. shows the actual spawning period of the *Macoma* populations living
on the intertidal flats, which is limited to the months April and May. The
year-to-year fluctuation is remarkably small. In June spawning is completed.

The above observations on gonad development and spawning are only for a minor
part not in agreement with the previous work of Caddy (8). Worth mentioning are:
1) development of the gonads in the Thames estuary occurs more rapidly; from
September onwards animals with mature oocytes were observed. Spawning occurs
one month earlier, and 2) any evidence for a second spawning period in autumn
was not found in the Wadden Sea.

Laboratory Experiments

Equipped with the above mentioned data efforts were made to initiate spawning
in the laboratory. From literature on bivalves (Ref. 11, 12) there was enough
evidence to suppose that changes in temperature play a role in the spawning
mechanism. Some years ago, when filming deposit-feeding in *Macoma*, a sudden
outburst of spawning was observed. Apparently the intense irradiance of the
photo lamps had triggered the spawning mechanism.

Of efforts to initiate spawning with light, thermal changes, mechanical and
osmotic shocks and the addition of sperm and eggs, all, but an increase in
temperature failed to produce results. However, a simple exceeding of a certain
threshold temperature was found not to be able to unlock the spawning mechanism.
From numerous pilot experiments we learned that the nature of such a
temperature rise, exceeding a critical level of about $10^{o}$ must be shock-wise.
This led to the adoption of a "standard" shock, which always forced a
temperature rise from 5 - 12.5$^{o}$ C within a time interval of 5 minutes. In this
way in many hundreds of ripe *Macomas* spawning could be induced. The
experimental animals, at weekly intervals collected on the flats, were at first
adapted to the basic temperature of 5$^{o}$ for at least 1 day. Figure 2 shows some
of the results obtained in animals of various ages.

Ejection of gametes never started earlier than 45 min. after the thermal shock
was administered. The peak activity is noticed 30 - 45 min. later. Then the
activity rapidly decreases and 2 and a half hours after the shock spawning is
completed. Emission of gametes in single animals takes about half an hour. In
the scope of this paper it is not well possible to describe the special
spawning behaviour of *Macoma*. Considering both sexes separately we found that
spawning in females is retarded some 15 min. as compared to males, but there
is no evidence that the sperm carries some chemical compound that will
stimulate other individuals, so that spawning in the whole group is
synchronized.

Additional experiments learned that this basic pattern could be changed in two
ways. The first manner is a slower administration of the thermal rise. This
will lower the percentages of spawning animals, while the peak height decreases.
The time-lapse, however, is not changed. In general a temperature rise slower

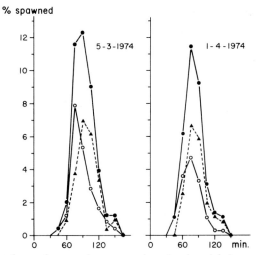

Fig. 2 Two examples of spawning experiments in which groups of animals (n=244 and n=358 resp.) were exposed to a standard thermal shock, offered at t=0. The graphs represent the total percentages of spawning animals (●), and of males (O) and females (▲) as a function of time. Occurring spawnings are summarized over periods of 15 minutes.

than $2^O$ per hour was found to be ineffective. The second manner is to start at a lower temperature level. This produces a shift of the whole curve to the right. Starting at a basic level of $2^O$ C causes a delay of at least two hours.

Another interesting observation is shown in Fig. 3. In animals in which the effect of a thermal rise was small or negative when it was offered the first time, positive results were often obtained when a similar shock was repeated a second or third time.

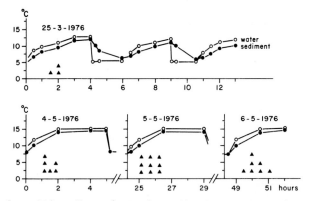

Fig. 3. Repeated positive thermal shocks - the temperature changes in water and sediment are indicated as a function of time - will produce enhanced spawning effects in *Macoma* when the intervals are long enough (in the order of 1 day). Black triangles indicate the observed spawnings. Too short intervals as shown in the upper graphs stay without extra results.

This points to an accumulation effect of repeated temperature rises and drops.
However, the intervals between the repeated shocks must be relatively long -
in the order of 1 day - to induce results. Repeated shocks, with short
intervals in between, produce negative results.
The response of *Macoma* to thermal shocks is generally slow and therefore it
seems likely that hormones play a role in the ultimate control of spawning.

Arranging now the results from the spawning experiments throughout 3 successive
years, the picture of Fig. 4 is obtained.

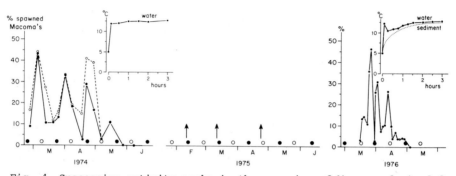

Fig. 4. Successive activity peaks in the spawning of *Macoma*, derived from
laboratory experiments in '74, '75 and '76. In 1975 the peaks are indicated
by arrows. The dotted line in 1974 gives the summarized effect of two
repeated shocks. Insets: nature of offered temperature shocks. Evidence
for a direct lunar periodicity is not present.

In 1974 and '75 only newly collected animals were used. A standard temperature
shock (inset Fig. 4) was offered. It appeared that the readiness to spawn in
mature animals was not equal during the spawning season. Three to four distinct
spawning peaks could be observed. For 1975 the exact percentages are not known.
In 1976 a standard shock was offered to burrowed animals. These animals were
collected in February and from that time kept in the laboratory at 5° C. Here
again a number of spawning peaks is found; the intervals, however, are smaller
and the whole spawning period is more compressed. The phenomenon of different
spawning peaks had already been observed by Caddy (8) who indentified periods
of sudden decline in the numbers of mature *Macomas* in the Thames estuary. Also
for other species, e.g. in oysters, frequency peaks in the numbers of larvae
produced are described (Ref. 13).

Amount and Calorific Value of the Gametes

For a quantitative collection of gametes in individuals, *Macomas* were isolated
in vessels and exposed to thermal shocks. As the gonads are not emptied during
one spawning, the individually marked animals were allowed to recover in
sediment and with intervals of some days used again and again until we thought
they were completely empty.

Table 1 shows the results from males and females, which had completely emptied.
The weight loss in males is somewhat higher as compared to females.
Irrespective sex or age, a weight loss of 25% of the soft parts due to spawning
seems a reasonable average. The importance of this weight loss is best illustrated when Fig. 5 is considered. Here, the seasonal weight change in a modal

TABLE 1

| sex | age (y) | shell length (mm) | animal weight (mg) | total wgt gametes (mg) | calc. % | mean |
|-----|---------|-------------------|--------------------|-----------------------|---------|------|
| males | 2 | 14.5 | 27.5 | 5.7 | 20.7 | |
| | 3 | 15.0 | 31.5 | 8.1 | 25.7 | |
| | 3 | 15.0 | 44.9 | 11.6 | 25.8 | |
| | 3 | 16.0 | 54.8 | 17.2 | 31.4 | |
| | 3 | 16.0 | 49.6 | 17.5 | 31.3 | |
| | 3 | 17.0 | 31.6 | 7.4 | 23.4 | |
| | 4 | 16.5 | 60.6 | 18.3 | 30.2 | 25.3 |
| | 4 | 18.0 | 56.7 | 13.0 | 22.9 | S.D.=4.1 |
| | 4 | 19.0 | 78.7 | 17.9 | 22.7 | |
| | 5 | 20.0 | 54.4 | 11.6 | 21.3 | |
| | 5 | 20.5 | 65.6 | 14.0 | 21.3 | |
| | 5 | 21.0 | 141.9 | 44.7 | 31.5 | |
| | 6 | 20.5 | 95.0 | 20.7 | 21.8 | |
| | 6 | 22.5 | 87.1 | 21.1 | 24.3 | |
| females | 3 | 16.0 | 39.1 | 10.8 | 27.6 | |
| | 3 | 16.5 | 25.2 | 2.2 | 8.7 | 22.9 |
| | 4 | 17.5 | 41.5 | 6.3 | 15.2 | S.D.=5.9 |
| | 5 | 19.0 | 95.6 | 27.8 | 29.1 | (20.9) |
| | 5 | 21.0 | 84.9 | 18.6 | 21.9 | (S.D.=7.6) |
| | 6 | 21.5 | 69.6 | 11.6 | 16.7 | |
| | 7 | 22.5 | 121.0 | 32.4 | 26.8 | |

Total amounts of gametes, obtained from successive spawnings in the laboratory.
The animal weight before spawning is derived from its ash free dry weight after
spawning to which the dry weight of the gametes is added. In the value of (20.9)
the extremely low value of 8.7 is included.

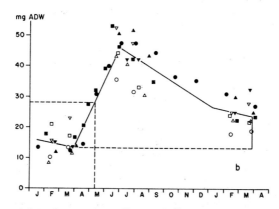

Fig. 5. Seasonal weight change in a "modal" *Macoma* after Beukema and de Bruin
(5). The weight loss due to spawning amounts about a quarter of the ash free
dry weight ($\sim$ 28 mg) of the animal. The vertical bar represents the net
weight increment during the whole year ($\sim$ 10 mg).

*Macoma* in its 3rd year, closely representing the average for the whole population, is shown. Its average weight in the middle of the spawning season amounts some 28 mg. of which 25% or 7 mg. will be spawned. Compared to the animal's net weight increment in the whole year of 10 mg, the spawned gametes represent an important share in the energy equation.

Table 2 shows the calorific values of the gametes. The mean value of sperm amounts 4.5 (S.D.=0.17); of eggs 5.9 (S.D.=0.24).

TABLE 2

|       | nr. of sample | dry wgt of sample in mg | calorific value (cal/mg) | mean |
|-------|---------------|-------------------------|--------------------------|-------|
|       | 1             | 17.4                    | 4.323                    |       |
|       | 2             | 17.2                    | 4.763                    |       |
| sperm | 3             | 20.9                    | 4.429                    | 4.529 |
|       | 4             | 17.4                    | 4.619                    |       |
|       | 5             | 13.2                    | 4.510                    |       |
|       | 6             | 19.2                    | 5.957                    |       |
|       | 7             | 25.6                    | 5.442                    |       |
| eggs  | 8             | 24.5                    | 5.951                    | 5.863 |
|       | 9             | 14.1                    | 5.975                    |       |
|       | 10            | 16.4                    | 5.991                    |       |

Calorific values of sperm and eggs of *Macoma balthica*.

Compared to an average calorific value for tissue homogenates of 5.3 (Beukema and de Bruin, pers. comm.) the value for sperm is very low and for eggs rather high. This is explained by the high lipid content of the eggs.

The Significance of Temperature Changes in the Field

Returning to the tidal flats again, the question rises how spawning occurs in the field situation and, moreover, to what extent the results from the spawning experiments fit into this situation.

The daily and seasonal variation of temperature in the mud-flats (1 cm) during the spawning seasons 1974 - 1976 is given in Fig. 6. During 2 years the maximum and minimum temperatures (obtained from in-situ recordings) in the upper sediment layer is shown; for 1975 only water temperatures were available. At the same time the spawnings actually observed, verified from declines in the gamete contents of the animals, are indicated (dashed areas). Each year at least 2 peaks are present. Spawning always coincided with periods characterized by the largest temperature fluctuations, provided that a threshold level of 10° (12°) is exceeded. Actual heat shocks, similar to the so-called "standard shock" are absent in nature. The in situ recordings show maximum temperature rises in the sediment in the order of 12° per day or 2° per hour. Such rises were experimentally found to be just sufficient to initiate spawning. In addition it is very likely that also the described cumulative effect of successive rises plays a part. The non-appearance of a spawning in the middle of April 1974, opposite to the spawnings in the first weeks of April and May is probably to be explained in this way.

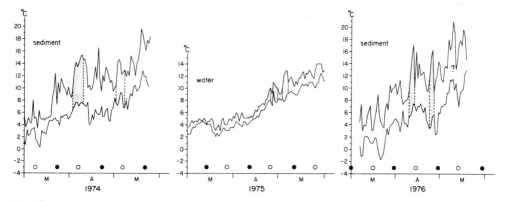

Fig. 6. Observed spawning periods of *Macoma balthica* in the western Wadden Sea (dashed areas) related to temperature. The extension of a third period in 1976 is not exactly known. Spawning always occurs in the months of April and May when large differences exist between daily maximum and minimum temperatures (drawn curves).

In general the frequency spectrum of temperature fluctuations at the earth's surface is dominated by annual and daily variations. According to Vught and Zimmerman (14) in a tidal mud-flat area the semi-diurnal lunar tide, interacting with the daily variation in solar radiation, gives rise to a third type of periodicity, with a period of 14.76 days. When the mud-flats at low tides are exposed to the sunlight during the middle of the day, the largest rise in temperature is to be expected. It is tempting to assume that these periodical temperature fluctuations have physiological significance for the spawning of *Macoma*. In that case spawning would be triggered in a period with low water around noon. A couple of hours later, when the release of gametes is finished, the fertilized eggs would be carried inward by the flood. Such a mechanism would assist in retaining the eggs within the intertidal area and reduce losses to the open sea.

The present results may throw some more light on the spawning mechanism of *Macoma* populations living on tidal flats. How spawning is triggered in subtidal populations as for example those off the Netherlands coast, only exposed to slow temperature fluctuations, remains a question. Perhaps reproduction in these animals is poor and populations are only stocked by 0-group spat derived from tidal populations in a way as described by de Vlas (15). Wolff (verb. comm.) observed that spawning of *Macoma* on the former tidal flats of the Grevelingen in the southwestern part of the Netherlands failed after the area had become a stagnant salt water lake.

It will be clear that for a proper understanding of the spawning of *Macoma* more details over the whole geographical range of the species are needed.

REFERENCES

(1)  J.J. Beukema, Biomass and species richness of the macro-benthic animals living on the tidal flats of the Dutch Wadden Sea, Neth. J. Sea Res. 10, 236-261 (1976).
(2)  W.C.M. Klein Breteler, Settlement, growth and production of the shore crab, *Carcinus maenas*, on tidal flats in the Dutch Wadden Sea, Neth. J. Sea Res. 10, 354-376 (1976).

384          P. A. W. J. de Wilde and E. M. Berghuis

(3)   B.R. Kuipers, On the ecology of juvenile plaice on a tidal flat in the
      Wadden Sea, Neth. J. Sea Res. 11, 56-91 (1977).
(4)   P.A.W.J. de Wilde, Influence of temperature on behaviour, energy
      metabolism and growth of *Macoma balthica* (l.), Proc. 9$^{th}$ Europ. Mar.
      Biol. Symp., 239-256 (1975).
(5)   J.J. Beukema and W. de Bruin, Seasonal changes in dry weight and chemical
      composition of the soft parts of the tellinid bivalve *Macoma balthica*
      in the Dutch Wadden Sea, Neth. J. Sea Res. 11, 42-55 (1977).
(6)   H.I. Battle, Rhythmic sexual maturity and spawning of certain bivalve
      mollusks, Contrib. Can. Biol. Fish. N.S. 7, 257-276 (1933).
(7)   J.J. Lammens, Growth and reproduction in a tidal flat population of *Macoma
      balthica* (L.), Neth. J. Sea Res. 3, 315-382 (1967).
(8)   J.F. Caddy, Maturation of gametes and spawning in *Macoma balthica* (L.),
      Can. J. Zool. 45, 955-965 (1967).
(9)   J.J. Beukema, Seasonal changes in the biomass of the macro-benthos of a
      tidal flat area in the Dutch Wadden Sea, Neth. J. Sea Res. 8, 94-107
      (1974).
(10)  C. Swennen and H.L. Ching, Observations on the trematode *Parvatrema
      affinis*, causative agent of crawling tracks of *Macoma balthica*, Neth. J.
      Sea Res. 8, 108-115 (1974).
(11)  V. Fretter and A. Graham in K.M. Wilbur and C.M. Yonge (1964), Physiology
      of Mollusca I, Acad. Press N.Y.
(12)  R.D. Purchon (1968) The biology of mollusca, Pergamon Press, Oxford.
(13)  E.W. Knight-Jones, Reproduction of oysters in the rivers Crouch and Rouch,
      Essex, during 1947, 1948 and 1949, Fish. Invest. Lond. 18, 1-48 (1952).
(14)  H.F. Vught and J.T.F. Zimmerman, Interaction between the daily heat
      balance and the tidal cycle, Nat. 255, 113-117 (1975).
(15)  J. de Vlas, Migratie via getijstromen van jonge nonnetjes *Macoma balthica*
      L., op en rond het Balgzand, N.I.O.Z. Int. Rap. (mimeogr.) 14, 1-30
      (1973).

# AUTHOR INDEX

# SUBJECT INDEX

This index is based on "key-words", and refers only to the initial page of each contribution.